The Four Ancient Books of Wales

The Cymric Poems attributed to the Celtic Bards of the Sixth Century – Welsh Folklore and Legends

By William F. Skene

PANTIANOS
CLASSICS

Published by Pantianos Classics

ISBN-13: 978-1-78987-207-1

First published in 1868

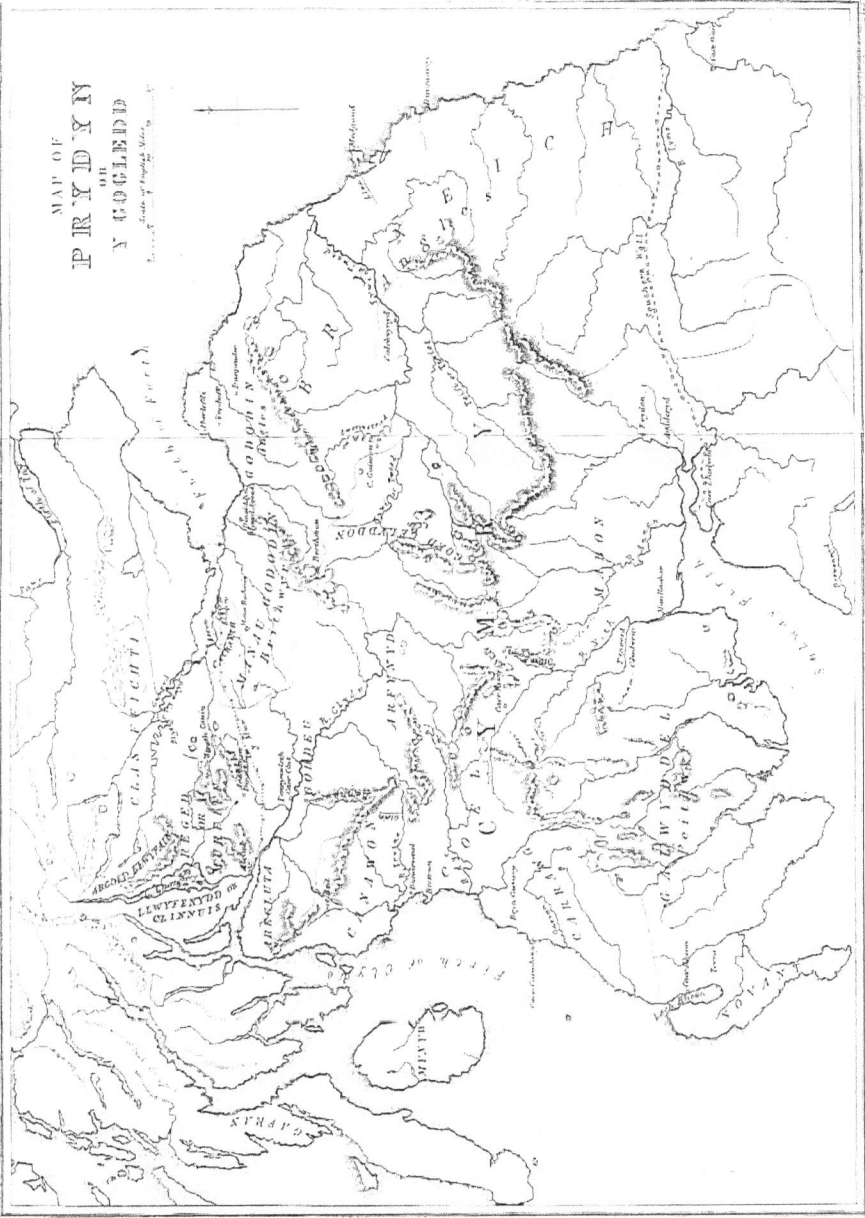

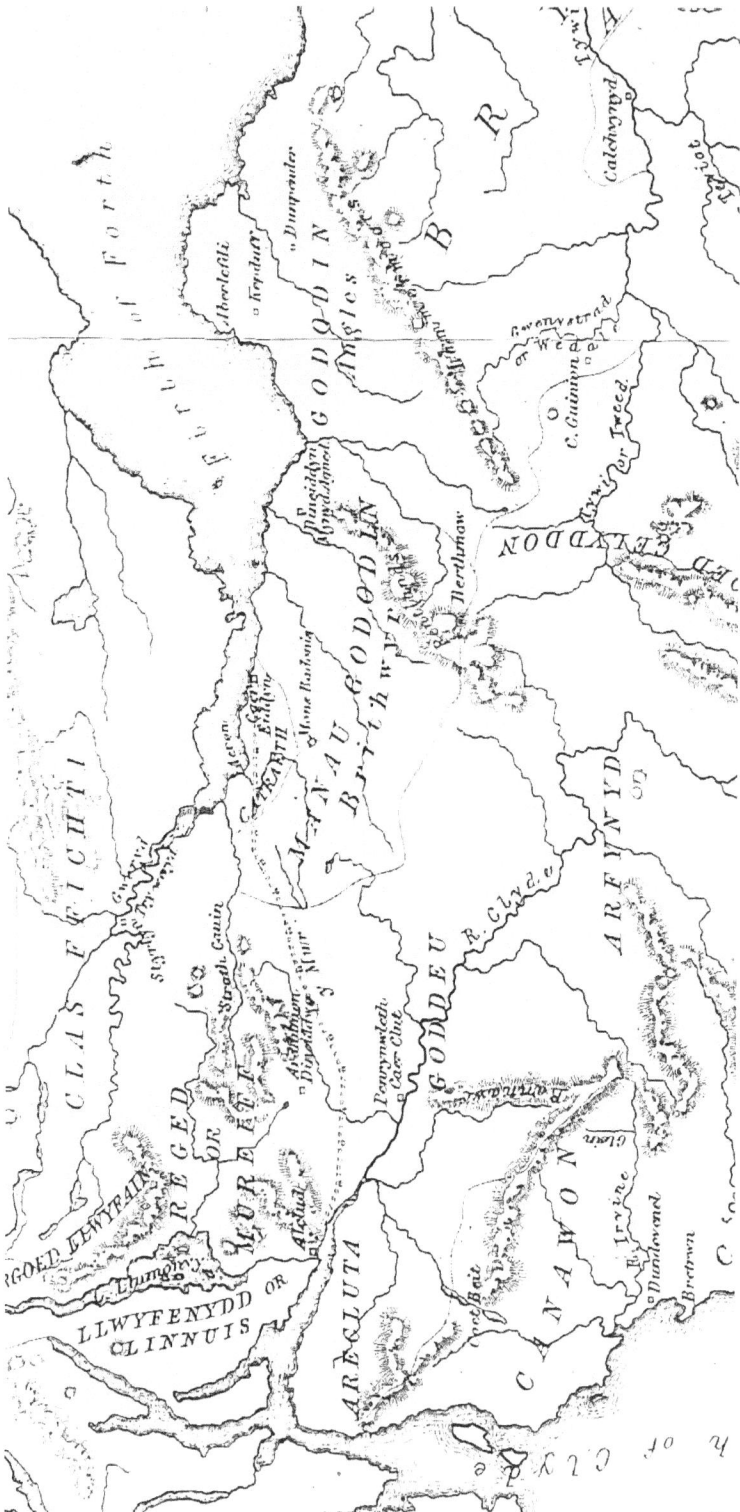

F R I T H   o f   F O R T H

B R

Caledonyd

Aberlessli
Kyndair
Dunpender

G O D O D I N

Migies

Gwenystrad
or Wedd

C. Guinion

Gwryd or Tweed

Dinsiddyn
Appeldonen

Merthrow

O E D   C E L Y D D O N

F

M A N A U   G O D O D I N

B r i t h w y r

A R F Y N I D

C L A S   F I C H T I

Mona Rodonig
Eiddyn

Mevan
Crch
TRAITH

R. Clyd e

G O D D E U

Strath. Gawin

Caer Clut
Penrymdeti

Battaile

C A N A W O N

R E G E D

M U R E I F

Aballon
Diggdiftye Mur

Avshial

Glasu

Irvine
Danlowod

Bratwm

R G O E D   E L W Y F A I N

L. Llunigin

L L W Y F E N Y D D   or
C L I N N U I S

A R E G L U T A

Car Bait

h   o f   C L Y D e

MEATH

Perth of

COED CELY

MABON

R. Nith

R. Anne

E. Fr
L. Ardd
Caer Llucherigh

Derwengd

Solway River

Manllodur

Fenoed
Cluberin

Dumfrond
Bretwn

Bryn Carvesa

Caer Carndoyn

CARRA

GALWYDDEL
Peith

Caer Rheon
Terra

Loch Rheon
Caer Rhun

NOVANT

Contents

Introduction

Chapter One - The Poems Contained in the Four Ancient Books of Wales

THE dissolution of the religious houses in Wales in the reign of Henry the Eighth, and the dispersion of their libraries, led to many Welsh MSS., which had been preserved in them, passing into the hands of private individuals; and collections of Welsh MSS. soon began to be formed by persons who took an interest in the history and literature of their country.

The principal collectors in North Wales were Mr. Jones of Gelly Lyvdy, whose collection was formed between the years 1590 and 1630, and Mr. Robert Vaughan of Hengwrt, author of a work termed *British Antiquities Revived*, published in 1662, who died at Hengwrt four years after, in 1666; and in South Wales, William Herbert, Earl of Pembroke, who formed a collection at Raglan Castle in 1590; and Sir Edward Mansel, whose father had received a gift of the priory of Margam in Glamorgan, in 1591.

The collections of Mr. Jones and Mr. Vaughan became united at Hengwrt, in arrangement having been made between them that the MSS. collected by each should become the property of the survivor. Mr. Jones having predeceased Mr. Vaughan, the united collection, consisting of upwards of 400 MSS., remained at Hengwrt till within the last few years, when it was bequeathed by Sir Robert Vaughan of Hengwrt to W. W. E. Wynne, Esq. of Peniarth, in whose possession it now is.

In the following century various collections were made, and among others some valuable MSS. became the property of Jesus College, Oxford. The collection of the Earl of Pembroke at Raglan Castle was destroyed by fire in the time of Oliver Cromwell; and a similar fate overtook two of those later collections, which had become the property of Sir Watkin Williams Wynne, and were preserved at Wynnstay, but which were likewise destroyed by fire. Other collections passed into the British Museum, and the principal collections of Welsh MSS. are now the Hengwrt collection at Peniarth, those in the British Museum, the MSS. at Jesus College, and those belonging to Lord Mostyn, Mr. Panton of Plas Gwyn, and others.

In the Hengwrt collection were preserved three ancient MSS., termed the Black Book of Caermarthen, the Book of Aneurin, and the Book of Taliessin, containing a considerable collection of Welsh poetry bearing marks of antiquity; and in the, library of Jesus College is a MS. which contains similar poems, termed the Red Book of Hergest. These poems are some of a historic character, and others not so, and are attributed, either by their rubric, by the title of the MS., or by tradition, to four bards termed Myrddin, Aneurin,

Taliessin, and Llywarch Hen, who are supposed to have lived in the sixth century.

Two of these MSS. are still in the Hengwrt collection, and of one of them we know the history: the Black Book of Caermarthen belonged to the Priory of Black Canons at Caermarthen, and was given by the Treasurer of the Church of St. Davids to Sir John Price, a native of Breconshire, who was one of the commissioners appointed by King Henry the Eighth; the other is the Book of Taliessin, and it is not known how it was acquired.

The Book of Aneurin is now the property of Sir Thomas Phillipps of Middlehill.

The Red Book of Hergest is said to have been so termed from its having been compiled for the Vaughans of Hergest Court, Herefordshire, and seems to have come to Oxford from the Margam Collection in South Wales.

It is these four MSS.--the Black Book of Caermarthen, written in the reign of Henry the Second (1154-1189); the Book of Aneurin, a MS. of the latter part of the thirteenth century; the Book of Taliessin, a MS. of the beginning of the fourteenth century; and the Red Book of Hergest, a MS. compiled at different times in the fourteenth and fifteenth centuries--that are here termed THE FOUR ANCIENT BOOKS OF WALES, and it is with the ancient poems contained in these four MSS. that we have now to do.

Numerous transcripts of these poems are to be found in other Welsh MSS., but undoubtedly it is in these four MSS. that the most ancient. texts of the poems are to be found; and, in most cases, those in the other MSS. are not independent texts, but have obviously, with more or less variation, been transcribed from these. The contents of these MSS. remained little known till the publication of the *Archæologia Britannica* in 1707, by Edward Lhuyd, who had examined all the collections which were accessible, and the account which he included in his work of the Welsh MSS. attracted some attention towards them, but none of the poems were printed till the middle of the century, when the publication of the poems of Ossian by James Macpherson, and the sudden popularity they acquired, gave a temporary value to Celtic poetry, and led to a desire on the part of the Welsh to show that they were likewise in possession of a body of native poems not less interesting than the Highland, and with better claims to authenticity. In 1764, the Rev. Evan Evans published his *Specimens of the Poetry of the Ancient Welsh Bards*; and though they mainly embraced poems written in the twelfth and subsequent centuries, translated in the style of Macpherson's Ossian, he annexed a Latin dissertation, *De Bardis*, in which he printed ten of the stanzas of the great poem of the Gododin, and a stanza from the Avallenau, as specimens of the older poems, with Latin translations. He was followed by Edward Jones, who, in his *Musical and Poetical Relies of the Welsh Bards*, published in 1784, printed a part of the Gododin, three of the poems of Taliessin--viz. the Battle of Argoed Llwyfain, the Battle of Gwenystrad, and the Mead song, one of the poems of Llywarch Hen, with metrical translations, and part of the Avallenau, with a more literal prose translation by Mr. Edward Williams. He was likewise assisted in his work by Dr. W. Owen, afterwards Dr. Owen Pughe, who, a few years afterwards, published five of the poems of Taliessin in the Gentleman's Magazine for the years 1789 and 1790, being the Ode to Gwallawg, the Death-Song of Owen, the Battle of Dyffryn Garant, the Battle of Gwenystrad, and the Gorchan Cynvelyn, with English translations. These translations, however, were too diffuse and too much tainted by a desire to give the passages a mystic meaning, to convey a fair idea of the real nature of the poems.

In 1792, Dr. Owen Pughe published *The Heroic Elegies, and other pieces of Llywarch Hen*, with a much more literal English version. The work contains a pretty complete collection of the poems attributed to Llywarch Hen, but it is not said from what MS. the text was printed, while the notes contain collations with the Black Book of Caermarthen and the Red Book of Hergest. [1]

At length, in the year 1801, the text of the whole of these poems was given to the world, through the munificence of Owen Jones, a furrier, in Thames Street, London, who, in that and subsequent years, published the *Myvyrian Archæology of Wales*, containing the chief productions of Welsh literature. He was assisted by Mr. Edward Williams of Glamorgan and Dr. Owen Pughe; but though the text of almost all of these poems is given, it is not said from what particular MSS. they were printed, and no materials are afforded for discriminating between what are probably old and what are spurious. The text is unaccompanied by translations.

If the publication of the poems of Ossian thus drew attention to these ancient Welsh poems, the controversy which followed on the poems drew forth an able vindication of the genuine character of the latter. Sharon Turner, in his *History of the Anglo-Saxons*, the first edition of which appeared in 1799, founded upon some of these poems as historical documents. He quoted the Death-Song of Geraint as containing the account of a real battle at Longporth, or Portsmouth, between Cerdic, the founder of the kingdom of Wesser, and the Britons. He referred to the poems of Taliessin on the battles of Argoed Llwyfain and Gwenystrad as real history, and he considered the great poem of the Gododin by Aneurin as describing a real war between the Britons and the Angles of Ida's kingdom. This drew upon him the criticism of the two chief opponents of the claims of Ossian--viz. John Pinkerton and Malcolm Laing--who declared that these Welsh poems, were equally unworthy of credit. In consequence of this attack, Turner published, in 1803, his *Vindication of the genuineness of the ancient British poems of Aneurin, Taliessin, Llywarch Hen, and Myrddin*. In this elaborate essay he endeavoured to demonstrate two propositions:--First, That these four bards were real men, and actually lived in the sixth century; and, secondly, that, with some exceptions, the poems attributed to them are their genuine works. He dealt, however, with the historical poems alone as sufficient for his purpose, and did not enter into any critical analysis of the poems as a, whole. This vindication, was, in the main, considered to be conclusive as to the poems being the genuine works of the bards whose name they bore; and it appeared to be now generally accepted as a fact, that a body of genuine poetry, of the sixth century, existed in the Welsh language which threw light upon the history of that century.

A new view was, however, soon taken of their real meaning; and some years after, the Rev. Edward Davies brought out, in his work called the *Mythology of the British Druids*, published in 1809, his theory that there was handed down in these poems a system of mythology which had been the religion of the Druids in the pagan period, and was still professed in secret by the bards, their genuine successors. The Gododin, he endeavoured to show by an elaborate translation, related to the traditionary history of the massacre of the Britons by the Saxons at Stonehenge, called the Plot of the Long Knives; and he appended to his work a number of the poems of Taliessin, with translations to show the mystic meaning which pervaded them. This theory was still further elaborated by the Honourable Algernon Herbert, in two works published anonymously: *Britannia after the Romans*, in 1836; and *The Neo-Druidic Heresy*, in 1838. He took the same view with regard to the meaning of the Gododin; and he combined with much ingenious and wild speculation regarding the post-Roman history of Britain, the theory that a lurking adherence to the old paganism of the Druids had caused a schism in the British church, and that the bards, under the name of Christians and the guise of Christian nomenclature, professed in secret a paganism as an esoteric cult, which he denominated the Neo-Druidic heresy, and which he maintained was obscurely hinted at in the poems of Taliessin. It would probably be difficult to find a stranger specimen of perverted ingenuity and misplaced learning than is contained in the works of Davies and Herbert; but the urgency with which they maintained their views, and the disguise under which the poems appeared in their so-called translations, certainly produced an impression that the poems of Taliessin did contain a mystic philosophy, while, at the same time, the Gododin of Aneurin and the poems of Llywarch Hen were generally recognised as genuine historical documents commemorating real historical events.

The Rev. John Williams, afterwards Archdeacon of Cardigan, an eminent Welsh scholar, and a man of much talent, announced, in 1841, a translation of the poems of Aneurin, Taliessin, and other primitive bards, with a critical revision and re-establishment of the text; but, although these poems had occupied a large share of his attention, I believe he never seriously prepared the materials for his edition, and he died in 1858, without having done anything towards carrying it out. I have frequently heard him give as a reason the great difficulty involved, and time and labour required, "in restoring the genuine text." What he meant by this we can see in the last work he published, termed *Gomer*, where (part ii. p. 33 *et seq.*), we have several specimens of how he meant to deal with the text. His plan obviously was to restore the orthography of the words from the existing text in the Myvyrian Archæology to what he conceived must have been their form when the respective poems were composed. His mind, too, appears to have been influenced in no slight degree by the school of Davies, and he was too ready to attach a mystic meaning to the text. In 1850, some time before the Archdeacon's death, a learned Breton, the Vicomte do la Villemarqué, published his *Poemes des Bardes Bretons du VI*. *Siecle, traduits pour la premiere fois, avec le texte en regard revu sur les plus anciens manuscrits*; and he, too, proceeded upon the same idea of restoring the original text. In his preface, after noticing the oldest copies of the poems, which he says formed the basis of his edition, he adds, "Apres le travail de collation, il restait a reproduire les textes avec l'orthographe convenable, mais la quelle suivre;" and he fixes upon the Breton orthography as the most ancient, and in this, which he terms "l'orthographe historique," presents us with the text of the poems which he translates. These poems are mainly the historical pieces, and he considers with Turner that they contain fragments of real history.

A more unfortunate idea than that of thus arbitrarily restoring the text never formed the basis of an important work; and while it has destroyed the value of Villemarqué's edition, it lessens the regret we should otherwise feel that the Archdeacon never carried his announced intention into effect. To present the poems in a different shape from what they appear in the oldest transcripts, and to clothe them with a supposed older orthography, is to confound entirely the province of the editor with that of the historic critic, and to exercise, in the character of the former, functions which properly belong to the latter, while it deprives him of the proper materials on which to exercise his critical judgment. Such restoration necessarily proceeds on the assumption by the editor that the poems are the genuine works of those to whom they are attributed, and existed in the same form and substance at the era at which their reputed authors lived; while the application of historical criticism to the poems as they now exist may lead to very different conclusions. It supersedes entirely the important work of the critic, by assuming the very questions which he has to solve. The true function of the editor is to select the oldest and best MSS., and to produce the text of the poems in the precise shape and orthography in which he there finds them: neither to tamper with, nor to restore them, but to furnish the critic with the materials on which he can exercise his skill in determining their true age and value. [2]

These remarks have likewise some bearing upon two very remarkable works which have inaugurated a new school of criticism of these poems, and subjected their claims to tests which they had not hitherto undergone. These two works are--*first, The Literature of the Kymry*, by Thomas Stephens, published in 1849; and, *secondly, Taliessin, or the Bards and Druids of Britain*, by D. W. Nash, published in 1858.

The main object of Mr. Stephens' work is to treat of the language and literature of the twelfth and two succeeding centuries; but it embraces likewise the poems attributed to the bards of the sixth century, in so far as he maintains that they are falsely so attributed, and are really the works of later bards. Mr. Stephens' work is written with much ability, and is, in fact, the first real attempt to subject these poems to anything like a critical analysis. He opens one of his chapters, to which he has put the title, "Poems, fictitiously attributed to Myrddin, Taliessin, Aneurin, Llywarch, Meugant, and Golyddan," with the following sentence:--"Reader! be attentive to what I am about to write, and keep a watchful eye upon the sentences as they rise before you, for the daring spirit of modern criticism is about to lay violent hands upon the old household furniture of venerable tradition;" and he certainly fulfils this promise, for he maintains that, with some exceptions, these poems contain allusions, and breathe forth a spirit and sentiment, which demonstrate that they were composed subsequent to the twelfth century; and he endeavours to indicate their real authors. Of the poems attributed to Aneurin he appears to admit the Gododin to be genuine. He considers the whole of the poems attributed to Myrddin, including even the Avallenau--which Turner maintained to be genuine--to be spurious, and the work of later bards, and endeavours to point out their real authors, hesitatingly in the text, but more decidedly in the title to one of his chapters, where he has "The Avallenau and Hoianau, composed by Prydydd y Moch. The Gorddodau, composed by Gruffydd ab Yr Ynad Coch;" and of seventy-seven poems attributed to Taliessin, he admits only twelve to be "historical and as old as the sixth century."

His admission that some of these poems are as old as the sixth century of course neutralises any argument drawn from their orthography and grammatical or poetical structure, unless he can show that the poems he maintains to be spurious differ materially in that respect from those he admits to be genuine; and his attempt to indicate their real authors breaks down in so far as the Avallenau and Hoianau, and other poems contained in the Black Book of Caermarthen, are concerned; for the poems in that MS. must have been already transcribed in the twelfth century, and Prydydd y Moch belongs to the succeeding century. So far as he shows that several of these poems contain direct allusions to events which occurred after the period when they are said to be composed, his criticism is successful, and may be received as well founded; but in his attempt to show that allusions, hitherto supposed to apply to events contemporaneous with the alleged date of the poem, were really intended to describe later events--which is, in fact, the main feature of his criticism--he is not equally successful. His reasoning appears to me to be quite inconclusive, the resemblances faint and uncertain, and the argument carries no conviction to the mind. For instance, in the poem attributed to Taliessin, termed Kerdd y Veib Llyr, where the lines occur--

"A battle against the lord of fame in the dales of Hafren,
  Against Brochwel Powys; *he loved my song*"--

it is a fair and legitimate inference that it could not have been composed prior to the time of Brochmail, who is mentioned by Bede as having been at the battle of Caerlegion, the true date of which is 613; but when the following lines occur in a subsequent part of the same poem—

"Three races, wrathful, of right qualities,
Gwyddyl, and Brython, and Romani,
Create war and tumult,"

it is not satisfactory to be told that "they refer to the ecclesiastic dispute between Giraldus and King John respecting the see of St. David's." It is therefore not without reason that the reader is exhorted to keep a watchful eye upon the sentences condemning the poems upon such grounds.

Mr. Nash, in his work, deals with the poems attributed to Taliessin only, and in the main he follows up the criticisms of Stephens. He goes, however, a step beyond him, as, without directly asserting it, he implies that none of the poems are older than the twelfth century, if he does not really assort that no earlier date can be assigned to them than the date of the oldest MS. in which they are found. Of the historical poems he sums up his criticism thus:-- "Without, therefore, venturing to decide that these 'Songs to Urien' were not re-written in the twelfth century, from materials originally of the date of the sixth, and that there are no poetical remains in the Welsh language older than the twelfth century, we may nevertheless assert that the common assumption of such remains of the date of the sixth century has been made upon very unsatisfactory grounds, and without a sufficiently careful examination of the evidence on which such assumption should be founded. Writers who claim for productions actually existing only in MSS. of the twelfth all origin in the sixth century, are called upon to demonstrate the links of evidence, either internal or external, which bridge over this great intervening period of at least five hundred years. This external evidence is altogether wanting, and the internal evidence, even of the so-called 'Historical Poems' themselves, is, in some instances at least, opposed to their claims to an origin in the sixth century." What he calls the mythological poems he entirely rejects, and appears to place them even in a much later age than Stephens has done.

While Mr. Nash's work must be admitted to be written with much ability, certainly the merit of candour cannot equally be attributed to it. It is less an attempt to subject the poems to a fair and just criticism than simply a very clever piece of special pleading, in which, like all special pleading, he proceeds to demonstrate a foregone conclusion by the usual partial and one-sided view of the facts--assuming whatever appears to make for his argument, and ignoring what seems to oppose it; while he makes conjectural alterations of the text when it suits his purpose, and the real sense of the poems which form the subject of his criticism is disguised under a version which he terms a translation, but which affords anything but a faithful or candid representation of their contents.

I consider that the true value of these poems is a problem which has still to be solved. Are we to attach any real historical value to them, or are we to set them aside at once as worthless for all historical purposes, and as merely curious specimens of the nonsensical rhapsodies and perverted taste of a later age?

Whether these poems are the genuine works of the bards whose names they bear, or whether they are the production of a later age, I do not believe that they contain any such system of Druidism, or Neo-Druidism, as Davies, Herbert, and others, attempt to find in them; nor do I think that their authors wrote, and the compilers of these ancient MSS. took the pains to transcribe, century after century, what was a mere farrago of nonsense, and of no historical or literary value. I think that these poems have a meaning, and that, both in connection with the history and the literature of Wales, that meaning is worth finding out; and I think, further, that if they were subjected to a just and candid criticism, we ought to be able to ascertain their true place and value in the literature of Wales. The criticism to which they have hitherto been subjected is equally unsatisfactory, whether they are maintained to be genuine or to be spurious, mainly because the basis of the criticism is an uncertain and untrustworthy text, and any criticism on the existing texts, in the shape in which they are presented in the Myvyrian Archæology, is, comparatively speaking, valueless; and because the translations by which their meaning is attempted to be expressed, are either loose and inaccurate, or coloured by the views of the translators. Those who deal with the poems as the genuine works of the bards whose names they bear, and view them as containing a recondite system of Druidism, or semi-pagan philosophy, present us with a translation which is, to say the least of it, mysterious enough in all conscience. Those, again, who consider them to be the work of a later age, and to contain nothing but a mere farrago of nonsense, have no difficulty in producing a translation which amply bears out that character.

The work of the editor must, however, precede that of the critic. An essential preliminary is to give the text of these poems in the oldest form in which it is to be found, and in the precise orthography of the oldest MSS., and to present a translation which shall give as accurate and faithful a representation of the meaning of the poems as is now possible as the basis of the work of the critic. The object of the present work. is to accomplish this. The contents of the four MSS., here called the *Four Ancient Books of Wales*, are printed as accurately as possible,--those of the first three completely, and as much of the last as contains any of these poems. It is in these four MSS. that the oldest known texts are to be found; and in order to secure a faithful and impartial translation, I resolved, in order to avoid any risk of its being coloured by my own views, to refrain from attempting the translation myself, and to obtain it, if possible, from the most eminent living Welsh scholars. With this view, I applied to the Reverend D. Silvan Evans of Llanymawddwy, the author of the *English and Welsh Dictionary* and other works, and the Reverend Robert Williams of Rhydycroesau, author of the *Biography of Eminent Welshmen* and the *Cornish Dictionary*, both distinguished Welsh scholars, who most kindly acceded to my request. Mr. Evans, has translated for me the poems in the Black Book of Caermarthen, the Book of Aneurin, and the Red

Book of Hergest, and accompanied them with valuable notes. Mr. Williams has translated for me the poems in the Book of Taliessin; and I beg to record my sense of the deep obligation under which they have laid me by the valuable assistance thus afforded. But while these eminent scholars an so far answerable for the translations, it is due to them to add that they are not responsible for any opinions expressed in this work except those contained in their own notes; and that, by permitting their names to be connected with this work, they must not be held as sanctioning the views entertained by myself, and to which I have given expression in the following chapters, or in the notes I have added. [3]

[1] It is remarkable that there is no reference to readings in the *Llyfr du* in the poems which are actually to be found there, while in six poems which are not in the *Black Book*, the foot of the page is full of references to the *Llyfr du* for various readings. These various readings, so far as I have been able to judge, correspond with the Red Book of Hergest, while those attributed to the *Llyfr coch* are not to be found there.

[2] In 1852, an edition of the Gododin was published, with a translation, by J. Williams, at Ithel. He adopts the historical view of this poem, and has given the text, such as he had it, with much fidelity; while the translation, though somewhat too free, is the first to give anything like a fair idea of the original.

[3] The Welsh text has been printed for some years. It was put in type as soon as the collation of the manuscript copy of the poems with the original MSS. was completed, and again collated in proof, and then thrown off, in order to facilitate the work of translation. The only request made to the translators was to make their version as literal and accurate as possible, even though the meaning might be obscured thereby; and the care and time requisite to prepare such a translation deliberately has delayed the appearance of the work since then. While engaged in the preliminary investigations, I from time to time communicated fragments of what was intended to appear in the Introduction and Notes in occasional papers to the *Archæologia Cambrensis*.

Chapter Two - The Literature of Wales Subsequent to the Twelfth Century

PRIOR to the twelfth century there are not many poems which claim to belong to the literature of that period, besides those attributed to Taliessin, Aneurin, Llywarch Hen, and Myrddin. The Black Book of Caermarthen contains a few attributed to Cuhelyn, Elaeth, and Meigant; and the Red Book of Hergest, one to Tyssilio, son of Brochwael Yscythrog; but the number of such poems is so small, that, if the poems attributed to the bards of the sixth century really belong to that period, there is an interval of several centuries, during which such a literature either never existed or has perished, till the twelfth century, from which period a mass of poetic literature existed in

Wales, and has been preserved to us. Of the genuine character of that poetry there seems to be no doubt.

In order, then, to estimate rightly the place which the poems attributed to the bards of the sixth century ought truly to occupy in the literature of Wales, it will be necessary to form a just conception of the character of her later literature subsequent to the twelfth century, as well as to grasp the leading facts of her history during the previous centuries in their true aspect.

In the eleventh century two events happened which seem to have had a material influence on the literature of Wales. The one was the return of Rhys ap Tewdwr, the true heir to the throne of South Wales, in 1077, and the other was the landing of Gruffyd ap Cynan, the true heir to the throne of North Wales, in 1080.

On the death of Edwal, the last of the direct line of the Welsh kings, in 994, leaving an only son in minority; and of Meredith, Prince of South Wales, in 994, leaving an only daughter, the government of both provinces of Wales fell into the hands of usurpers. Cynan, who represented the North Wales line, fled to Ireland in 1041, where he married a daughter of the Danish king of Dublin, and after two fruitless attempts to recover his inheritance by the assistance of the Irish, died in Ireland, leaving a son Gruffyd. Rhys ap Tewdwr, the representative of the South Wales line, took refuge in Armorica, whence he returned in 1077; and, laying claim to the throne of South Wales, was unanimously elected by the people. Gruffyd ap Cynan invaded Anglesea with a body of troops obtained in Ireland, and having been joined by Rhys ap Tewdwr, their combined forces defeated the army of Trahaearn, then King of Wales, their opponent, at the battle of Carno in 1080, where that prince was slain, and Rhys ap Tewdwr and Gruffyd ap Cynan were confirmed on the thrones of their ancestors.

The return of these two princes to Wales--the one from Ireland, where he had been born and must have been familiar with the Irish school of poetry, and the other from Armorica, where he probably became acquainted with Armoric traditions, created a new era in Welsh literature, and a great outburst of literary energy took place, which in North Wales manifested itself in a very remarkable revival of poetry, while in South Wales it took more the shape of prose literature between 1080 and 1400, Stephens enumerates no fewer than seventy-nine bards, many of whose works are preserved, and the Red Book of Hergest, concludes with a body of poetry transcribed apparently by Lewis Glyn Cothi, and attributed to bards, forty-five in number, who lived in a period ranging from 1100 to 1450. One of the earliest of these bards was Cynddelw, commonly called Prydydd Mawr, or the great bard. He was bard to Madog ap Meredyth, Prince of Powis, who died in 1159, and two elegies on his death, by Cynddelw, are contained in the Black Book of Caermarthen. There is every reason to believe that the latter part at least of this MS. was transcribed by him.

The influence produced upon Welsh literature by the return of Rhys ap Tewdwr to South Wales was of a different description; and it is probably from this period that the introduction into Wales of Armoric traditions may be dated. The appearance of the *History of the Britons*, by Geoffrey of Monmouth, was the first open manifestation of it. This work, which is written in Latin, at once attained great popularity, and made the fabulous history which it contained, with the romantic tales of Uthyr Pendragon, and Arthur with his Round Table, familiar to the whole world. There is prefixed to this history an epistle-dedicatory to Robert, Earl of Gloucester, son of Henry I. It must therefore have been compiled prior to his death in 1147. In this epistle he states that Walter, Archdeacon of Oxford, a man of great eloquence and learned in foreign histories, gave him a very ancient book in the British tongue (*quondam Britannici sermonis librum vetustissimum*), giving an account of the Kings of Britain from Brutus to Cadwaladyr, and that he had, it the Archdeacon's request, translated it into Latin; and he concludes his history by committing to his contemporary, Caradoc of Llancarvan, the history of the subsequent Kings in Wales, as he does that of the Kings of the Saxons to William of Malmesbury and Henry of Huntingdon, whom he advises to be silent concerning the Kings of the Britons, since they have not the book written in the British tongue (*librum Britannici sermonis*), which Walter, Archdeacon of Oxford, brought out of Britanny (*Britannia*), and which being a true history, he has thus taken care to translate. William of Malmesbury's history is likewise dedicated to Robert, Earl of Gloucester, and is brought down to the 28th year of Henry I., or 1125, in which year it appears to have been written. Henry of Huntingdon's history of the English is dedicated to Alexander, Bishop of Lincoln, and the first part terminates with the death of Henry I. in 1135, in which year it appears to have been written. Geoffrey must therefore have finished his translation, if his account be true, or compiled his work, if it is original, before these dates; but as in his epistle-dedicatory he invites his patron to correct his work, so as to make it more polished, it is possible that there may have been editions prior to the one finally given forth as the completed work, which this epistle and postscript accompanied.

That there was such a person as Walter, Archdeacon of Oxford, seems now admitted; but whether the talc of the Welsh book, brought from Britanny and translated into Latin, is a reality or one of those fictions occasionally prefixed to original works, is a question of very great difficulty; and it will be necessary to inquire whether any light is thrown upon it by the, Welsh versions termed *Brut y Brenhinoedd*, or the History of the Kings. Two of these versions are printed in the *Myvyrian Archæology*. The second is obviously a translation from the Latin edition, as we now have it, to which it closely adheres, and is there termed *Brut Geoffrey ap Arthur*. The first is said to be taken from the Red Book of Hergest; the narrative is shorter and simpler; the epistle-dedicatory is not prefixed to it, and it contains at the end of it this postscript, "I, Walter, Archdeacon of Oxford, did turn this book out of Welsh (*Cymraeg*) into Latin; and in my old age I turned it a second time out of Latin into Welsh." The editor considers this version to be the original Welsh book brought by Walter the Archdeacon from Britanny; and conjecturing that it belongs to in earlier period, and may have been written by Tyssilio, son of Brochwael, who is said to have written a history and to have lived in the seventh century, he has without any authority termed it *Brut Tyssilio*. It is the text from which the Rev. Peter Roberts translated his English version termed *The Chronicle of the Kings of Britain, translated from the Welsh copy attributed to Tyssilio*, and published in 1811.

Now, though the text of the so-called *Brut Tyssilio* is distinctly stated both by the editor of the *Myvyrian Archæology* and by Roberts to be taken from the Red Book of Hergest, no such text is to be found there. The text of the *Brut y Brenhinoedd* in the Red Book is the same as the second version termed *Brut G. ap Arthur*. There are two later MSS. in the library of Jesus College, containing a text similar to that of the *Brut Tyssilio*, and from which it was probably taken. They are exactly alike, but the one bears to have belonged to David Powell of Aberystwith in 1610, and is a MS. of that period, and the other to have been written by Hugh Jones, keeper of the Ashmolean Museum, in 1695, and seems to be a copy of it. Another copy is said to be preserved in the library at Downing in North Wales, having this note attached to it:-- "Walter, Archdeacon of Oxford, translated this part of the Chronicle from Latin into Welsh, and Edward Kyffin copied it for John Trevor of Trevalin, A.D. 1577;" and a copy is likewise contained in the *Book of Basingwerk*, the property of Thomas T. Griffith, Esq., Wrexham, which appears to be in the handwriting of Guttyn Owain and to have been written in 1461. This is the oldest known transcript of this version of the *Brut*.

In the British Museum (MS. Cott., Cleop. B. v.) there is a copy of the *Brut* which differs from this, but approaches more nearly to it than to the *Brut G. ap Arthur*. It has been written about the end of the thirteenth century, and it has the epistle-dedicatory, in which the book given by Walter is termed *Llyvyr Cymraec*, but in the postscript it is stated that the *Cymraec* book which Walter gave him had been translated by him from Latin into *Cymraec*, and again by Geoffrey from *Cymraec* into Latin. The text in the Red Book is, as I mentioned, closely allied to Geoffrey's Latin version, but there is no epistle-dedicatory, and the postscript here again varies from the others. It states that the book Walter had was a Breton book (*llyfr Brvtvn*) which he translated from Breton into Cymraeg (*o Brytanec yg Kymruec*), and which Geoffrey translated into Latin. The only other MSS. which have been accessible to me are those at Hengwrt. There are several copies, some complete and some imperfect, but only one that has the postscript. It is the same text, or nearly so, as that in the Red Book, but varies in the postscript. It states Walter's book to have been a *Cymraec* book, which he translated from *Cymraec* to Latin, and which Geoffrey likewise translated from *Cymraec* to Latin, and again from Latin to *Cymraec*.

There are thus three different Welsh texts—one represented by the first text in the Myvyrian Archæology, by the two late copies in Jesus College, the Downing MS., and the Book of Basingwerk; a second by the Cottonian MS. in the British Museum; and a third by the second text in the Myvyrian

19

Archæology, by the text in the Red Book of Hergest and the Hengwrt MS.; but all differ in the account given of the original MS. By one it is said to have been Latin, by another Cymraec, and by a third Breton. So far we may extricate some facts:--All the MSS. of the first text agree that it was a translation by Walter the Archdeacon from Latin to Welsh; on the authority of the Hengwrt MS., we may pronounce the third to be a translation into Welsh, by Geoffrey of Monmouth, of his Latin edition; the second text probably represents an intermediate stage of the work; all seem to imply that Walter's book was at all events in Latin before it reached Geoffrey; but whether the original was in, Breton, in Cymraec, or in Latin, or whether there ever was an original, there is certainly no text, either in Welsh or in Latin, which now represents it; and all of these texts must be placed in the first part of the twelfth century.

The MSS. containing the Welsh versions usually have a translation into Welsh of the history of Troy, by Dares Phrygius, prefixed to it. Those which represent the first and second texts have a chronicle termed *Brut y Saeson*, annexed to it, which is expressly said by the Cotton MS. to be the work of Caradauc of Llancarvan, and gives a chronicle of events in the history of Wales, interspersed with notices of the Saxon history; but the text in the Red Book is followed by a chronicle containing the Welsh events only, and to which, in a later hand, the title *Brut y Tywysogion* has been attached.

The Red Book of Hergest likewise contains the text of several prose tales and romances connected with the early history of Wales. They are eleven in number, and have been published, with an English translation, by Lady Charlotte Guest, in 1849, under the title of *The Mabinogion, from the, Llyfr Coch o Hergest, and other ancient Welsh manuscripts, with an English translation and notes*. It is justly remarked in the preface of this collection that "some have the character of chivalric romances, and others bear the impress of a far higher antiquity, both as regards the manners they depict and the style of language in which they are composed." So greatly do these Mabinogion differ in character, that they may be considered as forming two distinct classes; one of which generally celebrates heroes of the Arthurian cycle, while the other refers to persons and events of an earlier period, and it is not difficult to assign each tale to one or other of these two classes:--

To the older class belong--
The Tale of Pwyll, Prince of Dyfed. The Tale of Branwen, daughter of Llyr.
The Tale of Manawyddan, the son of Llyr. The Tale of Math, son of Mathonwy.
The Contention of Llud and Llevelys. The Story of Kilhwch and Olwen.
The Dream of Rhonabwy.

To the second class belong—

The Tale of the Lady of the Fountain. The Story of Peredur, son of Evrawc.
The Story of Geraint, son of Erbin. The Dream of Macsen Guledig.

Though the whole of these tales have been published under the title of Mabinogion, that name is applied in the Red Book solely to the first four, which form, in fact, one romance. The name of Arthur only occurs in the last two of this class, and it is in his earliest aspect. They are probably older than the *Bruts* as the substance of the tale called the Contention of Llud and Llevelys occurs in the earliest form of the *Brut*, and is omitted in the later.

The tales included in the second class certainly belong to the full-blown Arthurian Romance.

As early as the date of the Black Book of Caermarthen, some of the Welsh traditions appear under the form of short triads, and that MS. contains a fragment of what were probably the earliest--the Triads of the Horses. A MS. in the Hengwrt collection, which has apparently been written as far back as the year 1300, contains two sets of triads, one termed *Trioedd arbenic*--Chief or excellent Triads which are religious; and. another, called *Trioedd Arthur ac gwyr*--Triads of Arthur and his warriors. And in the Red Book of Hergest are two sets of triads, one called *Trioedd ynys Brydain*, or Triads of the Island of Britain, which contain these Triads of Arthur, with many others; and the other an enlarged edition of the Triads of the Horses. They are both published in the Myvyrian Archæology (vol. ii. p. 1); and to these may be added the *Bonhed y Seint*, or Genealogies of the Saints, which are usually found along with them.

Such is a sketch of the literature of Wales subsequent to the twelfth century, of which we know something of the history; but a branch of its literature still remains to be noticed which has exercised a powerful influence upon the history of the country, the true source and history of which, however, is wrapped in obscurity and encompassed with doubt.

One, of the editors of the Myvyrian Archæology, and a chief contributor of its contents, was Edward Williams, of Flimstone in Glamorgan. He maintained that there had existed at an early period, when bardism flourished as an institution of the country, four chairs or schools of bards, and that one of these chairs still remained--the chair of Glamorgan--of which he was himself the bardic president, and he adopted the bardic title of *Iolo Morganwg*. He declared that the succession of bards and bardic presidents could be traced back to 1300; that the traditions of bardism had been handed down by them in the chair of Glamorgan; that Llywelyn Sion, who was bardic president in 1580, and died in 1616, had reduced this system to writing under the title of the "Book of bardism, or the Druidism of the Bards of the Isle of Britain," which he professed to have compiled from old books in the collection of MSS. at Raglan Castle. Iolo Morganwg published, in 1794, his *Poems, Lyric and Pastoral*, in which he gave to the world some account of this system, and a work which he had prepared for the press, termed *Cyfrinach Beirdd ynys Prydain*, in the Welsh language and from the MS. of Llywelyn Sion, was published after his death by his son in 1829. A further instalment, termed *Barddas*, was printed, with a translation, for the Welsh, MS. Society in 1862.

Among the contributions made by him to the documents printed in the Myvyrian Archæology, were the so-called Historical Triads (vol. ii. p. 5 7) which have been so much founded upon in writing Welsh history, and the

21

Triads called the Wisdom of Catoc, (vol. iii. p. 1), and the Triads of the Bards of Britain and Institutes of the Bards of Dyfnwal Moelmud (vol. iii. pp. 199 and 283). A volume of documents prepared by him as an additional volume of the Myvyrian Archæology, was printed after his death, with a translation, for the Welsh MS. Society, in 1848, termed *The Iolo Manuscripts*.

But the most important document which issued from him, and which has exercised the greatest influence on the popular views of Welsh literature, was the prose tale or Mabinogi, termed *Hanes Taliessin*, and containing the so-called personal history of that bard. A fragment of the Welsh text was given in the first volume of the Myvyrian Archæology; but the whole tale, with a translation, was published by Dr. Owen Pughe, in 1833, in the *Cambrian Quarterly Magazine* (vol. v. p. 198). In his introductory remarks he states that the compiler, Hopkin Thomas Philip, wrote this piece about the year 1370. He lived in Morganwg or Glamorgan. The same tale was published by Lady Charlotte Guest in 1849, in the third volume of her Mabinogion; and she states that her copy was made up from two fragments--the one contained in a MS. of the library of the Welsh school in London, written in a modern hand, and dated in 1758; the other from a MS. belonging to Iolo Morganwg. The fragment in the Welsh school library was probably that printed in. the Myvyrian Archæology; and the MS. belonging to Iolo Morganwg, that used by Dr. Owen Pughe, as the latter states in his introductory remarks, "Of the narrative part but one version exists." Iolo Morganwg himself states that the romance entitled *Hanes Taliessin--i.e.* the history of Taliessin--was "written so late at least as the fourteenth, or rather the fifteenth, century," and that he used the expression fifteenth century in the loose sense of the century from 1500 to 1600 is plain, as he likewise states that Hopkin Thomas Philip flourished about 1560. This is the same Hopkin Thomas Philip who, Dr. Owen Pughe says, wrote it about 1370; but there is no real difference between them as to his true age, for in his *Cambrian Biography*, published in 1803, thirty years before, Dr. Owen Pughe, then Mr. William Owen, has the following: "Hopcin Thomas Phylip, a poet who flourished between A.D. 1590 and 1630." At that time, therefore, the compilation of the *Hanes Taliessin* was not placed further back than the end of the sixteenth or beginning of the seventeenth century. The prose narrative contains a number of poems stated to have been composed by Taliessin in connection with the events of his life, but these will be noticed when we come to deal with the poetry attributed to that bard.

It is a peculiarity attaching to almost all of the documents which have emanated from the chair of Glamorgan, in other words, from *Iolo Morganwg*, that they are not to be found in any of the Welsh MSS. contained in other collections, and that they must be accepted on his authority alone. It is not unreasonable, therefore, to say that they must be viewed with some suspicion, and that very careful discrimination is required in the use of them.

Chapter Three - Sources of The Early History of Wales

IN order to discriminate between what is true and what is fabulous in the early history of Wales as presented to us in the historic literature subsequent to the twelfth century, and to disentangle the fragments of real history contained in them, so as to enable us to form something like a true conception of its leading features, it is necessary to test it by comparing it with the statements in contemporary authorities of other countries, and by referring to such earlier native documents as have come down to us. Of the latter class there are only three, and it is requisite that we should form a right conception of their authority. The first are the works of Gildas, who wrote in Latin. They are usually considered as consisting of two pieces, the *Historia* and the *Epistola*, but they may be viewed as forming one treatise. Questions have been raised upon the lives of Gildas, as to whether there was one or two persons of the name--an earlier and a later; but, viewing the question in its literary aspect, it is of little consequence, for the treatise is evidently the work of one man, and there is evidence in the work itself of his date. The writer states that he was born in the year in which the battle of Badon was, fought, and that he wrote forty-four years after. [1] According to the oldest Welsh annals, the battle of Badon was fought in the year 516, which would place the composition of the treatise in the year 560; and the Irish annals record the death of Gildas in 570, ten years after.

Only three MSS. of Gildas are known to have existed, and the oldest of these has since perished. It was in the Cottonian. Library (Vit. A. vi.), but fortunately the text of Josseline's edition of Gildas in 1568 was printed from it, and, according to Mr. Petrie, so correctly that it may be taken as representing it. [2] The other two MSS. are in the public library at Cambridge (Dd, i. 17 and Ff, i. 27)--the one of the end of the fourteenth or beginning of fifteenth centuries, and the other of the thirteenth century. The first is said to have belonged to the monks of Glastonbury, and the second to the monks of Durham. This latter MS. inserts various passages which are not to be found in the other MSS. Thus the other MSS. mention that the Saxons were invited "superbo tyranno," and the Durham MS. inserts the words, "Gurthrigerno Britannorum duce." Again, where the other MSS. mention the "Obsessio Badonici montis," the Durham MS. inserts "qui prope Sabrinum ostium habetur." The work of Gildas had early found its way to the Northumbrian monks, as Bede evidently uses it in his history, and they are probably answerable for the additions contained in this MS. It has been remarked that the account given by Gildas of the departure of the Romans from Britain, and the events which followed, are inconsistent with the statements of contemporary Greek and Roman authors; but this appears to me to arise solely from Gildas having misplaced the only document directly quoted by him, which has forced upon his narrative a chronology inconsistent with the true sequence of events, and which, unfortunately, has likewise influenced Bede's history. Gildas narrates two devastations by the Picts and Scots, after each of which they were driven back by the Roman troops; then he states the final departure of the Roman army, followed by the occupation of the territory between the walls by the enemy. When he quotes this document, which purports to be a letter by the Britons, addressed "Actio ter consuli," imploring assistance against the "*Barbari*, who drive them to the sea, while the sea throws them back on the Barbari." He understands by these "Barbari" the Picts and Scots, and places after this latter the invitation to the Saxons, who first drive back the Picts and then unite with them to subjugate the Britons. Now the exact date when this letter must have been written can be at once ascertained, for Aetius was consul for the third time in 446, and the dates of the other events have been fixed in accordance with this; but while this postdates these events when compared with the other authorities, the sequence is the same, with the single exception of the place occupied by this letter. We know from Zosimus that the Roman army really left finally in 409. We see, from Constantius' *Life of St. Germanius* that the Saxons had already, in alliance with the Picts, attacked the Britons in 429; and Prosper, a contemporary authority, tells us that in 441 "Britanniæ usque ad hoc tempus variis cladibus evenitibusque latæ, in ditionem Saxonum rediguntur." It is impossible to mistake this language. The Saxons must have completed their conquest six years before the letter was written, and it follows that the "Barbari" to which it refers must have meant the Saxons, and that it was an appeal to the Romans to assist them against the Saxon invaders. The language of the letter, too, which seems exaggerated and inapplicable to the incursions of the Picts and Scots from the north, is much more natural if directed against the steady and permanent encroachment of the Saxons from the east. Take the letter from its present place, and place it after the narrative of the Saxons turning against the Britons and attacking them, and the order of events at once harmonises with the other authorities, while the necessity for postdating them in Gildas no longer exists. It was no doubt his misapprehending the meaning of this document, and misplacing it, which led to the arrival of the Saxons being supposed to have taken place after it, and to the date of 447, the succeeding year, being affixed to it by Bede.

The second document is the work usually termed Nennius' *History of the Britons*, and it is very necessary that we should form a right conception of this work, and a correct estimate of its authority. The *Origines*, of Isidorus of Seville, who died in 636, and which must have been compiled some considerable time earlier, soon became widely known, and led to works being written in many countries upon their early history, in which the traditions of the people were engrafted upon it. Either in the same century, or the beginning of the next, a work was compiled in Britain, termed *Historia Britonum*. The author of it is unknown, but the original work appears to have been written in Welsh and translated into Latin. It seems to have acquired popularity at once, and become the basis upon which numerous additions were made from time to time. The original work appears to have belonged more to the North than to Wales, or at least the latter part of it, as the events of that part are mainly connected with the North, and it terminates with the foundation of the Anglic kingdom of Northumbria by Ida. Soon after was added what is termed the *Genealogia*, being the descent of the Saxon kings of the different small kingdoms; but here too Northumbria predominates, and most of the events mentioned in it are connected with its history. It must have been compiled shortly after 738, as that is the latest date to which the history of any of the Saxon kingdoms is brought down; and it too bears the marks of being a translation into Latin from Welsh. An edition of the *Historia* seems to have been made in 823, the fourth year of Mervyn Frych, king of Wales, by Marc the Anchorite, when that part at least of the text which contains portions of the life of Germanus, and probably the legend of St. Patrick, must have been inserted. Another edition in 858 bears the name of Nennius. The original work was very early attributed to Gildas, but latterly the whole work bore the name of Nennius.

The oldest MSS. are of the tenth century, and are three in number. They represent two different editions of the work. The Vatican MS. bears the name of Marc the Anchorite, and contains the date of 946, and the fifth year of King Edmund. It is remarkable enough that this was the year in which that king conquered Cambria, and made it over to Malcolm, king of Scots. It would seem as if this conquest had brought it first under the notice of the Saxons, and this conjecture is further strengthened by the fact that the Paris MS. exactly corresponds with this, and that this MS. alone, of all the numerous MSS. which have come down to us, has the names, of the Saxon kings in the Saxon and not in the Welsh form.

The MS. which represents the other edition is one in the British Museum (Harl. 3856). It contains in it the date of 796, but there are additions to it not found in any other MS., which must have been compiled in the year 977. These, are, *first*, a later chronicle of Welsh events, from the year 444, and though the last event recorded is in 954, the "anni" have been written down to 977; the second is a collection of Welsh genealogies, commencing with that of Owen, son of Howel dda, king of South Wales, who reigned from 946 to 985,--both in the paternal and maternal line,--from which we may infer that the writer was connected with South Wales. The Chronicle was made the basis of two much later chronicles, in which the events are brought down to 1286 and 1288, and the whole have been edited under the name of *Annales Cambriæ*, but the two later chronicles have in reality no claim to be incorporated with it, as the differences are not various readings of one text, but later additions. The great value of this Chronicle arises from the fact that it was compiled a century and a half before the Bruts were written, and it detracts from that value to add to it later additions taken from chronicles compiled as many years after the Bruts, and which are obviously derived from them. It is also the source from which many of the entries in the Welsh *Brut y Saeson* and *Brut y Tywysogion* have been translated. It is obvious that both the Chronicle and the Welsh genealogies were additions intended to illustrate the *Genealogia* attached to the *Historia Britonum*, and to bring the Welsh history down to the date of the compiler. The Chronicle inserts the events in the *Genealogia* in the very words of the latter; and when the *Genealogia* enumerates four Welsh kings as fighting against one of the kings of Bernicia, the Welsh genealogies give the pedigree of these four kings, in the same order.

The *Historia Britonum* was translated into Irish by *Giollacaomhan*, an Irish Sennachy, who died in 1072, and various Irish and Pictish additions were incorporated in the translation.

The work, therefore, as it existed prior to the twelfth century, may be said to consist of six parts: *First*, The original nucleus of the work termed *Historia Britonum*; *second*, The *Genealogia*, added soon after 738; *third*, The *Memorabilia*; *fourth*, The Legends of St. Germanus and of St. Patrick, added by Mare in 823, the latter being merely attached to his edition, and incorporated in that of Nennius; *fifth*, The Chronicle and the Welsh genealogies, added in 977; and, *sixth*, The Irish and Pictish additions, by Giollacaomhan. [3] The MSS. of Nennius amount to twenty-eight in number; and of the later MSS. several seem to have been connected with Durham. To the monks of Durham many interpolations may be traced very similar to those in Gildas: in some MSS. they are written on the margin, and in others incorporated into the text. Thus, when the Mare Fresicum is mentioned, the Durham commentator adds, "quod inter nos Scotosque est." The result of my study of this work is to place its authority higher than is usually done; and, used with care and with due regard to the alterations made from time to time, I believe it to contain a valuable summary of early tradition, as well as fragments of real history, which are not to be found elsewhere.

The third native authority prior to the twelfth century is *The Ancient Laws and Institutes of Wales*. They were published by the Record Commission of England in 1841, and the oldest of them, the Laws of Howel dda, are of the tenth century.

Such are the native materials upon which, along with the old Roman and Saxon authorities, any attempt to grasp the leading features of the early history of Wales must be based.

[1] Bede understood this well-known passage as implying that the battle of Badon was fought forty-four years after the arrival of the Saxons; but it is now generally admitted that this is a mistaken construction of the passage, and that the true import is as above, to which I also give my adhesion.
[2] Josseline says it had belonged to Christ Church, Canterbury, and was 600 years old.
[3] The original work will be quoted under the title of the *Historia Britonum*, the second portion under that of the *Genealogia*, or both generally as Nennius, and the fifth as the Chronicle and Genealogies of 977. The Irish Annals will be quoted from the *Chronicles of the Picts and Scots*, recently published, being the first of the series of Scottish Record publications.

Chapter Four - State of The Country in the Sixth Century, and Its History Prior to A.D. 560.

THE State of Wales and the distribution of the Cymric population, between the termination of the Roman dominion and the sixth century, so far as we can gather it from these ancient authorities, does not accord with what we should expect from the ordinary conception of the history of that period, but contrasts in many respects strangely with it.

We are accustomed to regard the Cymric population as occupying Britain south of the wall between the Tyne and the Solway; as exposed to the incursions of the Picts and Scots from the country north of the wall, and inviting the Saxons to protect them from their ravages, who in turn take possession of the south of Britain, and drive the native population gradually back till they are confined to the mountainous region of Wales and to Cornwall. We should expect, therefore, to find Wales the stronghold of the Cymry and exclusively occupied by them; the Saxons in the centre of Britain, and the country north of the wall between the Tyne and Solway surrendered to the barbaric tribes of the Picts and Scots. The picture presented to us, when we first survey the platform of these contending races; is something very different. We find the sea-board of Wales on the west in the occupation of the *Gwyddyl* or Gael, and the Cymry confined to the eastern part of Wales only, and placed between them and the Saxons. A line drawn from Conway on the north to Swansea on the south would separate the two races of the Gwyddyl and the Cymry, on the west and on the east. In North Wales, the Cymry possessing Powys, with the Gwyddyl in Gwynned. and Mona or Anglesea; in South Wales, the Cymry possessing Gwent and Morganwg, with the Gwyddyl in Dyfed; and Brecknock occupied by the mysterious Brychan and his family.

On the other hand, from the Dee and the Humber to the Firths of Forth and Clyde, we find the country almost entirely possessed by a Cymric population, where ultimately a powerful Cymric kingdom was formed; but this great spread of the Cymric population to the north not entirely unbroken. On the north of the Solway Firth, between the Nith and Lochryan, was Galloway with its *Galwydel*; in the centre the great wood, afterwards forming the forests of Ettrick and Selkirk and the district of Tweeddale, extending from the Ettrick to the range of the Pentland Hills, and north of that range, stretching to the river Carron, was the mysterious Manau Gododin with its *Brithwyr*. On, the east coast, from the Tyne to the Esk, settlements of Saxons gradually encroaching on the Cymry.

A very shrewd and sound writer, the Rev. W. Basil Jones, now Archdeacon of York, struck with this strange distribution of the population in Wales, has, in his essay, *Vestiges of the Gael in Gwynedd*, revived a theory first suggested by Edward Lhuyd that the Gael preceded the Cymry in the occupation of the whole of Britain, and that these Gael in the western districts of Wales were the remains of the original population, seen, as it were, in the act of departing from the country before the presence of the Cymry; but, though maintained with much ingenuity, it runs counter both to the traditions, which indicate their presence and to the real probabilities of the case. Till the year 360 the Roman province extended to the northern wall which crossed the isthmus between the Forth and the Clyde, and the Cymric population was no doubt co-extensive; but in that year barbarian tribes broke into the province, which the Roman authors tell us consisted of the Picts, Scots, and Saxons, and, though driven back, renewed their incursions from time to time. The Saxons, of course, made their descents on the east coast, and Gildas tells us that the Picts came *ab aquilone*, the Scots *a circione*, implying that they came from different directions; while all authorities concur in making Ireland the head-quarters of the latter. The Saxons made their descents on the east coast, the Picts from the north, and the Scots from the West.

Gildas tells us that the Picts finally occupied the country up to the southern wall *pro indigenis*, and settled down in the northern regions; and Nennius, in his account of the arrival of the Scots in Ireland, adds four settlements of them *in regionibus Britanniæ*, one of which he expressly says was in Demetia, or South Wales, and terms the people expelled by Cunedda and his sons, Scotti. The Scots, therefore, probably effected a settlement on the west coast of Wales, as they did on that of Scotland; and these foreign settlements in the heart of the Cymric population of Wales and the North seem more probably to have been permanent deposits remaining from the frequent incursions of the so-called barbaric tribes on the Roman province, than vestiges of an original population.

Relieved from the erroneous chronology applied by Bode to the events narrated by Gildas, into which he was led by the false place occupied by the letter to Aetius, the statements of Gildas harmonise perfectly with the facts indicated by contemporary Roman and Greek authors. The barbaric tribes who broke into the province in 360 were driven back by Theodosius in 368, and the province restored to the northern wall. Then follows the usurpation of the title of Imperator by Maximus in 383, who takes the Roman troops over to Gaul. This is succeeded by the first *devastatio* by the Picts and Scots, when the Britons apply to the Romans for assistance. Stilicho sends a single legion, who drive them back and reconstruct the northern wall. Claudian records the defeat of the barbarian tribes, which he names Picts, Scots, and Saxons, the fortifying the wall, and the return of the legion, which was re-called in 402. Then follows the second *devastatio* by the Picts and Scots, and the second appeal for assistance, and a larger force is sent, by whom they are again driven back. The Roman troops then elect Marcus, after him Gratian Municeps, and finally Constantine, as Imperator, who likewise passes over to Gaul with the troops in 409, after having repaired the southern wall. Then follows the third *devastatio* by the Picts and Scots, and Honorius writes to the cities of Britain that they must protect themselves. The Picts settle down in the region north of the wall, the Scots return to Ireland, soon to reappear and again effect settlements on the western sea-board. The Saxons are appealed to for help, but unite with the Picts to attack the Britons, and finally bring the greater part of the country under their subjection in 441, and the Britons vainly appeal to Aetius for assistance in 446.

Such is a rapid sketch of the events which brought about the destruction of the Roman province, when the statements of Gildas are brought into harmony with those of the classical writers, and which produced the relative position of the different races presented to us soon after the final departure of the Romans.

Passing over the legends connected with Gortigern, as involving an inquiry into his real period and history, which has no direct bearing upon our immediate object, and would lead us beyond the, limits of this sketch, the first event that emerges from the darkness which surrounds the British history at this period, and which influenced the relative position of the different races constituting its population, is the appearance of Cunedda, his retreat from the north, and the expulsion of the Gael from Wales by his descendants. We are told in the *Historia Britonum* that the Scots who occupied Dyfed and the neighbouring districts of Gower and Cedgueli "expulsi sunt a Cuneda et a filiis ejus;" and in the *Genealogia* that "Maelcunus Magnus rex apud Brittones regnabat, id est, in regione Guenedote, quia atavus illias, id est, Cunedag, cum filiis suis, quorum numerus octo erat, venerat prius de parte sinistrali, id est, de regione que vocatur Manau Guotodin, centum quadraginta sex annis antequam Mailcun regnaret, et Scottos cum ingentissima clade expulerunt ab istis regionibus." As Mailcun was the first king to reign in Gwynedd after the Scots were driven out, and he was fourth in descent from Cunedda, it is clear that the expression, that they were expelled "a Cuneda cum filiis ejus," is used somewhat loosely, and that the actual expulsion must have been effected by his descendants. In point of fact, we know from other documents that the real agent in the expulsion of the Scots from Gwynedd was Caswallawn Law Hir, the great-grandson of Cunedda and father of Mailcun. If four generations existed between Cunedda and Mailcun, this interval is well enough expressed by a period of 146 years; but an unfortunate date in the Chronicle of 977 has perplexed the chronology of this period, and led to Cunedda being placed earlier than is necessary. The Chronicle has, under the year 547, "Mortalitas magna in qua pausat Mailcun rex Guenedote;" and if Mailcun died in 547, a period of 146 years from the beginning of his reign would take us back to the fourth century, and place Cunedda towards the end of it; but we know from Gildas that Mailcun did not die in 547, as he was alive and rapidly rising to power when Gildas wrote in 560, and the date in the chronicle seems to be a purely artificial date, produced by adding the period 146 years to the beginning of the century. Gildas mentions that Maglocunus or Mailcun had, some time previously, retired into a monastery, from whence he emerged not long before he wrote, and this is probably the true commencement of his reign. A period of 146 years prior to 560 brings us to 414; and some years before that must be considered the true era of the exodus of

29

Cunedda, with his sons, from Manau Guotodin. It thus coincides very closely with the period of the occupation of territory between the walls by the Picts on the final withdrawal of the Roman troops in 409.

Cunedda is termed in all Welsh documents *Guledig*, a name derived from the word *Gulad*, a country, and signifying Ruler. The same term is applied to Maximus, who is called in Welsh documents, *Maxim Guledig*. It is therefore equivalent to the title and position of Imperator conferred upon him by the troops in Britain. After Maximus, and before the Roman troops left Britain, they elected three Imperatores, the last of whom, Constantine, withdrew the army to Gaul. We know from the *Notitia Imperii* that the Roman legionary troops were mainly stationed at the Roman wall and on the Saxon shore, to defend the province from inroads of the barbarian tribes; and when the Roman army was finally withdrawn, and Honorius wrote to the cities of Britain that they must defend themselves, the Roman troops were probably replaced by native bodies of warriors, and the functions of the Roman Imperator continued in the British *Guledig*. If this view be correct, the real fact conveyed by Nennius' intimation, that Cunedda had left the regions in the north called Manau Guotodin 146 years before the reign of Mailcun, is that in 410, on the Picts conquering the land up to the southern wall, the Guledig had withdrawn from the northern to within the southern wall. In the Welsh documents there is also frequent mention of the *Gosgordd* or retinue in connection with the *Guledig*, which appears to have usually consisted of 300 horse. It was certainly a body of men specially employed in the defence of the borders, as the Triads of Arthur and his warriors--a document not subject to the same suspicion as the Historical Triads--mentions the "three *Gosgordds* of the passes of the island of Britain," and the *Gosgordd mur* or Gosgordd of the wall, is also mentioned in the poems. It seems to be equivalent to the body of 300 cavalry attached to the Roman legion; three times that number, or 900 horse, forming the horse of the auxiliary troops attached to a legion.

The next *Guledig* mentioned is the notice by Gildas, in a part of his narrative that indicates a time somewhat later, that the Britons took arms "duce Ambrosio Auerliano," a man of Roman descent. whose relations had borne the purple. The term "Aurelianus" is Gildas' equivalent for *Guledig*, as he afterwards mentions Aurelius Conanus, and both are known in Welsh documents by the names of *Emmrys Guledig* and *Cynan Guledig*; and Ambrosius must have been connected by descent with prior "Imperatores" created by the Roman troops. Gildas then adds that after this "nunc cives, nunc hostes, vincebant usque ad annum, obsessionis Badonici montis", and the date of this event is fixed by the chronicle attached to Nennius, which places it in the year 516, in which year Gildas was born.

The period between the success of Ambrosius and the siege of Badon Hill is filled up in the *Historia Britonum* with the account of twelve battles fought by Arthur, of which that of Badon Hill is the last. In the oldest form of the text he is simply termed Arthur, and the title only of "dux bellorum" is given him. It says, "Tunc Arthur pugnabat contra illos (*i.e.* Saxones), in illis diebus cum regibus Britannorum, sed ipse dux erat bellorum." He was not "dux" or "rex Britannorum," but "dux bellorum," a title which plainly indicates the *Guledig*. That he bears here a very different character from the Arthur of romance is plain enough. That the latter was entirely a fictitious person is difficult to believe. There is always some substratum of truth on which the wildest legends are based, though it may be so disguised and perverted as hardly to be recognised; and I do not hesitate to receive the Arthur of Nennius as the historic Arthur, the events recorded of him being not only consistent with the history of the period, but connected with localities which can be identified, and with most of which his name is still associated. That the events here recorded of him are not mentioned in the Saxon Chronicle and other Saxon authorities, is capable of explanation. These authorities record the struggle between the Britons and the Saxons south of the Humber; but there were settlements of Saxons in the north even at that early period, [1] and it is with these settlements that the war narrated in the *Historia Britonum* apparently took place.

The *Historia Britonum* records among the various bodies of Saxons who followed Hengist to Britain one led by his son Octa and his nephew Ebissa, to whom he promises "regiones que sunt in aquilone juxta murum qui vocatur Gual"--the name given by Nennius to the northern wall. They arrive with forty ships, and after ravaging the Orkneys and circumnavigating the Picts, they occupy "regiones plurimas usque ad confinia Pictorum." The Harleian MS. inserts; the words "ultra Frenessicum Mare," to which the Durham MSS. add, "quod inter nos Scotosque est," to show that the, Firth of Forth is meant. That they may have had settlements beyond the Firth is very probable, but the regions next the wall, as far as the confines of the Picts, can mean nothing but the districts lying between the Forth and Clyde, through which the northern wall passes, as far as the river Forth, which formed at all times the southern boundary of the kingdom of the Picts. These regions are nearly equivalent to the modern counties of Stirling and Dumbarton. All Welsh traditions connected with this war invariably designate Octa and Ebissa, or Eossa as they termed him, and their successors, as Arthur's opponents, and we shall see that the localities of his twelve battles, as recorded by Nennius, are all more or less connected with the districts in the vicinity of the northern wall.

The first battle was "in ostium fluminis quod dicitur Glein." There are two rivers of this name--one in Northumberland, mentioned by Bode as the river where Paulinus baptized the Angles in 627, and the other in Ayrshire. It rises in the mountains which separate that county from Lanarkshire, and falls into the Irvine in the parish of Loudoun. It is more probable that Arthur advanced into Scotland on the west, where he would pass through the friendly country peopled by the Cymry, than through Bernicia, already strongly occupied by bodies of Angles; and it is at the mouth of the latter river, probably, that he first encountered his opponents. It accords better, too, with the order of his battles, for the second, third, fourth, and fifth, were "super aliud flumen quod dicitur Dubglas et est in regione Linnuis." Here must have been the first severe struggle, as four battles were fought on the same river, and here he must have penetrated the "regiones juxta murum," occupied by the Saxons. Dubglas is the name now called Douglas. There are many rivers and rivulets of this name in Scotland; but none could be said to be "in regione Linnuis," except two rivers--the Upper and Lower Douglas, which fall into Loch Lomond, the one through Glen Douglas, the other at Inveruglas, and care both in the district of the Lennox, the Linnuis of Nennius. Here, no doubt, the great struggle took place, and the hill called Ben Arthur at the head of Loch Long, which towers over this district between the two rivers, perpetuates the name of Arthur in connection with it.

The sixth battle was "super flumen quod vocatur Bassas." [2] There is now no river of this name in Scotland, and it has been supposed to have been somewhere near the Bass Rock, the vicinity of which it is presumed may have given its name to some neighbouring stream. The name Bass, however, is also applied to a peculiar mound having the appearance of being artificial, which is formed near a river, though really formed by natural causes. There is one on the Ury river in Aberdeenshire termed the Bass of Inverury, and there are two on the bank of the Carron, now called Dunipace, erroneously supposed to be formed from the Gaelic and Latin words *Duni pacis*, or hills of peace, but the old form of which was *Dunipais*, the latter syllable being no doubt the same word Bass. Directly opposite, the river Bonny flows into the Carron, and on this river I am disposed to place the sixth battle.

The seventh battle was "in silva Caledonis, id est, Cat Coit Celidon"--that is, the battle was so called, for *Cat* means a battle, and *Coed Celyddon* the Wood of Celyddon. This is the Nemus Caledonis that Merlin is said, in the Latin *Vita Merlini*, to have fled to after the battle of Ardderyth, and where, according to the tradition reported by Fordun (B. iii. c. xxvi.), he met Kentigern, and afterwards was slain by the shepherds of Meldredus, a regulus of the country on the banks of the Tweed, "prope oppidum Dunmeller." Local tradition places the scene of it in Tweeddale, where, in the parish of Drumelzier, anciently Dunmeller, in which the name of Meldredus is preserved, is shown the grave of Merlin. The upper part of the valley of the Tweed was once a great forest, of which the forests of Selkirk and Ettrick formed a part, and seems to have been known by the name of the *Coed Celyddon*.

The eighth battle was "in Castello Guinnion." The word *castellum* implies a Roman fort, and *Guinnion* is in Welsh an adjective formed from *gwen*, white. The Harleian MS. adds that Arthur carried into battle upon his shoulders an image of the Virgin Mary, and that the Pagani were put to flight and a great slaughter made of them by virtue of the Lord Jesus Christ and of Saint Mary his mother. Henry of Huntingdon, who likewise gives this account, says the image was upon his shield; and it has been well remarked that the Welsh *ysgwyd* is a shoulder and *ysgwydd* a shield, and that a Welsh original had been differently translated. Another MS. adds that he likewise took into battle a cross he had brought from Jerusalem, and that the fragments are still preserved at Wedale. Wedale is a district watered by the rivers Gala and Heriot, corresponding to the modern parish of Stow, anciently called the Stow in Wedale. The name Wedale means "The dale of woe," and that name having been given by the Saxons implies that they had experienced a great disaster here. The church of Stow being dedicated to St. Mary, while General Roy places a Roman castellum not far from it, indicates very plainly that this was the scene of the battle.

The ninth battle was "in urbe Leogis" according to the Vatican, "Legionis" according to the Harleian text. The former adds "qui Britannice Kairlium dicitur." It seems unlikely that a battle could have been fought at this time with the Saxons at either Caerleon on the Esk or Caerleon on the Dee, which is Chester; and these towns Nennius terms in his list not Kaerlium or Kaerlion, but Kaer Legion. It is more probably some town in the north, and the *Memorabilia* of Nennius will afford some indication of the town intended. The first of his *Memorabilia* is "Stagnum Lumonoy," or Loch Lomond, and he adds "non vadit ex eo ad mare nisi unum flumen quod vocatur Leum"--that is the Leven. The Irish Nennius gives the name correctly *Leamhuin*, and the Ballimote text gives the name of the town, *Cathraig in Leomhan* (for *Leamhan*), the town on the Leven. This was Dumbarton, and the identification is confirmed by the *Bruts*, which place one of Arthur's battles at Alclyd, while his name has been preserved in a parliamentary record of David II. in 1367, which denominates Dumbarton "Castrum Arthuri."

The tenth battle was "in littore fluminis quod vocatur Treuruit." There is much variety in the readings of this name, other MSS. reading it "Trath truiroit," or the shore of Truiroit; but the original Cymric form is given us in two of the poems in the *Black Book*: it is in one *Trywruid*, and in the other *Tratheu Trywruid*. There is no known river bearing a name approaching to this. *Tratheu*, or shores, implies a sea-shore or sandy beach, and can only be applicable to a river having an estuary. An old description of Scotland, written in 1165 by one familiar with Welsh names, says that the river which divides the "regna Anglorum et Scottorum et currit juxta oppidum de Strivelin" was "Scottice vocata *Froch*, Britannice *Werid*." [3] This Welsh name for the Forth at Stirling has disappeared, but it closely resembles the last Part of Nennius' name, and the difference between *wruid*, the last part of the name Try-wruid, and Werid is trifling. The original form must have been Gwruid or Gwerid, the G disappearing in combination. If by the *tratheu Try-wruid* the Links of Forth are meant, and Stirling was the scene of this battle, the name of Arthur is also connected with it by tradition, for William of Worcester, in his *Itinerary*, says "Rex Arthurus custodiebat le round table in castro de Styrlyng aliter Snowdon West Castle."

The eleventh battle was fought "in monte qui dicitur Agned,"--that is in *Mynyd Agned*, or Edinburgh, and here too the name is preserved in *Sedes Arthuri* or Arthur's Seat. This battle seems not to have been fought against the Saxons, for one MS. adds "Cathregonnum," and another "contra illos que nos Catlibregyon appellamus." They were probably Picts.

The twelfth battle was "in Monte Badonis." This is evidently the "obsessio Montes Badonici" of Gildas, and was fought in 516. It has been supposed to have been near Bath, but the resemblance of names seems alone to have led to this tradition. Tradition, equally points to the northern Saxons as the opponents, and in Ossa Cyllellaur, who is always named as Arthur's antagonist, there is no doubt that a leader of Octa and Ebissa's Saxons is intended; while at this date no conflict between the Britons and the West Saxons could have taken place so far west as Bath. The scene of the battle near Bath was said to be on the Avon, which Layamon mentions as flowing past Badon Hill. But on the Avon, not far from Linlithgow, is a very remarkable hill, of considerable size, the top of which is strongly fortified with double ramparts, and past which the Avon flows. This hill is called Bouden Hill. Sibbald says, in his *Account of Linlithgowshire in* 1710:--"On the Buden hill are to be seen the vestiges of an outer and inner camp. There is a great cairn of stones upon Lochcote hills over against Buden, and in the adjacent ground there have been found chests of stones with bones in them, but it is uncertain when or with whom the fight was." As this battle was the last of twelve which seem to have formed one series of campaigns, I venture to identify Bouden Hill with the Mons Badonicus.

According to the view I have taken of the site of these battles, Arthur's course was first to advance through the Cymric country, on the west, till he came to the Glen where he encountered his opponents. He then invades the regions about the wall, occupied by the Saxons in the Lennox, where he defeats them in four battles. He advances along the Strath of the Carron as far as Dunipace, where, on the Bonny, his fifth battle is fought; and from thence marches south through Tweeddale, or the Wood of Celyddon, fighting a battle by the way, till he comes to the valley of the Gala, or Wedale, where be defeats the Saxons of the east coast. He then proceeds to master four great fortresses: first, *Kaerlium*, or Dumbarton; next, Stirling, by defeating the enemy in the *tratheu Tryweryd*, or Carse of Stirling; then *Mynyd Agned*, or Edinburgh, the great stronghold of the Picts, here called *Cathbregion*; and, lastly, Boudon Hill, in the centre of the country, between these strongholds.

The Bruts probably relate a fact, in which there is a basis of real history, when they state that he gave the districts he had wrested from the Saxons to three brothers--Urien, Llew, and Arawn. To Urien he gave Reged, and the district intended by this name appears from a previous passage, where Arthur is said to have driven the Picts from Alclyde into "Mureif, a country which is otherwise termed *Reged*," and that they took refuge there in Loch Lomond. Loch Lomond was therefore in it, and it must have been the district on the north side of the Roman wall or *Mur*, from which it was called *Mureif*. To Llew he gave Lodoncis or Lothian. This district was partly occupied by the Picts whom Arthur had subdued at the battle of *Mynyd Agned*; and this is the Lothus of the Scotch traditions, who was called King of the Picts, and whose daughter was the mother of Kentigern. And to Arawn he gave a district which they call *Yscotlont* or *Prydyn*, and which was probably the most northern parts of the conquered districts, at least as far as Stirling.

In 537, twenty-one years after, the Chronicle of 977 records, "Gweith Camlan in qua Arthur et Medraut coruere;" the battle of Camlan, in which Arthur and Medraut perished. This is the celebrated battle of Camlan, which figures so largely in the Arthurian romance, where Arthur was said to have been mortally wounded and carried to Avallon, that mysterious place; but here he is, simply recorded as having been killed in battle. It, is surprising that historians should have endeavoured to place this battle in the south, as the same traditions, which encircle it with so many fables, indicate very clearly who his antagonists were. Medraut or Modred was the son of that Llew to whom Arthur is said to have given Lothian, and who, as Lothus, King of the Picts, is invariably connected with that part of Scotland. His forces were Saxons, Picts, and Scots, the very races Arthur is said to have conquered in his Scotch campaigns. If it is to be viewed as a real battle at all, it assumes the appearance of an insurrection of the population of these conquered districts, under Medraut, the son of that Llew to whom one of them was given, and we must look for its site there. On the south bank of the Carron, in the very heart of these districts, are remains which have always been regarded as those of an important Roman town, and to this, the name of Camelon has long been attached. It has stronger claims than any other to be regarded as the Camlan where Arthur encountered Medraut, with his Picts, Scots, and Saxons, and perished; and its claims are strengthened by the former existence of another ancient building on the opposite side of the river--that singular monument, mentioned as far back as 1293 by the name of "Furnus Arthuri," and subsequently known by that of Arthur's O'on.

In thus endeavouring to identify the localities of these events connected with the names of Cunedda and of Arthur, I do not mean to say that it is all to be accepted as literal history, but as a legendary account of events which had assumed that shape as early as the seventh century, when the text of the *Historia Britonum* was first put together, and which are commemorated in local tradition.

[1] I may refer the reader on this subject to my paper on the "Early Frisian Settlements in Scotland," printed in the *Proceedings of the Society of Antiquaries* (vol. iv. p. 169). For the struggle in the south, the reader cannot do better than refer to Dr. Guest's very able papers in the *Archæological Journal*.
[2] The printed text of the Vatican MS. of Nennius has "Lussas," but this is a mistake. The original MS. reads "Bassas."
[3] *Chronicle of the Picts and Scots*, p. 136.--It may seem strange that I should assert that Gwryd and Forth are the same word. But *Gwer* in Welsh is represented by *Fear* in Irish, the old form of which was *For*, and final *d* in Welsh is in Irish *ch*, in Pictish *th*. The river which falls into the Dee near Bala, in North Wales, is called the Try-weryn, a very similar combination.

Chapter Five - State of Britain In A.D. 560 When Gildas Wrote, and Kings of the Line of *Dyfi*

GILDAS, in his epistle, written probably from Armorica, draws a dark picture of the state of Britain. The colours may be overcharged and the lines deepened; but, exaggerated though it may be by a Christian zeal, which may have driven him from the country, his language, if there is any reality in it at all, implies a great departure from the Christian faith, and a deep corruption of manners. The expressions which he employs regarding the state of the princes of Wales are but an echo of what is used by other writers regarding the more northern Cymry. In the oldest life of Saint Kentigern, Llew, or Lothus as he is there called, whose daughter was his mother, is described as "vir semipaganus;" and Joceline, who used older documents, calls him "secta paganissimi," and describes the infant church, which had been founded shortly before at Glasgow by Kentigern, as being oppressed by "quidam tyrannus vocabulo Morken," that he "viri Dei vitam atque doctrinam sprevit atque despexit," and that after his death his "Cognati" obliged him to take refuge in Wales, where, under Caswallawn law Hir, the father of Maelgun, Kentigern founded the monastery of Llanelwy, or St. Asaph's. He also says of the Picts, "Picti vero prius per Sanctum Ninianum ex magna parte; postea per Sanctos Kentegernum et Columbam fidem susceperunt; dein in apostasiam lapsi, iterum per predicationem Sancti Kentegerni, non solum Picti, sed et Scoti, et populi innumeri in diversis finibus Britanniæ constituti, ad fidem conversi vel in fide confirmati sunt." There is here indicated a wide-spread apostasy from the Christian church founded by Ninian, which drove Kentigern from Glasgow, and which, on his return from Wales, he was mainly instrumental in healing. His expulsion from Glasgow must have taken place between 540 and 560, as he was a considerable time in Wales and returned in 573. It therefore closely followed the battle of Camlan. Arthur was pre-eminently a Christian leader. The legends connected with the battle in which he carried the image of Saint Mary on his shield, and the cross he obtained from Jerusalem, indicate this. Medraut was the son of that "vir semipaganus" Llew or Loth, and his insurrection with his Pictish and Saxon allies seems like the outburst of a Pagan party. The arrival in 547, no long time after, of Ida, the Anglic king, and the consolidation of the Saxon settlements on the eastern sea-board of the north into the Anglic kingdom of Bernicia, stretching first from the southern wall to the Tweed, with Bainborough for its capital, and pushing its way north until it eventually reached the Firth of Forth, must have strengthened the increasing Paganism, both by the direct subjugation of British and Pictish population by a Pagan king, but also by the insensible influence of the vicinity of a Pagan power. A struggle seems to have taken place between the Christian and Pagan elements in the country, in which the latter at first prevailed, but which terminated in the triumph of the Christian party, and the consolidation of the various petty states into regular kingdoms under its leaders.

Gildas, in his Epistle, addresses five kings by name, and of those he sufficiently indicates the locality of three. The first is Constantine, whom he terms "The tyrannical whelp of the unclean lioness of Damnonia" (immundæ leænæ Damnoniæ tyrannicus catulus), and who must have reigned in Devon and Cornwall. The second is Aurelius Conanus, whom he addresses as "Thou lion's whelp" (Catule leonine). His title of Aurelius is equivalent to *Guledig*. The third was Vortipore, whom he calls "Thou foolish tyrant of the Demetians" (tyrannus Demetarum), and who must have ruled over Dyfed and the regions in South Wales rescued from the Scots by Cunedda and his sons. The fourth was Cuneglase, whom he, addresses as "Thou bear, thou rider and ruler of many, and guider of the chariot which is the receptacle of the bear" (urse multorum sessor aurigaque currus receptaculi ursi); and the fifth was Maglocunus, whom he calls "Thou dragon of the island" (insularis draco). This was Maelgun, who, we learn from the *Genealogia*, ruled in Gwynedd, and was called the Island Dragon, from Mona or Anglesea, from which his father Caswallawn law Hir had expelled the Gwyddyl. The two kings, whose possessions are not indicated, probably possessed the two eastern kingdoms of Powys and Gwent, and Conan, the former, as the genealogies attached to Nennius call Brochwail Powys, who fought in 613, son of Cynan or Conanus.

It is plain, from the language of Gildas, that Maglocunus was one who swayed between Christianity and Paganism, and was rapidly rising into power over the other kings. He describes, him as having "deprived many tyrants as well of their kingdoms is of their lives," as "exceeding many in power," and "strong in arms," and that the King of kings had made him, as well. in kingdom as in stature of body, higher than almost all the other chiefs of Britain. He also describes him as in the beginning of his youth oppressing with sword, spear, and fire, the king his uncle; then repenting "and vowing himself before God a monk," and taking refuge "in the cells where saints repose;" and then being seduced by a crafty wolf out of the fold, and returning to evil, slaying his brother's son and marrying his widow; and he concludes by an urgent appeal to him again to repent and be converted.

There is a curious legend preserved in the old Welsh Laws. It is as follows:-

After the taking of the crown and sceptre of London from the nation of the Cymry, and their expulsion from Lloegyr, they instituted an inquiry to see who of them should be supreme king. The place they appointed was on Traeth Maelgwn at Aber Dyvi, and thereto came the men of Gwynedd, the men of Powys, the men of South Wales, of Reinwg, Morganwg, and of Scissyllwg. And there Maeldav the elder, son of Unhwch Unachen, chief of Moel Esgidion in Meirionydd, placed a chair composed of waxed wings under Maelgwn, so when the tide flowed no one was able to remain excepting Maelgwn because of his chair. And by that means Maelgwn became supreme king, with Aberfraw for his principal court, and the Jarll Mathraval, and the Jarll Dinevwr, and the Jarll Kaer Llion, subject to him, and his word paramount over all, and his law paramount, and he not bound to observe their law. (P. 412)

The Dyvi or Dovey flows into the sea in Cardigan Bay, and terminates in an estuary which divides North from South Wales. On the north shore of the estuary rise the hills of Merioneth. On the south shore is an extensive and dreary moss, extending to the Cardigan hills in the background, and interspersed with a few green knolls rising here and there. Between this moss and the estuary is a flat sandy beach, left dry far into the estuary at low water. The moss is called *Corsfochno*, the sandy shore *Traeth Maelgwn*; and here some transaction took place--some struggle hidden under the disguise of this fable--by which Maelgwn made himself supreme over the other three kings of Wales. This struggle, I take it, was the *Gwaeth Corsfochno*, or the affair of Corsfochno, of the Bards.

But the true field of the contest between the Christian and semi-pagan chiefs was further north, where the great struggle for the mastery took place not long after. The chronicle of 977 records, in 573, "Bellum Armterid." About nine miles north of Carlisle, on the western bank of the river Esk, are two small rising grounds or knolls, called the Knows of Arthuret, and still further north is a ravine, in which a stream called the Carwinelow falls into the Esk. On the north side of that stream the ground rises till it reaches an elevation terminating abruptly in a cliff which overhangs the river Liddel, and on the summit of this cliff is a magnificent native stronghold, with enormous earthen ramparts, now called the Moat of Liddel.

Arthuret is the *Roddwyd Ardderyd*, or Pass of Ardderyd, forming the great western pass leading from the Roman wall into Scotland. Carwinelow is Caer Wendolew, or the city of Gwenddolew, so called from the adjacent stronghold; and here, in 573, was fought the great battle of Ardderyd, [1] between Gwenddolew, whose name is surrounded by bardic tradition with every type and symbol of a semi-pagan cult, and on the other side three leading chiefs, who each became the founder of a kingdom--Maelgwn Gwynedd, Rydderch Hael, and Aedan, son of Gafran, called Fradawg, or the treacherous. The importance of this battle may be inferred from the part it plays in bardic tradition, from the exaggeration with which it is attended when 80,000 Cymry are said to have been engaged in it, and, historically, from the results which followed. Rydderch Hael established himself in Alclyde, or Dumbarton, as the first monarch of the kingdom of Cambria, or Strathclyde, embracing all the petty Cymric states from the Derwent to the Firth of Clyde, and recalled Kentigern from Wales to resume his ecclesiastical primacy over that region, as Bishop of Glasgow and Aedan was solemnly inaugurated king of Dalriada by St. Columba in the island of Iona. [2]

The establishment of these kingdoms seems to have terminated the functions of the *Guledig*, and more thoroughly separated the north, or *Y Gogled*, from Wales, or *Cymru*--Rydderch Hael being now the monarch of the one, and Maelgwn Gwynedd of the other; but when we read in Bode of Aedan, the petty king of the small Scottish state of Dalriada, invading the kingdom of

Bernicia in 603 at the head of an immense and mighty army, it is difficult to avoid the suspicion that he was for the time the Dux Bellorum, or *Guledig*, in the north, and had ranged under him the whole Celtic force of the country. Maelgwn, however, by this time must have been dead, the latest date assigned by any writer for the termination of his reign being 586. According to the Bruts he did not transmit his kingdom to his son, and the subsequent history, as given by Welsh authorities, is as follows:--Maelgwn was succeeded in the sovereignty of Britain by Caredig, and in Gwynedd, or North Wales, by Iago, son of Beli, his great-grandson. Under Caredig, the Cymry were finally driven by the Saxons across the Severn, and confined to Cornwall and Wales. Ingo was slain in 603 by Cadavael, and was succeeded in North Wales by his son Cadvan, who joined Brochwel, Prince of Powis, and defeated Ethelfirth, king of Bernicia, on the banks of the Dee, in the year 607. Edwin, the son of Ella, had taken refuge with Cadvan, and was brought up along with his son Cadwallawn, who succeeded his father in the same year that Edwin obtained the throne--that is in 617. Cadwallawn was, after two years, expelled from his throne by Edwin, who defeated him in a great battle, and driven to Ireland; but after some years he obtained assistance from Salomon, king of Armorica, returned to Britain, and encountered Penda, king of Mercia, whom he defeated and took prisoner, but, having afterwards united with him, they jointly attacked Edwin, and defeated and slew him. During the reign of Oswald, Cadwallawn joined Penda in the war against him, which resulted in Oswald's defeat and death. He likewise took part in the war with his successor Oswy, when Penda was slain in 657, and died after a reign of forty-two years. This brings us to the year 659. Cadwaladyr succeeded him, and reigned twelve years, when the plague broke out in Britain, before which he fled to Armorica. The plague lasted eleven years, and these two periods bring us to the year 682. Cadwaladyr applies to Alan, king of Armorica, who sends his son Ivor, and his nephew Ynyr, with a large force, who carry on the war against the Saxons for twenty-eight years, while Cadwaladyr himself goes to Rome, where he dies. The date of his death is variously given in the Bruts as 12th May 687, 12th May 688, and 12th day before the kalends of May 689. It is necessary to give this narrative simply as we find it in the Bruts, without attempting to adjust it to the true history, as has been done in later authorities. The *Brut y Brenhinoed* terminates with the death of Cadwaladyr. The *Brut y Tywysogion* states that Ivor carried on the war for fifty-eight years, and was succeeded in 720 by Rodri Molwynog, son of Idwal Iwrch, son of Cadwaladyr.

This narrative will not stand the test of a comparison with older authorities, and the attempts to bring them more into harmony have not been very successful. The connecting links are of course the battles, which are likewise recorded by Bede. The first battle, or that fought with Brochwel on the banks of the Dee, is mentioned by Bede without the date being given, but both the Chronicle of 977 and the Irish Annals of Tighernac agree in assigning it to the year 613. It is plain, however, from Bede's narrative, that the Britons were not the victors, but were defeated, and the death of Iago, son of Beli., is placed by both chronicles in the same year. The Welsh Chronicle records in 616 the death of Ceretic, so that it is probable that a king of that name did succeed Maelgwn in the sovereignty over all Wales. In the following year the Chronicle records, "Etguin incipit regnare," which likewise indicates the year of Cadwallawn's accession, who thus appears to have succeeded Ceretig in the sovereignty of Britain, while his father Cadvan had succeeded Iago in 613 in the kingdom of Gwynedd, and his not having possessed the sovereignty of all Wales will account for his not being mentioned in the Chronicle. The Welsh Chronicle records, in 629, "Obsessio Catguollauni regis in insula Glannauc," which may indicate the war between him and Edwyn.

Bede narrates that, after a reign of seventeen years, Cadwalla, king of the Britons, rebelled against Edwin, being supported by Penda, a most warlike man of the royal race of the Mercians, and that a great battle was fought in the plain called Haethfelth, when Edwin was killed, on the 12th October 633, and all his army either slain or dispersed. This battle is called by Nennius "Bellum Meicen," in which he says Edwin and his sons were slain "ab exercitu Catguollauni regis Gwenedote regionis;" and the Welsh Chronicle records, in 630, "Gueith Meiceren et ibi interfectus est Etguin cum duobus filiis suis. Catguollaun autum victor fuit." Tighernac places it in 631, and says that Edwin was slain "a Chon rege Britonum et Panta Saxano."

Bede tells us that a great slaughter was made of the church or nation of the Northumbrians, and that Cadwalla ravaged the whole country for a long time. The kingdom of Deira had devolved upon Osric, son of Edwin's uncle Elfric, and the kingdom of Bernicia upon Eanfred, the son of Ethelfrid, who had, during Edwin's life, lived in banishment among the Picts or Scots, but Cadwalla slew them both. Osric the next summer, and Eanfred after Cadwalla had ruled over Northumberland for an entire year. Bede then tells us that after the death of his brother Eanfred, Oswald advanced with an army, small indeed in number, but strengthened by the faith of Christ, and that the "impious commander of the Britons" (infandus Britonum dux) was slain, though he had most numerous forces, at a place called Denises-burn near the Roman wall.

It has been assumed that this "infandus Britonum dux" was the same Cadwalla who had defeated Edwin, and that the Bruts misrepresent his history in continuing his reign through those of Oswald and Oswy when he was in reality slain in 634; but it is remarkable that while Bede names Cadwalla on every occasion when he has to record his previous acts, he does not do so here, but says simply that the "dux Britonum" was slain. Nennius calls this battle "Bellum Catscaul"--that is *Cad ys guaul*, the battle at the wall, and says the commander slain was "Catgublaun, rex Gwenedote regionis," while he calls Cadwalla, *Catguollaun*; and Tighernac still further varies the name, for in 632 he records a battle by *Cathlon*, "in quo Oswalt mac Etalfraith victor erat et Cathlon rex Britonum cecedit;" while he had named Cadwalla *Chon* in the previous year. There seems, therefore, some indication that the Cadwalla who defeated and slew Edwin, and the "dux Britonum" who was slain by Oswald, were different persons, and the probability is that the two kings--Cadvan king of Gwynedd, and Cadwallon king of Wales--reigned during some years together, that their real names approached each nearly in sound, and that it was Cadvan, the father, who was slain in 634, while the Bruts are in this instance not unworthy of credit in representing the reign of Cadwallawn, the son, as lasting many years longer. There is every reason to believe that he continued in successful hostility to the Angles at least as long as the war with Penda lasted, and the remark of Bede that the occupation of Northumbria by Cadwallawn was looked upon as so unhappy and hateful, that it had been agreed by all who have written about the reigns of kings to interdict the memory of those perfidious monarchs and to assign that year to the reign of the following king, Oswald, shows that there was a strong desire to suppress as much as possible the acts of Cadwallawn. It is therefore not unlikely that Cadwallawn assisted Penda in the war when Oswald was slain, and in the war between Oswy and Penda, in 655, when Penda was eventually slain. It is stated by Bede that Penda had thirty legions with him, led on by thirty commanders who had come to his assistance. Tighernac, in narrating the same event, calls them *reges*, and Nennius says that the "reges Britonum interfecti sunt, qui exierant, cum rege Pantha in expeditione," but that "solus autem Catgabail rex Guenedote regionis cum exercitu evasit de nocte consurgens." That the Britons largely assisted in this war is therefore plain, and by Catgabail here probably Cadwallawn is meant. His death four years after, in 659, as stated by the Bruts, seems to me, therefore, quite in accordance with probability.

No such view, however, can be taken of the two subsequent reigns. In them, as stated by the Bruts, there are the obvious marks of fabrication. Cadwaladyr goes to Rome, where he dies on the 12th day before the kalends of May 689. Ceadwealla, king of the West Saxons--a Saxon by birth and descent--likewise goes to Rome, where he dies on the 20th of April 689; and the actions of Ivor, Cadwaladyr's successor on the throne of Wales, precisely correspond with those of Ina, Ceadwealla's successor on the throne of Wessex. There are, therefore, the obvious signs of artificial construction here, and the process seems to have been this:--The plague or pestilence before which Cadwaladyr is said to have fled to Armorica really took place, as we learn from Bede and Tighernac, in 664, and it did not last for eleven, but for only one year; and Nennius states explicitly that Cadwaladyr died in it. "Dum ipse (Osguid) regnabat venit mortalitas hominum, Catgualart regnante apud Britones post patrem suum *et in ea periit*." As Osguid or Oswy died in 670, there can be no doubt that the plague in 664 is meant; but in the Chronicle of 977, it is advanced nearly twenty years, and there we read, in 682--"Mortalitas magna fuit in Britannia in qua Catgualart filius Catguollaun obiit." When this chronicle is woven into still later chronicles, instead of "in qua Catgualart filius Catguollaun obiit," we read, pro qua Catwaladir filius Cat-

41

wallaun in Minorem Britanniam aufugit;" and Geoffrey of Monmouth adds the pilgrimage to Rome, and his death there.

The steps are plain enough. First., the plague and the death of Cadwaladyr in it, advanced from 664 to 682; and secondly, the death denied, and Cadwaladyr said to have retired to Armorica; and thirdly, the incident which really terminated the life of Ceadwealla of Wessex adopted and applied to that of Cadwaladyr.

The motives which led to this fabrication are probably the same with those which led to the consensus of English historians to suppress the acts of Cadwalla. Cadwallawn was evidently a powerful king and had waged, in conjunction with Penda, a successful war against the Angles of Northumbria. For one year he had actually been in possession of the kingdom, and his successful career of upwards of twenty years must have raised the courage and the hopes of the, Cymry to the highest. Then came the disaster of 655, when Oswy crushed the combination against him, when Penda and most of his British auxiliaries were slain, and Cadwallawn only escaped with his life, and died four years after. The result of this victory was that Oswy brought the Britons into subjection under him--a subjection which continued during his reign and that of his successor Ecfrid, till the latter was slain in the battle of Dunnichen in 686, and as, in the case of Northumbria, the year of Cadwalla's occupation was added to the reign of Oswald, so the twenty years of this subjection was added, to the reign of Cadwaladyr. The fact that he had died in the pestilence was not altered, but the date of it was advanced from 664 to 682; and, subsequently, the death was denied, and he was said to have retired to Armorica, whence the Cymry looked for him to return and reestablish the supremacy over the Angles lost by the disaster of 655. When the battle of Dunnichen terminated this subjection, Bede records that, "Non-ulla pars Britonum"--some but not all--recovered their liberty, and this part was the kingdom of the northern Britons of Cumbria, for the Chronicle of 977 records no king of Wales between the death of Cadwaladyr in 664 and that of Rodri in 754, when it has the entry, "Rotri rex Britonum moritur," but during that period records the deaths of the kings of Strathclyde. In 722, "Beli filius Elfin moritur;" and, in 750, "Teudubr filius Beli moritur." This interval was filled up by the fictitious reign of Ivor the events of which were taken from those of Ina, the successor of Ceadwealla.

Rotri, or, as he is usually termed, Rodri Molwynog, was the first real king of Wales after the death of Cadwaladyr; and when the Chronicle of 977 records, in 722, "Bellum Hehil apud Cornuenses; Gueith Gartmailauc; Cat Pencon apud dextrales Brittones et Brittones victores fuerunt in istis tribus bellis," it probably narrates the successes which led to the termination of the subjection of the Britons to the Saxons, and the reestablishment of the Welsh kingdom in the person of Rodri. He died in 754, and was succeeded by his son Conan or Cynan Tindaethwy, whose death is recorded by the Welsh Chronicle in 816, "Cinan rex moritur," in whom the direct line of Cadwaladyr failed, and the marriage of his only daughter placed a new family on the throne.

Her husband was Morvyn Frych, king of Manau; or, as he is designated in the Cyvoesi, *o dir Manan*, from the land of Manau.

[1] For these identifications, see notice of the site of the battle of Ardderyd, *Proc. Ant. Soct.* vol. vi. p. 91.

[2] I cannot help suspecting that the advantages held, out by the ecclesiastics were the main cause of uniting these Celtic leaders against the paganism of the country. Columba certainly made Aedan the first independent king of Dalriada, Kentigern was closely leagued with Rydderch, and the Maeldav of the Welsh Laws was probably an ecclesiastic who had undertaken to make Maelgwn supreme king of Wales by some stratagem cloaked under the fable of the floating chair.

Chapter Six - Manau Gododin and the Picts

THE name of Manau was applied by the Welsh to the Isle of Man. Thus, in Nennius, "tres magnas insulas habet, quarum una vergit contra Armoricas et vocatur Inisgueith; secunda sita est in umbilico maris inter Hiberniam et Britanniam et vocatur nomen ejus Eubonia, id est, Manau." Thus the Latin form was Eubonia, the Cymric, Manau; but it appears from Nennius that this name of Manau was also applied to a district in North Britain, when he says that Cunedda with his sons "venerat prius de parte sinistrali, id est, de regione que vocatur Manau Guotodin."

The Irish name for the Isle of Man is Manand or Manann; and it appears from the Irish Annals that a district on the north was likewise known by that name, as they record in 711 a slaughter of the Picts by the Saxons *in Campo Manand*, or the Plain of Manann, as distinguished from the island. It is, of course, difficult to discriminate between the two places, and to ascertain whether an event recorded is taking place in Manau or Manann belongs to the island or the district. Events which really belong to the one are often attributed to the other; and the fact that there existed a district bearing this name, having become comparatively forgotten, has led to the presumption in almost every case that the events recorded in connection with the word Manau or Manann belong to the island. It may help us to discriminate between the two to refer to the legendary matter, both Irish and Welsh, connected with this name of Manau or Manann.

From Manau in Welsh is formed the word Manawyd, and from Manawyd the personal name Manawydan. From Manann in Irish is formed the personal name Manannan. Manawydan in Welsh and Manannan in Irish are synonymous terms. In a curious tract in the Irish MS., termed the Yellow Book of Lecan, is the following account of the different persons bearing the name of Manannan:--

There were four Manannans in it. It was not in the same time they were.

Manandan mac Alloit, a Druid of the Tuath De Danann, and in the time of the Tuath De Danann was he. Oirbsen, so indeed, was his proper name. It is he, that Manannan, who was in Arann, and it is of him it is called Eamain Ab-hlach. [1] And it was he that was killed in the battle of Cuilleann by Uilleann Abradhruadh, son of Caithir, son of Nuadad of the silver hand, in defending the sovereignty of Connaught. And when his grave was dug, it was there sprang forth Loch Oirbsen over the land, so that from him (is named) Loch Oirbsen. This was the first Manannan.

Manannan mac Cirp, king of the Isles and of Manann, in the time of Conaire, son of Edersecoil, was he. And it was he made the espousal of Tuaide, daughter of Conall Collamracli, the foster child of Conaire, and from him is named Tuagh Inbhir.

Manannan mac Lir, *i.e.* a celebrated merchant was he between Erin, and Alban, and Manann, and a Druid was he also, and he was the best navigator that was frequenting Erin, and it was he used to know through science, by observing the sky, the period that the calm or the storm should continue, and of him the one Manannan nominabatur et ideo Scoti et Britones eum dominum maris vocaverunt et inde filium maris esse dixerunt ut deum et ideo adorabatur a gentibus ut deum quia transformat se in multis formis per gentilitatem.

Manandan mac Atgnai was the fourth Manannan. He it was that came to avenge the children of Uisnech, and it was he that had sustained the children of Usnech in Alban, and they had conquered what was from Manann northwards of Alban, and it was they that drove out the three sons of Gnathal, son of Morgann--viz. Iathach, and Tuathach, and Mani Lamhgarbh--from these lands, for it was their father that had dominion of that country, and it was the children of Usnech that killed him--(*Yellow Book of Lecan*, Trin. Coll. Dub. H. 2. 16.)

An account of Manannan mac Llyr is found almost in the same words in Cormac's Glossary, and by other Irish traditions he is made the same person with Manannan mac Alloid, as in the following stanza in an old Irish poem.:--

Manannan, son of Lir, from the Lake,
Fought many battles:
Oirbsen was his name; after hundreds
Of victories, of death he died.

Both of them belong to the mythic people termed in Irish traditions, Tuatha De Danann. The second people who are said to have colonised Ireland, according to the oldest traditions, which seem to have furnished the account in Nennius, were the Nemedians or children of Nemeid. They were driven out of Ireland by the pirates called the *Fomoire*. They left in three bodies, commanded by the three grandsons of Nemeid. Simon Breac, son of Starn, son of Nemeid, went to Thrace with his band, and from him descended the Firbolg; Jobaath, son of Jarbhainel, son of Nemeid, went to the north of Europe, and from him descended the Tuatha De Danann; and Briotan Maol, the son of Fergus Leithdearg, son of Nemeid, went to Dovar and Iardovar in Alban, and dwelt there with his posterity; and this colony is mentioned in the Albanic Duan, where the Nemedians are said to have been the second people in Alban. The third colony in Ireland were the Firbolg, and the fourth the Tuatha De Danann, who came from the north of Europe to Alban, and remained seven years in Dovar and Iardovar, whence they went to Ireland. There they found the Firbolg and drove them out, a part of whom, according to Irish tradition, passed over into Manann, Ili or Isla, Recra, and other islands. The Irish Nennius mentions this occupation of Manann and other islands by the Firbolg; and it is obviously the same event which is stated in the Latin Nennius as one of the four settlements of Scots in Britain, "Builc autem cum suis tenuit Euboniam insulam et alias circiter."

The only other Irish traditionary notices of Manann are that Cormac Ulfata, a king of Ireland, said to have reigned in the third century, was so named from having banished the *Uladh*, or Picts of Ulster, from Ireland, and driven them to Manann; and that an ancient Irish tract in the Book of Ballimote mentions Scal balbh *Ri Cruithentuaith acus Manaind*--that is, king of Pictland in Alban and of Manann.

According to Welsh traditions, Manawydan was the son of a British king called Llyr Lediaith. It is hardly possible to doubt the identity of the Manannan mac Llir of the Irish legends, and Manawydan ap Llyr of the Welsh, and the epithet Lediaith indicates that he was not of a people speaking a pure Cymric dialect. There are three very significant words which are applied in Welsh to indicate the mutual relation of languages. These are--*Cyfiaith*, where two tribes have a common speech; *Lediaith*, or half-speech, where is a certain amount of deviation or dialectic difference; and *Anghyfiaith*, the opposite of *Cyfiaith*, where the languages are considered as foreign to each other; and the epithet of *Llediaith* indicates that Llyr belonged to a race who spoke a peculiar dialect of Cymric. One of the kings in the list of shadowy monarchs of Britain contained in the Bruts is Llyr. He is the King Lear of Shakespeare, and the father of Gonorylla, Ragan, and Cordeylla; but Creidylad, who is the same as Cordeylla, is by other traditions the daughter of Llud Law Ereint. There seems, therefore, to have been the same juggle between the names Llyr and Llud in the Welsh legends as between Lir and Alloit in the Irish.

Cunedda is said in the *Genealogia* to have gone with his sons from a *regio* in the north called Manau Guotodin, and in the Welsh genealogies attached to Nennius his eldest son Typipaun is said to have died "in regione que vocatur Manau Guodotin."

According to the *Bonhed y Saint* there were three holy families of Britain. The second was the family of Cunedda. The third was that of Brychan. He is said to have been the son of Anllech or Aullech, a Gwyddelian, who married Marchell, daughter of Tewdwr, king of Garthmadrin, the region afterwards known by the name of Brecknock which took its name from Brychan, and to have had twenty-four sons and as many daughters. It has been supposed that there were more persons than one of the name, and the families of different

45

Brychans have been combined by tradition in one; but be this as it may, some of the sons are connected with Manau and several of the daughters with the Men of the North. Thus Rhun Dremrudd and Rhawin, two of the sons, are said to have been slain by the Saxons and Picts, and to have founded churches in Manau. Another son, Arthen, was buried in Manau, and Rhun had a son Nevydd, who is said to have been a bishop in *y Gogledd*, where he was slain by the Saxons and Picts. Of the daughters, Nefyn was the wife of Cynvarch, and mother of Urien; Gwawr was the, wife of Eledyr Lydanwyn, and mother of Llywarch Hen; Lleian was the wife of Gafran, and mother of Aeddan; Nefydd was the wife of Tudwal, and a saint at Llech Celyddon in the north; Gwrgon Goddeu was the wife of Cadrod Calchvynydd, and Gwen was the wife of Llyr Merini, and mother of Caradawc. These were all of the *Gwyr y Gogledd*, or Men of the North, and Corth or Cymorth, another daughter, was wife of Brynach Wyddel, the father of Daronwy, and one of the Gwyddel of Gwynedd. In the *Cognatio de Brachan*, in the Cotton Library (Vesp. A. xiv.), the sepulchre of Brychan is said to be "in insula que vocata Enysbrachan que est juxta Manniam."

Lastly, we have in a poem, which is not in either of the Four Books, but is placed by Stephens in the tenth century, mention of the *Brithwyr du o Fanaw*, or Black Brithwyr from Manau.

That these notices of Manau or Manann in the Irish and Welsh legends do not all apply to the same place seems plain enough, and it remains to find a clue to disentangle them. That the second of the four Manannans belongs to the island, and the fourth to the region in Alban, seems obvious. The first and third, whether they are to be viewed as the same or different Manannans, equally belong to the legend of the Tuatha De Danann; and as they occupied a district in Alban, it is probable that they are associated with both island and region. The Manann colonised by the Firbolg was certainly the island; on the other hand, Cunedda came from the region in the north, and the family of Brychan, whose sons were slain in Manau by the Picts and Saxons, and whose daughters married Men of the North, also belongs to the region in the North.

The clue seems to be that the island was associated with the name of the Scots, and the region with that of the Picts. Nennius includes the settlement of "Builc cum suis," or of the Firbolg, in Man and other islands, among the colonies of the Scots in Britain; and Orosius, who wrote in the fifth century, says that "Mevania insula a Scotorum gentibus habitatur." On the other hand, the Picts seem peculiarly connected with the region of Manau in the north. Cormac drove Picts of Ulster to Manann, and it is connected with the kingdom of *Cruithentuath*, or Pictland in Alban. Nennius calls the people whom Arthur defeated at Mynyd Agned, or Edinburgh, *Cath Bregion*, and the *Brithwyr* are frequently mentioned in the poems. The words which form the root of these epithets are, *Brith*, forming in the feminine *Braith*, Diversicolor, Maculosus, and *Brych*--the equivalent in Cymric of the Gaelic *Breac*--Macula. Both refer to the name Picti, or painted; and Agned or Mynyd Agned probably comes from an obsolete word, *agneaw*, to paint, *agneaid*, painted. It is singular enough that in the pedigree of Cunedda, given in the Welsh genealogies as 977, it is deduced from a certain *Brith*guein, grandson of Aballec, son of Amelach, son of Beli Mawr, and the name of Brychan obviously comes from *Brych*.

The history of this region, so far as we can trace it, will likewise show the connection of these painted men, or Picts, with it. The first event that seems founded on some historic truth is the battle fought at Mynyd Agned, by which the people called the Cath Bregion were defeated, and the establishment of Llew as ruler over Lothian. He is the Lothus of the legends of Saint Kentigern, and is said to have been buried near Dunpender Law, in East Lothian. His daughter Thenew, the mother of Kentigern, after an attempt to put her to death, in one legend on Dunpender, in another on Kepduff, now Kilduff, is cast adrift in a boat from Aberlady Bay.

Some of the localities connected with this district also emerge in the legends of Saint Monenna or Darerca of Killsleibeculean, in Ulster, who is recorded by Tighernac as dying in the year 518. There are three lives of St. Monenna, but they do not differ much in the leading incidents of her life. She was born in Ireland, and associated eight virgins with her, and, according to all of the lives, a widow (una vidua), with her son Lugar. In Scotland, she founded, according to one life, a church in Galloway, called Chilnacase; according to another life, three churches in Galloway; and the following churches on the summits of several mountains in Scotland, in honour of St. Michael: one "in cacumine montis qui appellatur Dundevenel;" another "in monte Dunbretan;" a third "in Castello quod dicitur Strevelin;" a fourth "in Dunedene que Anglica lingua dicitur Edineburg," where she left five virgins; and a fifth on the "Mons Dunpeledur." The first was on Dundonald in Ayrshire, near the mouth of the Irvine, into which the Glen flows, where Arthur's first battle was fought; and the three next were on the three fortified rocks of Dumbarton, Stirling, and Edinburgh, where Arthur fought three of his battles; while Dunpeledur, on which she founded another, is associated with Llew or Lothus, on whom Arthur bestowed the territory of Lothian. As Arthur was pre-eminently a Christian hero fighting against pagan Saxons and apostate Picts, these foundations appear to synchronise with the re-establishment of the Christian church there; and as one of Monenna's churches was on Dunpender Law, it seems not improbable that Thenew, the mother of Kentigern, was, in point of fact, one of the virgins in that church. Kentigern must have been born about 518, which synchronises with the date of Monenna's death; and one of her virgins, called Tannat, is said in one of the lives to have died three days after her. Monenna's church was in that part of Ulster called Dalaraidhe, and peopled by the Irish Picts; and her foundations in Scotland being in Galloway and in the regions near Edinburgh, show that her mission mainly was to the Picts of Galloway and of Manann.

The connection between the Picts of Ulster and the Picts of Manann, obscurely shadowed forth in the legendary expulsion of the Ultonians to

Manann, by Cormac, king of Ireland, in the third century, appears to have existed at this time. An old notice, in some of the Irish MSS. states that Baedan, son of Cairill, king of Ulster, "cleared Manann of Galls or strangers, so that the sovereignty belonged to the Ultonians thenceforth, and the second year after his death the Gael abandoned Manann." [2] Baedan died, according to Tighernac, in 581. In 577, he records, "primum periculum *Ulad an Eaman*;" and, in 578, "abreversio Ulad do Umania." The Annals of Ulster give these names as Eufania and Eumania. It has been supposed that Eamania or Eaman, the old capital of Ulster, is meant; but the expression "abreversio" could hardly be used with reference to a place within Ulster, and the Irish annalists were not likely to pervert the name of a place so celebrated as that of Eamania. These names Eumania and Eufania are more probably attempts to express the Latin name Eubonia, and to refer to Manann, and to the expedition by which Baedan cleared it of Galls. Two years after his death the Gael are said to have left it; and, in 583, Tighernac records the battle of Manann by Aedan mac Gabran, king of Dalriada, which likewise appears in the old Welsh chronicle in 584 as "Bellum contra Euboniam." It was therefore a battle fought between Aedan and the people of Manann.

The next event recorded in connection with Manann is the war between Penda with the aid of the Britons, and Oswy, in which the former was overthrown and slain, and the latter extended his dominion over the Britons, and wrested from the Picts a part of their "Provincia." Bode tells us that in a year which he does not specify, but which must have been after the year 653, Oswy was exposed to the fierce and intolerable eruptions of Penda, king of the Mercians, and promised to give him more and greater royal ornaments than can be imagined to purchase peace, provided the king would return home and cease to ravage and destroy the provinces of his kingdom; but that Penda refused to grant his request, and resolved to destroy and extirpate all his nation. Whereupon Oswy attacked him with a small army, though he had thirty legions led on by most skillful commanders, the Pagans were defeated and. slain, the thirty royal commanders were almost all of them killed; and he adds, "The battle was fought near the river Winwaed." The same transaction is narrated by the author of the *Genealogia*, but it is obvious that he is making use of two separate accounts; for the second paragraph narrates what must have preceded the conclusion of the first, and in the one the king of Mercia is called Pantha, and in the other Penda. By this account, the thirty commanders were kings of the Britons, who go with Pantha on an expedition as far as the city of *Iudeu* (usque in urbem quo vocatur Iudeu), and Oswy gave to Penda all the wealth that he had in the city, even into Manau (reddidit divitias cum eo in urbe, usque in Manau, Pendæ), and Penda gave it to the British kings, and this was called *Atbret Iudeu*--the ransom of Iudeu. Oswy then attacked Penda, and slew the thirty kings, Catgabail alone escaping, and this was the "Strages Gai Campi." The one is the Anglic account, the other is the Cymric. By the latter, Oswy bought off the attack upon the city of Iudeu, and the city itself, and the battle which followed must have been in or near Manau. The two accounts are not inconsistent, except in so far as Bede says that Penda refused the redemption-money, while the Welsh account says he took it and gave it to the British kings. Both agree that he was attacked, and the thirty commanders slain. Bede does not say where this happened, except that the battle was near the river Winwaed. The Welsh account says it was in the north, and is corroborated both by Florence of Worcester, who says that Penda invaded Bernicia, and by Tighernac, who says that he was accompanied by thirty kings. Bede does not expressly say that Penda was slain in that battle, but in the next section he adds that Oswy brought the war to a conclusion by his slaughter, "in regione Loidis," on the 15th November in the thirteenth year of his reign, which represents in Bede the year 655; and the Chronicle of 977 implies that the two events were not the same, for it has in 656 "Strages Gai Campi," and in the following year, 657, "Pantha occisio."

This defeat was followed by the subjugation of the greater part of the Picts, who had probably aided Penda and Cadwalla, and not only Manau and Galwethia, or Galloway, became subject to Oswy, but a part of the "provincia Pictorum" on the north of the Firth of Forth. This subjection lasted for nearly thirty years, till the defeat of Ecfrid at Dunnichen in 686 enabled the Picts to regain that part of their provincia which had been wrested from them. Manau and Galloway seem, however, to have been considered still part of the Anglic kingdom, and their Pictish population subject to them, as we find the Angles establishing a Bishopric in Galloway after 686, and the Picts of Manann or Manau obviously rebelling against them. In 698 Tighernac records a "battle between the Saxons and the Picts, in which the son of Bernith, who was called Brechtraig, was slain," and the Saxon Chronicle mentions the same transaction under the year 699,--"In this year the Picts slew Beorht, the alderman." He was probably their Saxon governor. In 711, Tighernac also records "the slaughter of the Picts on the plain of Manann (in campo Manand) by the Saxons, where Findgaine, the son of Deleroith, perished by immature death;" and the Saxon Chronicle thus records the same event in 710,--"In the same year the alderman Deorhtfrith fought against the Picts between Haefe and Caere." Florence of Worcester says that "Berhfrid, the prefect of King Osred, fought against and overcame the Picts." Here again, Beorhtfrith appears as the Saxon Governor under the king of Northumberland, and the name of the leader of the Picts is also given as Findgaine, son of Deleroith. In the year 716, Osred, king of Northumberland, was slain; and in recording this event, the Annals of Ulster add that Garnat, son of Deleroith, obviously of the same Pictish family of Manann, died. In 729 a great battle was fought between the army of Angus, king of the Picts, and the host of Nechtain; and the annalist adds, that the "exactatores" of Nechtain fell--viz. Biceot son of Moneit, and his son, and Finguine son of Drostan, Ferot son of Finguine, and many others. This word "exactatores," or rather "exactores," was a word expressive of a Saxon officer, and was the Latin equivalent of "Gerefa," and the names show the connection of these leaders with the Picts of Manann, with whom the name of Finguine was especially connected.

We have no further notice of Manann. It owes its separate existence, and its loose connection with the Anglic kingdom, to its inhabitants possessing a community of race with the powerful kingdom of the Picts north of the Forth; and after the termination of that kingdom, when the name of Pict was merged in that of Scot, it too disappears as possessing any separate position from the other inhabitants of Lothian.

It has been necessary to be thus minute in giving these notices of Manau or Manann as its history as a separate region in North Britain has, in fact, to be reconstructed, and it will enable us now better to determine its precise situation and extent.

When the notices of the slaughter of the Picts in 710 by the Irish annalists and the Saxon historians are compared, they give us the situation of the "Campus Manann"--a battle fought on it was "between Haefe and Caere." It is impossible here to mistake the rivers Avon and Carron, which flow within some miles of each other; and the Avon rises in a moor called now Slamannan, and of old Slamannan Moor. This name is, in fact, *Sliabhmannan*, the moor or plain of Manann. *Mynyd Agned*, or Edinburgh, was in it, where the population of the region about it was called *Catbregion*. The Dovar and Iardovar of the Irish legends formed the whole or part of it. Bede tells us that of the two firths of the sea, one of which runs in far and broad into the land of Britain from the Eastern Ocean and the other from the Western, though they do not reach, so as to touch one another, the Eastern has in the midst of it the city *Giudi* (orientalis habet in medio sui urbem Giudi), the Western has on it, that is, on the right hand thereof, the city Alcluith, which in their language signifies the "rock Cluith," for it is close by the river of that name. Bede's city of *Giudi* is the same as Nennius' urbs *Iudeu*, the, G falling away in Welsh in combination, and in an old tract in the Book of Lecan ascribed to Angus the Culdee, who lived in the ninth century, Cuilennros or Culross is said to be between the *Sliabhnochel*, or range of the Ochils, and *Muir-n-Giudan*, or the Sea of Giudan (Reeves' *Culdees*, p. 124), and we learn from Simeon of Durham that the see of Lindisfarne, which marks the actual possessions of the Angles, extended to the river Esk, beyond which they only possessed settlements.

Manau or Manann, therefore, in its widest sense included Slamannan, and the western frontier proceeded in a line from thence to the Pentland Hills, so as to take in the great moor formerly called Cal*dover* Moor, consisting of what is now the three parishes of West, Mid, and East Calder, and thus included that mountainous region forming the west part of Linlithgowshire, embracing the parishes of Torphichen, Bathgate, and Whitburn. It probably also included that part of the range of the Pentland Hills called of old Pentland Moor, till it came down upon the North Esk, which formed its eastern boundary to the sea. On the northwest there lay between it and the Carron the district of Calatria or *Calathros*, containing on the coast the parishes of Kinnell and Carriden, while from Carriden to the Esk the coast would belong to Manann. At the point now called the Queensferry, it approaches within a short distance of the opposite coast, and the name of Clackmannan on the

50

northern shore indicates that that district likewise belonged to it. On some one of the islands in the Firth which lie between the mouth of the Esk and Carriden was the City of Giudi or Iudeu, which may have been founded by the people Bede terms the Jutes, while the fortified rock of Mynyd Agned or Dunedin was the great stronghold of its Pictish inhabitants.

Lying as this region did in the intermediate part of the country where the kingdoms of the Picts in the north, the Angles in the east, and the Cymry in the west, approached each other, and the Pictish, Anglic, and Cymric populations met, it could not but have had a mixed population. We see that an early colony of Saxons bad obtained settlements in this part of the country. Arthur fought several of his battles against them within its limits; and the king of Ulster cleared Manand of *Galls*. Here also dwelt the Picts of Lothian, known under the names of *Brithwyr* and of *Catbregion*. The former name comes from *Brith*, which in its primary sense means speckled or spotted; but in its secondary sense mixed, and may indicate a mixed people. Bregion comes from *Brych* or *Breac*, and this word crops up here and there over the district. Falkirk was in Gaelic, *Eglais Breac*, and in Saxon, *Fahkirk*, the spotted or brindled church; *Mynyd Agned*, the Painted Mount; while Caldovar Moss is bounded on the west by the river Brych. When Medrawd, the son of Llew, rebelled against Arthur, it was with a mixed army of Picts, Saxons, & Britons.

From this region Cunedda went with his sons, and gave a royal house to the throne of Wales in the person of Maelgwn and his descendants. When this house failed in the person of Cynan Tyndathwy, there is every reason to believe that the same region gave a second royal house to Wales, in the person of Mervyn *Frych*, and that he came from the region of Manau, and not from the island. His epithet of *Brych* points to this. He was the son of Gwriad, who married Nest, daughter of Cadell Deyrnllug, Prince of Powys, and *Gwriad* is the same name as the Pictish *Ferat*. His pedigree is deduced from Dwywc, a son of Llywarch Hen, and Llywarch Hen was one of the Men of the North, and his mother was a daughter of Brychan. Mervyn is said in the Cyvoesi to be *o dir Manau*, from the region of Manau, and not *o ynys Manau*, from the island of Manau. This derivation of the kings of the house of Mervyn Frych explains a passage in a tract contained in the text of the Irish Nennius, preserved in the Book of Ballemote, but which is not to be found elsewhere. After stating the first departure of the Romans, this text proceeds to say that Sarran then assumed the sovereignty of Britain, and established his power over the Saxons and Picts. That his eldest son was Luirig, and that Mucertach mac Erca having taken his wife, she bore him four sons, two of whom were Constantine and Gaidel Ficht, from whom descended the provincial kings of Britain and the kings of Cornwall. [3] This legend seems to apply to Manann, and if the house of Mervyn Frych sprang from its mixed population, we can understand in what sense the kings of Wales and Cornwall were said to be descended from Gaidel Ficht. Mervyn Frych married Essyllt, the daughter of Cynan, the last king of the house of Maelgwn Gwynedd, and inherited Powys through his mother, and acquired Gwynedd through his wife. His death is recorded in 844, so that he died in the very year that the kingdom of the Scots superseded that of the Picts, when all the old landmarks of the North British districts were changed, and the memory of Manau Gododin, as a region in the north distinct from the island of Manau, passed away for ever. Mervyn Frych was succeeded by his son Rodri Mawr, who acquired South Wales through his wife, and thus became king of all Wales. He divided Wales into three petty kingdoms among his three sons--Anaraut, Cadell, and Mervyn--the eldest, Anaraut, obtaining Gwynedd, with Aberfraw in Anglesea as his capital; Cadell, South Wales, with Dynevor for his capital; and Mervyn, Powis, with Mathraval for his capital; and the king of Gwynedd was to be supreme over the other two. He was succeeded by his eldest son Anarawd, who died in 913, and he by his son Edwal foel, after which Howel dda, son of Cadell, king of South Wales, obtained the dominion of the whole of Wales, from 940 to his. death in 948. After his death a struggle commenced between the descendants of Edwal foel and of Howel dda for supremacy in Wales till the year 1000, when the sovereignty was usurped by Aeddan ap Blegwred, and a period of confusion ensued both in North and South Wales, during which Cynan, the rightful heir of North Wales, took refuge in Ireland, and Rhys, the rightful heir of South Wales, in Armorica, and which was only terminated when Rhys ap Tewdwr succeeded in establishing himself in South Wales, in the year 1077, and Gruffudh, the son of Cynan, in North Wales, in 1080.

The kingdom of South Wales soon came to an end, in consequence of Jestin, the Lord of Glamorgan, having called in the assistance of Robert Fitzhamon, a Norman knight. Rhys ap, Tewdwr was defeated in battle and slain by him in 1090, and, according to the Brut y Tywysogion, "then fell the kingdom of the Britons," and Robert Fitzhamon, with his Norman knights, took possession of Glamorgan, and "the French came into Dyned and Ceredigion, which they have still retained, and fortified the castles, and seized upon all the land of the Britons." This was true of South Wales only, as in North Wales the native princes still ruled till the year 1282, when the death of Llywelyn, the last prince of North Wales, was followed by the subjugation of all Wales by King Edward the First.

Rhys ap Tewdwr had an only daughter, Nest, who had a son by King Henry the First, Robert, Earl of Gloucester. By marriage with the daughter of Robert Fitzhamon, he succeeded to all his possessions in South Wales; and, as the son of Nest, the only daughter of Rhys, was regarded by the Welsh as representing in some degree the princes of South Wales. He died in the year 1147.

[1] The island of Arran in the Firth of Clyde, here called Eamhain Ablach, or Eamania of the Apple Trees. Eamain is said in Cormac's Glossary to be derived from Eomain, and that from *Eo* i. *rind*, or breast-pin, and *Muin* i. *braige*, or neck. This word Muin is represented in Welsh by Mynyw, as St. David's is called in Irish Cillemuine, in Welsh, Mynyw. I conjecture, therefore, that Arran being called Eamain is the Insula Minau or Mynyw mentioned in the life of Gildas.

[2] *Chron. Picts and Scots*, p. 127.
[3] *Chron. Picts and Scots*, p. 54.

Chapter Seven - The Races of Britain and the Place of the Picts Among Them

SUCH being the aspect in which the leading features of the history of the Celtic population of Britain is presented to us, on a careful analysis of the authorities, it remains to inquire what they tell us of the mutual relation of the races of which it was composed, and of the true place of the Picts among them.

In human beings the recollections of infancy are the most vivid and tenacious, and every change of circumstance or of place in early years impresses itself with an indelible mark, on the memory, so that, while the recollections of middle life become faint and dim with advancing years, those of the nursery still stand out in the background with a clear and distinct light, and can be produced in all their original vividness. In like manner with races of men in an early stage of their social condition, the events of the infancy of the race, its migrations and settlements, seem to be indelibly impressed on the national memory, are the subject of songs and ballads, and become interwoven into such oral literature as they possess, while their history, after they become a settled people, may become to them a dreary blank, till the progress of civilization and society creates something like national annals among them.

Such ethnological traditions, however, in time lose the form of simple narrative, and assume a mythic and symbolic shape, which, though bearing the outward semblance of fable, still preserve the recollection of real ethnological fact. This mythic and symbolic form of the early ethnological traditions of the various tribes which form the population of the country, usually presents itself in two different aspects, according as the one idea or the other prevailed. According to the one, these tribes were a series of colonies arriving in the country at different times, and succeeding each other as occupants of the land, and their migrations from some distant land, in which some fancied resemblance in name or customs had fixed their origin, are minutely detailed. According to the other, each race is represented by an *eponymus*, or supposed common ancestor, bearing a name derived from that of the people, and the several *eponymi* representing the population of the country are connected in an ethnological genealogy, in which they appear as fathers, brothers, or cousins, according to their supposed relation to each other. We have a classical instance of this in the Greek traditions, where Hellen, the *eponymus* of the Hellenes, is father of Æolus Dorus, and Xuthus, and the latter of Achæus and Ionus, while the Æolians and Dorians appear in other traditions as successively overrunning the country. In Britain we have the same two-

53

fold myth; Brutus, the *eponymus* of the Britons, being, in the Bruts, father of Camber Locrinus and Albanactus, while, in the Triads, the Kymri, the Lloegri, and the Brython, are successive colonies which entered the country from different lands. It does not follow that, in the one case, the relationship was other than a geographical one, or, in the other, that the tribes were really of different origin, or inhabited the country at different times. These are but the adventitious, mythic, or symbolic forms, in which real ethnological relations had clothed themselves, under the operation of definite laws.

The earliest record of such ethnological traditions. connected with the British Isles is probably to be found in the *Historia Britonum*. In it the ethnological traditions are given in both shapes. In that in which they were symbolised by a genealogy, and which is certainly part of the original tract, the author states as his source "veteres libri veterum nostrorum," and concludes the chapter by stating, "Hanc peritiam inveni ex traditione veterum, qui incolæ in primo fuerunt Britanniæ." In this genealogy he says, "Hessitio autem habuit filios quatuor, hi sunt, Francus, Romanus, *Britto*, *Albanus*. . . . Ab Hesitione autem ortæ sunt quatuor gentes, Franci, Latini, *Albani*, et *Britti*."

In the Albanic Duan, which seems to have belonged to some collection of additions to Nennius, and which contains the oldest record of the ethnological traditions of Scotland, the brothers Brittus and Albanus appear as the *eponymi* of the two Celtic races inhabiting respectively Britain and Alban, or Scotland. Thus--

"O, all ye learned of Alban,
Ye well-skilled host of yellow hair,
What was the first invasion? Is it known to you?
Which took the land of Alban?
Albanus possessed it; numerous his hosts.
He was the illustrious son of Isacon.
He and *Briutus* were brothers without deceit.
From him Alban of ships has its name.
Briutus banished his active brother
Across the stormy sea of Icht.
Briutus possessed the noble Alban
As far as the conspicuous promontory of Fothudain." [1]

Here the two brothers, Brittus and Albanus, appear, and the latter is the *eponymus* of the inhabitants of Alban or Scotland, while the tradition of the retreat of the race of the one before that of the other seems to be preserved.

What races, then, were typified by the brothers Brittus and Albanus? A passage in one of the old poems preserved in the Book of Taliessin indicates this very clearly. The *Historia* had given us three of the sons of Hessitio-Romanus, Brittus, and Albanus; the brotherhood in such a genealogy implying no more than their mutual presence in the same country; and in the poem referred to there, is an obvious reference to the same tradition--

Three races, wrathful, of right qualities:
Gwyddyl and Brython and Romani,
Create war and tumult."

Here the *Romani* and *Brython* represent Romanus and Brittus, and *Gwyddyl* comes in place of Albanus.

This term *Gwyddyl*, though latterly used by the Welsh as synonymous with Irish, was formerly applied to the whole Gaelic race as distinguished from the Cymric. This is apparent from another poem in the Book of Taliessin, where the Celtic inhabitants of the British Isles are thus enumerated:--

"Let us make great rejoicing after exhaustion,
And the reconciliation of the Cymry and men of Dublin,
The Gwyddyl of Iwerdon, Mon, and Prydyn,
The Cornishmen and the Clydemen."

Here the Cymry of Wales and the Britons of Cornwall and Strathclyde are contrasted with the Gwyddyl of Ireland, Anglesea, and Scotland; in short, the Gaelic race in its full extension at that period, including Prydyn, or North Britain, and Mona, or Anglesea, as well as Ireland. To which of these two races then did the Picts belong, and was their language identical either with the Cymric or the Gaelic, or, if it was a different dialect, to which did it approach nearest?

Among the additions made to the *Historia Britonum*, some Pictish traditions seem to have been attached to it as early as the year 796; and these are preserved partly in the Irish translation of Nennius, and partly in the first part of the old chronicle in the Colbertine MS. usually called the *Pictish Chronicle*, and which bears evident marks of having been formed from such additions to the *Historia*. This chronicle contains a very important addition to the statement in the *Historia*. The *Historia* had said that Brittus and Albanus were brothers, and sons of Hessitio, and that from them proceeded the nations of the Britti and the Albani. The *Pictish Chronicle* adds, after quoting a passage from *Isidorus* giving the etymology of the name Albani. "*de quibus originem duxerunt Scoti et Picti;*" [2] that is, that both Scots and Picts belonged to the race of which Albanus was the *eponymus*.

Now the testimony of the entire literature of Wales is to the fact that the Picts belonged to the race of the Gwyddyl, and not to the Cymric race. To take, first, the perhaps doubtful authority of the *Triads*, in which the ethnology of the inhabitants of Britain is conveyed under the form of successive colonies, or invasions, they are thus represented: "Three social tribes of the Isle of Britain--the nation (*cenedl*) of the Kymry, the race (*al*) of the Lloegrwys and the Brython--and these are said to be descended from the original nation of the Cymry, and to be of the same language and speech. Three refuge-seeking tribes that came to the Isle of Britain--the tribe of Celyddon *yn y Gogled*, the race (*al*) of the Gwyddyl that are in Alban, and the men of Galedin. Three invading tribes that came to the Isle of Britain--the, Coraniaid, the

Gwyddyl Ffichti who came to Alban by the sea of Llychlyn, and the Saeson;" and it is added that the Gwyddyl Ffichti "are in Alban, on the shore of the sea of Llyddyn." "Three treacherous invasions of the Isle of Britain--the Gwyddyl *Coch o'r Iwerddon*, who came into Alban; the men of Llychlyn, and the Saesons." Here it will be observed that three tribes only are brought to Alban, and all three are said to have remained in it, and all are said to be. Gwyddyl or Gael. These are, *first*, the race of the Gwyddyl generally; *secondly*, the red Gwyddyl from Ireland; and *thirdly*, the Ffichti Gwyddyl. The red Gwyddyl are obviously the Gaelic Scots, who came from Ireland in the year 503, and settled in Dalriada or Argyll. The Gwyddyl Ffichti have been usually translated the Irish Picts, from the word Gwyddyl having been latterly used as synonymous with Irishman; and a very disingenuous use of this has been made by Mr. Herbert in his notes to the Irish Nennius; but the translation is erroneous, for the word Gwyddyl was at that time a name of race, and not a geographical term, and was applied to the whole Gaelic race; and, moreover, it is not an adjective, but a substantive; Gwyddyl Ffichti meaning the Ffichti or Pictish Gwyddyl, just as Gwyddyl Coch means the red Gwyddyl. That by these Ffichti Gwyddyl, the Picts of the Pictish kingdom in Scotland are meant, and not Irish Picts (in the sense of Picts dwelling in or emigrating from Ireland), is plain; for in the *Triad* they are said to have crossed the sea of Llychlyn, or German Ocean, to Alban or Scotland, and to dwell in Alban along the shore of the German Ocean. That it was applied to the Picts forming the great Pictish kingdom of Scotland, is also clear from the *Bruts* compared with each other and with the Irish annalist Tighernac. In the year 750 a great battle was fought between the Britons of Strathclyde and the Picts of Scotland, at a place called by the Welsh chronicles Magedaue or Maescdauc, now Mugdoch, in Dumbartonshire, the ancient seat of the Earls of Lennox, which is thus described by Tighernac: "A battle between the Pictones and the Britones--viz. Talorgan, the son of Fergus, and his brother, and the slaughter of the Piccardach with him." In the *Brut y Tywysogion* it is thus given:--"The action of Mygedawc, in which the Britons conquered the *Gwydyl Ffichti* after a bloody battle." Talorgan, who commanded them, was brother of Angus Mac Fergus, king of Fortren, or the Picts of Scotland, and they are here termed Gwyddyl Ffichti. Although the authority of the *Triads* is not unexceptionable, it is confirmed by the more authentic Triads of Arthur and his warriors, where "three tribes came into this island and did not again go out of it," and the second is "the tribe of the Gwyddyl Ffichti."

The statement here given of that form of the tradition which represents the ethnology of the inhabitants of North Britain under the form of successive colonies, so exactly accords with what we find in other statements of it as to leave little doubt that it is a faithful representation of this form of the tradition; and its harmony with the older statement of the other form of it in the *Historia Britonum*, is apparent. In the one we have Albanus, the *eponymus* of the Gwyddyl, called the brother of Brittus, and progenitor of the Albani from whom the Picti and Scoti took their origin. In the other we have the race of the Gwyddyl in Alban, and the successive colonies in Alban after them, the Gwyddyl Ffichti from Llychlyn, and the Gwyddyl Coch from Iwerdon or Ireland; the former being, as shown by the *Brut y Tywysogion*, the Picts of Scotland, and the latter the Scots of Dalriada.

The legend of the origin of the Picts, as contained in the *Bruts*, is that they came from Scythia and settled in Alban; that they asked wives of the Britons and were refused, and then married wives of the Gwyddyl. The text of the *Brut* in the Red Book of Hergest adds, "And their children and offspring increased, and the people multiplied. This people are the *Gwyddyl Ffichti*, and it is thus they came and were first continued in this island, and to this day have remained without going from it." Another text in one of the Hengwrt MSS. adds, "And thus arose this people; and this people were called *Gwyddyl Ffichtieit*, and this is the reason that they were called *Gwyddyl Ffichtieit*; and they are still a tribe among the Britons." [3] The tale that they were refused wives of the Britons and married wives of the Gwyddyl certainly implies that the Welsh considered that they did not speak a Cymric but a Gaelic dialect, for the legend is based upon the idea that the spoken language of a people was derived from their mothers, and is conveyed in the popular expression, the mother-tongue; and it is so understood in Layamon's *Brut*:--

"Through the same woman,
 Who there long dwelt,
 The folk 'gan to speak
 Ireland's speech."

And in one of the poems in the Book of Taliessin, where the Picts are symbolised by the expression, "y Cath Vreith," there is this line: "The Cat Vreith of *a strange language* (anghyfieithon) is troubled from the ford of Taradyr to Port Wygyr in Mona." There is no doubt that the allusion here is to the Picts.

The name of Gwyddyl Ffichti, as applied to the Picts, thus rests on better authority than that of the *Triads*. In the old poems, though the Picts are usually termed the Brithwyr, yet this. name of Gwyddyl Ffichti is also applied to them, as in a curious old poem in the Book of Taliessin: "Five chiefs there shall be of the Gwyddyl Ffichti." The Picts are thus clearly assigned by the Welsh authorities to the race of the Gwyddyl; and if they were really, according to the prevailing modern theory, a Cymric people speaking a Cymric dialect, it is hardly conceivable that the Cymri themselves should have thus so invariably classed them with the Gwyddyl, and attached that word to their name.

The whole testimony of the Britons themselves, and the inferences to be drawn from tradition, thus clearly range the Picts as a people with the Gwyddyl, or Gaelic division of the great Celtic, race, and not with the Cymric or British, and point to their race and language both being Gaelic; but though this may be true of the core or central body of the people, there are yet indications that the more outlying or frontier portions were extensively mixed with other people, and especially with the three races of the Saxons, the, Scots of Ireland, and the Britons.

And first of the Saxons. It is somewhat remarkable that when Ammianus Marcellinus narrates the first great outburst of the barbarian, or ex-provincial tribes, against the Romans in 360, he enumerates them as consist-ing of the "gentes Scotorum Pictorumque." In the second invasion, in 364, they were joined by two other nations, and consisted of the "Picti Sax-onesque, et Scotti et Attacotti;" and in the third invasion, in 368, of the "Picti in duas gentes divisi Dicaledones et Vecturiones, itidemque Atticotti bellicosa hominum natio, et Scotti per diversa vagantes." It is hardly possible to avoid the suspicion that the epithets applied here to each people point to charac-teristics connected with their name. In Cormac's glossary the old form of the name Scot is given as "Scuit." "Scuite" signifies wanderers; and the epithet "vagantes" is attached to the Scots. "Cath" (war) seems to enter into the name Atti*cotti*, and they are "bellicosa natio." So the peculiarity of the Picti was, that they were "in duas gentes divisi." This seems to imply that the "duæ gentes" were of different race. Now it is remarkable that while the Picti and the Saxones are connected together in the second invasion, the Saxones are omitted from the third; and the Picti then, for the first time, appear as com-posed of two "gentes;" while Claudian, in writing of the same invasion, ex-pressly mentions the Saxones along with the Picts as forming part of the rav-agers, and names the Orkneys as their seat.

"------- Maduerunt *Saxone* fuso
Orcades, incaluit *Pictorum* sanguine Thule
Scotorum cumulos flevit glacialis Ierne."

I have elsewhere shown [4] that the tradition given by Nennius, that Octa and Æbussa, the son and nephew of Hengist, led a body of Saxons past the Orkneys, and took possession of a part of Scotland, "usque ad confinia Picto-rum," indicated a real settlement of Saxons on the east coast of Scotland as early as the year 374; and it is not impossible that they may have allied with the Picts proper so closely as to form one of the two *gentes*, and that the Vec-turiones included them, a conjecture perhaps strengthened by the appear-ance of the Picts and Saxons in close union in 429 in Constantius' *Life of St. German*, by the fact that the ancestor of the Jutes, who were Octa's people, was Vecta, the son of Odin, and that another part of the same people were termed by Bede, Vectuarii. Be this as it may, there scent undoubtedly to have been settlements of Saxons at a very early period along the east coast of Scot-land among that part of the Picts.

But if there were Saxon settlements among the Picts on the east coast, the Scots made a settlement in their western district, in part of Argyllshire, which they called Dalriada. Bede gives the best indication of the nature of this settlement. He says of the Firth of Clyde that it was a "sinus maris permaximus, qui antiquitus gentem Brittonum a Pictis secernebat," that "Bri-tannia post Brittones et Pictos tertiam Scottorum nationem *in parte Pictorum recepit*," and that they settled "ad cujus videlicet sinus partem septentrionalem." We know that this mythic colony of the Scots represented an actual settlement of them in Dalriada, which took place in the year 503, if not earlier, and that they too settled among the Picts.

On their southern frontier they seem to have become mixed with the Britons. The indication afforded by the Albanic Duan of an early encroachment of the tribes represented by the name Britus upon those represented by Albanus, as far as Fifeness, has already been noticed. In several of the old poems contained in the Book of Taliessin, allusion is made to a combination between the Brython and the Gwyddyl, and the name of *Brithwyr*, which means mixed men as well as painted men, seems to have been applied to this mixed part of the Pictish nation. Higden, in his *Polychronicon*, in giving the fable of Carausius settling a body of Picts in Albania, adds, "*ubi permixti cum Britonibus* per subsequens ævum premanserunt," which implies that such a mixture of the two people had been known as a fact, and one of the Pictish legends preserved in the Irish Nennius indicates this also. One version of it bears that Cruthnechan mac Inge, the *eponymus* of the Picts, was sent from Ireland "to assist the Britons of Fortrenn to war against the Saxons, and they made their children and their swordland--*i.e.* Cruthentuaith--subject to them." Another versions bears, "And when they (the Picts) had cleared their swordland yonder among the Britons--viz. Magh Fortreinn *primo*, and Magh Girgin *postea*." [5] Now Fortren or Magh Fortren was the district lying between the river Forth and the river Tay, and is here said to have, been peopled by Britons, but afterwards obtained by the Picts who dwelt among them; and Magh Girgin is a district on the east coast, now called Mearns, which the Picts won when warring against the Saxons, and where they subjected their children. The presence, therefore, both of Britons and Saxons as part of the population of the districts which, under the name of Cruthentuaith, was the territory of the Pictish kingdom, is here indicated.

So far as race is concerned, therefore, the Pictish nation presents itself to us in the following aspect. The main body and centre of the nation, pure Albanic or old Gwyddyl, with the outlying parts mixed with other races--Saxons on the east coast, Scots in Argyll, and Britons south of the Tay--each having occasionally seen a king of their own race on the throne, and the Scots succeeding in converting the accession of one of their race to the throne, in right of his Pictish blood through his female descent, into their permanent supremacy over the Pictish population of the country--people and language gradually merging and disappearing under the general term of Scottish.

In endeavouring to determine the ethnological position of any people who, like the Picts, once existed as a distinctive element in the population of the country, but who have left no living representative to bear witness to their characteristics, there are other sources of information to which we may resort besides the evidence of writers contemporaneous with their existence as a known and distinct people, as to the particular race among the inhabitants of the country to which they belonged, or as to the existence among them of a living tradition of their origin. There is the evidence afforded by an analysis of such remains of their language as may have come down to us, indicating its philological relation to the languages spoken by the other races in the country; and there is likewise the inference to be derived from the topography of the districts which they are known to have occupied.

The evidence afforded by these three sources of information does not always correspond; and it is necessary carefully to discriminate between them in their bearing upon each other, and upon the problem to be solved.

Where a people remains unmixed in race, and has retained the spoken language originally peculiar to them, unmodified by foreign influences, and where that people has always formed the sole inhabitants of the districts occupied by them, the evidence afforded by each of these sources of information may be expected exactly to reflect the conclusions of the others. The traditions of the people, and the statements of contemporary writers, will refer them to a race speaking a language similar to their own; and the vocables which enter into the topography of the districts occupied by them will manifestly belong to the same original language. But where such a people forms merely one element in the population of a country made up of different races, and is not protected from foreign influences by any peculiar combination of physical, social, and political obstacles, this is rarely found to be the case, and the original harmony of race, language, and topography, soon ceases to be preserved in its integrity. Amid the clash of contending races, and the struggle for supremacy on the one hand, or for existence on the other, this condition suffers great modification. The race may remain pure and unmixed, and yet the language may suffer great modification from the influence of others. A part of the people may retain the old language; another part may have adopted the language of a people who have subjugated them; and the language of a third part may have become mixed with, or assimilated to, that of a neighbouring people speaking a kindred though not an identic dialect, through contact with them, or from the gradual spread of the one race into the territories of the other.

On the other hand, the people may have ceased to be a homogeneous race, from other races being intermingled with them; or a common name may have been applied to a combination of tribes originally distinct, but politically connected; and yet the language of one of these tribes may have spread over the whole nation, or a form of the spoken language may have been adopted as the medium of official intercourse, or selected for the purpose of conveying the knowledge of Christianity, and become the vehicle of instruction and civilisation; and the remains of the language which have come down to us, and with which we have to deal, may represent this form, or the written speech, only.

The topography, too, of the districts occupied by them may have retained unmixed the vocables of the language spoken by its earliest inhabitants; or it may have received the impress of foreign invading or immigrating races who may have, from time to time, occupied a part of the country, or have permanently succeeded the race in question; or it may have retained names which

60

belong to the language of a still older and more primitive people who may have preceded them.

It is necessary, therefore, in endeavouring to ascertain the ethnological position of a people long since passed away, to look separately at these three sources of information, and to weigh well their bearing upon each other, and upon the race to which the people belonged. The Picts unquestionably existed as a known people, and as an independent nation possessing a political organisation and a known till the middle of the ninth century. From that date till the twelfth century the name of the Picts is known as the denomination of one element in a population formed of two different races, but combined into one monarchy, and had no independent existence. After the twelfth century the name disappears as applied to, or borne by, any portion of the population of Scotland. Bede, who wrote prior to the ninth century, and during the first period, has the following passage: "Hæc (i.e. Britannia) in præsenti juxta numerum librorum quibus lex divina scripta est quinque gentium linguis unam eandemque summæ veritatis et verræ sublimitatis scientiam scrutatur et confitetur Anglorum, videlicet, Brittonum, Scottorum, Pictorum, et Latinorum quæ meditatione Scripturarum cæteris omnibus est facta communis." In another place he says of Oswald, king of Northumbria:--"Denique omnes nationes et provincias Britanniæ quæ in quatuor linguas, id est, Brittonum, Pictorum, Scottorum, et Anglorum divisæ sunt, in ditione accepit;" and afterwards, in narrating the letter written by Ceolfrid, abbot of Jarrow in Northumberland, to Naiton:--"Rex Pictorum qui septentrionales Britanniæ plagas inhabitant" in the year 710, that is, during his own lifetime; he says, "Hæc epistola cum præsente rege Naitono multisque viris doctoribus esset lecta ac diligenter ab his qui intelligere poterant in linguam ejus propriam interpretata." Henry of Huntingdon, who wrote about 1135, and therefore in the second period, repeats the statement of Bede:- "Quinque autem linguis utitur Britannia, Brittonum, videlicet, Anglorum, Scottorum, Pictorum, et Latinorum quæ doctrina Scripturarum cæteris omnibus est facta communis," but adds this qualification:--"quamvis Picti jam videantur deleti et lingua eorum ita omnino destructa ut jam fabula videatur quod in veterum scriptis eorum mentio invenitur."

Bede, therefore, knew of the Picts as an existing people, and of a language termed the Pictish, and, in his own day, tells of a letter translated into it as the language of the kingdom of Naiton or Nectan; and when Henry of Huntingdon wrote, the people and their language had apparently so entirely passed away that it appeared like a fable that any kingdom of the Picts, and any such language, had ever existed.

It seems strange that Henry of Huntingdon should have made this statement almost in the very year in which the Picts, as a body, formed an entire division of the Scottish army at the Battle of the Standard, and when Reginald of Durham, in the same century, refers to their language as then spoken at Kirkcudbright in Galloway; but the truth is, that, notwithstanding the language of Henry of Huntingdon, neither the people nor their language may, in point of fact, have ceased to exist in Scotland, the one as an element in the conglomerate of different races which composed the population of the monarchy, and the other as the *patois* of a district; nor does it follow, from the language of Bede, that the Picts must of necessity have been a different race, and their language a different language from any of the other peoples and languages enumerated in the same passage.

What, then, did Bede and Henry of Huntingdon mean when the former enumerated the Pictish as a separate and distinct language, and the latter said that this people and language were destroyed, while it is evident that large bodies of the people remained, and that a language called the Pictish was still spoken by some portion of the inhabitants of the country.

If the language referred to by Bede was the spoken language of a people of unmixed race, possessing but one common form of speech, then these statements certainly imply that it was something distinct as a language from that of the Angles, Scots, or Britains, and that in Henry's time the people called the Picts had been either entirely extirpated, or so completely subjugated that all distinctive character had been lost, and that they now spoke the language of their conquerors. If, however, the Picts were a people consisting of various tribes, politically combined into one nation, and the language referred to was that form of language adopted as the medium through which they had been instructed in knowledge, and in which all public affairs were carried on, then this by no means follows. Such a language might have perished when the kingdom was destroyed. It may have been merely a different form of a language analogous either to that of the Angles or Scots or Britains, and the spoken language of the Pictish tribes, or of some of them, may have remained as the vernacular dialect of those who survived the revolution which destroyed their independence.

The language referred to by Bede and Henry of Huntingdon, was a cultivated or literary language, which had been brought under the trammels of written forms. It was a language in which the word of God was studied, and we know how the dialect selected for the teaching of the Christian Church becomes elevated above the spoken dialects into a fixed standard for the whole nation. It was a language into which Ceolfrid's letter was translated by the "Viri doctores" of the court, and it was this same language which is stated to have ceased to exist in Henry's time. Its position, in this respect, is analogous to the German literary language, technically called New High German. Like the Celtic, the German spoken dialects fall into two classes, which are usually called High German and Low German. The differences between them are not so broad or so vital is those between the two types of the Celtic, the Gaelic, and the Cymric dialects, and they are more of a geographical than of a philological character. Grimm remarks this when he says that language is susceptible of a physical as well as an intellectual influence, and, though its principal elements remain the same, is, by long residence in mountains, woods, plains, or sea-coast, differently toned, so as to form separate subordinate dialects. "All experience shows, " says he, "that the mountain-air makes the sounds sharp and rough; the plain, soft and smooth. On the Alps the tendency is to diphthongs and aspirates; on the plain to narrow and thin vowels, and to *mediæ* and *tenues* among the consonants." The former represents the High German dialects; the latter the Low. The written language, however, or the literary German, is not identic with any one spoken dialect; it approaches more nearly to the High than to the Low German, but it is, in fact, an independent form of the language, the creation, in a sense, of Martin Luther, who, with the view of making his translation of the Bible adapted to all Germany, adopted as his medium a form of the language based upon the Upper Saxon and the official language of the German Empire, and this form of the language, stamped with the impress of his vigorous intellect, and popularised through the first Protestant version of the Bible, was adopted as the language of the literature of Germany, and, subjected to the cultivation it necessarily produced, became the language of the educated classes. The language of Holland or the Dutch is a Low German dialect, and is more nearly allied to the Low than the latter is to the High German; but it is an independent language, and has its own cultivation and literature, and its own translation of the Bible.

Now, a historian might well say that the word of God was studied in the five languages of the English, the French, the Dutch, the German, and the Latin, and yet one of them---the Dutch--would be closely allied to one form of the German. Again, if we could suppose Germany conquered by the Dutch, the German written and language would be superseded by the Dutch equally written and cultivated language; the Low German dialects would be as closely assimilated to the literary Dutch as the High German dialects now are to the literary German, and the latter would occupy the same position in which the Low German now is. In such a case we could well understand a writer, three centuries after the event, saying that the Germans had disappeared, and the German language was so completely destroyed that the mention of it and its literature in former writers appeared like fables. And yet the people and the spoken dialects of Germany would have remained unchanged and been there just as they always had been.

Substitute Scot for Dutch and Pict for German, and this is exactly the state of matters producing the phenomena noted by Bede and Henry of Huntingdon, and it is perfectly possible that the Picts may have been very nearly allied, both in race and language, with either the Britons or the Scots, who conquered them; and that the may have remained as in element in the population, and their language as the *patois* of a district, long after the days of Henry of Huntingdon, in a country in which both Scot and Briton entered so largely into its population. I have thought it necessary to enter at some length into the consideration of the meaning and import of these passages of Bede and Henry of Huntingdon, as a right understanding of them has a most material bearing, upon the question.

[1] *Chron. Picts and Scots*, p. 57. The Irish *f* is the *digamma* placed before an initial vowel; and the word *F*othudain seems to express Ptolemy's Ottadeni, who extended to the river Eden in Fife. The promontory of Fife, called Fifeness, is probably the promontory meant.
[2] *Chron. Picts and Scots*, p. 393.
[3] *Chron. Picts and Scots*, p. 123.
[4] The Early Frisian settlements in Scotland.
[5] *Chron. Picts and Scots*, pp. 319, 329.

Chapter Eight - The Celtic Dialects and the Probable Character of the Pictish Language

THERE is a fallacy which lurks in many of the arguments regarding the ethnological character of the old Celtic nations, based upon the modern languages. In arguing from the modern languages, it is always assumed that the language of each branch of the old Celtic race must be represented by one or other of the modern Celtic dialects. This fallacy pervades the writings of almost all of our ethnological writers, who argue as if, when a classical writer states that a difference existed between the language of two divisions of the old Celtic people, and when there is reason to suppose that the language of the one resembled the Welsh, then it must of necessity follow that the language of the other was the Gaelic. But this by no follows; nor is it at all self-evident that these modern Celtic languages represent all the ancient dialects. On the contrary, analogy and experience would lead us to a different conclusion. The ruder a language is, the more multiplied are its dialects; and the great medium for reducing their number is its cultivation. Before the introduction of writing, the means of such cultivation were to a great extent wanting. The Christian church was the great civiliser; and it was through its agency that these dialects received their cultivation, and one of their forms raised to the position of a written language. In the ante-Christian period of the Celtic language, the diversity of dialects must have been very great, and there may be many which have no direct representative among the modern languages. There may be many lost dialects on the Continent; and one such certainly existed, as we have seen in our own island, which has long ago disappeared--viz. the Pictish.

There run, however, through the whole of the modern Celtic, languages two great distinctive dialectic differences, which lie deep in the very groundwork of the language, and must have existed before their entrance into Great Britain, if not before their entrance into Europe. These differences separate these languages into two classes, each consisting of three of the spoken tongues. The one class, which we shall call the Cymric, consists of the Breton, the Welsh, and the Cornish;, the other, which we shall call the Gaelic, consists of the Irish, the Manx, and the Scotch Gaelic. The three Gaelic dialects are much more closely allied to each other than the three Cymric dialects; but each of the dialects composing the one class possesses in common those great distinctive differences which separate them from the three dialects composing the other class.

But while this great diversity exists, there are also analogies so close, vital, and fundamental, as to leave no doubt that they are all children of one common parent. Their vocabulary is, to a great extent, closely allied. A distinguished Welsh scholar of the present day estimates that two-thirds of the vocabulary of the six dialects are substantially the same; and I believe this conclusion to be correct. A number of the primitive adjectives expressing the simplest conceptions are the same. It is a peculiarity of both classes that the irregular forms bear a smaller proportion to the regular forms than is usual; but these irregular forms, which are, in fact, the deposit of an older stage of the language, bear a very remarkable analogy to each other.

The great and leading peculiarity in both classes of the Celtic languages, however, is the mutation of initial consonants; and while these initial mutations exist in each class, and are governed by the same laws, and thus afford additional evidence of their common origin, they at the same time present us with a means of discriminating between the different dialects, and distinguishing their mutual position as such, quite as effectual as Grimm's law has been among the German dialects. The consonants most readily affected by initial mutation are the mute consonants; and the following tables will show what the initial mutations in Welsh and Irish are:--

TABLE I.—INITIAL MUTATION OF MUTE CONSONANTS.

	WELSH.					IRISH.		
	Radical.	Medial.	Aspirate.	Nasal.		Radical.	Eclipsis.	Aspirate.
Labial	P	B	PH	MH	...	P	B	PH
Guttural	C	G	CH	NGH	...	C	G	CH
Dental	T	D	TH	NH	...	T	D	TH
Labial	B		F	M	...	B	M	BH
Guttural	G		—	NG	...	G	NG	GH
Dental	D		DD	N	...	D	N	DH
						F	BH	FH

But while these consonants thus undergo a change according to fixed laws *within* the limits of the language itself, there is also a similar interchange of sounds *between* the different spoken languages; and it is obvious that if the changes which the same words undergo in different dialects follow regular laws, the phonetic laws of these languages are of the utmost importance in discriminating their dialectic differences. The phonetic law which governs the relations of Welsh and Gaelic, so far as regards the mute consonants, is this:--Each mute consonant in Welsh has two changes in Gaelic, either into its own middle sound, or into another consonant of the same character, but of a different organ. Thus the labial *p* passes into its middle sound *b*, as in

Penn, a summit.　　　　*Beann*, a hill.
Prydydh　　*Breagha*, pretty.
Pincen　　　　*Beangan*, a sprig.

or into the guttural *c*, as in
Penn　Ceann, a head.
Pren　Crann, a tree.
Plant　Clann, children.
Pwy　Cia, who.

This latter change is deeply rooted in Welsh and Gaelic, and enters into the very life of the language, of which we have two very remarkable instances. The word *Pascha*, for Easter, can only have entered these languages after the establishment of the Christian church, when the languages, under the influence of its teaching, were passing into the fixed form of a written and cultivated speech; but while in Welsh it becomes *pasg*, in Gaelic, under the operation of this law, it becomes *casg*. On the other hand, St. *Ciaran*, an Irish saint, and the founder of Clonmacnois, passed over, in the sixth century, into Cornwall, and had no sooner put his foot on Cymric ground than he became St. *Pieran*.

In the next class of the mutes the converse takes place, for the Welsh guttural *g* either disappears or passes into the dental *d*, as in

Gel　　　　*Daoil*, a leech.
Gloin　　　*Dealan*, coal
Gwneyd　　*Deanadh*, to do.
Gobaith　　*Dobhchais*, hope.

There is here, however, a slight deviation from the general rule: *g* in Welsh is usually combined with *w*, and is in this combination the Welsh digamma; but instead of passing into *w*, according to the law, it becomes in Gaelic *f*; that is, the guttural in Welsh passes into an aspirated labial in Gaelic, as in

Gwyn　　　*Fion*, wine.
Gwyr　　　*Fior*, true.
Gwr　　　　*Fear*, a man.
Gwynn　　*Fionn*, White.

This is sufficient to illustrate the law of this double change; but it is rather remarkable that while the one change is into a different character of the same letter, and in strict accordance with the phonetic change within the language itself, the other change is from a letter of one organ to that of another, as from labial to guttural, and guttural to dental. The operating cause of this rather startling change is to be found within in the laws which govern the sounds of the whole languages of this class, and in consequence of which the same phenomenon presents itself in other members of the Indo-European family.

There are two influences at work at all languages, antagonistic and mutually destructive of each other--the etymologic and the phonetic. The one governs the formation of a language, the other aids in its disorganisation. The etymologic influence has reference to meaning only, and brings together sounds which do not harmonise. These are immediately assailed by the phonetic influence, and modified till they are brought to a more simple and harmonious sound. History knows nothing of the formation of languages, and the phonetic influence is at work, and language in a process of decay, before the people which speak it have entered the historic period; but when these phonetic laws have become known, we are able to trace back the sounds, however impaired, to their original constituent elements. These contrasts, then, of labial and guttural, and guttural and dental, draw us back to a time when there were complex sounds which the human ear could not long tolerate, and which, by the modification of one or other element, passed over into the more simple sound, and in their divorce from each, other present this great contrast. There was probably a complex sound composed of a guttural and labial; *k*, or hard *c*, and *v* or *p*. By one member of the family the *c* will be softened to *s*, and then disappear; while the *v* will be hardened to *p*, and remain alone. In another, the hard *c* will remain, and the *v* be softened to *u*, and then disappear, leaving the *c* alone. An instance of this is the word for a "horse," which runs through most of the languages of the Indo-European family. The original term must have been *acvas*; in Sanscrit it becomes *asvas*; in Zend, *aspas*; in Greek, *ippos*; and in Gaulish or old Celtic, *epo*. In Latin the hard *c* is retained, and *v* modified, and it becomes *equus*; and in Gaelic, *ech*. The same process would seem to have been gone through within the Celtic languages, as the old inscriptions indicate that the old Celtic word for a "son" was *maqvas*. By one branch of the race the hard *c* was softened, and then dropped; while the *v* was hardened to *p*, producing the Welsh *map* (a son). By the other, the hard *c* was retained, but the *v* softened to *u*, in which form we have it as *maqui*, and finally dropped, leaving the Gaelic *mac*. The digamma, too, was originally a complex sound, which in Welsh is *gw*, and in Latin *v*, and in Gaelic *f*.

The consonantal changes between Welsh and Gaelic are, then, as follows:--

TABLE II.—PHONETIC LAWS BETWEEN WELSH AND GAELIC.

P *into* C *or* B	G *into* D	W *into* O
C *into* T *or* G	GW *into* F	Y *into* E
B *into* G	H *into* S *or* F	E *into* EA

The vowel changes from Welsh to Gaelic are from *w* to *o* and *y* to *e*, which are likewise the masculine and feminine forms in Welsh, as--

WELSH.		GAELIC.
Trwm m	*Trom* f	*Trom*
Crwm m	*Crom* f	*Crom*
Bychan m	*Bechan* f	*Began*
Brych m	*Brech* f	*Breac*

The vowel *e* becomes *ea*, as in *pen* (a head), *ceann*, and *beann*, G. Such being the relations between Gaelic, and Welsh, it must be obvious that they are of a nature to enable us to fix, from the form of the words, the relative position of almost any Celtic dialect to these two great types of the twofold division of the language; and the question at once arises, whether they may not enable us to determine the position of that one Celtic dialect in Great Britain--of which we have no direct living representative--viz. the Pictish. Of this language only five words have been handed directly down to us; but still, if these words are of such a kind as to exhibit some of the phonetic laws of the language, we are not without the means of determining this question. These five words are--

1. PEANFAHEL.--Bede, who wrote in the eighth century, says that the Roman Wall commenced about two miles west of the monastery of Abercorn, "in loco qui sermone Pictorum Peanfahel, lingua autem Anglorum Penneltun appellatur;" and Nennius adds that the wall was called "Britannico sermone Guaul," and extended "a Penguaul quæ villa Scotice Cenail, Anglice vero Peneltun dicitur." This gives us *Penguaul* as the British form, *Peanfahel* as the Pictish, and *Cenail* as the Scottish.

2. UR.--One of the Pictish legends which had been added to the *Historia Britonum*, and has been preserved in the Irish *Nennius*, is expressly stated to have been taken from the books of the Picts, and has so important a bearing on this question that I insert it here entire:.--

"Of the origin of the Cruithneach here. Cruithne, son of Cing, son of Luctai, son of Partalan, son of Agnoin, son of Buain, son of Mais, son of Fathecht, son of Iafeth, son of Noe. He was the father of the Cruichneach, and reigned a hundred years. These are the seven sons of Cruithne--viz. Fib, Fidach, Fodla, Fortrend, warlike, Cait, Ce, Cirig--and they divided the land into seven divisions, as Columcille says:--

Seven children of Cruithne
Divided Alban into seven divisions:
Cait, Ce, Cirig, a warlike clan,
Fib, Fidach, Fotla, Fortrenn.

And the name of each man is given to their territories, as Fib, Ce, Cait, and the rest. Thirteen kings of them took possession. Fib reigned twenty-four years; Fidach, forty years; Fortrend, seventy years; Cait, twenty-two years; Ce, twelve years; Cirig, eighty years; Aenbecan, son of Cait, thirty years; Finecta, sixty years; Guidid Gadbre, *id est*, Geis, one year; Gest Gurid, forty years; Urges, thirty years; Brude Pont, thirty kings of them; and Brude was the name of each man of them, and of the divisions of the other men. They possessed an hundred and fifty years, *as it is in the Books of the Cruithneach.*

"Brude Pont, B. urpont, B. Leo, B. urleo, B. Gant, B. urgant, B. Gnith, B. urgnith, B. Fech, B. urfeich, B. Cal, B. urcal, B. Cint, B. urcint, B. Feth, B. urfeth, B. Ru, B. ero, B. Gart, B. urgart, B. Cind, B. urcind, B. Uip, B. uruip, B. Grith, B. urgrith, B. Muin, B. urnmin." [1]

Thus ends this very curious fragment, which undoubtedly contains a number of Pictish vocables. I shall advert to these afterwards; at present I have to do with only one. It will be observed that the names of the thirty kings descended from Bruide Pont consist of only fifteen vocables, each name being repeated with the syllable *ur* prefixed. We have something exactly analogous to this in the old Welsh genealogies annexed to the Harleian MS. of Nennius, and written in the year 977. The ancestry of Cunedda Guledig is there thus given:--Cunedda, son of Patern, son of Tacit, son of Cein, son of *Gwr*cein, son of Doli, son of *Gwr*doli, son of Duvn, son of *Gwr*duvn. This is evidently the same thing--*guor, gur,* or *gwr,* representing the Pictish *ur.* Again, one of the Pictish names is Urgest; and this name is repeated afterwards in the list of Pictish kings, where we twice have Ungust, son of Urgest; while the *Irish Annals* give the Irish equivalent as Aongus, son of Feargus--*fear* representing *ur.* We thus get the following forms:--Cymric, *gwr*; Pictish, *ur*; Gaelic, *fear.*

3. SCOLOFTH.--Reginald of Durham, in his *Libellus de admirandis Beati Cuthberti Virtutibus*--a work of the twelfth century--tells: of, a certain "Scolasticus Pictorum apud Cuthbrictiskchirch," or Kirkcudbright in Galloway; and says he was one of those "clerici qui in ecclesia illa commorantur qui, Pictorum lingua Scollofthes cognominantur." *Scolasticus* in Welsh is *yscolheic*; in Irish, *sgolog.*

4. CARTIT.--Cormac, in his old *Irish Glossary*, compiled in the ninth century, has--"*Cartit,* id est *delg,* id est *belra cruithnech,* id est *delg for a curtar a choss;*" that is; "*cartit,* a buckle, is a Pictish word. It is a buckle for putting on the foot." The Welsh equivalent is *gwaell*; the Irish is given by Cormac, *dealg.*

5. DUIPER.--In another of the Pictish fragments, which also formed part of the *Pictish Chronicle,* one of the mythic kings is thus given, "Gartnaidh Duiper." In the *Chronicle of the Priory of St. Andrew,* which contains a Scottish list of the same kings, the epithet is translated thus--"Gartnech *dives,*" or rich. "Rich" in Welsh is *goludog*; in Irish, *saoibher.*

From these five words we gather the following phonetic changes. In the first we see the initial *p* in Cymric and Pictish passing over into *c* in Gaelic, the Cymric *e* passing into *ea* in Pictish and Gaelic, and the Cymric *gu* passing into *f* in Pictish, and neutralised by aspiration in Gaelic. In the second, *gwr* becomes *ur* in Pictish, *fear* in Gaelic. In the third we see the final guttural in Cymric and Gaelic softened to the dental in Pictish. The fourth is a peculiar word, but the Welsh and Irish equivalents furnish an example of *g* passing into *d*. In the fifth, the Pictish *duiper* and the Gaelic *saoibher* are the same word, showing *d* passing into *s*.

From these examples, Pictish appears to occupy a place between Cymric and Gaelic, leaning to the one in some of its phonetic laws, and to the other in others. Thus in the initial of the first word we have a Cymric form. The vowel-changes are Gaelic, and the initial of the second syllable also Gaelic; and on comparing the first two, words we see, that, while gw in Cymric ought, according to the general law; to pass into *u* in Gaelic--but in reality passes into *f*--the Pictish law combines both; and the Pictish canon is that *gw* in Cymric before a consonant becomes *u* in Pictish, and before a vowel becomes *f* in Pictish as in Gaelic.

The other words do not help us, at this stage of the inquiry; but we have another source of information in the proper names, of which we have in the lists of the Pictish kings the Pictish forms in the Irish *Nennius* and the *Pictish Chronicle*, and the Irish or Gaelic forms in the *Chronicle of the Priory of St. Andrew* and the *Irish Annals*, while the Welsh genealogies furnish Cymric equivalents. The phonetic laws which govern these, are equally available for our purpose. First, the Pictish law which changes *gw* into *u* before a consonant and *f* before a vowel, appears in the Pictish names Urgest, Uroid, and Fingaine; the Cymric equivalents of which are Gwrgust, Gwriad, and Gwyngenau; and the Gaelic, Feargus, Ferat, and Fingon. Then in the Pictish Drust, Deriloi, and Dalorgan, the Cymric equivalents of which are Grwst, Gwrtholi, and Galargan, we have the *g* passing into *d*, which is a Gaelic form. In the Pictish Domnall, the Cymric equivalent of which is Dwfnwall, we have the vowel-change of *w* into *o*, also a Gaelic form. The following table will show the result of this analysis:--

TABLE III.—COMPARISON OF CYMRIC, PICTISH, AND GAELIC WORDS.

C	Penguaal	Gwr	Yscolheic	Gwaell	Goludog
P	Peanfahel	Ur	Scolofth	Cartit	Duiper
G	Cen(fh)ail	Fear	Sgolog	Dealg	Saoiber
C	Gwyngenau	Gwrgust	Dwfnwal	Grwst	Caran
P	Fingaine	Urgest	Domnall	Drust	Taran
G	Fingon	Feargus	Domnall		Sarran
C		Gwriad		Gwrtholi	
P		Uroid		Deriloi	
G		Ferat			
C				Galargan	
P				Dalorgan	
G					

The Pictish tradition which I have given at length, besides yielding the word *ur*, furnishes us with a series of Pictish vocables. These are, first, the seven sons of Cruithne. They are said to have divided the land into seven portions, and to have given their names to them. We can identify some of

70

them. "Fib" is plainly Fife, the old form of which was Fibh. "Fodla" is Atholl, the old form of which name was Ath*fodla*. "Fortrenn" is the well-known name of the central district of the Pictish kingdom, which has now disappeared. "Cirig" or "Circin," as in the *Pictish Chronicle*, is the district of Girgin or *Maghghirghin*; now corrupted into Mearns, or Kincardineshire. "Caith" is Caithness, as in the old poem in the Irish *Nennius*,--

From thence they conquered Alba,
The noble nurse of fruitfulness,
Without destroying the people or their homes,
From the region of Cait to Forcu;"

that is, from Caithness to the Forth, the southern boundary of the Pictish kingdom. "Ce" and "Fidach" I cannot identify. But it will be observed, of these seven sons, the names of four begin with *f*, and the other three with *c*, obvious Gaelic forms; and I am inclined to think that they mark out a division of the Pictish race into two, of which one affected the guttural *c*, and the other the softer sound of the *f*.

Of the six names which follow, Aenbecan and Finecta are Gaelic forms; Guidid, Cymric; Gest, Urgest, and Brude, Pictish, as distinguished from either; and the untranslated epithets, Gadbre, Geis, and Gurid, are probably Pictish words.

The names of the thirty Brudes yield also fifteen Pictish monosyllables. These are, alphabetically, Cal, Cint, Cind, Fech, Feth, Gant, Gart, Geis, Gnith, Grith, Leo, Muin, Pont, Ru, Uip; and here also the prevalence of the gutturals, *c*, *g*, and the soft *f* is apparent. Some of these monosyllables have a resemblance to the names of the old Irish letters which signify trees, as *cal*, the name for *c*, a hazel; *feth* seems the same as *pet*, the name for *p*; *gart*, like *gort* (ivy), the name for *g*; *muin*, the vine, is the name for *m*; and *leo* resembles *luis*, and *ru*, *ruis*, ash and alder, the names for *l* and *r*. In the same manner three of the names of the seven sons of Cruithne have a resemblance to three of the numerals; as fib, *pump*, five; ce, *se*, six; caith, *saith*, seven. These, however, may be casual resemblances.

The relation of the fifteen vocables to the proper names is more apparent. On analysing the proper names of the Cymri and the Gael we find that both are produced by the same process--viz. a certain number of monosyllables forms the first half of the name, and to these are affixed a certain number of endings, the combination of which forms the proper names. In Cymric the initial syllables are--Ael, Aer, Arth, Bed, Cad, Car, Col, Cyn, Dog, Dygvn, El, Eur, Gar, Gor, Gwen, Gwyn, Gwyd, Gwr, Id, Mael, Mor, Tal, Tud, Ty. The Irish initial syllables are--Aen, Ain, Air, Aid, Art, Cath, Con, Corb, Cu, Domh, Donn, Dubh, Dun, Each, Echt, Eoch, Er, For, Fian, Fin, Finn, Fedh, Fear, Fail, Flaith, Flann, Gorm, Ir, Laigh, Lear, Lugh, Maen, Muir, Ragh, Reacht, Ruadh, Rud, Saer, Tuath. It would be endless to enumerate the affixes; but the most common Cymric are--deyrn, varch, wyr, swys; as, Aelgyvarch, Cadvarch, Cynvarch,

Aerdeyrn, Cyndeyrn, Arthwys, Cynwys, etc.; and in Irish, cal, or in oblique case, gal and gusa; as, Aengus, Artgal, Ardgal, Congus, Congal, Dungus, Dungal, Feargus, Feargal, and so forth. Now these fifteen Pictish vocables likewise enter into the Pictish names, as Gart in Gartnaidh, and Dergart and Geis in Urgest; Leo in Morleo, Muin in Muinait, Uip in Uipog, and so forth. On the whole, the Pictish vocables coincide more with the Irish than with the Cymric, as Cal with Gal, Geis with Gusa, and so forth.

Further, on comparing the initial forms in Irish and in Cymric, we see in Cymric no words beginning with *f*, while in Irish there are nine; so that the vocables in Pictish with initial *f* are Gaelic. On the other hand, six vocables begin with *g* in Cymric, and only one in Irish; so that here the Pictish draws to the Cymric, and stands between the two with a greater leaning to the Gaelic.

The same fallacy which pervades the ethnological deductions regarding the Gauls also affects this Pictish question. It has been too much narrowed by the assumption that, if it is shewn to be a Celtic dialect, it must of necessity be absolutely identic in all its features either with Welsh or with Gaelic. But this necessity does not really exist; and the result I come to is, that it is not Welsh, neither is it Gaelic; but it is a Gaelic dialect partaking largely of Welsh forms.

It has always appeared to me that we can trace in the Celtic languages a twofold subordinate dialectic difference lying side by side, which is very analogous to some of the differences between high and low German. I do not mean to say that the differences between those subordinate Celtic dialects are absolutely parallel to those, between high and low German; but merely that they are of a nature which renders this nomenclature not inapplicable, while it affords a convenient term of distinction. A leading distinction between the high and low German is the preference of the latter for the sharp sounds, *p*, *t*, and *k*, instead of *f* or *pf*, *s* or *z* and *ch*; and the instance most familiar to us is the substitution of *t* for *s*, as *wasser* in high German becomes *water* in low, and water in English; *dasz* in high German is *dat* in low, and *that* in English.

Now, a similar distinction is, in one point of view, observable among the three dialects of the Cymric. Of these dialects, the Cornish and Breton are much nearer to each other than either is to the Welsh. It is, in fact, a mistake to suppose, as is frequently asserted, that a Welshman and a Breton can understand each other. One of our best Welsh scholars, Mr. Price, who visited Bretagne, remarks: "Notwithstanding the many assertions that have been made respecting the natives of Wales and Brittany being mutually intelligible through the medium of their respective languages, I do not hesitate to say that the thing is utterly impossible. Single words in either language will frequently be found to have corresponding terms of a similar sound in the other, and occasionally a short sentence deliberately pronounced may be partially intelligible; but as to holding a conversation, that is totally out of the question." Cornish and Breton are much more nearly allied. Now, it is remarkable that in many cases *d*, *dd*, and *t*, in Welsh, pass into *s* in Cornish and *z* in Breton, as in

W. *Tad.*   C. *Tas.*
W. *Goludog.*   C. *Gallosah.*
W. *Bleidd.*   B. *Bleiz.*
W. *Noeth.*   B. *Noz.*

which is exactly analogous to one of the leading differences between high and low German; and Welsh, like the latter, shows a great preference for the dentals and its aspirates. I am therefore inclined to introduce the same nomenclature among the Celtic languages, and to call Welsh "low Cymric," Cornish and Breton "high Cymric" dialects.

The three dialects which compose the Gaelic class are much more nearly allied to each other than even Cornish and Armoric, and may be held to represent the old Scottish. On the same analogy they all belong to a high Gaelic dialect. There are, to be found, however, among the synonyms in the Gaelic dialects, low Gaelic forms accompanying high Gaelic forms, as in

Suil,   *Duil*, hope.
Seangan,   *Deangan,* an ant.
Seas,   *Deas,* stay.
Samh,   *Damh,* learning.
Seirc,   *Deirc,* almsgiving.
Sonnach,   *Tonnach,* a wall.

which seems to indicate that a low Gaelic dialect has been incorporated or become blended with it.

The Pictish language appears to have approached more nearly to the old Scottish than even Breton to Welsh, according to Mr. Price's view; for Adomnan, who, in the seventh century, wrote the *Life of St. Columba*, the Scottish missionary to the Picts, describes St. Columba, the Scot, as conversing freely with the Picts, from the king to the plebeian, without difficulty, but when he preached to them the Word of God, he was obliged to make use of an interpreter: that is, he could make himself understood in conversing, but not in preaching; and, conversely, a Pict understood what he said in Scottish, but could not follow a Scottish sermon. This is a point, in fact, as to which there exists much misapprehension; and we are apt. to forget how very small a difference even in pronunciation will interpose an obstacle to mutual intelligence. Even in Breton and Cornish, the two Cymric dialects which most nearly approach each other, Norris, the highest Cornish authority, says, "In spite of statements to the contrary, the writer is of opinion that a Breton, within the historical existence of the two dialects could not have understood a Cornishman speaking at any length, or on any but the most trivial subjects;" and between Irish and Scotch Gaelic it would not require very much additional divergence to prevent the one from understanding the other.

Such being probably the mutual position of Pictish and Scottish, the few words we are able to compare show the difference between them to have been of the same character as between the high and low dialects; for we find *saoibher* (rich) in Irish represented by *duiper* in Pictish; and in proper names, Sarran by Taran, showing *s* in the one represented by *d* and *t* in the other; while the words *sgolofth*, *cartit*, and the proper names, *Bargoit*, *Wroid*, *Wid*, show the preference of the Pictish for dental in place of guttural terminations. I consider, therefore, that Pictish was a low Gaelic dialect; and, following out the analogy, the result I come to is, that Cymric and Gaelic had each a high and a low variety; that Cornish and Breton were high Cymric dialects, Welsh low Cymric; that old Scottish, spoken by the Scotti, now represented by Irish, Scotch Gaelic, and Manx, was the high Gaelic dialect, and Pictish the low Gaelic dialect.

This analogy is confirmed by the legendary origins of these different races, in which, under the form of a mythic migration, the traces of a rude and primitive ethnology often lie hid. The tendencies which produce the high and low German are, as we have remarked, associated with the character of the country peopled by them. The low German forms are connected with the level and marshy plains which border on the German Ocean, the high German with the more mountainous region of the south of Germany; but the same characteristics mark the mythic. migrations of the Celtic races which peopled Britain. In the Welsh traditions, the Cymry, which are represented by the Welsh or low Cymric people, are said to have crossed the German Ocean from the north of Germany; the Lloegrys, represented by the Cornish or high Cymric, are brought from the South. In the old Irish traditions, the different races said to have peopled Ireland fall into two classes: the one is said to have penetrated through Europe by the Rhiphaean Mountains to the Baltic, and to have crossed the German Ocean; and the other is brought by the Mediterranean and the south of Europe. [2] The former alone are said to have made settlements in Scotland; and Bode, in giving the tradition of the origin of the Picts, brings them likewise from the north of Germany across the German Ocean. This population which preceded the German races was, in fact, the race of the Celts, who seem to have been driven westward by the pressure of the Teutonic movement; and, like the German, to have shown a twofold minor difference, produced by the same physical influence, which is known by the names of "high" and "low" German.

The platform occupied by the Pictish people was not confined to Scotland alone, for they certainly extended over part of the north of Ireland, and formed, in all probability, an earlier population of the north half of Ireland, which became subjugated by the Scots. On the other hand, the Scots at an early period occupied the district of Argyll. In the north of Ireland and the west of Scotland the Picts must, at an early period, have become blended with the Scots, and their form of the Gaelic assimilated to the Scottish. In Scotland, south of the Tay, where they occupied the districts from the Tay to the Forth, the region of Manau or Manann, and Galloway, they came in contact with the Cymric people, and the one being a low Gaelic dialect, and the other a low Cymric dialect, their forms must have so far resembled each other as to lead to an admixture presenting that mixed language of low Gaelic with Cymric forms, known to Bode as the Pictish language.

[1] *Chron. Picts and Scots*, p. 24.
[2] The one class consists of the Nemedians and the Tuatha de Danaan; the other of Partholan and his colony, the Firbolg and the Milesians.

Chapter Nine - The Celtic Topography of Scotland, and the Dialectic Differences Indicated By It

THE etymology of the names of places in a country is either a very important element in fixing the ethnology of its inhabitants, or it is a snare and a delusion, just according as the subject is treated. When such names are analysed according to fixed laws, based upon sound philological principles and a comprehensive observation of facts, they afford results both important and trustworthy; but if treated empirically, and founded upon resemblance of sounds alone, they become a mere field for wild conjectures and fanciful etymologies, leading to no certain results. The latter is the ordinary process to which they are subjected. The natural tendency of the. human mind is to a mere phonetic etymology of names, both of persons and of places, in which the sounds of the name of the place appear to resemble the sounds in certain words of a certain language, the language from which the etymology is derived being selected upon no sound philological grounds, but from arbitrary considerations merely.

Unhappily, an etymology founded upon mere resemblance of sounds has hitherto characterised all systematic attempts to analyse the topography of Scotland, and to deduce ethnologic results from it. Prior to the publication of the *Statistical Account of Scotland* in 1792, it may be said, that no general attempt had been made to explain the meaning of the names of places in Scotland, or to indicate the language from which they were derived. We find occasionally, in old lives of the saints and in charters connected with church lands, that names of places occurring in them are explained; and these interpretations are very valuable, as indicating what may be termed the common tradition of their meaning and derivation at an early period. Of very different value are a few similar derivations in the fabulous histories of Boece, Buchanan, and John Major, which are usually mere fanciful conjectures of pedantry.

The first impetus to anything like a general etymologising of Scottish topography was given when Sir John Sinclair projected the *Statistical Account of Scotland*. In the schedule of questions which he issued in 1790 to the clergy of the Church of Scotland, the first two questions were as, follows:--

1. What is the ancient and modern. name of the parish?

2. What is the origin and etymology of the name?

This set every minister thinking what was the meaning of the name of his parish. The publication of the *Poems of Ossian*; and the controversy which followed, had tended greatly to identify national feeling and the history of the country with literature and language, and, with few exceptions, the etymology was sought for in that language. The usual formula of reply was, "The name of this parish is derived from the Gaelic," and then followed a Gaelic sentence resembling in sound the name of the parish, and supposed admirably to express its characteristics, though the unfortunate minister is often obliged to confess that the parish is remarkably free from the characteristics expressed by the Gaelic derivation of its name. These etymologies are usually suggested irrespective entirely of any known facts as to the history or population of the parish, and are purely phonetic.

After the publication of the Statistical Account, Gaelic was in the ascendant as the source of all Scottish etymologies, till the publication of Chalmers' *Caledonia* in 1807. John Pinkerton had indeed tried to direct the current of popular etymology into a Teutonic channel, but his attempts to find a meaning in Gothic dialects for words plainly Celtic were so unsuccessful that he failed even to gain a hearing. Chalmers was more fortunate. His theory was that a large proportion of the names of places in Scotland are to be derived from the Welsh, and indicate an original Cymric population. And this he has worked out with much labour and pains. In doing so, he was the first to attempt to show evidence of the dialectic difference between Welsh and Gaelic pervading the names of places, and to discriminate between them; but for almost all the names of places in the Lowlands of Scotland he furnishes a Welsh etymology, which, like his predecessors the Scottish clergy, he supposes to be expressive of the characteristics of the locality. His theory has, in the main, commanded the assent of subsequent writers, and is usually assumed to be, on the whole, a correct representation of the state of the fact. Yet his system was as purely one of a phonetic etymology, founded upon mere resemblance of sounds, is those of his predecessors. The MSS. left by George Chalmers show how he set about preparing his etymologies, and we now know the process he went through. He had himself no knowledge of either branch of the Celtic language, but he sent his list of names to Dr. Owen Pughe; and that most ingenious of all Welsh lexicographers, who was capable of reducing every word in every known language in the world to a Welsh original, sent him a list of Welsh renderings of each word, varying from twelve to eighteen in number, out of which Chalmers selected the one which seemed to him most promising. His other etymologies, are equally founded on a mere resemblance of sounds between the modern form of the word and the modern Welsh, as those of the clergy in the Statistical Account were between the modern form of the word and the modern Gaelic.

That system of interpreting the names of places, which I have called phonetic etymology, is, however, utterly unsound. It can lead only to fanciful renderings, and is incapable of yielding any results that are either certain or important. Names of places are, in fact, sentences or combinations of words originally expressive of the characteristics of the place named, and applied to it by the people who then occupied the country, in the language spoken by them at the time, and are necessarily subject to the same philological laws which governed that spoken language. The same rules must be applied in interpreting a local name as in rendering a sentence of the language. That system, therefore, of phonetic etymology which seeks for the interpretation of a name in mere resemblance of sound to words in an existing language, overlooks entirely the fact that such names were fixed to certain localities at a much earlier period, when the language spoken by those who applied the name must have differed greatly from any spoken language of the present day.

Since the local names were deposited in the country, the language itself from which they were derived has gone through a process of change, corruption, and decay. Words have altered their forms--sounds have varied--forms have become obsolete, and new forms have arisen, and the language in its present state no longer represents that form of it which existed when the local nomenclature was formed. The topographical expressions, too, go through a process of change and corruption, till they diverge still further from the spoken form of the language as it now exists. This process of change and corruption in the local names varies according to the change in the population. When the population has remained unchanged, and the language in which the names were applied is still the spoken language of the district, the names either remain in their original shape, in which case they represent an older form of the same language, or else they undergo a change analogous to that of the spoken language. Obsolete names disappear as obsolete words drop out of the language, and are replaced by more modern vocables. Where there has been a change in the population, and the older race are replaced by a people speaking a kindred dialect, the names of places are subjected to the dialectic change which characterises the language. There are some striking instances of this where a British form has been superseded by a Gaelic form, as, for instance, Kirkintulloch, the old name of which, Nennius informs us, was Caerpentalloch, *kin* being the Gaelic equivalent of the Welsh *pen*; Penicuik, the old name of which was Peniacop; Kincaid, the old name of which was Pencoed.

When, however, the new language introduced by the change of population is one of a different family entirely, then the old name is stereotyped in the shape in which it was when the one language superseded the other, becomes unintelligible to the people, and undergoes a process of change and corruption of a purely phonetic character, which often entirely alters the aspect of the name. In the former cases it is chiefly necessary to apply the philologic laws of the language to its analysis. In the latter, which is the case with the Celtic topology of the low country, it is necessary, before attempting to analyse the name, to ascertain its most ancient form, which often differs greatly from its more modern aspect.

It is with this class of names we have mainly to do, as presenting the phenomena I am anxious to investigate.

When the topography of a country is examined, its local names will be found, as a general rule, to consist of what may be called generic terms and specific terms. What I mean by generic terms are those parts of the name which are common to a large number of them, and are descriptive of the general character of the place named; and by specific terms, those other parts of the name which have been added to distinguish one place from another. The generic terms are usually general words for river, mountain, valley, plain, etc.; the specific terms, those words added to distinguish one river or mountain from another. Thus, in the Gaelic name Glenmore, *glen* is the generic term, and is found in a numerous class of words; *more*, great, the specific, a distinguished term, to distinguish it from another called Glenbeg. In the Saxon term Oakfield, field is the generic term, and oak the specific, to distinguish it from Broomfield, etc.

When the names of places are applied to purely natural objects, such as rivers, mountains, etc., which remain unchanged by the hand of man, the names applied by the original inhabitants are usually adopted by their successors, though speaking a different language; but the generic term frequently undergoes a phonetic corruption, as in the Lowlands, where Aber has in many cases become Ar, as in Arbroath, Arbuthnot; Ballin has become Ban, as in Bandoch; Pettin has become Pen, as in Pendriech; Pol has become Pow; and Traver has become Tar and Tra, as in Tranent.

On the other hand, where the districts have been occupied by different branches of the same race, speaking different dialects, the generic terms exhibit the dialectic differences when the sounds of the word are such as to require the dialectic change; thus in Welsh and Gaelic:--

Pen and Ceann--a head,

Gwynn and Fionn--white,

show the phonetic difference between these dialects.

The comparison of the generic terms which pervade the topography of a country affords a very important means of indicating the race of its early inhabitants, and discriminating between the different branches of the race, to which the respective portions of it belong. It was early observed that there existed in the Celtic generic terms a difference which seemed to indicate dialectic distinction. Even in the Old Statistical Account, the minister of the parish of Kirkcaldy remarks--

"To the Gaelic language, a great proportion of the names of places in the neighbourhood, and indeed through the whole, of Fife, may unquestionably be traced. All names of places beginning with Bal, Col or Cul, Dal, Drum, Dun, Inch, Inver, Auchter, Kil, Kin, Glen, Mon, and Strath, are of Gaelic origin. Those beginning with Aber and Pit are supposed to be Pictish, names, and do not occur beyond the territory which the Picts are thought to have inhabited,"

Chalmers states it still more broadly and minutely. He says--

"Of those words which form the chief compounds in many of the Celtic names of places in the Lowlands, some are exclusively British, as Aber, Llan, Caer, Pen, Cors, and others; some are common to both British and Irish, as Carn, Craig, Crom, Bre, Dal, Eaglis, Glas, Inis, Rinn, Ros, Strath, Tor, Tom, Glen; and many more are significant only in the Scoto-Irish or Gaelic, as Ach, Ald, Ard, Aird, Auchter, Bar, Blair, Ben, Bog, Clach, Corry, Cul, Dun, Drum, Fin, Glac, Inver, Kin, Kil, Knoc, Larg, Lurg, Lag, Logie, Lead, Letter, Lon, Loch, Meal, Pit, Pol, Stron, Tullach, Tullie, and others."

This attempt at classification is, however, exceedingly inaccurate. Two of the words in the first class, Llan and Caer, are common to both British and Irish; and a large, portion of the third class are significant in pure Irish, as well as in the Scoto-Irish or Gaelic. No attempt is made to show, by the geographical distribution of these words, in what parts of the country the respective elements prevail.

The most popular view of the subject, and that which has recently been most insisted. in, is the line of demarcation between a Cymric and a Gaelic population, supposed to be indicated by the occurrence of the words Aber and Inver. This view has been urged with great force by Kemble, in his *Anglo-Saxons*; but I may quote the recent work of Mr. Isaac Taylor, on words and places, as containing a fair statement of the popular view of the subject:--

"To establish the point that the Picts, or the nation, whatever was its name, that held central Scotland, was Cymric, not Gaelic, we may refer to the distinction already mentioned between *Ben* and *Pen*. *Ben* is confined to the west and north; *Pen* to the east and south. *Inver* and *Aber* are also useful test-words in discriminating between the two branches of the Celts. The difference between the two words is dialectic only; the etymology and the meaning is the same--a confluence of waters, either of two rivers or of a river with the sea. Aber occurs repeatedly in Brittany, and is found in about fifty Welsh names, as Aberdare, Abergavenny, Abergele, Aberystwith, and Barmouth, a corruption of Abermaw. In England we find *Aber*ford in Yorkshire, and *Ber*wick in Northumberland and Sussex; and it has been thought that the name of the Humber is a corruption of the same root. *Inver*, the Erse and Gaelic forms, is common in Ireland, where *Aber* is unknown. Thus, we find places called Inver in Antrim, Donegal, Mayo, and Invermore in Galway and in Mayo. In Scotland the *Invers* and *Abers* are distributed in a curious and instructive manner. If we draw a line across the map from a point a little south of Inveraray to one a little north of Aberdeen, we shall find that (with very few exceptions) the *Invers* lie to the north of the line and the *Abers* to the south of it. This line nearly coincides with the present southern limit of the Gaelic tongue, and probably also with the ancient division between the Picts and the Scots."

Nothing can be more inaccurate than this statement. *Ben* is by no means confined to the west and north; and as examples of *Pen* he refers, among others, to the Pentland Hills, Pentland being a Saxon word, and corrupted from Pectland; and to Pendriech in Perthshire, which is a corruption from Pittendriech. So far from Inver being common in Ireland, it is very rare. The *Index locorum* of the *Annals of the Four Masters* shows only six instances. On the other hand, Aber is not unknown in Ireland. It certainly existed formerly to some extent in the north of Ireland; and Dr. Reeves produces four instances near Ballyshannon.

The statement with regard to the distribution of Aber and Inver in Scotland here is, that there is a line of demarcation which separates the two words-- that, with few exceptions, there is nothing but Invers on one side of this line, nothing but Abers on the other; and that this line extends from a point a little south of Inveraray to a point a little north of Aberdeen. This is the mode in which the distribution of these two words is usually represented, but nothing can be more perfectly at variance with the real state of the case. South of this line there are as many Invers as Abers. In Perthshire, south of the Highland line, there are nine Abers and eight Invers; in Fifeshire, four Abers and nine Invers; in Forfar, eight Abers and eight Invers; in Aberdeenshire, thirteen Abers and twenty six Invers. Again, on the north side of this supposed line of demarcation, where it is said that Invers alone should be found, there are twelve Abers, extending across to the west coast, till they terminate with Abercrossan, now Applecross, in Ross-shire. In Argyllshire alone there are no Abers. The true picture of the distribution of these two words is--in. Argyllshire, Invers alone; in Inverness and Ross shires, Invers and Abers in the proportion of three to one and two to one; and on the south side of this supposed line, Abers and Invers in about equal proportions.

Again he, says, quoting Chalmers, "The process of change is shown by an old charter, in which King David grants to the monks of May 'Inverin qui fuit Aberin.' So Abernethy became Invernethy, although the old name is now restored." In order to produce the antithesis of Inverin and Aberin, one letter in this charter has been altered. The charter is a grant of "Petneweme et Inverin quæ fuit Averin;" and I have the authority of the first charter antiquary in Scotland for saying that this construction is impossible: "quæ fuit" does not, in charter Latin, mean "which was," but "which belonged to," and Averin was the name of the previous proprietor of the lands. Abernethy and Invernethy are not the same place, and the former never lost its name. Invernethy is at the junction of the Nethy with the Earn, and Abernethy is a mile further up the river.

When we examine these Abers and Invers more closely, we find, 1*st*, that in some parts of the country they appear to alternate, is in Fife--Inverkeithing, Aberdour, Inveryne, Inverlevin, and so forth; 2*d*, That some of the Invers and Abers have the same specific terms attached to them, as Abernethy and Invernethy, Aberuchill and Inveruchill, Abercrumbye and Invercrumbye, Abergeldie and Invergeldie; and 3*d*, That the Invers are always at the mouth of the river, close to its junction with another river, or with the sea; and the Abers usually a little distance up the river where there is a ford. Thus Invernethy is at the mouth of the Nethy; Abernethy a mile or two above. These and other facts lead to the conclusion that they are part of the same nomenclature, and belong to the same period and to the same people.

When we look to the south of the Forth, however, we find this remarkable circumstance that in Ayrshire, Renfrew, and Lanarkshire, which formed the possessions of the Strathclyde Britons, and were occupied by a British people till as late a period as the more northern districts were occupied by the Picts, there are no Abers at all. What we have, therefore, is the Scots of Argyll with nothing but Invers, the Picts with Abers and Invers together, and the Strathclyde Britons with no Abers.

As a mark of discrimination between races this criterion plainly breaks down, and the words themselves contain no sounds which, from the different phonetic laws of the languages, could afford an indication of a dialectic difference. The truth is, that there were three words expressive of the junction of one stream with another, and all formed from an old Celtic word, *Ber*, signifying water. These were *Aber*, *Inver*, and *Conber* (pronounced in Welsh *cummer*, in Gaelic *cumber*). These three words were originally common to both branches of the Celtic as derivations from one common word. In old Welsh poems we find not only Aber as a living word in Welsh, but Ynver likewise. [1] and Dr. Reeves notices an Irish document in which Applecross or Appurcrossan is called Conber Crossan. Ynver, however, became obsolete in Welsh, just as Cummer or Cumber and Aber became obsolete in Irish but we have no reason to know that it did so in Pictish. In the Pictish districts, therefore, the Abers and Invers were deposited when both were living words in the language. When the Scots settled in Argyll, Aber had become obsolete in their language, and Inver was alone deposited, and in Strathclyde both words seem to have gone into desuetude.

In the same manner *Dwfr* or *Dwr*, is quoted as a word for water, peculiar to the Welsh form of Celtic, and an invariable mark of the presence of a British people, but, the old form of this word in Scotland was *Doboir*, as appears from the Book of Deer, where Aberdour is written *Abber-doboir*, and in Cormac's Glossary of the old Irish, *Doboir* is given as an old Irish word for water. In another old Irish glossary we have this couplet:--

"Bior and An and Dobar,
  The three names of the water of the world."

These words, therefore, form no criterion of difference of race, and to judge by them is to fall into the mistake of the phonetic etymologists--viz. to apply to old names, as the key, the present spoken language, which does not contain words which yet existed in it in its older form.

In order to make generic terms a test of dialect, they must be words which contain sounds affected differently by the different phonetic laws of such dialects--such as *Pen*, *Gwynn*, *Gwern*, and *Gwydd* which all enter copiously into Welsh topography, and the equivalents of which in the Gaelic dialects are *Ceann*, *Fionn*, *Fearn*, and *Fiodh*. Such generic terms afford a test by which we can at once determine whether the Celtic topography of a country partakes most of the Cymric or the Gaelic character. The earliest collection of names in North Britain is to be found in Ptolemy's Geography in the second century, but we know too little of the origin of his names, whether they were native terms, or names applied by the invaders, to obtain from them any certain result. After Ptolemy, the largest collection of names in Great Britain is in the work of the anonymous geographer of Ravenna, a work of the seventh century. The exact localities are not given, but the names are grouped according to the part of Britain to which they belong. Those which commence the topography of Scotland are placed under this title: "Iterum sunt civitates in ipsa Britannia quæ recto tramite de una parte in alia, id est, de oceano in oceano existunt, ac dividunt in tertia portione ipsam Britanniam." They commence with the stations on the Roman wall between the Tyne and the, Solway, and then proceed northwards. Among these we find two names together, Tadoriton and Maporiton, and as *Tad* and *Map* are Cymric forms for father and son, we have no doubt that here we are on the traces of a Cymric population. The next group is arranged under this head:--"Iterum sunt civitates in ipsa Britannia recto tramite una alteri conexæ, ubi et ipsa Britannia plus angustissima, de oceano in oceano esse dinoscitur." This part of Britain, which is *plus angustissima*, is the isthmus between the Forth and the Clyde, and in proceeding with the names northwards we come to one called Cindocellum. The Ocelli Montes were the Ochills, and here the Gaelic form of Kin is equally unmistakable. When we apply to the present topography the testing words Pen, Gwynn, Gwern, and Gwydd, the Gaelic equivalents of which are Kin, Fionn, Fearn, and Fiodh, we find that, with one exception, Pen, though frequent south of the Forth, where there was a British population, does not occur north of the Forth, while it is full of Kins, and Gwynn, Gwern, and Gwydd occur only in their Gaelic equivalents.

Such then being the aspect in which the question really presents itself, it becomes important, with a view to ethnological results, to ascertain more closely the geographical distribution of the generic terms over Scotland, and in order to show this I have prepared a table of such distribution. The generic terms are taken from the index to the Scottish Record of Retours; and as this record relates to properties, and not to mere natural objects, the generic terms they contain are to a great extent confined to names of places connected with their possession by man, and more readily affected by changes in the population. For the purposes of comparison, I have framed a list of generic terms contained in Irish topography from the index to the *Annals of the Four Masters*, and of those in Welsh topography from a list in the *Cambrian Register*. I have divided Scotland into thirteen districts, so as to show the local character of the topography of each part of Scotland, and opposite each generic term in Scotch topography is marked--1*st*, if it occurs in Ireland, and how often; 2*d*, if it occurs in Wales; and 3*d*, I have marked the number of times it occur in each district of Scotland from the Index of Retours.

On examining this table, it will be seen that there are five terms peculiar to the districts occupied by the Picts. These are Auchter, Pit, Pitten, For, and Fin. Now none of these five terms are to be found in Welsh topography at all, and For and Fin are obviously Gaelic forms.

It is necessary, however, in examining these terms, which may be called Pictish, to ascertain their old form. Auchter appears to be the Gaelic *Uachter*, upper; and as such we have it in Ireland, and in the same form, as in Scotland Ochtertire, in Ireland Uachtertire. It does not occur in Wales.

The old form of Pit and Pitten, as appears from the Book of Deer, is *Pette*, and it seems to mean a portion of land, as it is conjoined with proper names, as Pette MacGarnait, Pette Malduib. But it also appears connected with Gaelic specific terms, as *Pette an Mulenn*, the Pette of the Mill, and in a charter of the Chartulary of St. Andrews, of the church of Migvie, the *terra ecclesiæ* is said to be vocatus Pettentaggart--"an taggart" being the Gaelic form of the expression "of the priest."

The old forms of For and Fin are Fothuir and Fothen. The old form of Forteviot is Fothuirtabaicht, and of Finhaven is Fothen-evin. The first of these words, however, discloses a very remarkable dialectic difference. Fothuir becomes For, as Fothuir-tabacht is Forteviot; Fothuir-duin is Fordun; but Fothuir likewise passes into Fetter, as Fothuiresach becomes Fetteresso; and these two forms are found side by side, Fordun and Fetteresso being adjacent parishes. The form of For extends, from the Forth to the Moray Firth-- that of Fetter from the Esk, which separates Forfar and Kincardine, to the Moray Firth.

An examination of some other generic terms will disclose a perfectly analogous process of change. The name for a river is Amhuin. The word is the same as the Latin Amnis. The old Gaelic form is Amuin, and the *m* by aspiration, becomes *mh*, whence Amhuin, pronounced Avon. In the oldest forms of the language the consonants are not aspirated, but we have these two forms, both the old unaspirated form and the more recent aspirated form, in our topography, lying side by side in the two parallel rivers which bound Linlithgowshire--the Amond and the Avon. There is also the Amond in Perthshire. We know from the Pictish Chronicle that, the old name was Aman, and the Avon, with its aspirated *m*, is mentioned in the Saxon Chronicle. It is a further proof that Inver is as old as Aber in the eastern districts, that we find Aman in its old form conjoined with Inver in the Pictish Chronicle in the name "Inveraman."

In Dumbartonshire we find the names Lomond and Leven together. We have Loch Lomond and Ben Lomond, with the river Leven flowing out of the loch through Strathleven; but we have the same names in connection in Fifeshire, where we have Loch Leven with the two Lomonds on the side of it, and the river Leven flowing from it through Strathleven. This recurrence of the same words in connection would be unaccountable, were it not in example of the same thing. Leven comes from the Gaelic *Leamhan*, signifying an elm-tree, but the old form is Leoman, and the *m* becomes aspirated in a latter stage of the language and forms *Leamhan*, pronounced Leven. Here the old form adheres to the mountain, while the river adopts the more modern.

A curious illustration of two different terms lying side by side, which are derived from the same word undergoing different changes, will be found in Forfarshire, where the term Llan for a church appears, as in Lantrethin. It is a phonetic law between Latin and Celtic, that words beginning in the former with *pl* are in the latter *ll*. The word Planum, in Latin signifying any cultivated spot, in contradistinction from a desert spot, and which, according to Ducange, came to signify Cimiterium, becomes in Celtic Llan, the old meaning of which was a fertile spot, as well as a church. In the inquisition, in the reign of David I., into the possessions of the See of Glasgow, we find the word in its oldest form in the name Planmichael, now Carmichael; and as we find Ballin corrupted into Ban, and Ballindoch becomes Bandoch, so Plan becomes corrupted into Pan, and we find it in this form likewise in Forfarshire, Panmure and Panbride. In the Lothians and the Merse this word has become Long, as in Longnewton and Longniddrie.

The Celtic topography of Scotland thus resembles a palimpsest, in which an older form is found behind the more modern writing. I shall not lengthen this chapter by going through other examples. The existence of the phenomenon is sufficiently indicated by those I have brought forward, and I shall conclude by stating shortly the results of this investigation.

1*st*, In order to draw a correct inference from the names of places as to the ethnological character of the people who imposed them, it is necessary to obtain the old form of the name before it became corrupted, and to analyse it according to the philological laws of the language to which it belongs.

2*d*, A comparison of the generic terms affords the best test for discriminating between the different dialects to which they belong, and for this comparison it is necessary to have a correct table of their geographical distribution.

3*d*, Difference between the generic terms in different parts of the country may arise from their belonging to a different stage of the same language, or from a capricious selection of different synonyms by separate tribes of the same race.

4*th*, In order to afford a test for discriminating between dialects, the generic terms must contain within them those sounds which are differently affected by the phonetic laws of each dialect.

5*th*, Applying this test, the generic terms do not show the existence of a Cymric language north of the Forth.

6*th*, We find in the topography of the north-east of Scotland traces of an older and of a more recent form of Gaelic--the one preferring labials and dentals, and the other gutturals; the one hardening the-consonants into tenues--the other softening them by aspiration; the one having Abers and Invers--and the other having Invers alone; the one a low Gaelic dialect--the other a high Gaelic dialect; the one I conceive the language of the Picts--the other that of the Scots. [2]

Generic Terms	Ireland	Wales	Angli		Britones				Picti					Scoti	
			Berwick, Roxburgh, Haddington.	Mid-Lothian, Linlithgow.	Selkirk, Peebles.	Dumfries.	Ayr, Renfrew, Lanark.	Stirling, Dumbarton.	Perth.	Fife, Kinross.	Forfar.	Kincardine, Aberdeen, Banff.	Elgin and Nairn, Inverness, Ross, and Sutherland.	Kirkcudbright, Wigton.	Argyll, Bute.
Aber	...	W	3	3	...	4	...	...	12	4	7	18	6	...	...
Ard	66	...	...	...	...	...	...	16	34	6	14	66	51	5	93
Arn	...	...	...	...	...	...	...	4	15	5	...	...	...	...	...
Ar	...	W	...	...	...	...	...	...	...	...	...	...	...	15	...
Auch	25	...	...	...	...	...	25	...	24	6	27	162	153	12	107
Auchin	...	...	...	4	...	23	88	34	30	...	22	8	25	...	...
Auchter	...	...	...	...	...	...	...	...	6	10	6	12	4	...	...
Auld	...	...	...	...	...	...	...	...	...	...	...	33	9	...	...
Bal	...	...	...	...	...	...	36	63	90	88	127	67	59	56	39
Balna	...	...	...	...	...	...	...	...	...	...	...	10	...	...	...
Ballie	104	...	...	...	...	...	...	...	...	...	...	...	...	...	...
Ballin	...	...	3	...	...	...	...	...	...	...	...	3	...	...	...
Belloch	36	W	...	...	...	9	...	...	...	...	...	...	...	...	...
Bellie	...	...	...	...	...	...	...	...	...	...	...	...	...	...	14
Ban	...	...	...	...	...	...	...	...	...	16	...	...	...	...	...
Bar	...	...	...	...	...	27	66	6	...	...	11	...	...	90	19
Barn	...	...	...	...	...	...	...	...	...	...	...	...	...	6	...
Blair	...	...	...	...	...	...	16	51	29	8	...	11	8	...	...
Bo	...	...	...	...	...	...	...	...	5	...	...	...	10	...	...
Carn	28	...	...	...	...	...	11	...	13	8	8	54	15	4	...
Car	...	W	8	6	...	12	36	12	7	18	10	18	5	15	...
Col	...	...	...	...	...	...	...	...	7	...	...	17	...	...	...
Corrie	...	...	...	...	...	...	...	...	9	...	...	...	8	...	...
Cambus	...	...	...	...	...	...	...	...	12	...	...	...	...	...	...
Clon	93	...	...	...	...	8	13	...	...	...	...	...	...	7	...
Craig	16	W	...	19	...	21	42	21	43	25	12	46	8	31	19
Cors	...	W	...	...	...	14	...	...	...	...	...	...	...	9	...
Cul	39	...	...	...	...	...	47	...	25	11	...	22	22	7	...
Cumber	...	...	...	...	...	6	...	4	...	...	...	...	...	...	...
Cult	...	...	...	...	...	...	...	...	10	...	...	...	...	...	...
Dal	10	W	...	...	...	20	82	8	52	...	...	...	...	24	...
Drum	64	...	...	4	...	30	50	26	51	33	25	56	36	57	25
Dun	95	...	3	6	...	14	16	17	26	11	17	...	20	...	14
Fetter	...	...	...	...	...	...	...	...	...	...	...	4	...	...	...
For	...	...	...	...	...	...	...	...	13	9	11	22	...	...	...
Fin	...	...	...	...	...	...	...	...	14	6	4	...	3	...	...
Glen	35	W	5	...	17	42	44	...	56	...	23	52	54	61	52
Gar	...	...	...	...	...	...	34	...	...	...	...	17	...	23	...
Garth	...	W	...	...	...	...	10	23	13	...	...	...	...	...	10
Inch	90	...	...	...	...	...	...	18	30	25	10	17	31	...	...
Iron	...	...	...	...	...	...	...	...	...	...	...	...	...	15	...
Inver	6	...	...	2	...	...	...	5	32	10	16	37	69	...	24
Kin	30	...	...	3	...	...	...	6	43	34	52	88	57	...	7
Knock	29	...	...	...	...	5	64	...	6	...	...	32	30	37	31
Larg	...	...	...	...	...	...	...	...	...	...	...	...	...	13	...
Lin	...	W	...	...	...	...	...	...	...	5	8	...	...	...	...
Lan	3	W	...	...	...	...	...	...	...	6	...	...	...	...	6
Lath	...	...	...	...	...	...	...	...	9	...	...	...	...	...	...
Loch	100	...	...	7	...	14	34	16	30	18	...	15	19	26	...
Locher	...	...	...	...	...	5	...	...	...	...	...	...	...	...	...
Led	...	...	...	...	...	...	...	6	6	...	...	...	...	...	...

| | | | SCOTLAND | | | | | | | | | | | | |
Generic Terms	Ireland	Wales	Berwick, Roxburgh, Haddington (Angli)	Mid-Lothian, Linlithgow (Angli)	Selkirk, Peebles (Angli)	Dumfries (Britones)	Ayr, Renfrew, Lanark (Britones)	Stirling, Dumbarton (Britones)	Perth (Picti)	Fife, Kinross (Picti)	Forfar (Picti)	Kincardine, Aberdeen, Banff (Picti)	Elgin and Nairn, Inverness, Ross, and Sutherland (Picti)	Kirkcudbright, Wigton (Picti)	Argyll, Bute (Scoti)
Mon	14	...	...	...	...	7	...	...	11	13	13	31	...	...	...
Mul	15	...	...	...	...	...	...	...	...	...	...	...	8	...	...
Pen	...	W	9	3	...	5	7	...	...	...	...	...	...	2	...
Penny	...	...	...	...	...	...	7	...	...	...	...	...	...	...	11
Pot	...	...	...	...	...	...	...	...	...	...	...	30	5	...	...
Pit	...	...	...	...	...	...	...	...	75	52	38	69	30	...	...
Pitten	...	...	...	...	...	...	...	...	7	9	...	...	...	...	...
Pol	...	...	...	...	...	13	7	6	9	...	...	...	17	9	...
Port	22	...	...	...	...	...	...	3	...	...	...	...	...	8	...
Ra	63	...	...	...	...	...	...	...	17	6	...	...	...	...	...
Strath	...	...	...	...	...	...	...	...	19	13	...	27	35	...	13
Stron	...	...	...	...	...	...	...	...	...	...	...	...	...	...	17
Stuck	...	...	...	...	...	...	...	8	...	...	...	...	...	...	6
Tar	...	...	...	...	...	...	...	...	...	...	...	14	...	...	...
Tra	...	...	...	...	...	...	...	...	...	...	...	...	...	5	...
Tom	...	...	...	...	...	...	...	11	...	...	...	...	...	...	...
Tor	...	...	...	11	...	11	...	...	...	9	...	21	22	10	19
Tullie	...	...	...	...	...	...	...	...	...	...	...	38	...	...	...
Tulli	...	...	...	...	...	7	...	...	25	...	11	42	7	...	...
Tulloch	17	...	...	...	...	...	...	5	...	...	...	10	...	...	...

[1] *Ynver* occurs twice in the Book of Taliessin.

[2] The substance of these three chapters has already appeared in a different shape in the *Archæologia Cambrensis*, and the last in the *Transactions of the Royal Society*. They were written with a view to this work.

Chapter Ten - Cumbria and the Men of The North

THE districts comprehended at an early period under the name of Cumbria were of considerable extent; and, as its name indicates, occupied by a Cymric population.

Joceline, who wrote about the year 1180, in his life of Kentigern, states that the limits of his bishopric were coextensive with those of the "regio Cambrensis," and extended from the Roman wall to the "flumen Fordense;" but it originally extended even further south than this, for Joceline was judging by the extent of the diocese of Glasgow, and Carlisle and the district surrounding it had, after the Norman Conquest of England, been formed into an earldom, and in 1132 erected into the diocese of Carlisle. In a document printed in the Iolo MSS., the extent of many of the old Welsh districts is given, and the district of Teyrnllwg is said to have extended from Aerven to *Argoed Derwennydd*--that is, to the Forest upon the Derwent. This river, which falls into the Western Sea at Workington, now divides the diocese of Chester from that of Carlisle; and as soon as we pass the Derwent, dedications of churches to

Kentigern commence. The district south of the Derwent had very early come under the power of the kings of Northumberland, and the independent states of the Cymry probably extended from the Derwent and from Stanmore to the Clyde, including Westmoreland (with the exception of Kendal), and the central districts in Scotland, of Teviotdale, Selkirk, and Tweeddale. It comprehended what afterwards formed the dioceses of Glasgow and Carlisle; and its Cymric population appears as a distinct people, even as late as the battle of the Standard, in 1130, where they formed one of the battalions in King David's army, consisting of the Cumbrenses and Tevidalenses.

They appear to have been composed of numerous small states under their petty kings.

There is a document in one of the Hengwrt MSS., transcribed about 1300, with the title of *Bonhed Gwyr y Gogledd*, or Genealogies of the Men of the North--a name used to designate these Northern Cymry. It gives the pedigrees of twelve families, and they fall into three groups--one consisting of six families, whose descent is traced from Ceneu, son of Coel; the second, of five families descended from Dyfawal Hen, or the aged, grandson of Macsen Guledig, the Roman Emperor; and the third, of one family connected with the north, apparently through the female line. The first group again falls into two branches respectively derived from two sons of Ceneu, son. of Coel, Gorwst Ledlwm, and Mar or Mor. To Merchion Gul, the son of Gorwst Ledlwm, are given two sons--Cynvarch, the father of Urien and Elidir Lydanwyn, father of Llywarch Hen. To Garthwys or Arthwys, son of Mor, are given four sons-- Ceidiaw, the father of Gwenddolew, Nudd, and Cov; Elivir Gosgorddvawr, or of the large retinue, the father of Gwrgi and Perodur; Pabo Post Prydain, or the pillar of Britain, the father of Sawyl Benuchel; Dunawd Vawr, and Carwyd; and Cynvelyn, the grandfather, by his son Cynwyd Cynwydion, of Clyddno Eiddyn, Cynan Genhir, Cadrod Calchvynydd, and Cynvelyn Drwsgl.

The second group, consisting of the descendants of Dyfnwal Hen, also falls into four branches, descended of four sons of Dyfnwal Hen:--Cedig, father of Tudwal Tudclud, the father of Rydderch Hael, Senyllt, father of Nudd Hael, and Servan, father of Mordav; Garwynwyn, father of Caurdav, father of Gwyddno Garanhir; Aeddan Vradog; and Gorwst Briodawr, father of Elidr Mwynvawr.

The genealogies annexed to Nennius in 977 do not greatly differ from this. In the first group of families descended from Coel they add the pedigrees of two additional families--that of Gwallawg ap Leenawg and of Morcant. In the second group, the most important variation is that the descent pf Dyfnwal Hen, the common ancestor is not brought from Macsen Guledig, but from a Caredig Guledic, whose pedigree is taken back to a Confer the Rich; and that the descent of the later kings of Strathclyde from Dyfnwal Hen is given.

Adding, therefore, the two additional families descended from Coel, we have eight in the first group, and five in the second--in all, thirteen; and the following tables will show their connection:--

TABLE OF THE THIRTEEN KINGS OF "Y GOGLEDD" IN THE NORTH.

TABLE I.

Kings of the Race of Coel Hen.

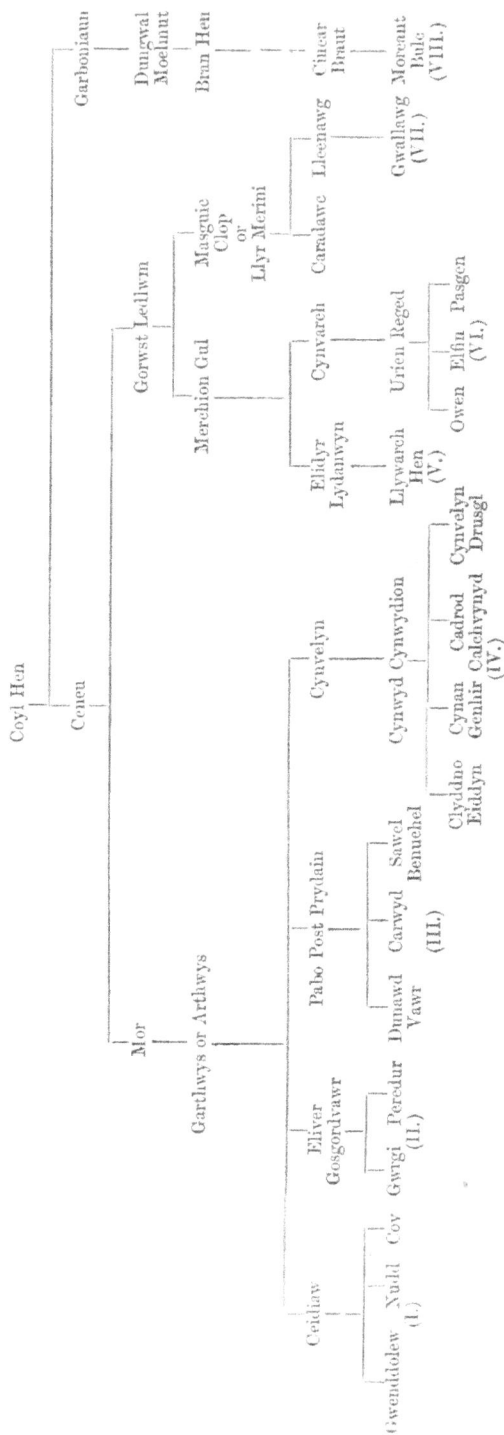

Coyl Hen

Ceneu

- Gorwst Ledlwm
  - Garbonian
    - Dunqwal Moelmut
    - Bran Hen
      - Cincar Braut
      - Morcant Bulc (VIII.)
  - Masguic Clop or Llyr Merini
    - Caradawc
      - Lleenawg
      - Gwallawg (VII.)
  - Meirchion Gul
    - Elidyr Lydanwyn
    - Cynvarch
      - Llywarch Hen (V.)
      - Urien Regel
        - Owen, Elfin, Pasgen (VI.)
- Mor
  - Gartlwys or Arthwys
    - Pabo Post Prydain
      - Dunawt Vawr
      - Carwyd
      - Sawel Benuchel (III.)
    - Cynvelyn
      - Cynwyd Cynwydion
        - Clydno Eiddyn
        - Cynan Genhir, Cadrod Calchvynyd (IV.), Cynvelyn Drusgl
    - Eliffer Gosgordvawr
      - Peredur (II.)
      - Gwrgi
  - Ceidiaw
    - Cov
    - Nudd (I.)
    - Gwenddolew

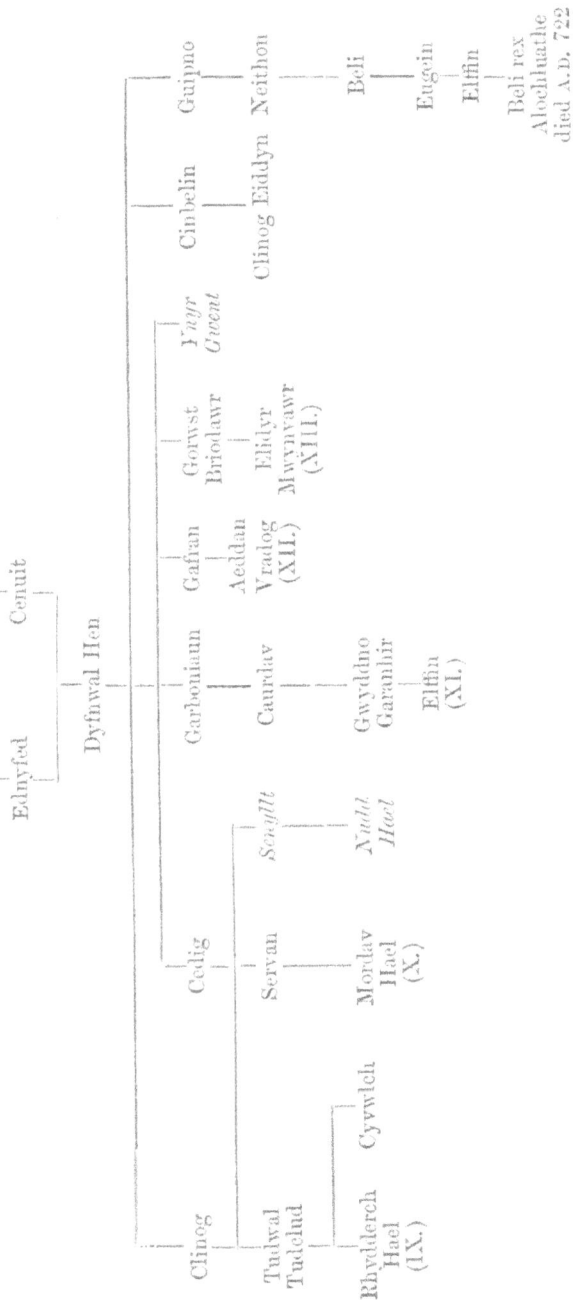

TABLE II.

Kings of the Race of Macsen Guledig.

Gen. of 1300. Macsen Guledig	*Gen. of* 977. Ceredig Guledig		
Ednyfed	Ceruit		
	Dyfnwal Hen		
Cedig	Garbouiaun	Cinbelin	Guipno
Servan	Caurdav	Clinog Eiddyn	Neithon
Scaglt	Gwyddno Garanhir		Beli
Morlav Hael (X.)	Nudd Hael	Elffin (XI.)	Eugein
Rhydderch Hael (IX.)	Cywlch		Elffin
Clinog	Tudwal Tutclud		Beli rex Alocliuathe died A.D. 722

Cafran / Aeddan Vradog (XII.)

Gorwst Briolawr / Elidyr Mwynvawr (XVIII.)

Ynyr Gwent

It is, of course, not maintained that those genealogies are, strictly speaking, historical, and that each link in the pedigree represents a real person; but they are valuable as conveying a general idea of the period, and tribal connection of these "Gwyr y Gogledd," or Men of the North. The thirteen families

89

no doubt represented as many petty states in Cumbria; and in the two groups we can see the mixture of two races--the provincial Roman and the native Cymric--and the small septs into which they were respectively divided.

There are indications, derived from their names, their history, and from local tradition, which connect most of these families with localities within the limits of Cumbria. Beginning with the first group, Ayrshire--divided into the three districts of Cuningham, Kyle, and Carrick--seems to have been the main seat of the families of the race of Coel, from whom indeed the district of Coel, now Kyle, is said traditionally to have taken its name. There is every reason to believe that Boece, in filling up the reigns of his phantom kings with imaginary events, used local traditions where he could find them; and he tells us "Kyl dein proxima est vel Coil potius nominata, a Coilo Britannorum rege ibi in pugna cæso;" and a circular mound at Coilsfield, in the parish of Tarbolton, on the highest point of which tire two large stones, and in which sepulchral remains have been found, is pointed out by local tradition as his tomb. He likewise connects two of his early kings with this part of the country. These are Caractacus and Corbredus Galdus, son of his brother Corbredus. He identifies the first with the British king Caractacus, and the second with Galgacus, who fought against Agricola; but he says of them--"Horum quæ de Carataco, Corbredo ac Galdo Scotorum regibus, his voluminibus memoriæ dedimus, *nonulla ex nostris annalibus*, at longe uberiora ex Cornelio Tacito sunt deprompta." While adapting the events from Tacitus, he likewise made use of native traditions. His Caratacus is obviously the name Caradawg; and his Galdus I believe to be taken from Gwallawg ap Lleenawg. It is curious that these two warriors of the "Gwyr y Gogledd" should have the same relationship of uncle and nephew. Now he says that in Carrick, one of the three divisions of Ayrshire, and lying to the south of Kyle, "erat civitas tum maxima a qua Caractani regio videtur nomen sortita. In ea Caratacus natus, nutritus, educatus." Of Galdus or Gwallawg he says that, on his death, "Elatum est corpus . . . in vicino campi ut vivens mandaverat, est conditum ubi ornatissimum ei monumentum patrio more, immensis ex lapidibus est erectum." Symson, in his *Description of Galloway*, written in 1684, says--"In the highway between Wigton and Portpatrick, about three miles westward of Wigton, is a plaine called the Moor of the Standing Stones of Torhouse, in which there is a monument of three large whinstones, called King Galdus's tomb surrounded, at about twelve feet distance, with nineteen considerable great stones, but none of them so great as the three first mentioned, erected in a circumference." And a similar monument is described in a MS. quoted by Dr. Jamieson, in his edition of Bellenden's *Boece*, as existing in Carrick:--"There is 3 werey grate heapes of stonnes, callit wulgarley the Kernes of Blackinney, being the name of the village and ground. At the suthermost of thir 3 cairnes are ther 13 great tall stonnes, standing upright in a perfyte circkle, aboute some 3 ells ane distaunt from ane other, with a gret heighe stonne in the midle, which is werily esteemid be the most learned inhabitants to be the buriall place of

King Caractacus." The names of Caradawg and of Gwallawg seem, therefore, connected with the district of Carrick and that of Wigton, extending between Carrick and the Solway Firth.

Gwenddolew, the son of Ceidiaw, is clearly connected with Ardderyd, now Arthuret, where his name still remains in Carwhinclow; and between this and the southern boundary of Cumbria, at the Derwent, others of the descendants of Coel may have had their seat. We have Urien connected with the district at the northern wall,. termed Mureif or Reged, in which Loch Lomond was situated. And of the, family of Cynwyd Cynwydion one son, Clyddno Eiddyn, is connected by his name with Eiddyn, or Caer Eiddyn, now Caredin, termed in the *Capitula* of Gildas "civitas antiquissima;" and another, Catrawd Calchvynyd, with Kelso. *Calchvynyd* is simply *Calch* Mountain, or chalk mountain; and Chalmers, in his *Caledonia* (vol. ii. p. 156), says: "It (Kelso) seems to have derived its ancient name of Calchow from a calcareous eminence which appears conspicuous in the middle of the town, and which is still called the Chalk Heugh."

The other group of families descended from Dyfnwal Hen are not so easily placed, as they soon acquired the supremacy over the whole region, but it is probable that they were more immediately connected with the central districts, Annandale, Clydesdale, Teviotdale, Yarrow, Selkirk, and Tweeddale. After Kentigern was recalled to Cumbria, it is stated by Joceline that he placed his episcopal seat for some time at Hoddelm or Hoddom in Annandale, where Rydderch's power may have been greatest, and his father's name of Tutgual Tut*clud* seems to connect him with the "flumen Clud," probably the upper part, as we read in the acts of St. Kentigern of a "regina de Caidzow" or Cadyow, the old name of the middle district of the vale of the Clyde, which indicates a separate small state. Between Strathclyde and Ayrshire lay the district of Strathgryf, now the county of Renfrew, and this part of Cumbria seems to have been the seat of the family of Caw, commonly called Caw Cawlwydd or Caw Prydyn, one of whose sons was Gildas. In one of the lives of Gildas he is said to be son of Caunus who reigned in Arccluta. In the old description of Scotland we are told that Aregaithel means Margo Hibernensium. The name Arecluta is similarly composed, and signifies a district lying along the Clyde, and Strathgrife or Renfrewshire lies in its whole extent along the south bank of the Clyde. In the life of St. Cadocus a singular legend is preserved. He is said to have visited Scotland, and while he was building a monastery there near the mountain Bannawc he found the grave of a giant, who rose and informed him that he was Caw of Prydyn, and that he had been a king who reigned beyond the mountain Bannawc, and in another legend we are told that this monastery was in regione Lintheamus (*Lives of Cambro British Saints*). Now the parish of Cambuslang, on the Clyde, is dedicated to St. Cadoc, and through the adjoining parish of Carmunnock, formerly Carmannock, runs a range of hills, now called the Cathkin hills, which separates Strathclyde from Ayrshire and terminates in Renfrewshire. This must be the mountain Bannawc, and the name is preserved in Carmannock, B passing into M in Welsh in combination, and Caw is thus represented in this legend also as reigning in Strathgryf or Renfrewshire. The name Lintheamus is probably meant for Lintheamus or Cambuslang.

There is a curious legend preserved in the Venedotian code of the old Welsh laws, which is as follows:

"Here Elidyr Muhenvaur, a man from the north was slain and, after his death, the "Gwyr y Gogled," or Men of the North, came here to avenge him. The chiefs, their leaders, were Clyddno Eiddin; Nudd Hael, son of Senyllt; and Mordaf Hael, son of Seruari, and Rydderch Hael, son of Tudwal Tudglyd; and they came to Arvon, and because Elidyr was slain at Aber Mewydus in Arvon, they burned Arvon as a further revenge. And then Run, son of Maelgwn, and the men of Gwynedd, assembled in arms, and proceeded to the banks of the Gweryd "yn y Gogledd," or in the north, and there they were long disputing who should take the lead through the river Gweryd. Then Run despatched a messenger to Gwynedd to ascertain who was entitled to the lead: some say that Maeldaf the elder, the Lord of Penardd, adjudged it to the men of Arvon; Joruerth, the son of Madog, on the authority of his own information, affirms that Idno the aged assigned it to the men of the black-headed shafts. And thereupon the men of Arvon advanced in the van, and were valorous there. And Taliessin sang--

"Behold! from the ardeney of their blades,
With Run, the reddener of armies,
The men of Arvon with their ruddy lances."
Old Welsh Laws, p. 50.

Elidyr Mwynvawr was the head of one of the families descended from Dyfnwal Hen, and so were. Rydderch Hael, Nudd Hael, and Mordav Hael, and Clyddno Eiddyn was of the race of Coel. They are called "Gwyr y Gogledd," or Men of the North, and the scene of the dispute as to who should lead was the banks of the river Forth, for the river Gweryd in the north is the Forth, it having been, according to the old description of 1165, called, "Britannice, Weryd."

The author of the *Genealogia* annexed to Nennius describes four of these kings of the north--Urien, Rydderch, Gwallawg, and Morcant--as warring against Hussa, son of Ida, the king of Bernicia, who reigned from 567 to 574; and the battle of Ardderyd, fought in 573, by which the anti-Christian party were finally crushed, resulted in the consolidation of these petty states into the kingdom of Cumbria or Strathclyde, and the establishment of Rydderch as king in the strong fortress of Alclyde or Dumbarton rock, which became from henceforth the chief seat of the kingdom. Here we find Rydderch established when he sent a message to St. Columba, to consult him, as supposed to possess prophetic power, whether he should be slain by his enemies, as recorded by Adomnan in his *Life of St. Columba*, who calls him "Rex Rodarcus filius Totail qui Petra Cloithe regnavit." St. Columba's reply--"De eodem rege et regno et populo ejus"--was, that he would not fall into the hands of his enemies, but die in his own house: which prophecy, adds Adomnan, as fulfilled, as he died a peaceful death.

If Joceline reports a real fact, when he says that he died in the same year as St. Kentigern, his death must have taken place either in the year 603 or 614, according to which is the true date of St. Kentigern's death; [1] during that time he consolidated his power, and re-established the bishopric of Glasgow.

The chronicle of 977 records, in 580, the death of Gwrgi and Peredur, the sons of Eliver Gosgorddvaur, another of these northern kings, and, in 593, the death of Dunawd, son of Pabo Post Prydain; and the *Genealogia* state that against Theodric, son of Ida, who reigned in Bernicia from 580 to 587, Urien with his sons fought valiantly, and adds, "In illo tempore aliquando hostes, nunc cives, vincebantur," showing the character of the struggle which was taking place between the Cymric population and the increasing power of the Angles.

In 603 a great effort appears to have been made by the Celtic tribes to drive back the Angles, under Aidan, king of the Scots who inhabit Britain, whom Bode describes as invading Bernicia with an immense and brave army, and being defeated and put to flight at Degsastan, now Dawston, in Liddesdale, where almost all his army were slain, and he himself escaped with a few only of his followers. This disaster must have crushed the efforts of the Celtic tribes to resist the Angles for the time, and enabled the latter to extend their territories unresisted, till in the reign of Edwin they reached the shores of the Firth of Forth.

After the death of Edwin, when Cadwallawn had established his power, Tighernac records, in 638, the battle of Glenmairison, in which the people of Donaldbrec were put to flight, "et obsessio Etain," and afterwards, in 642, that Donaldbrec was slain in the fifteenth year of his reign in the battle of Strathcauin by Ohan, king of the Britons, and in the same, year a battle between Oswy and the Britons. The same transactions are repeated at a later date in Tighernac, when the first battle is said to have been in *Calithros*, and the second in Strathcarn, while the name of the British king is given as Haan; but the first are the true dates.

Donaldbrec was the king of Dalriada, and the son of that Aidan who had been defeated in 603. Glenmairison must not be confounded with the glen called Glenmoriston on Loch Ness. It was in *Calithros*, and Calithros appears to have been the same with the district called Calatria, in which Callander is situated. It lay between the Carron and the Avon, extending on the west at least to the place called Carriden on the Avon, and bounded on the east by the Firth of Forth, including in its limits the parishes of Kineil and Careden; and within this district Glenmairison must have been situated, though it cannot now be identified. Etain was no doubt Eiddyn or Caereden, and the upper part of the valley of the Carron was called Strath Carron, in which there was a royal forest termed in old charters Stratheawin. These events then indicate a great struggle between Donaldbrec and the Britons, in which the former was defeated and finally slain in 642. If my conjecture is correct, that Aidan led a combined force of Scots and Britons, he was in fact for the time performing the functions of Guledig or "Dux Bellorum" in the north; and this struggle probably indicated an attempt on the part of Donaldbrec to maintain the same position. Who Ohan or Haan was, we do not know. He may have been a king of Alclyde and a successor of Rydderch, but it is more probable that he was no other than Cadwallawn himself, whom Tighernac calls Chon, and that the object of the war was whether Donald should retain his father's position, or whether Cadwallawn, who had now become powerful in the south, should extend his supremacy over the north likewise. [2]

The great defeat of the combined forces of the Mercians and Britons in 655 by Oswy, king of Northumbria, in which Penda, king of the Mercians, was slain, and Cadwallawn escaped with his life, terminated the power of the latter, and led to the subjection of the Cumbrian Britons to the kings of Northumbria, and two years afterwards the Annals of Ulster record the death of Gureit or Guriad, king of Alclyde. The subjection of the Britons to the Angles lasted till the year 686, when Ecfrid, king of Northumbria, was slain in the battle of Dunnichen, and during that time no king of Alclyde is recorded. It was also during this time that Ecfrid granted to Lindisfarne, Carlisle, with territory to the extent of fifteen miles round it; but the result of the defeat and death of Ecfrid was, as Bede tells us, that a part of the Britons recovered their liberty, and that this part was the British kingdom of Cumbria or Strathclyde appears from this, that the kings of Alclyde again appear in the Annals as independent kings.

In 694 died Domnall MacAuin rex Alochluaithe, and, in 722, Beli filius Elfin rex Alochluaithe. In the Welsh pedigrees annexed to Nennius, a genealogy is given, in which this Beli, son of Elfin, appears, and his descent is there given from Dyfnwal Hen, the ancestor of Rydderch Hael, and stem-father of the second group of northern families.

Although the Britons of Strathclyde had recovered, their liberty, and the Picts had regained that part of the "Provincia Pictorum" north of the Forth which the Angles had subjected, it would appear that the Pictish population south of the Forth still remained subject to them. The Picts of Manann had come under their power as early as the reign of Edwyn, and therefore still remained within the Anglic kingdom, as appears from their subsequently rebelling against its kings; and the Picts of Galloway seem likewise to have remained under their subjection, as Bede tells us that in 731, when he closes his history, four bishops presided in the province of the Northumbrians, one of whom was Pecthelm in the church which is called Candida Casa, or Whitehorn, "which," he says, "from the increased number of believers, has lately become an additional Episcopal see, and has him for its first prelate." This implies that Whitehorn still remained in the province of the Northumbrians; and in 750, we are told, in the chronicle annexed to Bede, that Ecbert, king of Northumbria, "Campum Cyil cum aliis regionibus suo regno addidit;" that is, Kyle and Carrick, which lay between it and Galloway, and possibly

Cuningham, forming modern Ayrshire.

In the same year, however, a great battle is recorded both in the Welsh and the Irish Annals between the Britons and the Picts, in which the Picts were defeated, and Talorgan, brother of Angus, the king of the Picts, slain. The place where this battle was fought is termed in the Chronicle of 977, Mocetauc, in the *Brut y Saeson*, Magdawc, and in the *Brut y Tywysogion*, Maesydawc. *Maes* is the Welsh equivalent for *Magh* in Gaelic, meaning a plain, and the place meant was no doubt Mugdock in the Parish of Strathblane, Stirlingshire, the ancient seat of the Earls of Lennox. In old charters it is spelt Magadavac. In the same year, according to the Welsh Chronicle, and two years after, according to Tighernac, died Teudwr, son of Bile, king of Alclyde, and in 756 Eadbert, king of Northumbria, and Angus, king of the Picts, appear to have united their forces, and we are told by Simeon of Durham that they le d their army "ad urbem Alewith, ibique Brittones inde conditionem receperunt, prima die mensis Augusti."

In 760 the Welsh Chronicle records the death of Dungual, son of Teudwr. From this date there is a blank in the kings of Alclyde for an entire century-- the first notice we have of them again being in 872, when Arthga "rex Britonum Strathcluaide" is slain, "Consilio Constantini filii Cinadon." This Constantine was king of the Scots, and Arthga or Arthgal appears in the Welsh genealogy as descendant in the fourth degree from Dungual. Alclyde is recorded, however, in the Annals of Ulster as having been burnt in 780 and besieged 870 by the Norwegian pirates, who, after a siege of four months, took and destroyed it. According to the Welsh Chronicle, "Arx Alclut a gentilibus fracta est." Strathclyde was again ravaged by them in 875. Arthgal appears to have been succeeded by his son Run, who is called in the Pictish Chronicle "rex Britonum," and said to be the father of Eocha, who reigned along with Grig, by a daughter of Kenneth MacAlpin. This is the last name given in the Welsh genealogy, and one of the copies of the *Brut y Tywysogion* has the following entry in 890, which, if containing a true fact, will explain this.

"The men of Strathclyde who would not unite with the Saxons were obliged to leave their country and go to Gwynned, and Anarawd (king of Wales) gave them leave to inhabit the country taken from him by the Saxons, comprising Maelor, the vale of Clwyd, Rhyvoniog, and Tegeingl, if they could drive the Saxons out, which they did bravely. And the Saxons came on that account a second time against Anarawd, and fought the action of Cymryd, in which the Cymry conquered the Saxons and drove them wholly out of the country; and so Gwynned was freed from the Saxons by the might of the 'Gwyr y Gogledd' or Men of the North."

That the British line of the kings of Strathclyde came to an end very soon is certain, for the Pictish Chronicle tells us that on the death of Donald "rex Britannorum," who must have died between 900 and 918, "Dunenaldus filiis Ede rex eligitur." He was brother to Constantine, the king of the Scots, and thus the Scottish line was established in the kingdom of Strathclyde. It must have been so much weakened by the loss of Kyle and the other regions wrested from it by the Saxons, and the attacks upon it by the Norwegian pirates, that we can well believe that, a large portion of the population fled to Wales for refuge, and that the influence of the new and powerful kingdom of the Scots led to a prince of that race being placed upon the throne.

In 946 it was overrun and conquered by Edmund, king of Wessex. He bestowed it upon Malcolm, king of the Scots, and from this time it became an appanage of the Scottish crown. The Saxon historians name the region conquered by Edmund as Cumbria, but that this kingdom of Strathclyde is meant, appears from the Chronicle of 977, now a contemporary record, which has, in 946, "Strat Clut vastata est a Saxonibus."

It is unnecessary for the purpose of this work to follow the history further. Suffice it to say that, in the reign of Malcolm Canmore, Carlisle and that part of Cumbria south of the Solway Firth belonged to the Norman conqueror, and was erected into an earldom for one of his followers; that, on the death of Edgar, that part of it which lay north of the Solway Firth was given to his brother, Prince David, and on his accession to the throne in 1124 became united to the Scottish crown; but that its population remained a distinct element in the population of Scotland for some time after, under the names of Cumbrenses, Brits, and Strathclyde Wealas.

[1] The Chronicle of 977 places Kentigern's death in 612; but the Aberdeen Breviary, in the Life of Baldred, places his death on Sunday, the 13th January 603. The 13th of January is St. Kentigern's day, and it fell upon a Sunday in 603 and also in 614. The first date is to be preferred.

[2] The passages quoted from Tighernac will be found in the Chronicles of the Picts and Scots, recently published in the series of Scottish Records, and an account of Calatria will be found in the introduction, p. lxxx.

Chapter Eleven - Recent Criticism of Mythological Poems Examined

SUCH then being, so far as we can gather it from the scanty materials afforded to us, the real position of the Cymric population, and the leading features of their history prior to the twelfth century, as well as of their literature subsequent to that period, the question before us is this, What place, does this very peculiar body of ancient poetry really occupy? Are we to regard them as ancient poems which have come down to us from an early period of Cymric literature, and possessing from their antiquity in historic value independently of their literary merit, if they have any? or are we to set them aside as so beset with suspicion, and as evincing such evidence of fabrication in a later age, as to render them valueless for all historic purposes?

That the bards to whom these poems are in the main attributed, are recorded as having lived in the sixth century, is certain. We have it on the authority of the *Genealogia* annexed to Nennius, written in the eighth century. That this record of their having lived in that age is true, we have every reason to believe, and we may hold that there were such bards as Taliessin, Aneurin, Llywarch Hen, and Myrddin, at that early period, who were believed to have written poems. That the poems which now bear their name do not show the verbal forms, and orthography of that age and that the form of the language of these poems has not the aspect which the language of the sixth century ought to exhibit, is equally certain. But this implies no more than that we do not possess transcripts of these poems made at that period. With the exception of two fragments, the oldest transcript we now possess is that in the Black Book of Caermarthen, a MS. of the twelfth century, and the orthography and verbal forms are those of that period, but this is not conclusive. All transcripts show the orthography and forms of their period. There may have been earlier transcripts, and if these had been preserved they would have shown earlier forms.

Before proceeding further, then, with this view of the subject, we may inquire whether these poems exhibit other marks of a later date, independently of the orthography and form of the language, so clear and decisive, as to lead us at once to the conviction that they could not belong to an earlier period than the date of the MS. in which we find the oldest text. If this question is answered in the negative, we may then inquire how far they show us clear and decisive marks of having been the work of au earlier age; and having determined their date, the literary question will become easily disposed of. If, on a fair and candid examination of these poems, it must be answered in the affirmative, *cadit quæstio*.

These poems have recently been arraigned at the bar of criticism by Mr. Stephens and Mr. Nash; and though they differ somewhat in the extent to which they answer this question in the affirmative, yet on the whole their verdict is against the antiquity of the poems, and the grounds upon which they arrive at this conclusion partake, to a great extent of one common character. It will, therefore, be convenient to deal with these works together as really forming one body of criticism, and to examine first the case for the prosecution, as it were, and the real bearing of that criticism upon the question.

Both of these writers group the poems into two classes, which they call Mythological and Historical, and the objections which they urge against them may be comprised under the three following propositions:--

1. The so-called mythological poems do not contain, as is supposed, a system of mystical and semi-pagan philosophy, handed down from the Druids, and preserved in these poems by their successors, the Bards of the sixth century, as an esoteric creed; but they are the work of a later age, and are nothing but the wild and extravagant emanations of the fancy of bards of the twelfth and subsequent centuries, and contain such allusions to the prose tales and romances of the middle ages as to show that they must have been written after these tales were composed.

II. The so-called historical poems not only contain direct allusions to later events, but it can be shown that other allusions, which have been supposed to apply to events of the sixth century, were really intended to refer to later events.

III. The orthography and poetic structure of these poems show that they could not have been written earlier than the date of the MSS. in which they first appear.

Mr. Stephens embraces in his criticism the whole of these poems; Mr. Nash deals with those of Taliessin alone and it may be as well to consider the bearing of this criticism on the poems attributed to Taliessin first.

Mr. Stephens, in his work on the Literature of the Cymry, does not go minutely into them, but deals with a few specimens only, and states the result of his examination of seventy-seven poems, attributed to Taliessin, in the following classification:--

HISTORICAL, AND AS OLD AS THE SIXTH CENTURY.

Gwaith Gwenystrad.	The Battle of Gwenystrad.
Gwaith Argoed Llwyfain.	The Battle of Argoed Llwyfain.
Gwaith Dyffryn Gwarant.	The Battle of Dyffryn Gwarant.
I Urien.	To Urien.
I Urien.	To Urien.
Canu i Urien.	A Song to Urien.
Yspail Taliessin.	The Sports of Taliessin.
Canu i Urien Rheged.	A Song to Urien Rheged.
Dadolwch Urien Rheged.	Reconciliation to Urien.
I Wallawg.	To Gwallawg (the Galgacus of Tacitus).
Dadolwch i Urien.	Reconciliation to Urien.
Marwnad Owain ap Urien.	The Elegy of Owain ap Urien.

DOUBTFUL.

Cerdd i Wallawg ap Lleenawg.	A Song to Gwallawg ap Lleenawg.
Marwnad Cunedda.	The Elegy of Cunedda.
Gwarchan Tutvwlch.	The Incantation of Tutvwlch.
Gwarchan, Adebon.	The Incantation of Adebon.
Gwarchan. Cynfelyn.	The Incantation of Cynvelyn.
Gwarchan Maelderw.	The Incantation of Maelderw.
Kerdd Daronwy.	The Song to Daronwy.
Trawsganu Cynan Garwyn.	The Satire on Cynan Garwyn.

ROMANCES BELONGING TO THE TWELFTH AND THIRTEENTH CENTURIES.

Canu Cyntaf Taliessin.	*Taliessin's first Song.*
Dehuddiant Elphin.	*The Consolation of Elphin.*
Hanes Taliessin.	*The History of Taliessin.*

Canu y Medd.	The Mead Song.
Canu y Gwynt.	The Song to the Wind.
Canu y Byd Mawr.	The Song of the Great World,
Canu y Byd Bach.	The Song of the Little World.
Bustl y Beirdd.	*The Gall of the Bards.*
Buarth Beirdd.	The Circle of the Bards.
Cad Goddeu.	The Battle of the Trees.
Cadeir Taliesin.	The Chair of Taliesin.
Cader Teyrnon.	The Chair of the Sovereign On.
Canu y Cwrwv.	The Song of the Ale.
Canu y Meirch.	The Song of the War-horses.
Addvwyneu Taliesin.	The Beautiful Things of Taliesin.
Angar Kyvynodawd.	The Provincial Confederacy.
Priv Cyfarch.	The Primary Gratulation.
Dehuddiant Elphin.	*Elphin's Consolation.*
Arymes Dydd Brawd.	The Day of Judgment.
Awdl Vraith.	*The Ode of Varieties.*
Glaswawd Taliesin.	The Encomiums of Taliesin.
Divregawd Taliesin.	*Past and Future Ages.*
Mab gyfreu Taliesin.	Taliesin's Juvenile Accomplishments.
Awdl Etto Taliesin.	*Another Ode by Taliesin.*
Kyfes Taliessin.	*The Confession of Taliessin.*

THESE SEEM TO FORM PORTIONS OF THE MABINOGI OF TALIESIN WHICH WAS COMPOSED By THOMAS AB EINION OFFEIRIAD.

Cadair Keridwen.	The Chair of Keridwen.
Marwnad Uthyr Pendragon.	The Elegy of Uthyr Pendragon.
Preiddeu Annwn.	The Victims of Annwn (Hell).
Marwnad Ercwlf.	The Elegy of Hercules.
Marwnad Mad. Ddrud ac Erov y greulawn.	The Elegy of Madoc the Bold and Erov the Fierce.
Marwnad Aeddon o Von.	The Elegy of Aeddon of Mon.
Anrhyveddodau Alexander.	The not wounding of Alexander.
Y Gofeisws Byd.	A Sketch of the World.
Lluryg Alexander.	The Lorica of Alexander.

PREDICTIVE, POEMS--TWELFTH AND SUCCEEDING CENTURIES.

Ymarwar Llud Mawr.	The Appeasing of the Great Llud.
Ymarwar Llud Bychan.	The Appeasing of Llud the Little.
Gwawd Llud Mawr	The Praise of Llud the Great.
Kerd am Veib Llyr.	Song to the Sons of Llyr.
Marwnad Corroi ab Dairy.	Elegy on Corroy, Son of Dayry.
Mic or Myg Dinbych.	The Prospect of Tenby.
Arymes Brydain.	The Destiny of Britain.

Arymes.	The Oracle.
Ayrmes.	The Oracle.
Kywrysedd Gwynedd a Debeubarth.	The Contention of North and South Wales.
Awdl.	*A Moral Ode.*
Marwnad y Milveib.	Elegy on a Thousand Saints.
Y Maen Gwyrth.	*The Miraculous Stone.*
Can y Gwynt.	The Song of the Wind.--Subject, Owen Gwynedd.
Anrhec Urien.	The Gift of Urien.

THEOLOGICAL--SAME DATE.

Plaeu yr Aipht.	The Plagues of Egypt.
Llath Moesen.	The Rod of Moses.
Llath Moesen.	The Rod of Moses.
Gwawd Gwyr Israel.	Eulogy of the Men of Israel.

NOTE.--The poems printed in italics are not in the Book of Taliessin.

Since the publication of that work, several papers have appeared in the *Archæologia Cambrensis*, in which he has given his more matured views of the poems, modifying somewhat this classification.

Mr. Nash deals with them in the two classes only, and on the whole considers the entire body of poetry connected with the name of Taliessin to belong to the twelfth and subsequent centuries.

It is with the poems attributed to Taliessin that the objections under the first proposition mainly deal. The great body of those included under the head of mythological poems bear his name, or are said to be composed by him, and to these the school of Owen Pughe and Edward Williams, of Davies and Herbert, has given a mystic sense, and has supposed that a species of Druidic superstition was handed down in them. Now, I go a certain length with them in this objection. I agree with them in thinking that these poems do not contain any such esoteric system of semi-pagan philosophy, and so far as their criticism goes to demolish the fancies of this school, I think it is well. founded. But there I stop. It does not follow that because the poems are not what Davies and Herbert represent them to be, that they are therefore not genuine. It does not follow that because a mistaken meaning has been applied to them, therefore they can have no rational meaning whatever. Like all poems of this description, they are full of obscure allusions and half-expressed sentiments, and where the real drift of the poem is not understood, it will of course have the aspect of meaningless verbiage, just as the ritual of a church, to one who does not know what it is intended to convey or to symbolise, appears mere mummery; but as soon as a clue is obtained to the real meaning of the poet, the allusions in the poem, however obscure they appear, become intelligible and consistent; and before the critic can justly urge this objection, he must be very sure that he has grasped the real meaning of the poet, as well as comprehended the true bearing and place in literature of the poems he is dealing with. That these poems are really intended to convey a definite meaning I do not doubt. They will be found to harmonise with the history and intellectual character of the place and period to which they belong, and the first work of the critic is to ascertain, on definite grounds, what that place and period really is.

The other ground given for doubting these poems is more tangible--viz. that they contain such allusions to the prose tales and romances of the middle ages as to show that they must have been written after these tales were composed, and here Mr. Nash makes a special case against the poems attributed to Taliessin. He states that a prose tale, containing the personal history of Taliessin and his transmigrations, was composed in the thirteenth century, and that a copy of this tale contained in the Red Book of Hergest has been published, with an English translation, by Lady Charlotte Guest, in her collection of Mabinogion. His prose tale is interspersed with poems said to have been sung by Taliessin, and Mr. Nash maintains that it is in the main the basis from which the greater part of the so-called poems of Taliessin has sprung, and that a large number, besides those contained in the Mabinogi of Taliessin, derive their inspiration from it.

It seems rather strange that so severe a critic am Mr. Nash, who will accept none of the poems which are the subject of his criticism as ancient or genuine, except upon the clearest evidence, should yet assume at once the genuineness and antiquity of the Mabinogi of Taliessin. It is beyond question, that the only text of it before him is written in much more modern Welsh than any of the poems it is supposed to have given birth to, and yet he makes no difficulty. It is further strange that in founding upon this prose tale as the very basis of his argument throughout, and his most formidable weapon, he should not have taken means to ascertain whether it really is in the Red Book of Hergest. No copy of this tale is to be found in the Red Book of Hergest at all, and as that valuable MS. contains all the other prose tales of that period, this of itself is an argument against its authenticity.

But, moreover, no copy of it is to be found in any known MS. prior to the eighteenth century. Owen Pughe, who published it in 1833, says explicitly that there was but one version of the prose narrative, and that version was furnished by Iolo Morganwg. Every notice regarding it upon which Mr. Nash founds emanates from him, and is not to be found elsewhere. Even if we accept the account given by Dr. Owen Pughe, his explicit statement is, that it was composed by Hopkin Thomas Philip, and it cannot be taken farther back than 1590 or 1600, long after every poem we are dealing with had been transcribed; but its history is so questionable as to lead to the suspicion that it had no earlier origin than the school which produced it, and it is quite as necessary for Mr. Nash, before be can legitimately found upon it, to bridge over the interval between Einion Offeiriad in the thirteenth century, if he lived then, or if he ever lived at all, and Dr. Owen Pughe in the nineteenth, as it is for the advocates of the authenticity of the poems to bridge over the interval between the sixth century and the Black Book of Caermarthen.

So much for the prose narrative. With regard to the poems imbedded in it, whether naturally or artificially, the text published by Dr. Pughe in 1833 contains eleven poems; that published by Lady Charlotte Guest in 1849, fourteen, but in the notes we are informed that four of these poems were added to her edition from the Myvyrian Archæology, and were not in the MSS. from which she printed. Now, of these eleven poems contained in the MSS. of the prose tale printed by Dr. Owen Pughe and Lady Charlotte Guest, not one is to be found in the Book of Taliessin; and of the four poems which she added from the Myvyrian Archæology, only two are in that Book.

At the time, therefore, when the Book of Taliessin was transcribed, the poems inserted in the prose tale had either not been written, or were known to be spurious, and not to belong to the body of poems at that time attributed to Taliessin. Moreover, several of these poems are said to have been in reality the work of *Jonas Athraw o Fynyw*, or Jonas, the Doctor or Divine of St. Davids, of whom, however, and thc true period in which he lived, we know really nothing, but one of these poems appears among the poems transcribed in the end of the Red Book of Hergest in the fifteenth century. The poems attributed to Jonas Athraw of St. David's are--

1. Hanes Taliessin, beginning "Prifardd Cyffredin."
2. Fustl y Veirdd, beginning "Cler o gam."
3. Dyhuddiant Elfin, beginning "Gognawd Gyrra."
4. Divregwawd Taliessin, beginning "Goruchel Dduw." This is the poem contained in the Red Book of Hergest.
5. Yr awdl Fraith, beginning with the line "Ef a wnaith Panton."

it is the last of these poems from which the well-known sentiment has been so often quoted, as a saying of Taliessin--

Eu nor a volant	Their God they shall adore,
Eu hiaith a gadwant	Their language they shall keep,
Eu tir a gollant	Their country they shall lose,
Ond gwyllt Walia.	Except Wild Wales.

Indeed, it is generally considered that the history of Wales cannot be referred to with any propriety without quoting those lines.

None of these poems, however, appear in the Book of Taliessin; and a verse in this poem might have shown that it made no claim to being the genuine work of the bard whose name it bears:--

Joannes the Divine
Called me Merddin;
At length every king
Will call me Taliessin.

And called Taliessin it has been ever since, and it has been subjected by Mr. Nash, along with the other spurious poems, to one common criticism with those which are to be found in the Book of Taliessin, and the estimate formed of the spurious poems maintained equally to invalidate those professing to be genuine. These poems are all included in Mr. Stephens's third class; and the criticism, so far as based upon them, may now be set aside as having little or no bearing upon the real question.

Having thus disposed of the so-called Mabinogi, or romance of Taliessin, which plays so great and illegitimate a part in modern criticism, we must now advert to the allusions said to be made to the other prose tales really contained in the Red Book of Hergest, and usually called the Mabinogion, and which it is maintained show that the poems containing such allusions must have been written after these prose tales were composed. It is admitted that these allusions are made to the Mabinogion of the oldest class only, and they certainly possess a considerable antiquity. Here, the first feature in this proposition which startles us is, that if well founded, it inverts the usual sequence in the early literature of most countries, and supposes that prose tales were first composed, and poems afterwards written from them. We usually find the reverse of this. The literature of most countries commences with lays in which the traditions and knowledge of the people in the infancy of their society are handed down to succeeding generations; and then, as cultivation advances, and the intellect of the nation developes, it passes over into chronicles and prose romances. In Wales we must suppose the progress to be different. If the poems we are dealing with belong to a later age, none others have come down to us, and we must suppose that the fancies and dim imaginings of the people in their earlier stages first developed themselves in prose romances. The fallacy which leads to this is the assumption that these tales are so far fictions, invented romances, in which, though the names may be real, the incidents are fictitious, and thus that any allusion to them, however slight, or even any mention of the more names of the heroes of them, infallibly demonstrates a later composition of the poem which contains them. It is in this spirit that Mr. Stephens deals with them, and he sends ruthlessly every poem to a later age in which the mere name of Arthur occurs, as having been composed after the Arthurian romance was introduced from Britanny.

But these tales are, equally with the poems, founded to some extent upon older legends and traditions, and the germ of their narrative had a prior existence in the earlier oral tales of the people. It is true that there is a marked difference in character between the older legend and the romantic tale founded upon it. The former is part of a more primitive literature, running parallel to and in harmony with the history and progress of the people. Tales and incidents connected with their history were the subject of lays and poetic narratives, and the early philosophy of the people, the common-sense of the nation in the primitive meaning of the term, became crystallised into proverbs. Symbolical and figurative language was largely used. Revolutions and invasions were compared to convulsions of nature and the ravages of monsters; tyrants were denounced by obscure epithets, sentiments were conveyed in proverbs, and fragments of real history were encrusted in them, like the masses of primitive rock protruding through a later formation, or the boulders deposited upon its surface; while the oral transmission of this early poetic literature was secured by a complicated system of metre and an intricate rhyme which enabled the writer more readily to employ the right expressions. With a fixed and unalterable number of syllables in the line, a rhyme recurring in the middle of one line and the end of another, with one stanza commencing with the last word of the preceding stanza, or with certain words commencing with the same letter, it was difficult for the reciter to misplace a letter or sentence; the right word must be found, and the general sentiments expressed were retained in his mind by their taking the shape of proverbs.

This is what we should expect early poetry of this description to be, and this, to a great extent, characterises the poems with which we are dealing; but when the period arrives when prose tales or romances are preferred, the recollection of the real incidents alluded to, the real events symbolised, has passed away; the taste of the age soon requires social tales rather than historical romances, the incidents become trivial, the heroes dwindle down to ordinary mortals, the ancient warriors, to private lords of a district, the symbolic representations become real convulsions of nature and actual wild beasts, and what originally sprang from some great internal change or some external invasion, now becomes the hunt of a wild animal or a quest after some treasure. The names of the heroes of these legends are retained in the prose tales, but the events in which they figure are changed, and assume a totally different character and aspect.

This to a great extent characterises the Mabinogion, and if we find evidence in them of the characteristics of this stage in the literature, why are we to presume that the earlier stages had no existence? In point of fact, we do find traces of the earlier existence of the germs of these tales. Thus, in the tale of Llud and Llefelys, at the end of the narrative as printed by Lady Charlotte Guest, is this notice--"And this tale is called the *Story* of Llud and Llevelys, and thus it ends. "The expression in the original Welsh, however, is "Ar chwedyl hwnn aelwir *Kyfranc* Llud a Llevelys." The word "Kyfranc" does not mean a story, but a quarrel or contention, and the reason of this great alteration is, that there is not a trace throughout the whole tale of any quarrel or contention between the two brothers Llud and Llevelys; on the contrary, they are represented as a perfect model of two affectionate brothers, living in perfect harmony with and mutually aiding one another. The tale, as it stands, is as old as the first edition of the Bruts where the substance of it occurs, and there must apparently have been an earlier legend, the facts of which had been forgotten while the name was recollected and applied to the later tale. Now, one of the poems attributed to Taliessin (B. T. 54, Ymarwar Lludd Bychan) is condemned because it is supposed to contain an allusion to this tale. The whole of the allusion is simply this: "Before the reconciliation of

104

Llud and Llefelys." But there cannot be a reconciliation without a previous contention, and it is obvious that the reference here is to the earlier legend. There is, however, one striking difference between the poem and the tale. In the prose tale one of the chief incidents is the invasion of a mysterious people called Corraniad, who use enchantments and possess magic powers; but when we refer to the poem, it is the real invasion of the Romans which forms the chief incident.

Another of the Mabinogion supposed to be referred to is that of Kilhwch and Olwen. The chief incident in this curious tale is the hunt of the Twrch Trwyt, or the Boar Trwyt. The poem called the Gorchan Cynvelyn is supposed to refer to it, but, like the other poem, the allusion is comprised in a few lines:--

Stalks like the collar of Twrch Trwyth,
Monstrously savage, bursting and thrusting through,
When he was attacked on the river,
Before his precious things.

The allusion to the legend is plain enough, but the more fact of Arthur and his warriors being represented in the prose tale as finding the boar with seven young pigs in Ireland, and hunting him to Dyfed and through the whole of Wales, and then by the Severn into Cornwall, whence he was driven into the sea again, shows that this is a tale in which what were originally figurative and symbolical representations of real events have been converted into realities. Even in its present shape the legend is old, for in the *Memorabilia* of Nennius he mentions a stone bearing the mark of a dog upon it, and explains, "Quando venatus est, *porcum Troit* impressit Cabal, qui erat canis Arthuri militis, vestigium in lapide."

A poem in the Black Book of Caermarthen (No. 31) is also supposed to refer to it. This poem certainly mentions many of the characters in it, but not one syllable of the plot of the prose tale; neither Kilhwch and Olwen, the hero and heroine, nor the hunt of the boar, the chief incident, are once alluded to. The real allusions are to two of Arthur's battles, and the scenery is in the north--*Try-weryd*, *Mynyd Eiddyn* or Edinburgh, and *Manauid* or Manau Guotodin.

The other tales supposed to be alluded to, are the four which form what is strictly speaking the Mabinogi, and are all connected with one another. They are the following:--

The Tale of Pwyll, Prince of Dyfed; The Tale of Branwen, daughter of Llyr; The Tale of Manawyddan, the son of Llyr; The Tale of Math, son of Mathonwy.

The supposed allusions run through a considerable number of the poems attributed to Taliessin, and form an important group of these poems. Now there is this peculiarity in these four tales forming the Mabinogi proper, that they do not mainly refer to Wales as the country of the Cymry, but to the period when Mona and Arvon were possessed by a Gwyddel population, and it is the legendary kings of the Gwyddel who are the main actors in the tales. These are probably the oldest of the tales, but the previous remarks as to the form in which such legends appear in the prose tales are here equally applicable. The characters which appear in these tales are, in the first, Pwyll, prince of Dyfed, and Arawn, king of Annwfn or Hell; in the second, Bran and Manawyddan, the sons, and Branwen, the daughter, of Llyr, and Matholwch, king of Ireland; in the third, Manawyddan, son of Llyr, and Pryderi, son of Pwyll; and in the fourth, Math, son of Mathonwy, king of Arvon and Mona, Gwydyon ap Don, and Arianrod his sister, Llew Law Gyffes and Dylan eil Ton, her sons, the first of whom became king of Gwynedd, and Pryderi, son of Pwyll, king of Dyfed. Pwyll is only mentioned in one poem (B. T. 30), called Preiddeu Annwfn), and it bas no reference to the Mabinogi. Arawn is one of the three brothers, Llew, Arawn, and Urien, whom I have already noticed in the historical sketch, and whom we found obtaining lands conquered from the Saxons by Arthur. Arawn is said to have obtained the most northern portion, and from the expressions used he must have been seated almost beyond the limits of the Cymric population. This northern region must always have been viewed by the more southern population as a dreary and barren wilderness, and invested with superstitious attributes. Even as early as the time of Procopius, who flourished in the sixth century, he thus describes it:--

"In this isle of Britain men of ancient time built a long wall, cutting off a great portion of it, for the soil and the men, and all other things, are not alike on both sides; for on the eastern (southern) side of the wall there is a wholesomeness of air, in conformity with the seasons, moderately warm. in summer and cool in winter. Many men inhabit here, living much as other men. The trees, with their appropriate fruits, flourish in season, and their cornlands are as productive as others, and the district appears sufficiently fertilised by streams. But on the western (northern) side all is different, insomuch indeed that it would be impossible for man to live there even half-an-hour. Vipers and serpents innumerable, with all other kinds of wild beasts, infest that place, and what is most strange, *the natives affirm that if any one passing the wall should proceed to the other side, he would die immediately*, unable to endure the unwholesomeness of the atmosphere. Death also, attacking such beasts as go thither, forthwith destroys them. But as I have arrived at this point of my history, it is incumbent on me to record a tradition very nearly allied to fable, which has never appeared to me true in all respects, though constantly spread abroad by men without number, who assert that themselves have been agents in the transaction, and also hearers of the words. I must not, however, pass it by altogether unnoticed, lest when thus writing concerning the island Brittia I should bring upon myself an imputation of ignorance of certain circumstances perpetually happening there. *They say, then, that the souls of men departed are always conducted to this place*."

And when the Cymric population looked northwards to these mountain-barriers, shrouded often with mist, from whose bosom poured the wintry blasts, and from whose recesses issued those fearful bands of Pictish savages, we may well suppose that they regarded it with awe and terror, and could give *Uffern* itself no more terrible an epithet than to call it "A cold hell." Whether Arawn's territory really bore the name of Annwfn, as its opposite Dwfn certainly did enter into that of the Damilonii, who are placed in that part of Scotland by Ptolemy, we can only conjecture.

The oldest legends connect Manawyddan ap Llyr with Manau or Manauid. He is only mentioned in two poems. In one (B. B. 31) he is mentioned in connection with Arthur's battles in the north:--

Manawyddan, the son of Llyr,
Deep was his counsel.
Did not Manauid bring
Perforated shields from Trywruid?

In the Other (B. T. 14 Kerdd am veib Llyr) the references are as follow:--
A battle against the sons of Llyr at Eber Henvelen.
I have been with Bran in Ywerddon,
I saw when was killed Mordwydtyllon,
Is it known to Manawyd and Pryderi?

Of Gwydyon ap Don and Llew, the former is associated with in the legends connected with the settlements of the Gwyddyl, and the latter is one of the three brothers in the north. He was placed over Lothian, including part of the county occupied by Pictish tribes, and is the Lothus, king of the Picts, of Scottish tradition. Now throughout these poems we find allusion to a confederacy or union between Brython and Gwyddel, in connection with the names of Llew and Gwydyon. In one poem (B. T. 14) we have:--

I have been in the battle of Godeu with Llew and Gwydion,
I heard the conference of the Cerddorion (British Bards),
And the Gwyddyl, devils, distillers.

In another (B. T. 1, and R. B. 23):--

Truly Llew and Gwydyon
Have been skilful ones.
Thou wilt remember thy old Brython,
And the Gwyddyl, furnace distillers.
Again, in the Cad Goddeu--
Minstrels were singing,
Warriors were hastening,
The exaltation to the Brython,
Which Gwydion made.

This was the alliance between the Brython represented by Llew, and the Gwyddel by Gwydyon, which resulted in the insurrection of Medraut, son of Llew, against Arthur with his combined army of Picts, Britons, and Saxons, and which arose from a section of the Britons in the north being drawn over to apostasy by the pagan Saxons and semi-pagan Picts.

These poems then contain, under figurative and symbolic language, allusions to real facts; but when we come to the Mabinogi all is changed. The heroes mentioned may be the same. The events are, of a totally different character. Bran goes to Ireland to resent a slap given by Matholwch to Branwen. There is no battle against the sons of Llyr at Eber Henvelen, but they gaze at it from a window after waking from an enchanted sleep. There is no slaughter of Mordwydtyllon. Math, son of Mathonwy, is there the leading figure, and Gwydion is a mere adventurer, stealing pigs and forcing Arianrod to acknowledge her son Llew by enchantments, while Arawn is placed under the earth as king of Annwfn, which represents the actual region of departed spirits. [1]

Mr. Nash, in his criticism on the Cad Godeu, quotes from the Myvyrian Archæology a fragment which he thus translates--

"ENGLYNION, OR VERSES ON THE CAD GODDEU.

"These are the Englyns that were sung at the Cad Goddeu, or, as others call it, the Battle of Achren, which was on account of a white roebuck and a whelp; and they came from Annwn, and Amathaon ap Don brought them. And therefore Amathaon ap Don, and Arawn, king of Annwn, fought. And there was a man in that battle, unless his name were known he could not be overcome; and there was on the other side a woman called Achren, and unless her name were known her party could not be overcome. And Gwydion ap Don guessed the name of the man, and sang the two Englyns following:--

"Sure-hoofed is my steed before the spur,
  The high sprigs of alder were on thy shield,
  Bran art thou called of the glittering branches."
"And thus--
"Sure-hoofed is thy steed in the day of battle,
  The high sprigs of alder are in thy hand,
  Bran, with the coat of mail and branches with thee,
  Amathaon the good has prevailed." [2]

and maintains that this is a fragment of a story or romance called Cad Godeu, and that this real Cad Godeu must not be confounded with the Cad Godeu ascribed to Taliessin, which he adds is one of the very latest of these productions, and very inferior in style and spirit to the compositions worked up by Thomas ab Einion.

I am exactly of the opposite opinion. Mr. Nash, as usual, assumes the genuineness of the prose document; but there is no indication of where it came from. It exists in no known MS., and I doubt not came from the same workshop as the so-called compositions of Thomas ab Einion; but assuming it to be a fragment of a prose tale, it truly bears out the remarks I have made. The poem called "Cad Godeu" contains no description of a battle, but Godeu is repeatedly mentioned in other poems, and always in close connection with Reged, which takes us to the "Gogledd," as do also the names of Llew and Arawn. It describes in highly figurative language a hateful appearance in Britain, passing before the Guledig, "like horses in the middle--like fleets full of wealth--like a monster with great jaws--and a hundred heads--like a toad with black thighs and a hundred claws--like a speckled snake." The word *breith*, or "speckled," betrays its character. It was the exaltation Gwydion gave to the Brython--the alliance with the speckled race of the Picts--which filled the bard with these gloomy pictures, and this idea runs through the whole poem.

When we come to the prose tale, if it be one, it is a battle between Amathaon and Arawn, king of Annwfn, for a whelp and a white roebuck, and which was settled by the device of Gwydion guessing the name of a man.

[1] I do not here notice the poem (B. T. 16, Kadeir Kerrituen), as I consider it of later date, and to belong to a different period and class of poems.
[2] The translation is Mr. Nash's.

Chapter Twelve - Recent Criticism of Historical Poems Examined

THE objections under the second proposition apply mainly to the poems classed by Mr. Stephens and Mr. Nash as historical. Mr. Stephens maintains that there are not only in some of these poems direct allusions to persons and events of a later date than the period when the poems must have been composed, if they are genuine, but also that, in most of the poems, it can be shown that allusions which have been supposed to refer to early events were really intended to apply to those of a later date, and that later persons are indicated under the names of earlier heroes.

Now, here also I go along with the objection, so far as direct allusions are made to later persons and events, but there I stop.

When I find in the Black Book a poem on the death of Howel ap Goronwy, in which he is named, I can have no difficulty in believing it to apply to Howel ap Goronwy, who died in 1103, and that it must have been written after that date. The poems in the Black Book bearing to be the composition of Cynddelw are of course not within the scope of our inquiry. The poem in the Red Book attributed to Myrddin, which mentions *Coch o Normandi*, I can have no doubt refers to William Rufus, as I find him called *Y Brenhyn Coch* in the *Brut y Tywysogion*. The poems referring to Mab Henri, or the son of Henri, I can have equally little doubt proceeded from Glamorgan, and refer to Robert, Earl of Gloucester, the son of King Henry I.; and the Hoianau, which mentions the five chiefs from Normandy, and the fifth going to Ireland, must have been composed, either in whole or in part, in the reign of Henry II.

The attempt which Mr. Stephens makes, however, and in which he is followed by Mr. Nash, to show that the greater proportion of these poems contain indirect allusions to later events, is, in my opinion, unsuccessful, and will not bear examination. it is this criticism which mainly affects a large number of the poems attributed to Taliessin, and it appears to me to be superficial and inconclusive in its reasoning, and based upon fancied resemblances, which have no true foundation in fact. Mr. Stephens, in a series of articles on the poems of Taliessin, which appeared in the *Archæologia Cambrensis* subsequent to the publication of the *Literature of the Cymry*, has, to some extent, modified the views expressed in the latter work. Of the poems which he there classed as doubtful he now removes three, and, of those in the fifth class, two, to the first class of genuine poems; but the mere fact that he does so on a more careful examination will show how superficial the grounds must have been on which he made that classification.

The mode in which he has dealt with two of the poems will afford a good illustration of the character of this criticism. Among the poems in the Book of Taliessin is one called *Marwnad Corroi m. Dayry*, or the death-song of Corroi, son of Dayry (B. T. 42). In his *Literature of the Kymry* Mr. Stephens places this poem in his fifth class of "Predictive poems, twelfth and succeeding centuries," but in a paper in the *Archæologia Cambrensis* (vol. ii. p. 151) he gives his more matured views, and reverses this verdict. He now considers it to have been written about 640. The grounds upon which he comes to this conclusion are these. The poem alludes to a contention between Corroi and Cocholyn (*Kyfranc Corroi a Cocholyn*). Here is his own account of his process:--"The name of Corroi's opponent piqued my curiosity. I forthwith went in search of his history in the Anglo-Saxon Annals, and, much to my delight, the personage whom I sought appeared in good company, being Cuichelm, one of the West Saxon kings." He then gives extracts from the Anglo-Saxon Chronicle of the event, connected with Cuichelm from A.D. 611 to 626, when he died. He confesses he can make nothing of Corroi, but he immediately identifies Cocholyn with Cuichelm, and forthwith removes the date of the composition of the poem from the twelfth to the seventh century. This is a good specimen of the mode in which this kind of criticism is made to tell upon the dates of the poems. If there is any poem in which we can predicate with certainty of the subject of it, it is this; and if Mr. Stephens, instead of betaking himself to the Saxon Chronicle, had gone to Ireland for his hero, he would have been more successful. Cocholyn is no other than the celebrated Ossianic hero Cuchullin, and Corroi, son of Dayry, was the head of the knights of Munster. They are mentioned together in an old: Irish. tract, which says, "This was the cause which brought Cuchulain and Curoi son of Daire from Alban to Erin." [1] The allusions in the poem are to the events of a legendary tale in which these heroes figure, and there are none to any other events. The poem belongs to a period when there was more intercommunion between the different branches of the British Celts, and when they had a common property in their early myths.

The other poem is one in the Red Book of Hergest commonly called Anrhec Urien (R. B. 17). It is likewise placed by Mr. Stephens in the same class of predictive, poems of the twelfth century, and in an article in the same volume of the *Archæologia Cambrensis* (p. 206), Mr. Stephens adheres to this opinion as to its date, and maintains that it refers to events of the eleventh century. These events are supposed to be contained in a series of extracts from the Anglo-Saxon Chronicle and the *Brut y Tywysogion*, ranging from 1055 to 1063, but the reader will seek in vain for anything but the most vague and general resemblance, which might be equally well traced between the allusions in the poem and any other series of events. Mr. Nash makes much shorter work of it. His argument is this:--The poem mentions a battle of Corsfochno. The Hoianau also refers to a battle of Corsfochno. The Hoianau was written in the twelfth century, therefore this poem also was written in the twelfth century! Admitting that the Hoianau was written in the twelfth century, does it follow that a poem of that date may not refer to an event of an earlier period? The Hoianau mentions likewise Rhydderch Had and the battle of Argoed Llwyfain, and both belong to an early period. There can be no doubt as to Rhydderch Hael being a real person in the sixth century, and as little that the battle of Argoed Llwyfain was a real event of the same century. Both Mr. Stephens and Mr. Nash admit it. Mr. Stephens, in his *Literature of the Kymry*, says, with his usual candour: "Corsfochno is in Cardiganshire, but I can find no other notice of this battle than another prediction;" but in his article on this poem he endeavours to find a notice of it in some lines of Gwalchmai, who flourished in the twelfth century, and Mr. Nash adopts the. conclusion at once. Corsfochno, however, was a real place, and these lines only refer to events in South Wales having been *tra Corsfochno*, beyond Corsfochno.

Let us now see whether another construction may not be put upon this poem, which is, to say the least of it, equally well borne out. The poem opens with a greeting of Urien Reged. It then mentions three of the sons of Llywarch Hon--Jeuaf, Ceneu, and Selev. It then alludes to a competition between " four men maintaining their place with four hundred, with the deepest water." One of these is mentioned as A Dragon from Gwynedd of precipitous lands and gentle towns. Surely this was enough to have indicated at once Maelgwn Gwynedd, whom Gildas calls "the insular dragon," as the person probably alluded to. Then another is thus alluded to as

A Bear from the South, he will arise,

and Cyneglas is called by Gildas a "Bear and the Charioteer of a Bear." If two of the four men thus indicate two of Gildas's kings, we may, well presume that the four men meant are his four kings of Wales. It is said of the Dragon of Gwynedd--

Killing and *drowning* from Eleri (a river in Corsfochno) to Chwilfynydd,
A conquering and unmerciful one will triumph;
Small will be his army on returning from the (action of) Wednesday.
And again--

He that will escape from the affair of Corsfochno will be fortunate. Now, does not this contest between the four men, in which the deep waters play a part, and the Dragon of Gwynedd triumphs, and which is said to be the affair of Corsfochno, very plainly refer to the transaction at Corsfochno, whatever it really was, by which Maelgwn Gwynedd, the insular dragon, became supreme sovereign of Wales, and in which these northern chiefs may have taken a part? The reference to Urien at the end—

Urien of Reged, generous he is and will be,

And has been since Adam.

He, proud in the hall, has the most wide-spreading sword

Among the thirteen kings of "Y Gogledd," or the North--is conclusive as to the antiquity of the poem. If it had been composed in the twelfth century, when all memory of the Cymric states in the north had passed away, Urien would have been brought to South Wales, where the later bards had provided a Reged for him between the Tawy and the Towy.

It is needless to examine more of this criticism. These two specimens will suffice, and the notes to the poems will indicate, as far as possible, the real events referred to. The real character and bearing of this criticism upon the poems may be sufficiently indicated by a short illustration. Let us suppose that the question is the genuinuess of the poem called *The Wallace*, attributed to a popular minstrel Blind Harry. Why, we might suppose Mr. Stephens and Mr. Nash would say, Here is a battle fought by Wallace against the English at Falkirk. We know the real battle of Falkirk was fought against the English by Prince Charles Edward in 1746. Wallace heads an insurrection against the English, so does Prince Charles. It is quite clear that the battle of Falkirk in 1746 is the real battle; under the name of Wallace, an ancient hero, Prince Charles is meant, and we must bring down the age of the poem to the eighteenth century. In using this illustration I do not think I am caricaturing this branch of the recent criticism.

The objections taken to these poems under the third proposition are, that the orthography and verbal forms are not older than the date of the MSS. in which they were transcribed, and that the poetical structure and the sentiments they breathe are analogous to the poetry of a later age. Mr. Stephens, by admitting that some of the poems are genuine, neutralises the first branch of this objection entirely, and the second to some extent. If some of the poems are pronounced to be ancient, notwithstanding the orthography being of a later date, so may all, and Mr. Stephens is bound to show that there is a marked difference between the poetical form and the sentiments of the poems he rejects and those he admits to be genuine, before he can found upon such an argument. Mr. Nash, however, goes further. He does not absolutely deny that some of the poems may be genuine, but he does not admit that any are older than the MSS. in which they appear, and he throws upon the advocates of their authenticity the burden of proving that they are older, notwithstanding their structure and orthography.

It may be admitted that these poems, as well as all such documents, what-ever their age may be, usually appear, in so far as their orthography and ver-bal forms are concerned, in the garb of the period when the MS. in which they appear was transcribed. The scribes of those times had not the spirit of the antiquaries of the present, which leads them to preserve the exact spelling and form of any ancient document they print. When such poems were handed down orally, those who recited them did not do so in the older forms of an earlier period, but in the language of their own. In their vernacu-lar forms, a process of phonetic corruption and alteration was going on, but it was a gradual and insensible one, and the language of the poems was easily adapted to it as their spoken idiom. The reciters and the hearers both wished to understand the historic and national lays they were, dealing with; and the reciter no more thought it necessary, in transcribing them from older MSS., to preserve their more ancient form, than he did, in reciting them orally, to preserve any other form of the, language than the one in which he heard them repeated. This is not peculiar to Welsh MSS., but is true of all such rec-ords. The only exception was when the scribe did not understand the piece which he was transcribing, and retained the old forms, and hence arise those pieces which appear in an obsolete form of the language with glosses. There was also this peculiarity in Welsh MSS., that there had been at intervals great and artificial changes in the orthography, and the scribe was no doubt wed-ded to the orthographic system of the day.

It is fortunate, however, that these poems are contained in MSS. of differ-ent dates, as it affords at once a test of the soundness of this objection. Be-tween the Black Book of Caermarthen and the Red Book of Hergest there is an interval of two centuries, and the Books of Aneurin and Taliessin stand between them. Now, there are poems in the Red Book of Hergest and in the Book of Taliessin which are also to be found in the Black Book of Caermar-then. Had this latter MS. not been preserved, there would have been no older text of these poems than in the two former MSS., and Mr. Nash's argument as to their being no older than the MS. in which they appear would have applied with equal force, but here we have the same text nearly two centuries earlier.

Let us then compare a few lines of the same poem in each Book:--

BLACK BOOK OF CAERMARTHEN.

Adwin caer ẏssit ar lan llẏant
   Adwin ẏd rotir ẏ pauper ẏ chwant.
   Gogẏwarch de gwinet boed tev wẏant,
   Gwaewaur rrin. Rei adarwant.
   Dẏv merchir. gueleisse guir ẏg cvinowant.
   Dẏv iev bv. ir. guarth. it adcorssant.
   Ad oet brẏger coch. ac och ar dant.

Oet llutedic guir guinet. Dit ẏ deuthant.
   Ac am kewin llech vaelvẏ kẏlchuẏ wriwant
   Cuẏtin ẏ can keiwin llv o carant.

BOOK OF TALIESSIN.

Aduúyn gaer yssyd ar lan lliant.
   Aduúyn yt rodir y paúb ychwant.
   Gogyfarch ti vynet boet teu uúyant.
   Gúaywaúr ryn rein a derllyssant.
   Duú merchyr gúeleis wyr

ygkyfnofant.

Dyfieu bu gúartheu a amugant

Ac yd oed vriger coch ac och ar-
dant.

Oed lludued vynet dyd y doethant

Ac am gefyn llech vaelúy kylchúy
vriwaut

Cúydyn ygan gefyn llu o garant.

BLACK BOOK OF CAERMARTHEN.

Rac gereint gelin kýstut

Y gueleise meirch can crinvrut

A gwidý gaur garv achlut

RED BOOK OF HERGEST.

Rae gereint gelyn kýthrud

Gúeleis y veirch dan gymryd

A gúedy gaúr garú achlud.

But there are indications in the Black Book of Caermarthen that in some of the poems the writer had transcribed from some older record, and had not always understood what he wrote. The fact that no older record has come down to us, is no proof that it never existed; and had such record been preserved, we no doubt would have found a difference between its text and that of the Black Book, analogous to the difference between the latter and the Red Book of Hergest. Had we the Book that Scolan confesses to have drowned, it might have settled the question.

But though we have no older record of any of the existing poems than the Black Book of Caermarthen, we have two fragments of other poems of older date, and these may help us to penetrate still a little further back. The first is a verse preserved in the old Welsh Laws, and there expressly said to have been sung by Taliessin. The other is the short poem preserved in the Cambridge Juvencus. It is not attributed to any bard, but it approaches so closely, in style, structure, and sentiment, to one of the poems attributed to Llywarch Hen, as to leave no rational doubt that they are by the same author. Though we cannot compare them with the same passages in the later MSS., we may place them in contrast with passages as nearly approaching to them in metre and style as we can find.

In comparison with the first, let us take three lines in the same metre out of the first poem in the Book of Taliessin, which is also to be found in the Red Book of Hergest. And with the other let us compare a few stanzas in the poems of Llywarch Hen which most nearly approach it:--

OLD WELSH LAWS.

Kickleu odures eu llaueneu

Kan Run en rudher bedineu

Guir Aruon rudyon euredyeu

BOOK OF TALIESSIN.

Achyn mynhúyf derwyn creu

Achyn del ewynuriú ar vyggeneu

Achyn vyghyfalle ar y llathen preu

RED BOOK OF HERGEST.

A chynn mynnúyf deruyn creu

A chynn del ewynriú ar vynggeneu

A chynn vyngkyualle ar llathen preu

CAMBRIDGE JUVENCUS.

Niguorcosam nemheunaur

Henoid. Mitelu nit gurmaur.

Mi. amfranc dam amcalaur

Nicanu niguardam nicusam

Henoid. Cet iben med nouel.

Mi amfranc dam an patel

RED BOOK OF HERGEST.

Stauell gyndylan ystywyll

Heno. Heb dan heb gannwyll

Namyn duú púy am dyry púyll

114

Stauell gyndylan ystywyll	Oct re rereint dan vortuid
Heno. Heb dan heb oleuat.	Gereint. Garhirion gratin guenith
Elit amdaú am danat	Rution ruthir eririon blith.
Pan wisgei garanmael, gat peis kynndylan	Oct re rerient dan vortuid
A phyrydyaú y onnen	Gereint. Garhirion graun ae bú
Ny chaffei *ffranc* tranc oe benn	Rution ruthir eriron dú.

There can be no doubt that the analogy here carries us back to the ninth century, but before we can advance further it will be necessary to revert to the historic argument as to the true date and place of these poems in Cymric literature.

To enter into an inquiry with regard to the metrical structure and poetic character of these poems, in order to show the extent to which they indicate that they are the work of an earlier age, and the essential difference between them and the poetry of the twelfth and succeeding centuries, would exceed the limits of this work. It would involve a detailed examination of the whole of these poems, which is here impossible. The examples above given will show that the metre of most of the poems attributed to Llywarch Hen, and which is usually called the Triban Milwyr, or warrior's triplet, is at least is old as the ninth century, and one of Taliessin's metres as the tenth.

There is a remarkable admission by Iolo Morganwg himself as to the difference in character between the genuine and the spurious poems attributed to Taliessin. He says of the Mabinogi of Taliessin--

"This romance has been mistaken by many for true history; but that it was not, might have been easily discovered by proper attention to the language and its structure to the structure of the verse in the poems attributed in this fiction to Taliessin having nothing but the externals of the verse of the genuine Taliessin, and nothing of its internal rhythm and other peculiarities."

No one knew better than Iolo Morganwg where these spurious poems really came from.

The poems attributed to Taliessin have been subjected to criticism both by Mr. Stephens and by Mr. Nash, but the poems attributed to Myrddin, with which Mr. Nash does not profess to deal, are likewise included within the scope of Mr. Stephens' criticism. We have only to deal with those, the texts of which are to be found in the four ancient MSS. There are four in the Black Book of Caermarthen, and two in the Red Book of Hergest, and no doubt the legendary connection of the name of Caermarthen with that of Myrddin led to their occupying a prominent place in the former MS. The first poem in that book (B. B. 1) is a dialogue between Myrddin and Taliessin, the last stanza--

Since I, Myrdin, after Taliessin
Let my prophecy be made common,

indicates Myrddin as the author. The subject is the Battle of Ardderyd, and one of Arthur's battles--that at Trywruid--is alluded to in it; but there is one allusion in it which marks great antiquity--that to a place called *Nevtur*--

which can be no other than *Nemhtur*, the most ancient name of Dumbarton, and one not applied to it, or indeed known, after the eighth century.

The other three are Nos. 16, 17, and 18, the two last being the Avallenau and the Hoianau. Mr. Stephens considers both to be spurious, and the work of Llyward Prydydd y Moch, the bard of Llywellyn, prince of North Wales from 1194 to 1240, but the poems had evidently been already transcribed before his time: Mr. Stephens is of course dealing with the text in the Myvyrian Archæology; but while the texts of the Hoianau in the Black Book and in the Myvyrian Archæology are substantially the same, there is a great difference between the two texts of the Avallenau. That in the Archæology contains twenty-two stanzas, while the text in the Black Book has only ten, and the order is different; but further, the stanzas omitted in the Black Book are just those upon which Mr. Stephens founds his argument for its later date. While, therefore, I agree with Mr. Stephens in considering the Hoianau as a spurious poem written in imitation of the Avallenau, I consider that his criticism is not applicable to the text of the latter as we have it in the Black Book, and that it is an old poem to which the stanzas founded upon by Mr. Stephens have been subsequently added. The poem No. 16 I rank along with the Hoianau.

The two poems contained in the Red Book of Hergest are the first two in the MS. The first is the Cyfoesi Myrdin, but this poem will be more conveniently considered in the next chapter, in connection with the historical argument. The second is the Guasgardgerd Vyrddin; and from the direct allusions to a king under the name of *Coch o Normandi*, who can be no other than William Rufus, as he is invariably termed in the Bruts *Y Brenhin Coch*, and to *Mab Henri*, or the son of Henri, whom I believe to be intended for Robert, Earl of Gloucester, son of Henry the First, I can have no hesitation in assigning it to the beginning of the twelfth century.

None of these three poems, which I consider to be unquestionably spurious, ought in my opinion to be assigned to any bard of North Wales. They, along with some other poems of the same class contained in the Red Book of Hergest, emanate very plainly from South Wales, and probably from Glamorgan.

[1] *Chron. Picts and Scots*, p. 319.

Chapter Thirteen - True Place of The Poems in Welsh Literature

HAVING thus examined the recent criticism, by which the poems attributed to the bards of the sixth century are maintained really to belong to a much later period, so far as the limits of this work will permit, we have now to approach the true problem we have to solve, and endeavour to assign to them their real place in Cymric literature; and the first question is, Do the poems themselves afford any indications by which we may judge of their antiquity? It is obvious, viewed in this light, that if these poems are genuine they ought to reflect the history of the period to which they belong. If we find that they do not re-echo to any extent the fictitious narrative of the events of the fifth and sixth centuries as represented in the Bruts, but rather the leading facts of the early history of Cymry, as we have been able to deduce them from the older authorities, it will be a strong ground for concluding that they belong themselves to an earlier age. This is an inquiry which of course can only affect the so-called historical poems, with such others of the class of mythological poems as contain historical allusions; but when their true place and period are once ascertained, the other poems must be judged of by their resemblance to these in metrical structure, style, and sentiment.

Following, then, the course of the history, as we have traced it, we have first the *Marwnad* or Death-song of Cunneddaf (B. T. 46). Cunedda, as we know, was Guledig in the fifth century, and retired from the northern wall to beyond the southern. In the poem we are told--

There is trembling from fear of Cunedda the burner,

In Caer Weir and Caer Lliwelydd;

that is, in Durham. and Carlisle--two towns, the one behind the west end, and the other the east end of the wall. And again--

He was to be admired in the tumult with nine hundred horse.

[paragraph continues] Here he is represented as commanding 900 horse, the exact amount of auxiliary cavalry attached to a Roman legion. The Roman wall, or *mur*, is likewise alluded to in two other of those death-songs (B. T. 40, 41)--one where Ercwlf is called the Wall-piercer, and the other where Madawg, the son of Uthyr, is called the Joy of the Wall.

It is very remarkable how few of these poems contain any notice of Arthur. If they occupied a place, as is supposed, in Welsh literature, subsequent to the introduction of the Arthurian romance, we should expect these poems to be saturated with him and his knights, and his adventures, but it is not so. Out of so large a body of poems, there are only five which mention him at all, and then it is the historical Arthur, the Guledig, to whom the defence of the wall was entrusted, and who fights the twelve battles in the north and finally perishes at Camlan. In one of them, the Cadeir Teyrnon (B. T. 15), this idea pervades the whole poem. Arthur is the

Person of two authors of the race
Of the steel Ala.He is mentioned as being
Among the Gosgordd of the wall. The Bard asks
Who are the three chief ministers
That guarded the country? And finally
From the destruction of Chiefs,
In a butchering manner;

117

From the loricated Legion
Arose the Guledig.

In another, the poem in the Black Book which has been supposed to refer to the Mabinogi of Kilhwch and Olwen, Arthur again appears as the warrior fighting in the north, and two of his twelve battles are mentioned--
In Mynyd Eiddyn
He contended with Cynvyn. And again--
On the strands of Trywruyd
Contending with Garwluyd,
Brave was his disposition.
With sword and shield. And the same body of legionary cavalry is alluded to--
They were stanch commanders
Of a legion for the benefit of the country,
Bedwyn and Bridlaw,
Nine hundred to them would listen. Again, in the Spoils of Annwfn. (B. T. 30), in which, in its historical sense, an expedition to the dreary region north of the wall would be intended--
Thrice twenty Canhwr stood upon the mur or wall. *Canhwr* is a *centuria*, or body of 100 men, and there were sixty centuries in the Roman legion, here represented as stationed at the wall.
In the *Historia Britonum*, the author describes the Britons as having been, for forty years after the Romans left the island, "sub metu," which expression he afterwards explains as meaning, "sub metu Pictorum et Scotorum," and the memory of these fearful and destructive outbursts of ravaging and plundering bands of Picts from beyond the wall must have long dwelt in their recollection. This we might also expect to find reflected in the poems.
When a poem opens with these lines:--

How miserable it is to see
Tumult and commotion,
Wounds and confusion,
The *Brithwyr* in motion,
And a cruel fate,
With the impulse of destiny,
And for the sake of Heaven,
Declare the discontinuance of the disaster--

is it possible to doubt that that poem was written in a time when the country was still smarting from the recollection of their ravages? Thus, in another poem (R. B. 23), we have

Let the chief architects
Against the fierce Picts
Be the Morini Brython--

alluding to the attempt by the Britons to protect themselves by the wall. Then, in two other poems, One commonly called the Mic Dinbych (B. T. 21), where the billows which surround one of the cities are said

To come to the green sward from the region of the Ffichti;

and in another (B. T. 11), where, it is said--

Hearndur and Hyfeid and Gwallawg,

And Owen of Mona of Maelgwnian energy,

Will lay the *Peithwyr* prostrate--

is it possible to doubt that they must have been written when the Picts were still a powerful people in Britain, and before their kingdom was merged in that of the Scots?

The mode in which Mr. Nash deals with these passages is characteristic. He ignores the first poem altogether, and he so disguises the other passages in his translation as to banish the Picts as effectually from them as they were ever expelled by the Roman troops from the province. In the passage quoted from the second poem, he translates the line--*Rac Ffichit leuon*, before twenty chiefs. Now, *Ffichit* does not mean twenty in Welsh, but *Fichead* means twenty in Gaelic; and he would rather suppose that the bard had introduced a Gaelic word than that he could have alluded to such embarrassing people as the Picts.

In the next passage he translates the line--*Adaw hwynt werglas o glas Ffichti*, "promised to them are the drinking-cups of painted glass." If *A daw hwynt* means they came, *Adaw* means a promise; but how *Gwerlas* call mean drinking-cups I cannot conceive.

It is always used as meaning "the green sward." Then he evidently supposes that *glas* is the English word "glass," instead of the middle form of *clas*, a region; and thus here, too, he would rather suppose that the bard had used the English word "glass," and. the Latin word "pictus" in its corrupt form *ffichti*, than that the Picts could have been mentioned; but the technical use in Welsh of *Ffchti* for the Picts is quite established.

The last passage he thus translates:--"Hearnddur and Hyfeid Hir, and Gwallawg and Owen of Mona, and Maelgwn of great reputation, they would prostrate the foe;" thus quietly suppressing the word *Peithwyr*, which certainly does not mean. simply "foe." [1]

Nennius mentions the Picts whom Arthur defeated at the battle of *Mynyd Eiddyn*, or Edinburgh, by the strange and unusual name of *Catbregion*; but we find them appearing under that name in another poem in the Book: of Taliessin (50):--

The *Catbreith* of a strange language will be troubled,

From the ford of Taradyr to Portwygyr in Mona.

The ford of Taradyr is the ford of Torrador, across the river Carron, the northern boundary of the Picts of Manau, near Falkirk.

This poem, too, is ignored by Mr. Nash.

Another portion of these poems must evidently have been known to the author of the *Genealogia*, written in the eighth century. After narrating the reign of Ida, king of Northumbria, who died in 559, he says:--"Tunc Talhaern Cataguen in poemate claruit et Neirin et Taliesin et Bluchbard et Cian qui vocatur Gueinthgwant simul uno tempore in poemate Britannico claruerunt." Of these four who shone in British poetry, it is admitted that the first three are Aneurin, Taliessin, and Llywarch Hen, and being mentioned in the course of his notice of Bernicia, they must have been connected with the north. The expression used with regard to them is remarkable. It does not simply say that they flourished then but "*in poemate Britannico* claruerunt." Could he have used that expression had there not been *poemata Britannica*, Welsh poems, then well known and then connect with this some of the subsequent notices, "Contra illum (*i.e.* Hussa) quatuor regis Urbgen et Ridderch Hen et Guallaue et Morcant dimicaverunt." The idea that runs through these notices, and accounts for the otherwise apparently unconnected and intrusive mention of the bards, is this. Aneurin, Taliessin, and Llywarch Hen, wrote Welsh poems, and it was against Hussa that Urien, Ridderch Hen, Gwallawg, and Morcant fought. Add to this, that the subject of a number of the poems of Taliessin and Llywarch Hen was the wars of these very heroes against the Saxons; and can we reasonably doubt that these poems were known to the writer? The next notice is still more significant "Deodric, contra illum Urbgen cum filiis dimicabat fortiter." There is but one poem in which Urien is mentioned as fighting along with any of his sons. It is the Battle of Argoed Llywyfain, attributed to Taliessin (B. T. 35), in which Urien and his son Owen are attacked by Flamddwyn, the Saxon king, and fight valiantly against him. Must this poem not have been in the mind of the writer when he here notes--It was against Deodric that Urien and his sons fought,--thus identifying him with Flamddwyn? There is another allusion of the same kind equally significant. After narrating the war between Oswy and Penda, with the thirty British kings who assisted him, and their slaughter in Campo Gai, he adds, "Et nunc facta est strages Gai Campi." Is the idea not this--And it was now that the well-known slaughter of *Catraeth* took place? for *traeth*, a shore, is here rendered by Campus and *Ca*, forming in combination *Ga*, as in *Gatraeth*, is the adjective Gaus agreeing with Campus, and the great poem of the Gododin, including the mixed portion, which belongs to this period, must have been known to the writer. If these inferences are at all legitimate, a body of historical poems attributed to the same bards, and narrating the same events by the same warriors as those which we now have, must have been in, existence when the author of the *Genealogia* wrote--that is, in the eighth century.

Further, in examining these poems,. we find that there runs through the poems in each of the four books a date indicated in the poem itself, which is nearly the same in all, and is comprised within the first sixty years of the seventh or immediately preceding century. Thus, in the Book of Caermarthen, there is what I conceive to be the text of the Avallenau in its original shape, and in this text the bard says--

Ten years and forty, with my treasures,
Have I been sojourning among ghosts and sprites. And the first poem tells us
that, after the battle of Ardderyd,
Seven score generous ones become ghosts.
In the wood of Celyddon they came to an end. he battle of Ardderyd was
fought in the year 573, and ten years and forty will bring us to 623, not long
after which the poem may have. been composed.

In the Book of Aneurin, the bard who wrote the last part of the Gododin
tells us that "from the height of Adoyn he saw the head of Dyfnwal Brec de-
voured by ravens;" but Dyfnwal Brec is no other than Donald Brec, king of
Dalriada, and the year of his death is a fixed era. It was in 642;

In the Book of Taliessin there is a poem (49) which has been much misun-
derstood. It contains these verses:--

Five chiefs there will be to me
Of the Gwyddyl Ffichti,
Of a sinner's disposition,
Of a race of the knife;
Five others there will be to me
Of the Norddmyn place;
The sixth a wonderful king,
From the sowing to the reaping;
The seventh proceeded
To the land over the flood;
The eighth, of the line of *Dyfi*,
Shall not be freed from prosperity.

The *Dyfi* or Dovey flows past Corsfochno and the *Traeth Maelgwn*, where
Maelgwn Gwynedd. established the sovereignty in his family, is on its shore.
The kings of his race are the only kings who could be said to be of the line of
Dyfi or Dovey. The word *Norddmyn* is probably the word translated by the
author of the *Genealogia*, where he calls Oswald "Rex Nordorum." It is only
used on this one occasion, and seems, during his reign, to have been applied
to the kings of the Nordanhymbri. We know that the Saxons of Bernicia su-
perseded a Pictish population; and there is but one king of the line of *Dyfi*
who became a king of Bernicia, and he was Cadwallawn, a descendant of
Maelgwn Gwynedd. The passage, therefore, appears to refer to Bernicia,
which lay south of the Firth of Forth. We have first five kings of the Gwyddyl
Ffichti, then five kings of the Norddmyn--Ida, Ella, Ethelric, Ethelfred, and
Edwin. The sixth, from the sowing to the reaping--that is, from spring to har-
vest--was Osric, who only reigned a few months, when he was slain in au-
tumn by Cadwallawn. The seventh was Eanfrid, who crossed the flood--that
is, the Firth of Forth--from the land of the Picts, where he had taken refuge,
and was likewise slain by Cadwallawn, who is the eighth king of the line of

Dyfi, and the poem must have been written before his reverse of fortune in 655. In the poem called Cerdd y Vab Llyr (B. T. 14) there is this line--

A battle against the lord of fame in the dales of Severn,
Against Brochmail of Powys, who loved my *Awen*.

which implies that the bard was contemporary with Brochmail, who is mentioned by Bede as being present at the battle fought in 613. In the Red Book of Hergest, in the historical poems attributed to Llywarch Hen, there occurs throughout a current of expressions which imply that the bard witnessed the events he alludes to, and must have lived during the period extending from the death of Urien to that of Cadwallawn in 659. But what was this period thus indicated in so many of the poems, and running through the four ancient books? It was that of the great outburst of energy on the part of the Cymry under Cadwallawn, when they even, for the time, obtained supremacy over the Angles of Northumberland, and throughout his life presented a formidable front to their Saxon foes--when their hopes must have been excited, and their exultation equally great, till, after the first reverse in 655, they were finally quenched by the death of Cadwaladyr, in the pestilence of 664, who, they fondly hoped, would have re-established the power they had enjoyed under his father.

The first poem in the Red Book of Hergest is the Cyvoesi Myrddin, and its peculiar form requires special consideration. It is a species of chronicle written in the shape of a dialogue between Myrddin and his sister Gwendydd, in which the latter appeals to her brother's prophetical power to foretell the successive rulers over Britain. This is a device of which there are other examples, and it is a favourite one in rude times. A record of past events is written in the shape, of a prophecy of future events, and the period of its composition is indicated by the termination of a distinct and literal record, and the commencement of one clothed in figurative and obscure language. This is a species of poetic chronicle which, is peculiarly adapted to addition and interpolation. A few imitative verses in the same style can be inserted or added, bringing the record from time to time further down.

The Cyvoesi commences with Rydderch Hael, in whose time the prophecy is supposed to be uttered, and the bard foretells the rule of Morcant after him; after. Morcant, Urien; and after Urien, Maelgwn Hir. He then takes the line of Maelgwn's descendants down to Cynan Tindaethwy, when he introduces Mervyn *o dir Manau*, and follows his descendants to Howel dda. The record then changes its character, and proceeds to foretell a succession of kings under descriptive names, until it announces the coming again of Cadwaladyr, who is said to reign 303 years and 3 months, and to be succeeded by Cyndaf; and after some further obscure references, the poem assumes a more personal character, in which the bard is described as having been imprisoned beneath the earth, and concludes.

It has been supposed that this poem must have been composed in the reign of Howel dda, who died in 948, as after his name the style of the poem changes from the direct mention of historic kings under their real names to that of a list of apparently imaginary kings, designated by obscure epithets; but Mr. Stephens does not admit this, and maintains that these obscure epithets can be so easily identified as to show that the bard was in fact recording the historic successors of Howel dda. An example of this identification will suffice: The bard, when asked, Who will rule after Howel? answers *Y Bargodyein*, the borderers. Mr. Stephens thinks this word plainly indicates Jevan and Jago, the sons of Edwal Voel, king of North Wales, because their claim to the throne which they usurped only *bordered* on a rightful title. [2]

There is reason to think, however, that parts of this poem were compiled at an earlier date than the reign of Howel dda. It may in fact be divided into four parts--the first, from the beginning to the end of the 26th stanza, containing the stanza mentioning Cadwaladyr; the second, from the 26th stanza to the 65th; the third, from the 66th stanza to the 102d; and the fourth, from the 102d stanza to the end.

Now there is this peculiarity in the first part of the poem, that it names as the kings who ruled before Maelgwn, Urien, Morcant, and Rydderch Hael. Is it possible to conceive that any chronicle containing such a succession of kings could have been composed in Wales even so early as the tenth century? Would the author not have given, in preference, the kings said to have ruled in Wales? Its connection, how ever, with Nennius and with Bernicia is apparent. Nennius states that the British kings who fought against the Bernician kings were Urien, Rydderch, Gwallawg, and Morcant, and the Cyvoesi begins its list with three of them--Rydderch, Morcant, and Urien--and then says that Maelgwn reigned over Gwynedd only. This part of the chronicle must have been composed in the north, but after Cadwaladyr there is an obvious break. Throughout the previous part, the questions and answers alternate, each answer being followed by a question, Who ruled next? But the verse naming Cadwaladyr is not followed by a question. The verses are as follows—

25 Though I see thy cheek is direful,
It comes impulsively to my mind
Who will rule after Cadwallawn.
26 A tall man holding a conference,
And Britain under one sceptre:
The best of Cymro's sons, Cadwaladyr.
27 He that comes before me mildly,
His abilities are they not worthless?
After Cadwaladyr, Idwal.

The question before this last stanza is omitted, but if we go on to the mention again of Cadwaladyr, in the 102d stanza, which commences the fourth portion of the Cyvoesi, we shall find that it must originally have immediately succeeded the 26th stanza. Let us place them together:--

215 Though I see thy check is direful,
It comes impulsively to my Mind
Who will rule after Cadwallawn.
26 A tall man *holding a conference*,

And Britain under one sceptre:

The best of Cymro's sons, Cadwaladyr.
102 Do not separate abruptly from me,
From a dislike *to the conference*.
Who will rule after Cadwaladyr?
103 To Gwendydd I will declare,
Age after age I will predict,
After Cadwaladyr, Cyndav.

As Cyndav is an imaginary king, I hold that the original poem, of which we have a part in the first 26 stanzas, must have been composed before the death of Cadwaladyr, while he was still the hope of the Cymry, and must have belonged to the north.

The second part, which contains the real names of the kings to Howel dda, and a list of imaginary kings after, him, must, I think, notwithstanding Mr. Stephens' attempt to identify them, have been added in the reign of Howel dda; and this is confirmed by the fact that the, successor of Cadwaladyr is made to be his son Idwal, and that there is no appearance of Ivor from Armorica, who would certainly have been mentioned had the poem been composed after the appearance of the Bruts.

The third portion, extending from stanza 66 to stanza 102, has probably been added in South Wales in the twelfth century. The lord of eight fortresses, mentioned in the 65th stanza, may have been Robert Fitz-Hamon, the first Norman who obtained Glamorgan, and built castles; and *Mab Henri*, in the 68th stanza, Robert, Earl of Gloucester, who succeeded him in Glamorgan, and was son of Henry the First.

This part of the poem contains a prophecy that Cadwaladyr would reappear with a powerful host to defend the men of Gwynedd, that he would descend in the vale of Tywi, and would reign 303 years.

There were, however, two very distinct forms in which this prophecy of the reappearing of Cadwaladyr was conveyed. The first we find in the Afallenau, the text of which, as it appears in the Black Book, I consider to be that of an old poem.

The poem in that text concludes with this stanza:--

Sweet apple-tree, and a tree of crimson hue
Which grows in concealment in the wood of Celyddon,
Though sought for their fruit, it will be in vain,
Until Cadwaladyr comes from the conference of the ford of Rheon,

And Cynan to meet him advances upon the Saxons.
The Cymry will be victorious, glowing will be their leader;
All shall have their rights, and Britons will rejoice,
Sounding the horns of gladness, and chanting the song of peace and happiness.

The other form of the prophecy we find in the Hoianau, which I agree with Mr. Stephens in considering to be spurious.
In it the expressions are as follows:--

And I will predict that two rightful princes,
Will produce peace from heaven to earth--
Cynan and Cadwaladyr--thorough Cymry,
May their councils be admired.

. . . .

And when Cadwaladyr comes to the subjugation of Mona,
The Saxons will be extirpated from lovely Britain.

. . . .

Stout Cynan appearing from the banks of the Teifi,
Will cause confusion in Dyfed.

The form of the prophecy in the Hoianau is obviously the same with that in the third part of the Cyvoesi, which I consider to have been produced in South Wales in the twelfth century. In the one, Cadwaladyr comes to Mona, and Cynan from the valley of the Teifi in *Dyfed* or South Wales, in the other, Cadwaladyr comes to Gwynedd, and descends in the vale of the Tywi in South Wales.

But the form of the prophecy in the Avallenau is very different. There Cadwaladyr comes from a conference at *Ryd Rheon*, or the ford of Reon, and this is evidently the same place as *Llwch Rheon*, which we can identify with Loch Ryan in Galloway, and he goes to the wood of Celyddon to meet Cynan.

In the later form of the prophecy Cynan and Cadwaladyr come from Armorica. Thus, in the *Vita Merlini*, Geoffrey says—

The Britons their noble kingdom,
Shall for a long time lose through weakness,
Until from Armorica Conan shall come in his car,
And Cadwaladyr, the honoured leader of the Cymry.

And the prophecy can only have assumed this shape after the fictitious narrative of Cadwaladyr taking refuge in Armorica was substituted for his death in the pestilence, and the scene of his return is placed in South Wales, whence this form of the prophecy emerged.

But the prophecy which connects his reappearance with the conference at the ford of Loch Ryan, and places the meeting with Conan in the wood of Celyddon, must be much older, and the Cumbrian form of the prophecy; and with this form of it, the first passage in the Cyvoesi is obviously connected, which describes Cadwaladyr as a tall man holding a conference.

[1] In noticing Mr. Nash's so-called translations, I may remark that he invariably translates Welsh on the principle that, if any Welsh word resembles an English word, it must be the English word that is used. He carries this so far as to translate the well-known word for a ford in Welsh, *rhyd*, by the English word "road." He appears to me to translate Welsh somewhat in the same fashion as Hood's School-boy translated the first line of Virgil--Arma, virumque cano--An arm, a man, and a cane.
[2] The italics are Mr. Stephens'.

Chapter Fourteen - Result of the Examination of the Poems, and Their Classification

OF, a large proportion, then, of the historical poems, the scenery and events lie in the north; the warriors whose deeds they celebrate were "Gwyr y Gogled," or Men of the North. They are attributed to bards connected with the north, and there is every reason to believe them older than the tenth century. They are, in point of fact, the literature of the Cymric inhabitants of Cumbria before that kingdom was subjugated by the Saxon king in 946.

As soon as this view of their birthplace and home is recognised, localities are identified, warriors recognised, and allusions heretofore obscure become intelligible. During the last half-century of the Roman dominion in Britain, the most important military events took place at the northern frontier of the province, where it was chiefly assailed by those whom they called the barbarian races, and their troops were massed at the Roman walls to protect the province. After their departure, it was still the scene of a struggle between the contending races for supremacy. It was here that the provincial Britons had mainly to contend under the Guledig against the invading Picts and Scots, succeeded by the resistance of the native Cymric population of the north to the encroachment of the Angles of Bernicia.

Throughout this clash and jar of contending races, a body of popular poetry appears to have grown up, and the events of this never-ending war, and the dim recollections of social changes and revolutions, seem to have been reflected in national lays attributed to bards supposed to have lived at the time in which the deeds of their warriors were celebrated, and the legends of the country preserved in language, which, if not poetical, was figurative and obscure.

It was not till the seventh century that these popular lays, floating about among the people, were brought into shape, and assumed a consistent form. The sudden rise of the Cymric population to power under Cadwallawn, and the burst of national enthusiasm and excited hope, found vent in poetry. The

Cymry were stimulated to combined effort by the voice of the bards, and poems were composed, and the more ancient lays either adapted to their purpose, or embedded as fragments in their own compositions. It is in the seventh century that I place these poems in their earliest consistent shape, and I do not attempt to take them further back.

The hopes excited by the success of Cadwallawn, and the expectations formed of his son Cadwaladyr, were extinguished by the final defeat of the former in 655, and the subjection of the Britons to the Angles, which lasted nearly thirty years as to the northern Britons, and probably much longer as to the southern; and we may well suppose that during this subjection the national spirit was kept alive by these popular lays, and by prophetic strains as to a possible future regeneration of the Cymry, accompanied by the usual fable that the king on whom they built so much and who was said to have perished in the pestilence of 664, had not really died, but would re-appear to renew the success of his father.

The accession to the throne of Wales of Mervyn Frych, from the northern region of Manau, seems to have brought the knowledge of the *Historia Britonum*, to Wales, and the emigration of large bodies of the Cymric population to Wales during the reign of Anaraut, and the termination of their kingdom in 946, when Howel dda, Prince of South Wales, occupied the throne of all Wales, probably made them acquainted with these poems.

But they appear to have found their new home in South Wales. By degrees the memory of the Northern Cymric kingdom passed away, the name of "Y Gogledd" was transferred from Cumbria to Gwynedd, and much of the traditionary history of the north, obscurely reflected in these poems, was applied to North Wales, while the warriors celebrated in them had new homes found for them in South Wales. To' adopt the language of an able modern writer:-- "To the inhabitants of the south, Gwynedd (of the past) was an unknown land. Their imagination filled it with giants, fairies, monsters, and magicians. The inhabitants exercised strange arts; they had cauldrons of like virtue with that which renewed the youth of Aeson; a red dragon and a white were buried as a palladium of their metropolis. Among their monarchs was a veritable cat, the offspring of a wandering sow. Their chief philosopher was of gigantic stature, and sat on a mountain-peak to watch the stars. Their wizard-monarch, Gwydion, had the power of effecting the strangest metamorphoses. The simple peasant, dwelling on the shore of Dyfed, beheld across the sea those shadowy mountain-summits pierce the air--guardians, as it seemed, of some unearthly region. Thence came the mists and storms; thence flashed aloft the northern streamers; thence rose through the silent sky the starry path of Gwydion."

It is to this period that I attribute the composition of the oldest group of the prose tales and romances, and especially those peculiarly called the Mabinogi; and while, soon after, a new school of Welsh poetry, which speedily, assumed large, dimensions and exercised a powerful influence, arose in North Wales, the literary spirit of South Wales manifested itself more in prose composition and in the gradual appearance of spurious poetry, written in the style and sentiments of this older poetry of Cumbria.

The introduction of the Arthurian romance into South Wales from Armorica led to the appearance of the Bruts and to the later class of prose tales and romances, and when the kingdom of South Wales terminated by the death of Rhys ap Tewdwr, and the occupation of Glamorgan by the Normans, the extent to which the affections. of the people seem to have centred upon Robert, Earl of Gloucester, as the son of Nest, the daughter of their last king, Rhys ap Tewdwr, by Henry the First, manifested itself in the last Phase of this poetry.

There are therefore four eras connected with these poems, each of which was succeeded by a period of confusion or national depression:--

The era of Cadwallawn and Cadwaladyr, in which they were first brought into shape; that of Howel dda when they were transferred to South Wales, and when some of the later poems in the Book of Taliessin may have been composed; that of Rhys, ap Tewdwr and his grandson Robert Mab Henri, when much of the spurious poetry was written, none of which, however, appears in the Book of Taliessin; and the reign of Henry the Second, when some of these poems, with others of the period, were first transcribed in the Black Book of Caermarthen.

The translation of these poems contained in this work comprises the whole of the poems attributed to these ancient bards, whether genuine or spurious, as we find them in the four books--the Black Book of Caermarthen, the Look of Aneurin, the Book of Taliessin, and the Red Book of Hergest; but in these MSS. they do not appear in chronological order, or in any systematic shape. They are transcribed without reference to date, subject, or supposed author, and are interspersed with poems by authors of the later period. To print the translations in the exact order in which they appear in the MSS. would be to present them in a confused and unintelligible shape, and where the same poem appears in more than one MS., would lead to double translations. It has been thought better, therefore, while the translation has been made as literal and exact a representation of the text in the MSS. as possible, to group the poems so as to bring those which relate to the same subject together, and thus afford the means of easy comparison as well as facilitate a sounder criticism, based upon a true conception of their character in their mutual bearing upon each other.

The translations are therefore printed in the following order:--The poems which are either, strictly speaking, historical, or which contain historical allusions, are separated in each of the four books from those which contain merely the sentiments of the poet, and the latter are classed under the head of "Miscellaneous Poems." Those that maybe called "Historical" fall into two divisions. The first comprises those which contain allusions to early traditions or events prior to the year 560 when Gildas wrote, and to the time when the warriors fought with the kings of Bernicia, whose names are recorded by the author of the *Genealogia*. This division contains the whole of those poems which contain allusions to the persons mentioned in the oldest class of the prose tales or Mabinogion. There are, first, grouped together under letter A, five poems which refer to early traditions; under letter B, four poems which mention Arthur by name; and it is somewhat remarkable that out of this large body of popular poetry there are only these four preserved, and one other, placed in another group, which mention him at all. Under letter C, eight poems, which refer to Llew and Gwydion, and the combination of the Brython and Gwyddyl, or to the Brithwyr. Under letter D has been placed a poem in the Black Book of Caermarthen relating to Gwyddno Garanhir and the mythic Gwynn ap Nudd. Under the letter E four poems in the Book of Taliessin, which belong to a later period; one of these, "the Kadeir Kerritwen," mentions the Books of Beda, and must have been written after his death; another mentions the line of Anaraut, who died in 913; and the other two contain illusions to the name of Hu, who belongs to a later school. One poem in the Black Book attributed to Gwyddneu is also included in this group. And under letter F are placed five poems, two relating to cities of the Cymry, either real or symbolical, and three relating to the legendary heroes generally, and consisting of the Triads of the Heroes in the Black Book of Caermarthen, the Song of the Horses in the Book of Taliessin, and the Graves of the Warriors in the former book.

The second division comprises the poems more strictly. historical, and alluding to events subsequent to 560. Under letter G are placed four poems attributed to Llywarch Hen, in which the war between his son Mechyd and Mwg Mawr Drefydd is referred to. Under letter H are three poems relating to Gwallawg ap Lleenawg, one of the four kings recorded to have fought against Hussa, who reigned from 567 to 574. Under letter I are nine poems relating to Urien, another of the four kings, concluding with his Death-song. And under letter J are three poems relating to his son Owen, one of the sons who was recorded to have fought with their father Urien against Theodric, who reigned from 580 to 587, and concluding with the Death-song of Owen.

Under letter K is the first poem in the Book of Caermarthen, which relates to the battle of Ardderyd, fought in 573, and the Avallenau. which is placed appropriately after it. Under letter L are the poems relating to the Gododin and the battle of Catraeth. Under letter M are three poems relating directly to Cadwallawn, and concluding with his Death-song; and under letter N the two poems termed *Arymes*, or the Omen, and another prophetic poem relating to Cadwaladyr. Under letter O are two poems relating to events in Powys--one from the Book of Taliessin, and the other from the Red Book of Hergest. Under letter P the Cyvoesi is first placed, which, as we have seen, ranges in its composition from the time of Cadwaladyr in the seventh to that of Robert, Earl of Gloucester, in the twelfth centuries; and after it are placed six poems, which I conceive to have emerged from South Wales. And this concludes the group of poems which I denominate historical.

The "Miscellaneous poems" consist first of those in the Black Book of Caermarthen, and are placed in three groups. Under letter Q are placed five poems attributed to other bards--Meigant, Cuhelyn, and Elaeth. Under letter

R ten anonymous poems on religious subjects; and under letter S two poems, which seem connected, and the first of which is the curious poem relating to Yscolan.

There is only one poem in the Book of Aneurin, the Gorchan Adebon, which is not historical. It is placed under letter T.

The "Miscellaneous poems" from the Book of Taliessin are placed under three groups. Under letter U are twelve poems, containing allusions to the personal history of Taliessin, or expressing his opinions on philosophy or religion. Under letter V four poems, containing allusions to the history of the Israelites. Under letter W two poems, relating to the legends connected with Alexander the Great.

The "Miscellaneous poems" from the Red Book of Hergest consist of three groups--one, under letter X, of seven poems attributed to Llywarch Hen, which are not historical; under letter Y, of two poems, beginning Eiry Mynyd, one of which is called the Colloquy of Llywelyn and Gwrnerth; and under letter Z, of two other anonymous poems, the last of which is termed the Viaticum of Llevoed Wynebglawr.

Translation of The Poems

I. Historical Poems Containing Allusions to Events Prior to A.D. 560

A. Poems Referring to Early Traditions

I. THE RECONCILIATION OF LLUD THE LESS. - BOOK OF TALIESSIN LIV.

IN the name of the God of Trinity, of knowing charity,
A tribe numerous, ungentle their arrogance,
Have overrun Prydain, chief of isles.
Men of the land of Asia, and land of Gafis.
A people of perfect prudence, their country is not known,
Their mother country; they deviated on account of the sea.
Flowing their coats; who is like them?
With discretion let the work of foes be brought about,
Europin, Arafin, Arafanis.
10 The Christian unmindful was impelled certainly
Before the reconciliation of Llud and Llevelys..
The possessor of the fair isle trembled
Before the chief from Rome, of splendid terror.
Neither hesitating nor crafty the king, fluent his speech.
Who has seen what I have seen of the strange speech?
There were formed a square mast, the clarions of journey,
Before the presence of Roman leader there is conflagration.
The son of Gradd, of fluent speech, retaliated,
Cymry burning: war on slaves.
20 I will consider, I will deliberate who caused them to go.
The Brythonic energy arose.

II. THE DEATH-SONG OF CORROI, SON OF DAYRY. - BOOK OF TALIESSIN XLII.

I. THY large fountain fills the river,
Thy coming will make thy value of little worth,
The death-song of Corroy agitates me.
If the warrior will allure, rough his temper.
And his evil was greater than its renown was great,
To seize the son of Dayry, lord of the southern sea,
Celebrated was his praise before she was entrusted to him.

II. Thy large fountain fills the stream.
Thy coming will cause saddling without haste,
The death-song of Corroi is with me now,
If (the warrior) will allure.
III. Thy large fountain fills the deep.
Thy arrows traverse the strand, not frowning or depressed.
The warrior conquers, great his rank of soldiers,
And after penetrating enters towns
And . . . the pure stream was promptly whitened.
Whilst the victorious one in the morning heaps carnage;
Tales will be known to me from sky to earth,
Of the contention of Corroi and Cocholyn,
Numerous their tumults about their borders,
Springs the chief o'er the surrounding mead of the somewhat gentle wood.
A Caer there was, love-diffusing, not paling, not trembling.
Happy is he whose. soul is rewarded.

III. THE DEATH-SONG OF EROF. - BOOK OF TALIESSIN XL.

WERE changed the elements
Like night into day,
When came the gloriously-free,
Erewlf chief of baptism.
Erewlf said,
That he valued not death.
Shield of the Mordei
Upon him it broke.
Erewlf the arranger,
10 Determined, frantic.
Four columns of equal length;
Ruddy, gold along them.

The columns of Erewlf
Will not dare a threatening,
A threatening will not dare.
The heat of the sun did not leave him.
No one went to heaven
Until went he,
Erewlf the wall-piercer.
20 May the sand be my covering,
May the Trinity grant me
Mercy on the day of judgment,
In unity without want.

IV. - BOOK OF TALIESSIN XLI.

MADAWG, the joy of the wall,
Madawg, before he was in the grave,
Was a fortress of abundance
Of games, and society.
The son of Uthyr before he was slain,
From his hand he pledged thee.
Erof the cruel came,
Of impotent joy;
Of impotent sorrow.
10 Erof the cruel caused
Treacheries to Jesus.

Though he believed.
The earth quaking,
And the elements darkening,
And a shadow on the world,
And baptism trembling.
An impotent stop
Was taken by fierce Erof,
Going in the course of things
20 Among the hideous fiends
Even to the bottom of Uffern.

V. - BOOK OF TALIESSIN XLVI.

I AM Taliesin the ardent;
I will enrich the praise of baptism.
At the baptism of the ruler, the worshipper wondered,
The conflict of the rocks and rocks and plain.
There is trembling from fear of Cunedda the burner,
In Caer Weir and Caer Lliwelydd.
There is trembling from the mutual encounter.
A complete billow of fire over the seas, .
A wave in which the brave fell among his companions.
10 A hundred received his attack on the earth,
Like the roaring of the wind against the ashen spears,
His dogs raised their backs at his presence.,
They protected, and believed in his kindness.
The bards are arranged according to accurate canons.
The death of Cunedda, which I deplore, is deplored.
Deplored be the strong protector, the fearless defender,
He will assimilate, he will agree with the deep and shallow,
A deep cutting he will agree to.
(His) discourse raised up the bard stricken in poverty,
20 Harder against an enemy than a bone.
Pre-eminent is Cunedda before the furrow (*i.e.* the grave)
And the sod. His face was kept
A hundred times before there was dissolution. A door hurdle
The men of Bryniich carried in the battle.
They became pale from fear of him and his terror chill-moving.
Before the earth was the portion of his end.
Like a swarm of swift dogs about a thicket.
Sheathing (swords is) a worse cowardice than adversity.
The destiny of an annihilating sleep I deplore,
30 For the palace, for the shirt of Cunedda;
For the salt streams, for the freely-dropping sea.
For the prey, and the quantity I lose.
The sarcasm of bards that disparage I will harrow,
And others that thicken I will count.
He was to be admired in the tumult with nine hundred horse.
Before the communion of Cunedda,
There would be to me milch cows in summer,
There would be to me a steed in winter,
There would be to me bright wine and oil.
40 There would be to me a troop of slaves against any advance.
He was diligent of heat from an equally brave visitor.
A chief of lion aspect, ashes become his fellow-countrymen,
Against the son of Edern, before the supremacy of terrors,

He was fierce, dauntless, irresistible,
For the streams of death he is distressed.
He carried the shield in the pre-eminent place,
Truly valiant were his princes.
Sleepiness, and condolence, and pale front,
A good step, will destroy sleep from a believer.

B. Poems Referring to Arthur the Guledig

VI. THE CHAIR OF THE SOVEREIGN. - BOOK OF TALIESSIN XV.

THE declaration of a clear song,
Of unbounded Awen,
About a warrior of two authors,
Of the race of the steel Ala.
With his staff and his wisdom,
And his swift irruptions,
And his sovereign prince,
And his scriptural number,
And his red purple,
10 And his assault over the wall,
And his appropriate chair,
Amongst the retinue of the wall.
Did not (he) lead from Cawrnur
Horses pale supporting burdens?
The sovereign elder.
The generous feeder.
The third deep wise one,
To bless Arthur,
Arthur the blessed,
20 In a compact song.
On the face in battle,
Upon him, a restless activity.
Who are the three chief ministers
That guarded the country?
Who are the three skilful (ones)
That kept the token?
That will come with eagerness
To meet their lord?
High (is) the virtue of the course,
30 High will be the gaiety of the old,
High (is) the horn of travelling,
High the kine in the evening.
High (is) truth when it shines,

Higher when it speaks.
High when came from the cauldron
The three awens of Gogyrwen.
I have been Mynawg, wearing a collar,
With a horn in my hand.
He deserves not the chair
40 That keeps not my word.
With me is the splendid chair,
The inspiration of fluent (and) urgent song.
What the name of the three Caers,
Between the flood and the ebb?
No one knows who is not pressing
The offspring of their president.
Four Caers there are,
In Prydain, stationary,
Chiefs tumultuous.
50 As for what may not be, it will not be.
It will not be, because it may not be.
Let him be a conductor of fleets.
Let the billow cover over the shingle,
That the land becomes ocean,
So that it leaves not the cliffs,
Nor hill nor dale,
Nor the least of shelter,
Against the wind when it shall rage.
The chair of the sovereign
60 He that keeps it is skilful.
Let them be sought there!
Let the munificent be sought.
Warriors lost,

I think in a wrathful manner.
From the destruction of chiefs,
In a butchering manner,
From the loricated Legion,
Arose the Guledig,
Around the old renowned boundary.
70 The sprouting sprigs are broken,
Fragile in like manner.

Fickle and dissolving.
Around the violent borders.
Are the flowing languages.
The briskly-moving stream
Of roving sea-adventurers,
Of the children of Saraphin.
A task deep (and) pure
To liberate Elphin.

VII. BLACK BOOK OF CAERMARTHEN XXXI.

WHAT man is the porter?
Glewlwyd Gavaelvawr.
Who is the man that asks it?
Arthur and the fair Cai.
How goes it with thee?
Truly in the best way in the world.
Into my house thou shalt not come,
Unless thou prevailest,
I forbid it.
10 Thou shalt see it.
If Wythnaint were to go,
The three would be unlucky:--
Mabon, the, son of Mydron,
The servant of Uthir Pendragon;
Cysgaint, the son of Banon;
And Gwyn Godybrion.
Terrible were my servants
Defending their rights.
Manawydan, the son of Llyr,
20 Deep was his counsel.
Did not Manawyd bring
Perforated shields from Trywruid?
And Mabon, the son of Mellt,
Spotted the grass with blood?
And Anwas Adeiniog,
And Llwch Llawynnog--
Guardians were they
On Eiddyn Cymminog,
A chieftain that patronised them.
30 He would have his will and make
redress.
Cai entreated him,
While he idled every third person.
When Celli was lost

Cuelli was found; and rejoiced
Cai, as long as he hewed down.
Arthur distributed gifts,
The blood trickled down.
In the hall of Awarnach,
Fighting with a hag,
40 He cleft the head of Palach.
In the fastnesses of Dissethach,
In Mynyd Eiddyn,
He contended with Cynvyn;
By the hundred there they fell,
There they fell by the hundred,
Before the accomplished Bedwyr.
On the strands of Trywruid,
Contending with Garwlwyd,
Brave was his disposition,
50 With sword and shield;
Vanity were the foremost men
Compared with Cai in the battle.
The sword in the battle
Was unerring in his hand.
They were stanch commanders
Of a legion for the benefit of the coun-
try--
Bedwyr and Bridlaw;
Nine hundred would to them listen;
Six hundred gasping for breath
60 Would be the cost of attacking
them.
Servants I have had,
Better it was when they were.
Before the chiefs of Emrais
I saw Cai in haste.
Booty for chieftains

Was Gwrhir among foes,
Heavy was his vengeance,
Severe his advance.
When he drank from the horn,
70 He would drink with four.
To battle when he would come
By the hundred would he slaughter;
There was no day that would satisfy
him.
Unmerited was the death of Cai.
Cai the fair, and Llachau,
Battles did they sustain,

Before the pang of blue shafts.
In the heights of Ystavingon
Cai pierced nine witches.
80 Cai the fair went to Mona,
To devastate Llewon.
His shield was ready
Against Cath Palug
When the people welcomed him.
Who pierced the Cath Palug?
Nine score before dawn
Would fall for its food.
Nine score chieftains.

VIII. BOOK OF TALIESSIN XXX.

I. I WILL praise the sovereign, supreme king of the land,
Who hath extended his dominion over the shore of the world.
Complete was the prison of Gweir in Caer Sidi,
Through the spite of Pwyll and Pryderi.
No one before him went into it.
The heavy blue chain held the faithful youth,
And before the spoils of Annwvn woefully he sings,
And till doom shall continue a bard of prayer.
Thrice enough to fill Prydwen, we went into it;
Except seven, none returned from Caer Sidi.
II. Am I not a candidate for fame, if a song is heard?
In Caer Pedryvan, four its revolutions;
In the first word from the cauldron when spoken,
From the breath of nine maidens it was gently warmed.
Is it not the cauldron of the chief of Annwvn? What is its intention?
A ridge about its edge and pearls.
It will not boil the food of a coward, that has not been sworn,
A sword bright gleaming to him was raised,
And in the hand of Lleminawg it was left.
And before the door of the gate of Uffern the lamp was burning.
And when we went with Arthur, a splendid labour,
Except seven, none returned from Caer Vedwyd.
III. Am I not a candidate for fame with the listened song
In Caer Pedryvan, in the isle of the strong door?
The twilight and pitchy darkness were mixed together.
Bright wine their liquor before their retinue.
Thrice enough to fill Prydwen we went on the sea,
Except seven, none returned from Caer Rigor.
IV. I shall not deserve much from the ruler of literature,
Beyond Caer Wydyr they saw not the prowess of Arthur.

Three score Canhwr stood on the wall,
Difficult was a conversation with its sentinel.
Thrice enough to fill Prydwen there went with Arthur,
Except seven, none returned from Caer Golud.
V. I shall not deserve much from those with long shields.
They know not what day, who the causer,
What hour in the serene day Cwy was born.
Who caused that he should not go to the dales of Devwy.
They know not the brindled ox, thick his head-band.
Seven score knobs in his collar.
And when we went with Arthur, of anxious memory,
Except seven, none returned from Caer Vandwy.
VI. I shall not deserve much from those of loose bias,
They know not what day the chief was caused.
What hour in the serene day the owner was born.
What animal they keep, silver its head.
When we went with Arthur of anxious contention,
Except seven, none returned from Caer Ochren.
VII. Monks congregate like dogs in a kennel,
From contact with their superiors they acquire knowledge,
Is one the course of the wind, is one the water of the sea?
Is one the spark of the fire, of unrestrainable tumult?
Monks congregate like wolves,
From contact with their superiors they acquire knowledge.
They know not when the deep night and dawn divide.
Nor what is the course of the wind, or who agitates it,
In what place it dies away, on what land it roars.
The grave of the saint is vanishing from the altar-tomb.
I will pray to the Lord, the great supreme,
That I be not wretched. Christ be my portion.

IX. GERAINT, SON OF ERBIN. - BLACK BOOK OF CAERMARTHEN XXII. - RED BOOK OF HERGEST XIV.

I. BEFORE Geraint, the enemy of oppression,
I saw white horses jaded and gory,
And after the shout, a terrible resistance.
II. Before Geraint, the unflinching foe,
I saw horses jaded and gory from the battle,
And after the shout, a terrible impulsion.
III. Before Geraint, the enemy of tyranny,
I saw horses white with foam,
And after the shout, a terrible torrent.

IV. In Llongborth I saw the rage of slaughter,
And biers beyond all number,
And red-stained men from the assault of Geraint.
V. In Llongborth I saw the edges of blades in contact,
Men in terror, and blood on the pate,
Before Geraint, the great son of his father.
VI. In Llongborth I saw the spurs
Of men who would not flinch from the dread of the spears,
And the drinking of wine out of the bright glass.
VII. In Llongborth I saw the weapons
Of men, and blood fast dropping,
And after the shout, a fearful return.
VIII. In Llongborth I saw Arthur,
And brave men who hewed down with steel,
Emperor, and conductor of the toll.
IX. In Llongborth Geraint was slain,
A brave man from the region of Dyvnaint,
And before they were overpowered, they committed slaughter.
X. Under the thigh of Geraint were swift racers,
Long-legged, with wheat for their corn,
Ruddy ones, with. the assault of spotted eagles.
XI. Under the thigh of Geraint were swift racers,
Long their legs, grain was given them,
Ruddy ones, with the assault of black eagles.
XII. Under the thigh of Geraint were swift racers,
Long-legged, restless over their grain,
Ruddy ones, with the assault of red eagles.
XIII. Under the thigh of Geraint were swift racers,
Long-legged, grain-scattering,
Ruddy ones, with the assault of white eagles.
XIV. Under the thigh of Geraint were swift racers,
Long-legged, with the pace of the stag,
With a nose like that of the consuming fire on a wild mountain.
XV. Under the thigh of Geraint were swift racers,
Long-legged, satiated with grain,
Grey ones, with their manes tipped with silver.
XVI. Under the thigh of Geraint were swift racers,
Long-legged, well deserving of grain,
Ruddy ones, with the assault of grey eagles.
XVII. Under the thigh of Geraint were swift racers,
Long-legged, having corn for food,
Ruddy ones, with the assault of brown eagles.
XVII. When Geraint was born, open were the gates of heaven,
Christ granted what was asked,
Beautiful the appearance of glorious Prydain.

C. Poems Referring to Gwydyon Ap Don and His Gwyddyl and the Brithwyr

X. DARONWY. - BOOK OF TALIESSIN X.

GOD preserve the heavens
From a flood wide spreading.
The first surging billow
Has rolled over the sea-beach.
What tree is greater
Than he, Daronwy?
I know not for a refuge
Around the proud circle of heaven,
That there is a mystery which is greater.
10 The light of the men of Goronwy.
Perhaps it may be known,
The magic wand of Mathonwy,
In the wood when it grows.
Fruits more profitable,
On the bank of Gwyllyonwy.
Cynan shall obtain it,
At the time when he governs.
There will come yet
Over the ebb and over the strand,
20 Four chief sovereignties,
And the fifth not worse.
Men vehement, extensive.
Over Prydain (their) purpose.
Women shall be eloquent,
Strangers shall be captive,
A torrent of longing
For mead and horsemanship.
There will come two ladies,
A widow, and a slender single one;
30 Iron their wings,
On warriors brooding.

Chieftains will come,
From about the land of Rome.
Their song will harmonise,
Their praise will spread abroad.
The nature of the oak and thorns
In song will harmonise.
A dog to draw,
A horse to move.
40 An ox to gore; a sow to turn up.
The fifth fair young beast Jesus made
From the apparel of Adam to proceed.
The foliage of trees, fair to behold them,
Whilst they were, and whilst it was.
When the Cymry shall commit transgressions,
A foreigner will be found, who will love what was?
I have leaped a leap from a clear leap,
Good has been dispersed abroad, if a person finds no evil.
The funeral-pile of Run, it is an expiation,
50 Between Caer Rian and Caer Rywg,
Between Dineiddyn and Dineiddwg
A clear glance and a watchful sight.
From the agitation of fire smoke will be raised,
And God our Creator will defend us.

XI. THE PRAISE` OF LLUDD THE GREAT - BOOK OF TALIESSIN LII.

THE best song they will dispraise,
Eight numbers they will protect,
Monday, they will come,
Devastating they will go.

Tuesday, they will portion
Anger against the adversary.
Wednesday, they will reap.
Pomp in excess.

Thursday, they will part with
10 The undesired possessor.
Friday, a day of abundance.
In the blood of men they will swim.
Saturday
Sunday, certainly,
Assuredly there will come
Five ships and five hundred
That make supplication--
  O Brithi, Brithi!
  Co-occupancy or battle.
  20 *Brithi, Brithanai!*
  Before battle, battle of spears in the
field.
Son of the wood of Cogni,
There will be an adventuring of
Everyone to Adonai.
On the sward of Pwmpai.
An intimation they prophesy,
A long cry against overwhelming,
Long the public harmony
Of Cadwaladyr and Cynan.
30 The world's profit (is) small,
The heat of the sun is lost.
The Druid will prophesy
What has been will be.
Sky of Geirionydd,
I would go with thee
Gloomy like the evening,
In the recesses of the mountain.
When should be the full length
The Brython in chasing.
40 To the Brython there will be
Blood of glorious strenuousness,
After gold and golden trinkets.
The devastation of Moni and Lleeni,
And Eryri, a dwelling in it.
It is a perfect prophecy,
With dwellings laid waste.
The Cymry of four languages
Shall change their speech.
Until shall come the cow, the speck-
led cow
50 That shall cause a blessing
On a fine day lowing,
On a fine night being boiled,
On the land of the boiler,
In the ships of the consumer.
Let the song of woe be chaunted.
Around the encircling border of
Prydain.
They will come, with one purpose,
To resist a maritime disgrace.
Be true the happiness
60 Of the sovereign of the world.
The worshippers adored together,
To the dale of grievous water it was
gone.
A portion full of corn
Invites conflagration.
Without Eppa, without a cow-stall.
Without a luxury of the world.
The world will be desolate, useless.
The deceitful will be fated.
Activity through freshness.
70 Small men are almost deceived
By the white-bellied trotter.
A hawk upon baptism
The swords of warriors will not
pierce Cyllellawr.
They had not what they wished for.
Violent is the grasp of the townman,
And to warriors there is a love of
blood.
Cymry, Angles, Gwyddyl, of Prydyn.
The Cymry, swift in mischief,
Will launch their ships on the lake.
80 The North has been poisoned by
rovers
Of a livid hateful hue and form.
Of the race of Adam the ancient.
The third will be brought to set out,
Ravens of the accurate retinue,
The sluggish animals of Seithin.
On sea, an anchor on the Christian.
A cry from the sea, a cry from the
mountain,
A cry from the sea, they vigorously
utter.
Wood, field, dale, and hill.

90 Every speech without any one attending,
High minded from every place
There will be confusion.
A multitude enraged,
And distress diffused
Vengeances through ready belief abiding.
That the Creator afflicts, the powerful God of exalted state.
A long time before the day of doom.
There will come a day
And a reader will rise,
100 In the pleasant border of the land of Iwerdon,
To Prydain then will come exaltation,
Brython of the nobility of Rome.
There will be to me a judge unprejudiced, void of guile;
The astrologers (or diviners) prophesy,

In the land of the lost ones.
Druids prophesy
Beyond the sea, beyond the Brython.
The summer will not be serene weather,
The noblemen shall be broken,
110 It will come to them from treachery
Beyond the effusion of the father of Ked.
A thousand in the judgment of exalted Prydain,
And within its united boundary.
May I not fall into the embrace of the swamp,
Into the mob that peoples the depths of Uffern.
I greatly fear the flinty covering
With the Guledig of the boundless country.

XII. - BOOK OF TALIESSIN XIV.

I WILL adore the love-diffusing Lord of every kindred,
The sovereign of hosts manifestly round the universe.
A battle at the feast over joyless beverage,
A battle against the sons of Llyr in Ebyr Henvelen.
I saw the oppression of the tumult, and wrath and tribulation,
The blades gleamed on the glittering helmets,
A battle against the lord of fame, in the dales of the Severn,
Against Brochwel of Powys, that loved my Awen.
A battle in the pleasant course early against Urien,
10 There falls about our feet blood on destruction.
Shall not my chair be defended from the cauldron of Ceridwen?
May my tongue be free in the sanctuary of the praise of Gogyrwen.
The praise of Gogyrwen is an oblation, which has satisfied
Them, with milk, and dew, and acorns.
Let us consider deeply before is heard confession,
That is coming assuredly death nearer and nearer.
And round the lands of Enlli the Dyvi has poured,
Raising the ships on the surface of the plain.
And let us call upon him that hath made us,
20 That he may protect us from the wrath of the alien nation.
When the isle of Mona shall be called a pleasant field,

Happy they the mild ones, the affliction of the Saxons.
I came to Deganwy to contend
With Maelgwn, the greatest in delinquencies,
I liberated my lord in the presence of the distributor,
Elphin, the sovereign of greatly aspiring ones.
There are to me three chairs regular, accordant,
And until doom they will continue with the singers.
I have been in the battle of Godeu, with Lleu and Gwydion,
30 The changed the form of the elementary trees and sedges.
I have been with Bran in Iwerdon.
I saw when was killed Morddwydtyllon.
I heard a meeting about the minstrels,
With the Gwyddyl, devils, distillers.
From Penryn Wleth to Loch Reon
The Cymry are of one mind, bold heroes.
Deliver thou the Cymry in tribulation.
Three races, cruel from true disposition,
Gwyddyl, and Brython, and Romani,
40 Create discord and confusion.
And about the boundary of Prydain, beautiful its towns,
There is a battle against chiefs above the mead-vessels,
In the festivals of the Distributor, who bestowed gifts upon me.
The chief astrologers received wonderful gifts.
Complete is my chair in Caer Sidi,
No one will be afflicted with disease or old age that may be in it.
It is known to Manawyd and Pryderi.
Three utterances, around the fire, will he sing before it,
And around its borders are the streams of the ocean.
50 And the fruitful fountain is above it,
Is sweeter than white wine the liquor therein.
And when I shall have worshipped thee, Most High, before the sod
May I be found in covenant with thee.

XIII. THE BATTLE OF GODEU - BOOK OF TALIESSIN VIII.

I HAVE been in a multitude of shapes,
Before I assumed a consistent form.
I have been a sword, narrow, varie-
gated,
I will believe when it is apparent.
I have been a tear in the air,
I have been the dullest of stars.
I have been a word among letters,
I have been a book in the origin.
I have been the light of lanterns
10 A year and a half.
I have been a continuing bridge,
Over three score Abers.
I have been a course, I have been an
eagle.
I have been a coracle in the seas:
I have been compliant in the banquet.
I have been a drop in a shower;
I have been a sword in the grasp of
the hand:

142

I have been a shield in battle.
I have been a string in a harp,
20 Disguised for nine years.
In water, in foam.
I have been sponge in the fire,
I have been wood in the covert.
I am not he who will not sing of
A combat though small,
The conflict in the battle of Godeu of sprigs.
Against the Guledig of Prydain,
There passed central horses,
Fleets full of riches.
30 There passed an animal with wide jaws,
On it there were a hundred heads.
And a battle was contested
Under the root of his tongue;
And another battle there is
In his *occiput*.
A black sprawling toad,
With a hundred claws on it.
A snake speckled, crested.
A hundred souls through sin
40 Shall be tormented in its flesh.
I have been in Caer Vevenir,
Thither hastened grass and trees,
Minstrels were singing,
Warrior-bands were wondering,
At the exaltation of the Brython,
That Gwydyon effected.
There was a calling on the Creator,
Upon Christ for causes,
Until when the Eternal
50 Should deliver those whom he had made.
The Lord answered them,
Through language and elements:
Take the forms of the principal trees,
Arranging yourselves in battle array,
And restraining the public.
Inexperienced in battle hand to band.
When the trees were enchanted,
In the expectation of not being trees,
The trees uttered their voices

60 From strings of harmony,
The disputes ceased.
Let us cut short heavy days,
A female restrained the din.
She came forth altogether lovely.
The head of the line, the head was a female.
The advantage of a sleepless cow
Would not make us give way.
The blood of men up to our thighs,
The greatest of importunate mental exertions
70 Sported in the world.
And one has ended
From considering the deluge,
And Christ crucified,
And the day of judgment near at hand.
The alder-trees, the head of the line,
Formed the van.
The willows and quicken-trees
Came late to the army.
Plum-trees, that are scarce,
80 Unlonged for of men.
The elaborate medlar-trees,
The objects of contention.
The prickly rose-bushes,
Against a host of giants,
The raspberry brake did
What is better failed
For the security of life.
Privet and woodbine
And ivy on its front,
90 Like furze to the combat
The cherry-tree was provoked.
The birch, notwithstanding his high mind,
Was late before he was arrayed.
Not because of his cowardice,
But on account of his greatness.
The laburnum held in mind,
That your wild nature was foreign.
Pine-trees in the porch,
The chair of disputation,
100 By me greatly exalted,

143

In the presence of kings.
The elm with his retinue,
Did not go aside a foot;
He would fight with the centre,
And the flanks, and the rear.
Hazel-trees, it was judged
That ample was thy mental exertion.
The privet, happy his lot,
The bull of battle, the lord of the world.
110 Morawg and Morydd
Were made prosperous in pines.
Holly, it was tinted with green,
He was the hero.
The hawthorn, surrounded by prickles,
With pain at his hand.
The aspen-wood has been topped,
It was topped in battle.
The fern that was plundered.
The broom, in the van of the army,
120 In the trenches he was hurt.
The gorse did not do well,
Notwithstanding let it overspread.
The heath was victorious, keeping off on all sides.
The common people were charmed,
During the proceeding of the men.
The oak, quickly moving,
Before him, tremble heaven and earth.
A valiant door-keeper against an enemy,
His name is considered.
130 The blue-bells combined,
And caused a consternation.
In rejecting, were rejected,
Others, that were perforated.
Pear-trees, the best intruders
In the conflict of the plain.
A very wrathful wood,
The chestnut is bashful,
The opponent of happiness,
The jet has become black,
140 The mountain has become crooked,
The woods have become a kiln,
Existing formerly in the great seas,
Since was heard the shout:--
The tops of the birch covered us with leaves,
And transformed us, and changed our faded state.
The branches of the oak have ensnared us
From the Gwarchan of Maelderw.
Laughing on the side of the rock,
The lord is not of an ardent nature.
150 Not of mother and father,
When I was made,
Did my Creator create me.
Of nine-formed faculties,
Of the fruit of fruits,
Of the fruit of the primordial God,
Of primroses and blossoms of the hill,
Of the flowers of trees and shrubs.
Of earth, of an earthly course,
When I was formed.
160 Of the flower of nettles,
Of the water of the ninth wave.
I was enchanted by Math,
Before I became immortal,
I was enchanted by Gwydyon
The great purifier of the Brython,
Of Eurwys, of Euron,
Of Euron, of Modron.
Of five battalions of scientific ones,
Teachers, children of Math.
170 When the removal occurred,
I was enchanted by the Guledig.
When he was half-burnt,
I was enchanted by the sage
Of sages, in the primitive world.
When I had a being;
When the host of the world was in dignity,
The bard was accustomed to benefits.
To the song of praise I am inclined,
which the tongue recites.
I played in the twilight,

180 I slept in purple;
I was truly in the enchantment
With Dylan, the son of the wave.
In the circumference, in the middle,
Between the knees of kings,
Scattering spears not keen,
From heaven when came,
To the great deep, floods,
In the battle there will be
Four score hundreds,
190 That will divide according to
their will.
They are neither older nor younger,
Than myself in their divisions.
A wonder, Canhwr arc born, every
one of nine hundred.
He was with me also,
With my sword spotted with blood.
Honour was allotted to me
By the Lord, and protection (was)
where he was.
If I come to where the boar was
killed,
He will compose, he will decompose,
200 He will form languages.
The strong-handed gleamer, his
name,
With a gleam he rules his numbers.
They would spread out in a flame,
When I shall go on high.
I have been a speckled snake on the
hill,
I have been a viper in the Llyn.
I have been a bill-hook crooked that
cuts,
I have been a ferocious spear
With my chasuble and bowl
210 I will prophesy not badly,
Four score smokes

On every one what will bring.
Five battalions of arms
Will be caught by my knife.
Six steeds of yellow hue
A hundred times better is
My cream-coloured steed,
Swift as the sea-mew
Which will not pass
220 Between the sea and the shore.
Am I not pre-eminent in the field of
blood?
Over it are a hundred chieftains.
Crimson (is) the gem of my belt,
Gold my shield border.
There has not been born, in the gap,
That has been visiting me,
Except Goronwy,
From the dales of Edrywy.
Long white my fingers,
230 It is long since I have been a
herdsman.
I travelled in the earth,
Before I was a proficient in learning.
I travelled, I made a circuit,
I slept in a hundred islands.
A hundred Caers I have dwelt in.
Ye intelligent Druids,
Declare to Arthur,
What is there more early
Than I that they sing of.
240 And one is come
From considering the deluge,
And Christ crucified,
And the day of future doom.
A golden gem in a golden jewel.
I am splendid
And shall be wanton
From the oppression of the metal-
workers.

XIV. BOOK OF TALIESSIN I. RED BOOK OF HERGEST XXIII.

PRIMITIVE and ingenious address,
when thoroughly elucidated.
Which was first, is it darkness, is it
light?
Or Adam, when he existed, on what
day was he created?

145

Or under the earth's surface, what the foundation?
He who is a legionary will receive no instruction.
Est qui peccator in many things,
Will lose the heavenly country, the community of priests.
In the morning no one comes
If they sing of three spheres.
10 Angles and Gallwydel,
Let them make their way.
Whence come night and day?
Whence will the eagle become gray?
Whence is it that night is dark?
Whence is it that the linnet is green?
The ebullition of the sea,
How is it not seen?
There are three fountains
In the mountain of roses,
20 There is a Caer of defence
Under the ocean's wave.
Illusive greeter,
What is the porter's name?
Who was confessor
To the gracious Son of Mary?
What was the most beneficial measure
Which Adam accomplished?
Who will measure Uffern?
How thick its veil?
30 How wide its mouth?
What the size of its stones?
Or the tops of its whirling trees?
Who bends them so crooked?
Or what fumes may be
About their stems?
Is it Lleu and Gwydyon
That perform their arts?
Or do they know books
When they do?
40 Whence come night and flood?
How they disappear?
Whither flies night from day;
And how is it not seen?
Pater noster ambulo

Gentis tonans in adjuvando
Sibilem signum
Rogantes fortium.
Excellent in every way around the glens
The two skilful ones make inquiries
50 About Caer Cerindan Cerindydd
For the draught-horses of pector David.
They have enjoyment--they move about--
May they find me greatly expanding.
The Cymry will be lamenting
While their souls will be tried
Before a horde of ravagers.
The Cymry, chief wicked ones,
On account of the loss of holy wafers.
There will long be crying and wailing,
60 And gore will be conspicuous.
There came by sea
The wood-steeds of the strand.
The Angles in council
Shall see signs of
Exultation over Saxons.
The praises of the rulers
Will be celebrated in Sion.
Let the chief builders be
Against the fierce Ffichti,
70 The Morini Brython.
Their fate has been predicted;
And the reaping of heroes
About the river Severn.
The stealing is disguised of Ken and Masswy
Ffis amala, ffur, ffir, sel,
Thou wilt discern the Trinity beyond my age
I implore the Creator, hai
Huai, that the Gentile may vanish
From the Gospel. Equally worthy
80 With the retinue of the wall
Cornu ameni dur.
I have been with skilful men,
With Matheu and Govannon,
With Eunydd and Elestron,

In company with Achwyson,
For a year in Caer Gofannon.
I am old. I am young. I am Gwion,
I am universal, I am possessed of penetrating wit.
Thou wilt remember thy old Brython
90 (And) the Gwyddyl, kiln distillers,
Intoxicating the drunkards.
I am a bard; I will not disclose secrets to slaves;
I am a guide: I am expert in contests.
If he would sow, he would plough; he would plough, he would not reap.
If a brother among brothers,
Didactic Bards with swelling breasts will arise
Who will meet around mead-vessels,
And sing wrong poetry
And seek rewards that will not be,
100 Without law, without regulation, without gifts.
And afterwards will become angry.
There will be commotions and turbulent times,
Seek no peace--it will not accrue to thee.
The Ruler of Heaven knows thy prayer.
From his ardent wrath thy praise has propitiated hint
The Sovereign King of Glory addresses me with wisdom:--
Hast thou seen the dominus fortis?
Knowest thou the profound prediction domini?
To the advantage of Uffern
110 Hic nemo in por progenie
He has liberated its tumultuous multitude.
Dominus virtutum
Has gathered together those that were in slavery,
And before I existed He had perceived me.
May I be ardently devoted to God!
And before I desire the end of existence,
And before the broken foam shall come upon my lips,
And before I become connected with wooden boards,
May there be festivals to my soul!
120 Book-learning scarcely tells me
Of severe afflictions after death-bed
And such as have heard my bardic books
They shall obtain the region of heaven, the best of all abodes.

XV. DEATH-SONG OF DYLAN SON OF THE WAVE. BOOK OF TALIESSIN XLIII.

ONE God Supreme, divine, the wisest, the greatest his habitation
When he came to the field, who charmed him in the hand of the extremely liberal.
Or sooner than he, who was on peace on the nature of a turn.
An opposing groom, poison made, a wrathful deed,
Piercing Dylan, a mischievous shore, violence freely flowing.
Wave of Iwerdon, and wave of Manau, and wave of the North,
And wave of Prydain, hosts comely in fours.
I will adore the Father God, the regulator of the country, without refusing.
The Creator of Heaven, may he admit us into mercy.

HORSEMAN resorts to the city,
With his white dogs, and large horns;
I, who have not before seen thee,
know thee not.
II. A horseman resorts to the river's
mouth,
On a stout and warlike steed;
Come with me, let me not be refused.
III. I will not go that way at present;
Bear with the conduct of the delayer;
And may the blessing of heaven and
earth come (upon thee).
IV, Thou, who hast not seen me daily,
And who resemblest a prudent man,
How long wilt thou absent thyself,
and when wilt thou come?
V. When I return from Caer Seon,
From contending with Jews,
I will come to the city of Lleu and
Gwidion.
VI. Come with me into the city,
Thou shalt have wine which I have
set apart,
And pure gold on thy clasp.
VII. I know not the confident man,
Who owns a fire and a couch;
Fairly and sweetly dost thou speak.
VIII. Come with me to my dwelling,
Thou shalt have high foaming wine.
My name is Ugnach, the son of Myd-
no.
IX. Ugnach! a blessing on thy throne!
And mayst thou have grace and hon-
our!
I am Taliessin who will repay thee
thy banquet.
X. Taliessin, chief of men.
Victor in the contest of song,
Remain here until Wednesday.
XI. Ugnach! the most affluent in rich-
es,
Grace be to thee from the highest re-
gion;
I will not deserve blame; I will not
tarry.

HOW miserable it is to see
Tumult, commotion,
Wounds and confusion,
The Brithwyr in motion,
And a cruel fate.
With the impulse of destiny,
And for heaven's sake
Declare the discontinuance of the
disaster!
It is not well that a son should be
born:
10 His youthful destiny
Will necessarily be unbelief
And general privation:--
The Lloegrians declare it.
Alas! for the utter confusion
Until the end of the seventh
From the hard Calends.
True it is, deliverance will come
By means of the wished-for man.
May he throw open the White Mount,
20 And into Gwynedd make his entry!
The forces of the Cymry
Will be of one course with the light-
ning:
The signal of their deliverance
Will be a true relief, to the bosom:
The guarantee being Reged,
Whose share will be glorious.
Glorious will be our portion.
To me has been given sway,
I have become a predicting bard:
30 Camlan will be heard again
Scenes of groaning will again be seen,
And dismal lamentations,
And mischievous contention,

And the child will grow
Strong in battle, even when small.
People will see battles,
And the increase of fortresses;
Many a banner will be shattered:
A red banner I know there is,
40 It will be death to vanquish it
A signal of their coming,--
The heroic warriors,
Who will defend their fame.
Active their swords before thee,
Before me their virtues.
They shall receive their portion be-
fore death.
The day of causing blood-streams,
The day of assailing walls,
Will come for certain,

50 And fleets on the water,
Neither tax nor tribute
Nor service will succeed,
Nor the entreaties of the weak will
avail,
Under the sway of the rulers.
May hens be relics
From Mona to Mynneu!
Believe in the living God for benefits,
Who will dispense us free blessings.
By imploring saints,
60 And the thorough comprehension
of books,
May we obtain, an Thursday, a, por-
tion
In the blissful region, the splendid
place of rest!

D. Poem Referring to Gwyddno and Gwynn Ap Nudd

XVIII. BLACK BOOK OF CAERMARTHEN XXXIII.

I, BULL of conflict was he, active in dispersing an arrayed army,
The ruler of hosts, indisposed to anger,
Blameless and pure his conduct in protecting life.
II. Against a hero stout was his advance,
The ruler of hosts, disposer of wrath.
There will be protection for thee since thou askest it.
III. For thou hast given me protection
How warmly wert thou welcomed!
The hero of hosts, from what region thou comest?
IV. I come from battle and conflict
With a shield in my hand;
Broken is the helmet by the pushing of spears.
V. I will address thee, exalted man,
With his shield in distress;
Brave man, what is thy descent?

VI. Round-hoofed is my horse, the torment of battle,
"Whilst I am called Gwyn, the son of Nud,
The lover of Creurdilad, the daughter of Llud.
VII. Since it is thou, Gwyn, an upright man,
From thee there is no concealing;
I also am Gwydneu Garanhir.
VIII. He will not leave me in a parley with thee,
By the bridle, as is becoming;
But will hasten away to his home on the Tawy.
IX. It is not the nearest Tawy I speak of to thee,
But the furthest Tawy;
Eagle! I will cause the furious sea to ebb.
X. Polished is my ring, golden my saddle and bright:

To my sadness
I saw a conflict before Caer Vandwy.
XI. Before Caer Vandwy a host I saw,
Shields were shattered and ribs broken
Renowned and splendid was he who made the assault.
XII. Gwyn ab Nud, the hope of armies,
Sooner would legions fall before the hoofs
of thy horses, than broken rushes to the ground.
XIII. Handsome my dog and round-bodied,
And truly the best of dogs;
Dormach was he, which belonged to Maelgwn.
XIV Dormach with the ruddy nose! what a gazer
Thou art upon me! because I notice
Thy wanderings on Gwibir Vynyd.
XV. I have been in the place where was killed Gwondoleu,
The son of Ceidaw, the pillar of songs,
When the ravens screamed over blood.
XVI. I have been in the place where Bran was killed,
The son of Gweryd, of far-extending fame,
When the ravens of the battle-field screamed.
XVII. I have been where Llachau was slain,
The son of Arthur, extolled in songs,
When the ravens screamed over blood.
XVIII. I have been where Meurig was killed,
The son of Carreian, of honourable fame,
When the ravens screamed over flesh.
XIX. I have not been where Gwallawg was killed,
The son of Goholeth, the accomplished,.
The resister of Lloegir, the son of Lleynawg.
XX. I have been where the soldiers of Prydain were slain,
From the East to the North;
I am alive, they in their graves!
XXI. I have been where the soldiers of Prydain were slain,
From the East to the South
I am alive, they in death!

E. Poems Referring to Early Traditions Which Belong to a Later School

XIX. THE CHAIR OF CERIDWEN - BOOK OF TALIESSIN XVI.

SOVEREIGN of the power of the air, thou also
The satisfaction of my transgressions.
At midnight and at matins
There shone my lights.
Courteous the life of Minawg ap Llen,
Whom I saw here a short while ago.
The end, in the slope of Lleu.
Ardent was his push in combats;
Avagddu my son also.
10 Happy the Lord made him,
In the competition of songs,
His wisdom was better than mine,
The most skilful man ever heard of.
Gwydyon ap Don, of toiling spirits,
Enchanted a woman from blossoms,
And brought pigs from the south.
Since he had no sheltering cots,

Rapid curves, and plaited chains.
He made the forms of horses
20 From the springing
Plants, and illustrious saddles.
When are judged the chairs,
Excelling them (will be) mine,
My chair, my cauldron, and my laws,
And my pervading eloquence, meet
for the chair.
I am called skilful in the court of Don.
I, and Euronwy, and Euron.
I saw a fierce conflict in Nant
Frangeon
On a Sunday, at the time of dawn,
30 Between the bird of wrath and
Gwydyon.
Thursday, certainly, they went to
Mona
To obtain whirlings and sorcerers.

Arianrod, of laudable aspect, dawn of
serenity,
The greatest disgrace evidently on
the side of the Brython,
Hastily sends about his court the
stream of a rainbow,
A stream that scares away violence
from the earth.
The poison of its former state, about
the world, it will leave.
They speak not falsely, the books of
Beda.
The chair of the Preserver is here.
40 And till doom, shall continue in
Europa.
May the Trinity grant us
Mercy in the day of judgment.
A fair alms from good men.

XX. THE DEATH-SONG OF UTHYR PENDRAGON - BOOK OF TALIESSIN XLVIII.

AM I not with hosts making a din?
I would not cease, between two hosts, without gore.
Am I not he that is called Gorlassar?
My belt was a rainbow to my foe.
Am I not a prince, in darkness,
(To him) that takes my appearance with my two chief baskets?
Am I not, like Cawyl, ploughing?
I would not cease without gore between two hosts.
Is it not I that will defend my sanctuary?
10 In separating with the friends of wrath.
Have I not been accustomed to blood about the wrathful,
A sword-stroke daring against the sons of Cawrnur?
Have I not shared my cause.
A ninth portion in the prowess of Arthur?
Is it not I that have destroyed a hundred Caers?
Is it not I that slew a hundred governors?
Is it not I that have given a hundred veils?
Is it not I that cut off a hundred heads?
Is it not I that gave to Henpen
20 The tremendous sword of the enchanter?
Is it not I that performed the rights of purification,
When Hayarndor went to the top of the mountain?

I was bereaved to my sorrow. My confidence was commensurate.
There was not a world were it not for my progeny.
I am a bard to be praised. The unskilful
May he be possessed by the ravens and eagle and bird of wrath.
Avagddu came to him with his equal,
When the bands of four men feed between two plains,
Abiding in heaven was he, my desire,
30 Against the eagle, against the fear of the unskilful.
I am a bard, and I am a harper,
I am a piper, and I am a crowder.
Of seven score musicians the very great
Enchanter. There was of the enamelled honour the privilege,
Hu of the expanded wings.
Thy son, thy barded proclamation,
Thy steward, of a gifted father.
MY tongue to recite my death-song.
If of stone-work the opposing wall of the world.
40 May the countenance of Prydain be bright for my guidance,
Sovereign of heaven, let my messages not be rejected.

XXI. BOOK OF TALIESSIN XLV.

DISTURBED is the isle of the praise of Hu, the isle of the severe recompenser
Mona of the good bowls, of active manliness. The Menei its door.
I have drunk liquor of wine and bragget, from a brother departed.
The universal sovereign, the end of every king, the ruinator.
Sorrowful (is) the Dean, since the Archdeacon is interred.
There has not been, there will not be in tribulation his equal.
When Aeddon came from the country of Gwydyon, the thickly coveted Seon.
A pure poison came four nightly fine-night seasons.
The contemporaries fell, the woods were no shelter against the wind on the coast.
10 Math and Eunyd, skilful with the magic wand, freed the elements.
In the life of Gwydyon and Amaethon, there was counsel.
Pierced (is) the front of the shield of the strong, fortunate, strong irresistibly.
The powerful combination of his front rank, it was not of great account
Strong (in) feasting; in every assembly his will was done.
Beloved he went first; while I am alive, he shall be commemorated.
May I be with Christ, so that I may not be sorrowful, when an apostle,
The generous Archdeacon amongst angels may he be contained.
Disturbed (is) the isle of the praise of Hu, the isle of the severe ruler.
Before the victorious youth, the fortress of the Cymry remained tranquil.
20 The dragon chief, a rightful proprietor in Britonia.
A sovereign is gone, alas! the chief that is gone to the earth.
Four damsels, after their lamentation, performed their office.

Very grievous truly on sea, without land, long their dwelling,
On account of his integrity (it was) that they were not satiated with distress.
I am blameable if I mention not his good actions.
In the place of Llywy, who shall prohibit, who shall order?
In the place of Aeddon, who shall support Mona's gentle authorities?
May I be with Christ, that I may not be sorrowful, for evil or good.
Share of mercy in the country of the governor of perfect life.

XXII - THE PRAISE OF TALIESSIN - BOOK OF TALIESSIN XII.

MESSENGERS to me are come, so numerously are they sent,
We shall bring a mutual conflict, so great is my bosom.
Like the effect of the oar in the brine is the liquor of Beli,
Like a light shield on the back of a shadow.
Like wrath and indignation from the protection
Of a Caer, and nine hundred governors became dead.
There will be a battle on Menei, a vehement retribution.
There will be more on Conwy, the scar of angry strife shall cause it
Cold death the destiny of the ready muse,
10 From the vehement blade by the stroke of Edyrn.
Three elegant unrestrainable, fell, heavily laden with forces,
There fleets in the stream, an omen of the day of gloom.
Three evenings of battle for three proper
Countries: a boat was made a burying place.
Three of every three: three sins
And Eryri a hill of judgment.
A host of Saxons: the second they were, a third affliction.
In Cymry widowhood awaits women.
Before the presence of Cynan fire broke out.
20 Cadwaladyr will bewail him.
He injured the country with pain,
Straw; and roof of houses; the house he burnt.
There will be a wonder.
A man with the daughter of his brother.
They will cite what is steel
Of the lineage of Anarawd.
From him proceeded
Coch, wise his prudence.
He will not spare nor defend
30 Either cousin or brother.
At the voice of the warrior's horn,
Nine hundred (were) anxious,
Of universal affliction.
Thou wilt be calling forth verdancy from affected praise,
It will run to such as is oppressed in bosom.

I. SEITHENHIN, stand thou forth,
And behold the billowy rows;
The sea has covered the plain of Gwydneu.
II. Accursed be the damsel,
Who, after the wailing,
Let loose the Fountain of Venus, the raging deep.
III. Accursed be the maiden,
Who, after the conflict, let loose
The fountain of Venus, the desolating sea.
IV. A great cry from the roaring sea arises above the summit of the rampart,
To-day even to God does the supplication come!
Common after excess there ensues restraint.
V. A cry from the roaring sea overpowers me this night,
And it is not easy to relieve me;
Common after excess succeeds adversity.
VI. A cry from the roaring sea comes upon the winds
The mighty and beneficent God has caused it!
Common after excess is want.
VII. A cry from the roaring sea
Impels me from my resting-place this night;
Common after excess is far-extending destruction.
VIII. The grave of Seithenhin the weak-minded
Between Caer Cenedir and the shore
Of the great sea and Cinran.

F. Poems Relating to Cities of The Cymry and Their Legendary Heroes

XXIV. BLACK BOOK OF CAERMARTHEN XV.

I. DINAS MAON, may God the blessed Sovereign defend it!
What the sun will dry, Edar will moisten.
II. Dinas Maon, the dislike of Sovereigns, where kings were hewed down in the obstinate conflict.
What the sun will dry, Mervin will moisten.
III. Dinas Maon, the security of the country, may the protection of God surround it!
What the sun will dry, Nynaw will moisten.
IV. Mad put his thigh on Merchin the gray steed,
The fort of the brave will defend me.
What the sun will dry, Maelgwn will moisten.

I. I WILL pray God to deliver the people of the fair (town),
The owner of heaven and earth, ill-wise pervader.
A pleasant Caer there is on the surface of the ocean.
May be joyful in the splendid festival its king.
And the time when the sea makes great audacity.
The crowns of bards are usual over mead-vessels.
A wave will come, in haste, speed unto it,
That will bring them to the green sward from the region of the Ffichti.
And may I obtain, O God, for my prayer,
When I keep the covenant of conciliation with thee.
II. A pleasant Caer there is on a broad lake,
A fortress impregnable, the sea surrounds it.
Prydain greets thee: how will these agree?
The point of the lake of the son of Erbin; be thine the oxen.
There has been a retinue, and there has been song, in the second place,
And an eagle, high in the sky, and the path of Granwyn,
Before the governing sovereign, that refuses not to start,
The dispersed of renown, and a leader, they form themselves.
III. A pleasant Caer there is on the ninth wave,
Pleasant its denizens in guarding each other.
They will not take them if it be through disgrace.
It is not their custom to be hard.
I will not speak falsely, upon my privilege,
Than the tenants of the two strands better the serfs of Dyved,
An associate, if he gives a banquet of deliverers,
Will contain between every two the best multitude.
IV. A pleasant Caer there is, it will be made complete
By meads, and praise, and mountain-birds.
Smooth its songs, on its festival,
And my intelligent Lord, a splendid distributor,
Before he went into his grave, in the boundary of the Llan,
He gave me mead and wine from a crystal cup.
V. A pleasant Caer there is on the shore of the gulf,
Pleasantly is given to every one his share.
I know in Dinbych, white with sea-mews,
A mild associate, the lord of Erlysan.
He was my law, on New Year's eve,
His song (was) solace, the king of splendid war.
And a veil of green colour, and possessing a feast.
This may I be, a tongue over the bards of Prydain.
VI. A pleasant Caer there is, that is supported with gifts,
Mine were its fords, should I have chosen.
I will not speak of the progress of the law that I had kept,

He deserves not a New Year's gift that knows not this.
The writing of Prydain, anxious care,
While the waves continue to be agitated about it,
If necessary, far into a cell I would penetrate.
VII. A pleasant Caer there is, rising up,
May we have shares in its meads and praises.
Pleasant on its boundary the sending forth of its chieftains.
A cormorant approaches me, long its wings,
There comes to the top of the scream of the sea-birds.
Wrath within fate, let it penetrate the sands and stones,
And the gray wolf the best of conflicts.
May there be derived from above the banquet accordant reasonings.
The blessing of the beneficent Ruler of Heaven's harmonious heights (be)
Upon them; may He make denizens (there) the worthies of Owain.
VIII. A pleasant Caer there is on the margin of the flood.
Pleasantly is given to every (one) his desire.
Address thou Gwyned, be thine the increase.
The dartings of the terrible spears were poured forth.
Wednesday, I saw men in distress,
Thursday, to their disgrace they returned.
And there were crimsoned hair, and clamorous woe.
Exhausted were the men of Gwyned the day that they came.
And on Cevn Llech Vaelwy shields they will break.
They fell at the Cevn, a host of kinsmen.

XXVI. BLACK BOOK OF CAERMARTHEN VIII.

I. THE three depredatory horses of the Isle of Prydain:--
Carnawlawg, the horse of Owain the son of Urien;
Bucheslwm Seri, the horse of Gwgawn Gleddyvrudd;
And Tavawd hir Breich-hir, the horse of Cadwallawn the son of Cadvan.
II. The three draught-horses of the Isle of Prydain:--
Arvul Melyn, the horse of Pasgen the son of Urien;
Du Hir Terwenydd, the horse of Selyv the son of Cynan Garwyn;
And Drudlwyd, the horse of Rhydderch Hael.
III. The three spirited horses of the Isle of Prydain:--
Gwineu Goddwf Hir, the horse of Cai;
Rhuthr Eon Tuth Blaidd, the horse of Gilbert the son of Cadagyffro;
And Ceincaled, the horse of Gwalchmai.
IV. The three high-mettled horses of the Isle of Prydain:--
Lluagor, the horse of Caradawg;
And Melynlas, the horse of Caswallawn the son of Beli.

IT broke out with matchless fury.
The rapid vehement fire.
Him we praise above the earth,
Fire, the fiery meteor of the dawn.
Above the high gale,
Higher than every cloud.
Great his animal.
He will not delay
Nor the wedding-feast of Llyr.
10. His path is like a water-course,
Thy rage in the chief streams.
The dawn smiles, repelling gloom,
At the dawn with violence,
At every meet season,
At the meet sea-son of his turnings,
At the four stages of his course,
I will extol him that judges violence,
Of the strong din, deep his wrath.
I am not a man, cowardly, gray,
20. A scum, near the wattle.
The illusion of my two relatives,
Two groans of affliction without ap-
petite.
From my hand to thy hand God will
give naught.
Thrice three protections,
Returning to the old places,
With a steed used to the field.
And the steed of Genethawg,
And the steed of Caradawg,
Perfect for travelling.
30. And the steed of Gwythur,
And the steed of Gwarddur,
And the steed of Arthur.
Dauntless to cause an ache,
And the steed of Taliessin,
And the steed of Lleu half domesti-
cated,
And of Pebyr, the dark gray of the
grove.
And Grei, the steed of Cunin.
Cornan stubborn in the conflict,
Of ardent desires,

40. The Black, from the seas famous,
The steed of Brwyn, betrayer of the
country.
And the three cloven-footed ones
They will not go a journey conven-
iently,
The terrible steed of Ceidaw,
A hoof with bribery on it.
Mottle-shouldered Ysgodig
The steed of Llemenig
The horse of Rhydderch Rhyddig
Of the gray colour of a pear.
50. And Llamre, full of inherent vig-
our,
And Froenvoll of a vigorous growth,
The steed of Sadyrnin,
And the steed of Constantine.
And others handling,
For the country, the smart of foreign-
ers.
The good Henwyn brought
A tale from Hiraddug.
I have been a sow, I have been a buck,
I have been a sage, I have been a
snout,
60. I have been a horn, I have been a
wild sow,
I have been a shout in battle.
I have been a torrent on the slope,
I have been a wave on the extended
shore.
I have been the light sprinkling of a
deluge,
I have been a cat with a speckled
head on three trees.
I have been a circumference, I have
been a head.
A goat on an elder-tree.
I have been a crane well filled, a sight
to behold.
Very ardent the animals of Morial,
70. They kept a good stock.
Of what is below the air, say the hate-

ful men,
Too many do not live, of those-that

know me.

XXIX. THE VERSES OF THE GRAVES. - BLACK BOOK OF CAERMARTHEN XIX.

I. THE graves which the rain bedews?
Men that were not accustomed to afflict me:-
Cerwyd, and Cywryd, and Caw.
II. The graves which the thicket covers?
They would not succumb without avenging themselves:
Gwryen, Morien, and Morial.
III. The graves which the shower bedews?
Men that would not succumb stealthily:--
Gwen, and Gwrien, and Gwriad.
IV. The grave of Tydain, father of the Muse, in the region of Bron Aren:
Where the wave makes a sullen sound
The grave of Dylan in Llan Beuno.
V. The grave, of Ceri Gledyvhir, in the region of Hen Eglwys,
In a rugged steep place
Tarw Torment in the enclosure of Corbre.
VI. The grave of Seithenhin the weak-minded
Between Caer Cenedir and the shore
Of the great sea and Cinran.
VII. In Aber Gwenoli is the grave of Pryderi,
Where the waves beat against the land;
In Carrawg is the grave of Gwallawg Hir.
VIII. The grave of Gwalchmai is in Peryddon,
Where the ninth wave flows:
The grave of Cynon is in Llan Badarn.
IX. The grave of Gwrwawd the honourable is
In a lofty region: in a lowly place of repose,
The grave of Cynon the son of Clydno Eiddyn.
X. The grave of Run the son of Pyd is by the river Ergryd,
In a cold place in the earth.
The grave of Cynon is in Ryd Reon.
XI. Whose is the grave beneath the hill?
The grave of a man mighty in the conflict--
The grave of Cynon the son of Clydno Eiddyn.
XII. The grave of the son of Osvran is in Camlan,
After many a slaughter
The grave of Bedwyr is in Gallt Tryvan.
XIII. The grave of Owain ab Urien in a secluded part of the world,
Under the sod of Llan Morvael;
In Abererch, that of Rhydderch Hael.

XIV. After wearing dark-brown clothes, and red, and splendid,
And riding magnificent steeds with sharp spears,
In Llan Heledd is the grave of Owain.
XV. After wounds and bloody plains,
And wearing harness and riding white horses,
This, even this, is the grave of Cynddylau.
XVI. Who owns the grave of good connections?
He who would attack Lloegir of the compact host--
The grave of Gwen, the son of Llywarch Hen, is this.
XVII. Whose is the grave in the circular space,
Which is covered by the sea and the border of the valley?
The grave of Meigen, the son of Run, the ruler of a hundred.
XVIII. Whose is the grave in the island,
Which is covered by the sea with a border of tumult?
The grave of Meigen, the son of Run, the ruler of a court
XIX. Narrow is the grave and long,
With respect to many long every way:--
The grave of Meigen, the son of Run, the ruler of right,
XX. The grave of the three serene persons on an elevated hill,
In the valley of Gwynn Gwynionawg--
Mor, and Meilyr, and Madawg.
XXI. The grave of Madawg, the splendid bulwark
In the meeting of contention, the grandson of Urien,
The best son to Gwyn of Gwynlliwg.
XXII. The grave of Mor, the magnificent, immovable sovereign,
The foremost pillar in the conflict,
The son of Peredur Penwedig.
XXIII. The grave of Meilyr Malwynawg of a sullenly-disposed mind.
The hastener of a fortunate career,
Son to Brwyn of Brycheinawg.
XXIV. Whose is the grave in Ryd Vaen Ced
With its head in a downward direction?
The grave of Run, the son of Alun Dywed.
XXV. The grave of Alun Dywed in his own region,
Away he would not retreat from a difficulty--
The son of Meigen, it was well when he was born.
xxvi. The grave of Llia the Gwyddel is in the retreat of Ardudwy,
Under the grass and withered leaves
The grave of Epynt is in the vale of Gewel.
XXVII. The Grave of Dywel, the son of Erbin, is in the plain of Caeaw;
He would not be a vassal to a king;
Blameless, be would not shrink from battle.
XXVIII. The Grave of Gwrgi, a hero and a Gwyndodian lion;
And the grave of Llawr, the regulator of hosts.
In the upper part of Gwanas the men are!

XXIX. The long graves in Gwanas--
Their history is not had,
Whose they are and what their deeds.
XXX. There has been the family of Oeth and Anoeth--
Naked are their men and their youth--
Let him who seeks for them dig in Gwanas.
XXXI. The grave of Llwch Llawengin is on the river Cerddenin
The head of the Saxons of the district of Erbin
He would not be three months without a battle.
XXXII. The graves in the Long Mountain--
Multitudes well know it--
Are the graves of Gwryen, Gwryd Engwawd, and Llwyddawg the son of Lli-
welydd.
XXXIII. Who owns the grave in the mountain?
One who marshalled armies--
It is the grave of Ffyrnvael Hael, the son of Hyvlydd.
XXXIV. Whose grave is this? The grave of Eiddiwlch the Tall,
In the upland of Pennant Twrch,
The son of Arthan, accustomed to slaughter.
XXXV. The grave of Llew Llawgyffes under the protection of the sea,
With which he was familiar;
He was a man that never gave the truth to any one.
XXXVI. The grave of Beidawg the Ruddy in the vicinity of Riw Llyvnaw;
The grave of Lluosgar in Ceri;
And at Ryd Bridw the grave of Omni.
XXXVII. Far his turmoil and his seclusion;
The sod of Machawe conceals him
Long the lamentations for the prowess of Beidawg the Ruddy.
XXXVIII. Far his turmoil and his fame--
The sod of Machawe is upon him--
This is Beidawg the Ruddy, the son of Emyr Llydaw.
XXXIX. The grave of a monarch of Prydain is in Lleudir Gwynasedd,
Where the flood enters the Llychwr;
In Celli Briafael, the grave of Gyrthmwl.
XL. The grave in Ystyvachau,
Which everybody doubts.
The grave of Gwrtheyrn Gwrthenau.
XLI. Cian wails in the waste of Cnud,
Yonder above the grave of the stranger--
The grave of Cynddilig, the son of Corcnud.
XLII. Truly did Elffin bring me
To try my primitive bardic lore
Over a chieftain--
The grave of Rwvawn with the imperious aspect.

XLIII. Truly did Elffin bring me
To try my bardic lore
Over an early chieftain--
The grave of Rwvawn, too early gone to the grave.
XLIV. The grave of March, the grave of Gwythur,
The grave of Gwgawn Gleddyvrudd;
A mystery to the world, the grave of Arthur.
XLV. The grave of Elchwith is by the rain bedewed,
With the plain of Meweddawg under it;
Cynon ought to bewail him there.
XLVI. Who owns this grave? this grave? and this?
Ask me, I know it;--
The grave of Ew, the grave of Eddew was this,
And the grave of Eidal with the lofty mien.
XLVII. Eiddew and Eidal, the unflinching exiles,
The whelps of Cylchwydrai:
The sons of Meigen bred war-horses.
XLVIII. Whose is this grave? It is the grave of Brwyno the Tall,
Bold were his men in his region.
Where he would be, there would be no flight.
XLIX. Who owns this grave--not another?
Gwythwch, the vehement in the conflict,
While he would kill thee, he would at thee laugh.
L. The grave of Silid the intrepid is in the locality of Edrywfy;
The grave of Llemenig in Llan Elwy,
In the swampy upland is the grave of Eilinwy.
LI. The grave of a stately warrior; many a carcase
Was usual from his hand,
Before he became silent beneath the stones;
Llachar, the son of Run, is in the valley of the Cain.
LII. The grave of Talan Talyrth
Is at the contention of three battles,
A hewer down of the head of every force,
Liberal was he, and open his gates.
LIII. The grave of Elisner, the son of Ner,
Is in the depth of the earth without fear, without concern;
A commander of hosts was he, so long as his time lasted.
LIV. The grave of a hero vehement in his rage
Llachar the ruler of hosts, at the confluence of noisy waters,
Where the Tawne forms a wave.
LV. Whose are graves in the fords?
What is the grave of a chieftain, the son of Rygenau,
A man whose arms had abundant success.

LVI. Whose is this grave? The grave of Braint
Between Llewin and Llednaint--
The grave of a man, the woe of his foes.
LVII. Whose is the grave on the slope of the hill?
Many who know it do not ask;
The grave of Coel, the son of Cynvelyn.
LVIII. The grave of Dehewaint is on the river Clewaint,
In the uplands of Mathavarn,
The support of mighty warriors.
LIX. The grave of Aron, the son of Dewinvin, is in the land of Gwenle;
He would not shout after thieves,
Nor disclose the truth to enemies.
LX. The grave of Tavlogau, the son of Ludd,
Is far away in Trewrudd; and thus to us there is affliction;
He who buried him obtained an advantage.
LXI. Who owns the grave on the banks of Ryddnant?
Run his name, his bounties were infinite;
A chief he was! Riogan pierced him.
LXII. He was like Cyvnyssen to demand satisfaction for murder,
Ruddy was his lance, serene his aspect:
Who derived the benefit? The grave of Bradwen.
LXIII. Whose is the quadrangular grave
With its four stones around the front?
The grave of Madawg the intrepid warrior.
LXIV. In the soil of the region of Eivionydd,
There is a tall man of fine growth,
Who would kill all when he was greatly enraged.
LXV. The three graves on the ridge of Celvi,
The Awen has declared them to me:--
The grave of Cynon of the rugged brows,
The grave of Cynvael, and the grave of Cynveli.
LXVI. The grave of Llwid Llednais in the land of Cemmaes,
Before his ribs had grown long,
The bull of conflict brought oppression thither.
LXVII. The grave of the stately Siawn in Hirerw,
A mountain between the plain and the oaken forest,
Laughing, treacherous, and of bitter disposition was he.
LXVIII. Who owns the grave in the sheltered place?
While he was, he was no weakling:--
It is the grave of Ebediw, the son of Maelur.
LXIX. Whose is the grave in yonder woody cliff?
His band was an enemy to many;--
The bull of battle--mercy to him!
LXX. The graves of the sea-marsh.
Slightly are they ornamented!

There is Sanawg, a stately maid;
There is Run, ardent in war;
There is Earwen, the daughter of Hennin;
There are Lledin and Llywy.
LXXI. The grave of Hennin Henben is in the heart of Dinorben;
The grave of Aergwl in Dyved,
At the ford of Cynan Gyhored.
LXXII. Every one that is not dilatory inquires--
Whose is the mausoleum that is here?
It is the grave of Einyawn, the son of Cunedda;
It is a disgrace that in Prydain he should have been slain.
LXXIII. Who owns the grave in the great plain?
Proud his hand upon his lance:--
The grave of Beli, the son of Benlli Gawr.

II. Historical Poems Containing Allusions to Events Subsequent to A.D. 560.

G. Poems Referring to War Between Sons of Llywarch Hen and Mwg Mawr Drefydd

XXX. NAMES OF THE SONS OF LLYWARCH HEN. - BLACK BOOK OF CAERMARTHEN XXXIX.

I. SWEETLY sings the bird on the fragrant tree
Over the head of Gwen; before his covering over with sod,
He used to fracture the armour of (Llywarch) Hen.
II. The three best men in their country,
To defend their homesteads,--
Eithir, and Erthir, and Argad.
III. The three sons of Llywarch, three intractable ones in battle.
Three fierce contenders,--
Llew, and Araw, and Urien.
IV. Better may it fare for my concerns,
That he be left on the banks of the river,
With a host of warlike men.

V. The bull of conflict, conductor of the war,
The support of battle, and the lamp of benevolence,
Father of heaven, increase Thou his energy!
VI. The best three men under heaven
To defend their homes,--
Pyll, and Selyv, and Sandev.
VII. The morning with the dawn of day,
When Mwg Mawr Drefydd was assaulted,
The steeds of Mechydd were not trained up.
VIII. They met around Cavall;
A corpse is there in blood through injustice,

163

From the rencounter of Rhun and the other hero.

IX. A shout will be uttered on the top of Mount Llug
Over the grave of Cynllug;
The reproach is mine; it was I that caused it.

X. Let the snow descend and cover the vale,
Warriors will hasten to battle;
I do not go; infirmity leaves me not.

XI. Thou art not a scholar, thou art not a recluse
Thou wilt not be called a monarch in the day of necessity;
Alas! Cynddilig, that thou wert not a woman.

XII. Far away is Aber Llyw,
Further are the two Cyvedlyws;
Talan, this day thou hast paid me with tears.

XXXI. BLACK BOOK OF CAERMARTHEN XXX.

I. KEEN is the gale, bare the hill,
It is difficult to find a shelter;
The ford is turbid, frozen is the lake,
A man stands firm with one stalk.

II. Wave after wave rolls towards the shore;
Loud the shoutings in front of the heights of the hill,
If one but just stands out.

III. Cold is the place of the lake-before the winter storm;
Dry the stalks of broken reeds;
Lucky is he who sees the wood in the chest.

IV. Cold is the bed of fish in the shelter of a sheet of ice;
Lean the stag; the topmost reeds move quickly;
Short the evening; bent the trees.

V. Let the white snow fall in deposits;
Warriors will not leave their duty;
Cold are the lakes without the appearance of warmth.

VI. Let the white snow fall on the boar frost;
Idle is the shield on the shoulder of the aged;
The wind is very high; it has certainly frozen.

VII. Let the snow fall on the surface of the ice;
Gently sweeps the wind the tops of thick trees;
Firm is the shield on the shoulder of the brave.

VIII. Let the snow descend and cover the vale
Warriors will hasten to battle;
I shall not go;--infirmity will not let me!

IX. Let the snow fall from the side of the slope
Prisoner is the steed, lean the cattle
Cold is no pleasure to-day.

X. Let the snow fall; white is the mountain-region;
Bare the timber of the ship on sea;
A host of men will cherish many counsels.

XI. Golden hands are around the horns, the horns in agitation;
Cold the stream, bright the sky,
Short the evening, bending are the tops of trees.
XII. The bees (live) on their store; small the clamour of birds,
The day is dewless;
The hill-top is a conspicuous object; red the dawn.
XIII. The bees are under cover; cold also is the ford,
Let the frost freeze as long as it lasts:
To him that is soft may dissolution happen!
XIV. The bees are in confinement this very day;
How withered the stalks, hard the slope;
Cold and dewless is the earth to-day.
XV. The bees are in shelter from the wet of winter;
Blue the mist, hollow the cow-parsnip;
Cowardliness is a bad quality in a man.
XVI. Long the night, bare the moor, hoary the cliff;
Gray the fair gull on the precipice;
Rough the seas; there will be rain to-day.
XVII. Dry the wind, wet the road,
The vale assumes its former appearance.
XVIII. Cold the thistle-stalks; lean the stag;
Smooth the river; there will be fine weather.
XIX. Foul the weather on the mountain; the rivers troubled;
Flood will wet the ground in towns;
The earth looks like the ocean!
XX. Thou art not a scholar, thou art not a recluse;
Thou wilt not be called a monarch in the day of necessity.
Alas! Cynddilig, that thou wert not a woman!
XXI. Let the crooked hart bound at the top of the sheltered vale;
May the ice be broken; bare are the lowlands;
The brave escapes from many a hardship.
XXII. The thrush has a spotted breast,
Spotted the breast of the thrush;
The edge of the bank is broken
By the hoof of the lean, crooked, and stooping hart.
XXIII. Very high is the loud-sounding wind;
It is scarcely right for one to stand out.
XXIV. At All-Saints it is habitual for the heath-tops to be dun;
High-foaming is the sea-wave,
Short the day:--Druid, your advice!
XXV. If the shield, and the vigour of the steed,
And of brave, fearless men, have gone to sleep,
The night is fair to chase the foe.

XXVI. The wind is supreme; sore and bare the trees,
Withered the reeds; the hart is bounding;
Pelis the False, what land is this?
XXVII. If it poured down snow as far as Arvwl Melyn,
Gloom would not make me sad;
I would lead a host to the hill of Tydwl.
XXVIII. For thou knowest, with equal ease, the causeway,
The ford, and the ascent, if snow were to fall,
When thou, Pelis, art our guide.
XXX. Anxiety in Prydain will not cause me to-night
To march upon a region where there is the greatest wailing,
From following after Owain.
XXXI. Since thou bearest arms and shield upon thee,
Defender of the destructive battle,
Pelis, in what land wast thou fostered?
XXXI. The man whom God releases from a very close prison,
Ruddy will be his spear from the territory of Owain,
Lavish of his entertainments.
XXXII. Since the chieftain is gone to earth,
Pursue not his family;
After mead seek no disgrace.
XXXIII. The morning with the dawn of day,
When Mwg Mawr Drefydd was assaulted,
The steeds of Mechydd were not trained up.
XXXIV. Joy will be to me of no benefit,
Owing to the news which apprises me
That a wooden cover is upon Mechydd!
XXXV. They met around Cavall;
A corpse is there in blood through injustice,
From the rencounter of Rhun and the other hero.
XXXVI. For the staffers of Mwg have slain Mechydd;
Drudwas did not perceive the day;
Creator of heaven! thou hast caused me severe affliction!
XXXVII. Men are in the shout (of war); the ford is frozen over;
Cold the wave, variegated the bosom of the sea;
The eternal God give us counsel!
XXXVIII. Mechydd, the son of Llywarch, the undaunted chief,
Fine and fair was his robe of the colour of the swan,
The first that fastened a horse by the bridle.

XXXII. BLACK BOOK OF CAERMARTHEN XXXIV.

THOUGH I love the strand, I hate the sea.
How the wave covered the stone of Camwr!
The brave, the magnanimous, the amiable, the generous, and the energetic,
Are as stepping-stones to the bards of the world, and an advantageous shel-

ter.

The fame of Heilyn proved a benefit to the solicitous.
To the day of judgment may his celebrity remain!
Though I love the strand, I hate the wave.
The wave has done violence, dismal the blow to the breast.
He will complain as long as he believes on its account.
10 It is a cheerful work to bathe on my bosom,
Though it (the water) fills the cavity, it does not disturb the heart.
And in the direction of Cyhaig did the wave arise.
Sorry we are for his concerns,
When Pebrwr from afar hastened to his death.
The brave and courageous multitude will affect us both;
As the water bearing the leaves shows it thee.
Mechydd is sad on account of thy coming.
I will not receive thee to my receptacle.
From my part I sold a horse for thee.
20 Cyhaig will revenge for the delay of his enjoyment,
And for the sweet strains.
O dwarf! for thy anger to me there have been enemies.

XXXIII. RED BOOK OF HERGEST XI.

I. I WAS formerly fair of limb, I was eloquent in speech:
What is not wonderful will be extolled
The men of Argoed have ever supported me.
II. I was formerly fair of limb, I was bold,
I was admitted into the congress-house
Of Powys, the paradise of the Cymry.
III. I was formerly fair of limb, I was comely;
Throbbing was concomitant with my spear:
My back (now) curved was first in vigour--I am heavy, I am wretched.
IV. Wooden crook! is it not the time of harvest,
When the fern is brown, and the reeds are yellow?
Have I not once disliked what I now love!
V. Wooden crook! is not this winter,
When men are noisy over the beverage?
Is not my bedside void of greeting visits!
VI. Wooden crook! is it not the spring,
When the cuckoos are brownish, when the foam is bright?
I am destitute of a maiden's love.
VII. Wooden crook! is it not the beginning of summer,
Are not the furrows brown, are not the corn-blades curled?
It is refreshing to me to look at thy beak!

VIII. Wooden crook! thou contented branch
That supportest a mourning old man!
Llywarch of pleasant talk!
IX. Wooden crook! thou hardy branch
That bearest with me--God protect thee!
Thou art justly called the tree of wandering.
X. Wooden crook! be thou steady,
So that thou mayest support me the better--
Am not I Llywarch known to many far away?
XI. Surely old age is uniting itself with me,
From my hair to my teeth,
And the glowing eyeball which the young ones loved!
XII. Surely old age is uniting itself with me,
From my hair to my teeth,
And the glowing eyeball which the women loved!
XIII. The wind grinningly blusters out, white is the skirt of the wood,
Lively is the stag, there is no moisture on the hill;
Feeble is the aged, slowly he moves!
XIV. This leaf, is it not driven by the wind?
Woe to it as to its fate!
It is old, this year was it born.
XV. What I loved when a youth are hateful to me now:
A stranger's daughter, and a gray steed.
Am not I for them unmeet?
XVI. The four most hateful things to me through life,
Have met together with one accord:--
Cough and old age, sickness and grief.
XVII. I am old, I am lonely, I am decrepit and cold,
After the sumptuous bed of honour:
I am wretched, I am triply bent!
XVIII. I am triply bent and old, I am fickly bold,
I am rash, I am outrageous:
Those that loved me, love me not.
XIX. Young maidens love me not, I am visited by none,
I cannot move about--
Ah! death, that he does not seek me!
XX. I am sought by neither sleep nor gladness;
After the slaughter of Llawr and Gwen,
I am outrageous and loathsome, I am old.
XXI. Wretched was the fate decreed to Llywarch
On the night he was born;
Long pain without being delivered of his load of trouble.
XXII. Array not thyself after waiting; let not thy mind be vexed;
Sharp is the gale, and bleak the spring!--
Accuse me not, my mother--I am thy son!

XXIII. Do I not recognise by my Awen,
My descent, sway, and kindred:
Three themes of the harmonious Awen?
XXIV. Sharp is my spear, furious in the onset;
I will prepare to watch the ford;
Support against falling may God grant me.
XXV. Shouldst thou run away, I will weep for thee;
Shouldst thou be slain, I shall mourn thee:
Lose not the countenance of the men of conflict.
XXVI. I will not lose thy countenance, prone to warfare,
From the time that the hero puts on harness for the course;
I will hear the pang ere I quit the spot.
XXVII. Gliding is the wave along the beach;
I perceive that the design of that battle will be frustrated,
It is usual for the talkative to run away.
XXVIII. Of that which concerns me I will speak;
There is breaking of spears about the place where I am;
I will not say but that I may retreat.
XXIX. Soft is the bog, the cliff is hard,
Before the hart's hoof the edge of the bank breaks,
A promise not fulfilled is none at all.
XXX. The streams will divide around the wall of the Caer,
And I will prognosticate--
A shield with a fractured front before I skulk.
XXXI. The horn given to thee by Urien,
With the wreath of gold around its rim,
Blow in it, if thou art in danger.
XXXII. For the terror of death from the base men of Lloegyr
I will. not tarnish my honour;
I will not dispraise maidens.
XXXIII. Whilst I was of the age of yonder youth,
That wears the golden spurs,
I was active in thrusting the spear.
XXXIV. Truly thy young man is faithful,
Thou art alive, and thy witness is slain,
The old man that is now feeble was not so in his youth.
XXXV. Gwen, by the Llawen, watched last night,
And success did not fail him:
The battle progressed on the green embankment.
XXXVI. Gwen, by the Llawen, watched last night,
With the shield on the shoulder;
As he was my son, he did not retreat.
XXXVII. Gwen with the lowering look, troubled is my mind,
Thy death greatly provokes my wrath--
It is not kindred (only) that will speak of thee!

XXXVIII. Gwen with thigh of wide opening watched last night
On the border of the ford of Morlas;
And as he was my son, he did not retreat.
XXXIX. Gwen, I knew thy inherent disposition;
In the assault like the eagle at fall of rivers thou wert;
If I were fortunate thou wouldst have escaped.
XL. Let the face of the ground be turned up, let the assailants be covered,
When chiefs repair to the toil of war;
Gwen, woe to him that is over old, for thee he is indignant.
XLI. Let the face of the ground be turned up, and the plain be covered,
When the opposing spears are lifted up.
Gwen, woe to him that is over old, that he should have lost thee.
XLII. My son was a man, splendid was his fame;
And he was the nephew of Urien;
On the ford of Morlas, Gwen was slain.
XLIII. The shrine of the fierce overbearing foe,
That vanquished the circularly compact army of Lloegr;
The grave of Gwen, the son of Llywarch Hen, is this!
XLIV. Four-and-twenty sons have been to me,
Wearing the golden chain, leaders of armies;
Gwen was the best of them.
XLV. Four-and-twenty sons have been to me,
Wearing the golden chain, leaders of battle;
Gwen was the best son of his father.
XLVI. Four-and-twenty sons to me have been,
Wearing the golden chain, leading princes;
Compared with Gwen they were but striplings.
XLVII. Four-and-twenty sons were in the family of Llywarch,
Of brave men fall of the wrath of war;
Their march was a rush, immense their fame.
XLVIII. Four-and-twenty were my sons complete;
My flesh they have caused to wither;
It is well that my budget of misfortune is come!
XLIX When Pyll was slain, gashing was the wound;
And the blood on the hair seemed horrible;
And on both banks of the Ffraw there was violence.
L. A room might be formed for the wings of shields,
Which would hold one standing upright,
That were broken in the grasp of Pyll.
LI. The chosen man amongst my sons,
When each assaulted the foe,
Was fair Pyll, impetuous as a fire through a chimney.
LII. Gracefully he placed his thigh over the saddle.
Of his horse, on the near and far side--
Pyll, impetuous as the fire through a chimney.

LIII. He was gentle, with a hand eager for battle;
He was second to no treasure;
He was a bulwark on the course--
Fair Pyll! fearful is his covering of separation.
LIV. When he stood at the door of his tent,
On the dark-gray steed,
At the sight, the wife of Pyll would recognise a hero.
LV. There was fractured before Pyll a strong skull;
Seldom would the silent coward be concealed from him;
The weak is satisfied without anything.
LVI. Fair Pyll, widely spread his fame:
Am. I not invigorated since thou hast existed
As my son, and joyful to have known thee?
LVII. The best three men under heaven
That guarded their habitation,--
Pyll, and Selyv, and Sandev.
LVIII. A shield I gave to Pyll;
Before he slept was it not perforated?
To promise it carelessly was to depreciate it.
LIX. Should Cymry come, and the predatory host of Lloegr,
And many from distant parts,
Pyll would show them conduct.
LX. Nor Pyll nor Madawg would be long lived,
If they preserved the custom.
Would they surrender? they would not surrender! they would never ask for
truce!
LXI. Behold here the grave of a faultless one and warlike;
With the Bards his fame went, where would not have gone,
Pyll, if longer he had continued?
LXII. Maen, and Madawg, and Medel, valiant men,
And brothers not refractory,
Sclyv, Heilyn, Llawr, and Lliver.
LXIII. The grave of Gwell is in Rhiw Velen;
The grave of Sawyl in Llangollen;
Llawr protects the pass of Llorien,
LXIV. The grave of Rhudd, is it not covered with sods?
The earth of Ammarch does not conceal
The grave of Llyngedwy, the son of Llywarch.
LXV. Far from hence is Aber Llyw,
Farther are the two Cyvedliws:
Talan, thou hast repaid my tears to-day.
LXVI. I have drunk wine from the goblet;
He would rush forward against the lance-bearer;
Like the wings of the dawn were the gleamings of the spear of Duawg.

LXVII. I have repented of the time that I entreated
That thou shouldst not have thy choice;
It would have been generous to have life prolonged a month.
LXVIII. I know the voice of distress:--
When he descended into the congress-house,
Chief of men, a goblet of wine he deserved.

H. Poems Relating to Gwallawg Ap Lleenawg

XXXIV. - BLACK BOOK OF CAERMARTHEN XXXII.

I. ON a fine night Pen Gethin heard
the shout of a host,
When he took a long leap;
Unless the ground be guarded he will
not cease.
II. Since Coegawg is so rich as this in
gold,
Close to the court of Gwallawg
I also shall be wealthy.
III. Accursed be the tree
Which pulled out his eye in his pres-
ence,
Gwallawg ab Lleenawg, the ruler.
IV. Accursed be the black tree
That pulled out his eye from its place,
Gwallawg ab Lleenawg, the chief of
armies.

V. Accursed be the white tree
That pulled out his eye from his head,
Gwallawg ab Lleenawg, the sover-
eign.
VI. Accursed be the green tree
That pulled out his eye when a youth,
Gwallawg ab Lleenawg, the honoura-
ble. [1]

[1] On the margin:
No one that was eminent went
In the way that Gwallawg did,
With his steel into the meadow.
No one that was honourable went
In the way that Meurig did,
With a bandage to the woman in three
folds.

XXXV. BOOK OF TALIESSIN XI.

IN the name of the Ruler of heaven, the mighty one
The supporter of his friends shall keep possession of his towns,
Splendid his princely spear.
Warlike kings spear-scouting.
He will defend the pleasant plain of Lleenawg;
The ruthless pushing shafts are broken.
Long they will experience
The gratitude of Prydain.
From the bush of Maw and Eiddyn,
10 They would not take opposition.
Friendly the aid of Clydwyn.
May I be satisfied! He supplied his fleet
From spears until the shafts were heated.
A coffin to every one his ambition.

172

They cannot reckon the battles fought
By Gwallawg. Better is wild food than a she-bear.
A battle in Agathes in defence,
Praise his active judgment caused.
A battle in the region of Bretrwyn with heat,
20 A great fire. Limited is his vehemence.
A battle, there was a rule of general benefit.
A battle, a battle of trembling in Aeron.
A battle in Arddunion and Aeron.
Bring reproach to the youths.
A battle in the wood of Beit at the close of the day.
Thou didst not think of thy foes.
A battle in the presence of Mabon.
He will not mention the contradiction of the saved.
A battle in Gwensteri, and thou subduest Lloegyr.
30 A darting of spears there is made.
A battle in the marsh of Terra with the dawn,
Easily broken (was) the terrible arch,
At the first littering of the word,
Of kings who were extinguished in the war.
Men with full intent to obtain cattle.
Haearddur and Hyveidd and Gwallawg,
And Owen of Mona of Maelgwnian quality,
Will lay the Peithwyr prostrate,
At the end of the wood of Cleddyfein,
40 From which there will be pierced corpses,
And the ravens wandering about.
In Prydain, in Eiddyn, acknowledged.
In Gafran, in the retreat of Brecheinawc.
In energy, in exalted covering.
He sees not a hero, who saw not Gwallawg.

XXXVI. BOOK OF TALIESSIN XXXVIII.

IN the name of the Ruler of the high powers of heaven,
They sing of, they deplore the prince;
He rejected uniform ranks of the rulers,
Of the hosts of Run and Nudd and Nwython.
I will not praise contrary to the custom of the Bards of the Brython.
Wonderfully liberal of the knowledge of astrologers.
One station of the complete songster; excellent of song,
I ardently desire; I will sing to the Guledig,
In the country where he was trembling,
10 he will not cause me to be unable to form the lay.
It is difficult to utter odes;

That will not be deficient to the Guledig that does not refuse.
Of looking at a heavy ode of sovereignty
In his life will not come the advantage of the grave.
They will not be satisfied with the gratification of their lives.
Harder the torment of a liberal course,
A multitude present beyond Prydain.
Thy excessive care of the too sprightly is corrupted.
Let it be corrupted. He shall be cut to pieces, he shall be judged.
20 He will judge all, the supreme man.
With his will as a judge; and let him be benefited,
Not the man that claims the mortuary.
A youth violent that regrets the milky food,
Like the herald of Gwallawg guiding on.
Of a forbearing aspect is the countenance of Gwallawg.
He inquires of no one what he has done.
Is he not my chief? Is there not sold to you
Thick mead in the end of summer?
There will not increase save six.
30 Sweeter to thee is conversation from elders.
Talkative is the privileged orator
Of king s ill the luxuriant circle of the good mead.
Like the sun, the warm animator of summer, let him sound the greatest song.
I will sing the wise song, the song of the host of harmony.
They will be, thou wilt be a Druid in summer time, the aspect of the son
Of Lleenawg, with a flowing manly robe.
Light, a robe of heat; vapour of heat, heat of vapour.
Whilst it rose it was contained without disgrace.
A sword will destroy the swordsman's horse;
40 His host will not break me to theft,
The native country of a slave is not free to him,
They will perforate the fronts of shields before the fronts of horses.
From his steed of tumult, Morial shall appear before the host
Fiercely impassioned. They shall pledge the rich plains
From Caer Clud to Caer Caradawg,
The support of the land of Penprys and Gwallawg,
The king of the kings of tranquil aspect.

I. Poems Relating to Urien Reged

XXXVII. RED BOOK OF HERGEST XVII.

I HAVE freely greeted, I will freely greet, the familiar greeter of
Urien Reged. May he diffuse his joy abroad!
Gold and silver, how great their consumption and destruction.
(Even) before they could come between the hands of the scatterer!

Ieuav caused loss and sorrow for horses daily;
Ceneu his brother, dilatory in the conflict, was not skilful;
Urien made retaliation for the dishonour
Of Cynin the active, ignominious was their execution.
About Aerven, all uncovered precipice, there will come an army.
10 Selev has been captured; he was incensed for what was to come.
It will fare worse with the free and the bond on their account,
Blades will be reddened, through proud words for the fruit of their trees.
The four men will maintain the place of four hundred,
With the deepest water. I would bless the corrupt in the enclosure on their account;
And whoever obtains it, may he be blessed for ever!
There will befall a loss from confiding in the claimant;
And hands without thumbs, and blades on the flesh, and a poor muster.
Puerile age will not be harmonious in the distraction.
There will be no fellowship, nor confidence in any toward others.
20 A dragon from Gwynedd of precipitous lands and gentle towns,
To the Lloegrians will go, when the report of him will spread abroad.
Stonework will be broken, with terrible destruction, in the encounter;
And more will be lost than spared of the Gwyndodians.
From mutual counselling, there will be means of deliverance by sea and land.
There will arise from concealment a man that will be a blessing to the Gwyndodians;
And the Brythyon, though a remnant, will be victorious over the ungentle multitude.
There will come a time when song will not be cherished, nor will it be elaborate;
The ruler will love wealth, and one sister will be bearish to another.
Killing and drowning from Eleri as far as Chwilvynydd,
30 A conquering and unmerciful one will triumph;
Small will be his army in returning from the (action of) Wednesday.
A bear from the south, will arise, meet
The Lloegrians, and kill vast numbers of Powysians.
The affair of Cors Vochno, he that will escape from it will be fortunate;
There will be twelve women, and no wonder, for one man.
The age of youth will fare unbecomingly worse;
After the tumultuous extermination, a bearded man in a hundred will not be a warrior.
Urien of Reged, generous he is, and will be,
And has been since Adam.
40 He, proud in the hall, has the most wide-spreading sword
Among the thirteen kings of the North.
Do I know his name--Aneurin the poet with the flowing song,
I being Taliesin, from the borders of the lake of Geirionnyidd?
May I not, when old,

Support my sore necessity,
If I praise not Urien. Amen.

XXXVIII. BOOK OF TALIESSIN XXXI.

THE men of Catraeth arose with the dawn,
About the Guledig, of work a profitable merchant.
This Urien, without mockery is his regret.
He sustains the sovereignty and its demands.
Warlike, the grandeur of a perfect prince of baptism.
The men of Prydain hurtful in battle array,
At Gwenystrad, continuously offerers of battle.
Protected neither the field nor woods
The people with shelter, when tribulation comes.
10 Like the wave loud roaring over the beach,
I saw valiant men in battle array,
And after the morning, battle-mangled flesh.
I saw a tumult of three limits slain,
A shout active in front was heard.
In defending Gwenystrad was seen
A mound and slanting ground obstructing.
In the pass of the ford I saw men gory-tinted,
Dropping their arms before the pallid miserable ones.
They join in peace as they were losers.
20 Hand on the cross they wail on the gravel bank of Garanwynyon.
The tribes revel over the rising wave.
The billows protect the hair of their captures.
I saw men of splendid progress
With blood that clotted on the garments,
Toiling energetically and incessantly in battle.
The covering battle, where there was no flight, when contrived.
The ruler of Reged, I am astonished at what was dared.
I saw a brow covered with rage on Urien,
When he furiously attacked his foes at the white stone
30 Of Galystem. His rage was a blade;
The bucklered men were sustained in need.
May a desire of battle come on Euirwyn.
And until I fail in old age,
In the sore necessity of death,
May I not be smiling,
If I praise not Urien.

XXXIX. BOOK OF TALIESSIN XXXII.

URIEN of the cultivated plain,
The most generous man of baptism,
Abundance has been given
To the men of earth.

As it has been gathered,
It has been scattered.
Joyful the bards of baptism
Whilst thy life continues.
There is greater joy
10 For the high-famed, and liberal of praise.
It is greater glory,
That Urien and his children should exist.
And he especially
The supreme Guledig.
In a distant city,
A principal pilgrim,
The Lloegrians know him,
When they converse.
Death they had,
20 And frequent vexation,
Burning their homesteads,
And drawing their coverings.
And loss,
And great incomprehension,
Without obtaining deliverance
From Urien Reged.
The protector of Reged,
The praise of Ior, the anchor of the country.
My inclination is on thee,
30 Of every hearing.

Heavy thy spear-throwing,
When the battle is heard,
When they resort to battle,
A smarting is made.
Fire in houses before day,
Before the sovereign of the cultivated plain,
The most fair cultivated plain,
And its most generous men.
The Angles are accustomed to be without homage
40 From most valiant king.
A most valiant progeny,
Thine is the best.
Of those who have been, or will be,
There is not thy match.
When he is looked upon,
Very great is the terror.
It is usual to look for him,
For an active king.
Around him a modest demeanour,
50 And the varied multitude,
The splendid prince of the North,
The choicest of princes.
And when I fail in age,
In the sore necessity of death,
May I not be smiling,
If I praise not Urien.

XL. BOOK OF TALIESSIN XXXIII.

IN rest,
A song I kept.
Respect and plenty
And mead I possessed.
I possessed mead.
His triumph,
And fair lands,
A great wonder.
And gold and hour,
10 And hour and treasure,
And plenty
And esteem.
And giving a desire,

A desire of giving it,
To encourage me.
He slays, he plagues,
He cherishes, he honours,
He honours, he cherishes,
He slays before him.
20 Presence was given
To the bards of the world.
Ever certainly
To thee they say
According to thy will.
God hath caused to thee
The shoulder of kings

Against despicable fear.
Incitement of battle
The protection of a country.
30 The country protected
Battle of incitement
Usual about thee
The tumult of capering,
The capering of tumult
And drinking of ale.
Ale for the drinking,
And a fair homestead,
And beautiful clothing,
To me has been extended.
40 The lofty Llwyvenydd,

And requests open.
In one dwell
Great and little.
Taliessin's song
Thou comfortest it.
Thou art the best
Of those that have heard
His vehement animosities.
I also will praise
50 Thy deeds,
And until I fail in old age,
In the sore necessity of death,
May I not be smiling
If I praise not Urien.

XLI. BOOK OF TALIESSIN XXXIV.

IN one year
One that provides
Wine and bounty and mead,
And manliness without enmity,
And a musician excelling,
With a swarm of spears about him.
With ribbands at their heads,
And their fair appearances.
Every one went from his presence,
10 They came into the conflict,
And his horse under him.
Purposing the affair of Mynaw.
And more harmony,
Advantage flowing about his hand.
Eight score of one colour
Of calves and cows.
Milch cows and oxen.
And every fair need.
I should not be joyful
20 If Urien were slain.
He is dear before he went.
A Saxon shivering, trembling,
With hair white-washed,
And a bier his destiny,
With a bloody face.
For the blood of men a little protect-
ed.
And a man of the intrenchment per-

severing,
Whose wife is a widow.
Mine is the wine of the prince,
30 Mine is the wine of frequent par-
ties,
My chance, my aid, my head.
Since the rising up will not cause
A striking fronting one another.
Porter, listen.
What is the noise: is it the earth that
quakes?
Or is it the sea that swells?
Whitened, clinging together, against
the infantry.
If there is a cry on the hill,
Is it not Urien that terrifies?
40 If there is a cry in the valley,
Is it not Urien that pierces?
If there is a cry in the mountain,
Is it not Urien that conquers?
If there is a cry on the slope,
Is it not Urien that wounds?
If there is a sigh on the dyke,
Is it not Urien that is active?
A cry of a journey over the plain,
A cry in every meandering vale.
50 Nor will one sneeze or two
Protect from death.

He would not be on famine
With spoils surrounding him.
Over-querulous, trailing, of a blue tint.
Like death was his spear,

Killing his enemy.
And until I fail in old age,
In the sore necessity of death,
May I not be smiling,
60 If I praise not Urien.

XLII. BOOK OF TALIESSIN XXXVI.

EXTOL the career of the kings of Reged.
Was I not an expense to thee, though I am thine?
They brandished the blade of battle, and spears of battle,
Men brandished under the round shield; lights
White gulls trampled.
It was not fell fought. A false king is not good.
The Guledig will prepare himself against contusions.
He will not drive the business of those that seek him.
We shall have a nimble horseman, of Gwirion's fame,
10 A leader of fair promise, wise as Don.
Until Ulph came with violence on his enemies.
Until Urien came in the day to Aeron.
He was not an agressor, there appeared not
The uplifted front of Urien before Powys.
Was not easily treated the heat of the compact elf the tribes,
Hyveidd and Gododin and the lion prince.
Bold in patience, and journey of joint summons.
Without pollution he drew blood in his veins.
(He) that saw Llwyvenydd humbly will tremble,
20 A conspicuous banner in the second place,
A battle in the ford of Alclud, a battle at the Inver.
The battle of Cellawr Brewyn. The battle of Hireurur.
A battle in the underwood of Cadleu, a battle in Aberioed.
He interposes with the steel loud (and) great.
The battle of Cludvein, the, affair of the head of the wood.
A tribe attracted of dogs to a plentitude of blood.
To destroy supreme felicity is the aim
Of the Angles, a hostile crew.
Ruddy-stained from the conflict with Ulph at the ford.
30 Better is born the Guledig, forward was born his lord,
Prydain's chief proprietor, harmonious his lord.
He bare not clothes, either blue or gray,
Or red or green; he will not honour the ground.
He placed not his thigh over Moel Maelaur,
On horses of the speckled race of Mor Greidiawl.
Summer until winter, and gently in hand,
On ford, and course exercising them.

And a guest under songs and exalting one's-self,
And until the end of the world was perceived the band.
40 They arrange, they sweep about chainless for an image,
Uncowardly about lights did I not mangle?
I strove against the fall of spears on shoulders.
Shield in hand, Godeu. and Reged protecting;
Did I not see a man folding cattle?
A serpent of enchantment, a comely trampler of the ground.
Do I not know a war wherein he was lost,
And how much I lose by his perishing?
I shall not be extremely angry to possess mead-liquor.
From the heroic Hyveidd, of hospitable course.
50 Wit not I that was permitted (to have) shelter of the battle.
My kings were broken off from cheerful graces,
Shelter of the country good to the oppressed.
And until I fail in age,
In the sore necessity of death,
May I not be smiling,
If I praise not Urien.

XLIII. THE SATISFACTION OF URIEN. - BOOK OF TALIESSIN XXIX.

THE lion will be most implacable;
I will not deplore him.
Urien I will approach,
To him I will sing.
When will come my surety,
I shall obtain admission.
Of the very best part,
Under the flow of melody,
It concerns me not much,
10 The everlasting lineage which I see.
I will not go to them, I will not be with them.
I will not address the North
And the kings of the plain.
Though there should be for many
That I should see a mutual pledging.
I have no need of affection:
Urien will not refuse me
The lands of Llwyvenydd.
Mine is their wealth,
20 Mine are the festivals,
Mine is the produce,
Mine are the metals,
And its rich productions.
Mead out of buffalo-horns
And good in abundance,
From the best prince,
The most generous that has been heard of.
The chiefs of every language
To thee are all captive.
30 For thee there will be lamentation when thy death is certain.
Though I should have preferred him
After being benefited, I would grow old.
There was not one that I loved better,
(Of those) that I knew before.
At times I see
The amount of what I shall have.
Except to God supreme,
I will not renounce
Thy royal sons,
40 The most generous of men,
Their spears shall resound

In the land of their enemies.
And until I fail in old age,
In the sore necessity of death,

May I not be smiling,
If I praise not Urien.

XLIV. THE SPOILS OF TALIESSIN, A SONG TO URIEN. - BOOK OF TALIESSIN XXVII.

IN manliness he will greet my trouble,
Should I be bled, I should evidently get better;
Truly I saw. no one before, who saw not in me
Every indisposition, he will cultivate his business.
I saw a feeding about a lion for plants,
I saw leaves of luxuriant growth.
I saw a branch with equal blossoms.
Did I not see a prince? most liberal his customs,
I saw the ruler of Catraeth beyond the plains
10 Be my oak *(i.e.* prince) the gleaming spirit *(i.e.* lightning) of the Cymry.
The value of my cry great will be its advantage to degrees.
The chief of men, shield of warriors.
The extensive booty of the ashen shaft is my fair Awen.
A shield before a prince, bright his smile,
Heroic, aspiring, the most heroic is Urien.
A merchant will not oppose me. Tumultuous
The slothful one, brightly shines the blue of the enamelled covering; prolific and highly exalted
Every one; a step without skill on the side of the watery fronts of the Mordei.
A chief excessively active to us he will come of thy will.
20 Active the yellow-gray one in the hall.
Full of people. A protector in Aerou.
Great his energy, his poets, and his musicians,
Very fierce is Ial against his enemies.
May great strength of men be connected with Brython.
Like the wheeling of a fiery meteor over the earth.
Like a wave that governs Llwyvenydd.
Like the harmonious ode of Gwen and Gweithen,
Like Mor the greatly courteous is Urien.
In his early career an intrepid hero.
30 He is such a ruler of kings as Dyawr,
He is one (i.e. unequalled) as a chaser of the swift horses of the multitude.
In the beginning of May in Powys, in battle array,
He is one, coming when he visits his people.
Eagle of the land, extensive thy glance.
I would have requested an active courser
Of vigorous trot, the price of the spoil of Taliessin.
One is the violent course on the bottom and the summit,

One is the gift of a baron to a lord.
One is the herd of stags in their flight,
40 One is the wolf not covetous of broom,
One is the country where a son is born,
And of one form and one sound is the battle-place of warriors.
Of one sound they will evilly yoke
And Ceneu and Nudd Hael, and an extensive country under him.
And if I obtain for myself a smile,
He will make the bards ever joyful,
Before that I could wish dead the sons of Gwyden,
May the happy country of Urien be filled with blood.

XLV.RED BOOK OF HERGEST XII.

I. LET the furious Unhwch lead me on
To the front of the mutual conflict--
'Tis better to be killed than parley on terms.
II. Let the furious Unhwch lead me on--
It was said in the Pass of Llech,--
"Dunawd the son of Pabo will not lurk."
III. Let the furious Unhwch lead me on--
Like the sullen agitation of the sea was the war-expanding tumult.
Of Urien with the ardent grasp.
IV. The eagle of Gal, Unhwch, bold and generous,
Wrathful in war, sure of conquest,
Was Urien with the ardent grasp.
V. The eagle of Gal, Unhwch,
The possessor of the energetic soul . . .
The cell of the sea of smooth inlets with green surface.
VI. A head I bear by my side,
That has been an assaulter between two hosts--
The magnanimous son of Cynvarch was its possessor.
VII. A head I bear by my side,
The head of Urien, the mild leader of his army--
And on his white bosom the sable raven is perched.
VIII, A head I bear in my shirt,
The head of Urien who governed a court in mildness--
And on his white bosom the sable raven gluts.
IX. A head I bear in my hand,
He that was a soaring eagle, whose like will not be had,
His princely breast is assailed by the devourer.
X. A head I bear by the side of my thigh,
That was the shield of his country,
That was a wheel in battle,
That was a ready sword in his country's battles.
XI. A head I bear on my sword:
Better his being alive than that he should go to the grave;
He was a castle for old age.
XII. A head I bear from the bordering land of Penawg,
Wide extended was his warfare:
Urien the eloquent, whose, fame went far.
XIII. A head I bear on my shoulder,
That would not bring on me disgrace--
Woo to my hand that my lord is slain.

XIV. A head I bear on my arm,
He that overcame the land of Bryneich--
But after being a hero, now on the hearse.
XV. A head I bear in the grasp of my hand,
Of a chief that mildly governed a country;
The head, the most powerful pillar of Prydain.
XVI. A head I bear that supported me,
Is there any known but he welcomed?
Woe my hand, gone is be that sustained me.
XVII. A head I bear from the Riw,
With his lips foaming with blood--
Woe to Reged from this day!
XVIII. My arm has not flagged; my bosom is greatly troubled;
Ah! my heart, is it not broken?
A head I bear that was my support.
XIX. The delicate white corpse will be covered to-day,
Under earth and stones:
Woe my hand, that the father of Owain is slain!
XX. The delicate white corpse will be covered to-day,
Amidst earth and oak:
Woe my hand, that my cousin is slain!
XXI. The delicate white corpse will be covered to-night;
Under stones let it be left:
Woe my hand, what a step has fate decreed me!
XXII. The delicate white corpse will be covered to-night
Amidst earth and green sods:
Woe my hand, that the son of Cynvarch is slain!
XXIII. The delicate white corpse will be covered to-day
Under the greensward and a tumulus:
Woe my hand, that my lord is slain!
XXIV. The delicate white corpse will be covered to-day,
Under earth and sand:
Woe my hand, the step that is decreed to me!
XXV. The delicate white corpse will be covered to-day
Under earth and nettles:
Woe my hand, that such a step could have happened to me!
XXVI. The delicate white corpse will be covered to-day
Under earth and blue stones:
Woe my hand, the step that has befallen me!
XXVII. A master-feat of the world the brother has been in pursuit of;
For the horns of the buffalo, for a festive goblet
He was the depredator with the hounds in the covert of Reged!
XXVIII. A master-feat of the world the brother has eagerly sought,
For the equivocal horn of the buffalo;
He was the chaser with the hounds with the men of Reged.
XXIX. Eurdyl will be joyless this night,
And multitudes (will be so) besides:
In Aber Lleu has Urien been slain.
XXX. Eurdyl will be sorrowful from the tribulation of this night,
And from the fate that is to me befallen;
That her brother should be slain at Aber Lleu.
XXXI. On Friday I saw great anxiety
Among the hosts of Baptism,
Like a swarm without a hive, bold in despair.
XXXII. Were there not given to me by Run, greatly fond of war,
A hundred swarms and a hundred shields?

But one swarm was better far than all.

XXXIII. Were there not given to me by Run, the famous chief,
A cantrev, and a hundred oxen?
But one gift was better far than those.

XXXIV. In the lifetime of Run, the peaceless ranger,
The unjust will wallow in dangers;
May there be irons on the steeds of rapine.

XXXV. The extreme I know of my trouble:
Is what all will hear in every season of warfare;
No one can charge me with anything.

XXXVI. Dunawd, the leading horseman, would drive onward,
Intent upon making a corpse,
Against the onset of Owain.

XXXVII. Dunawd, the chief of the age, would drive onward,
Intent upon making battle,
Against the conflict of Pasgen.

XXXVIII. Gwallawg, the horseman of tumult, would drive onward,
Intent upon trying the sharpest edge,
Against the conflict of Elphin.

XXXIX. Bran, the son of Mellyrn, would drive onward,
Collecting men to burn my ovens:
A wolf that looked grimly by the banks of Abers.

XL. Morgant and his men would drive onward,
Collecting a host to burn my lands:
He was a mouse that scratched against a rock.

XLI. I pushed onward when Elgno was slain;
The blade which Pyll brandished would gleam terribly,
If tents were pitched in his country.

XLII. A second time I saw, after a conflict,
A golden shield on the shoulder of Urien;
A second to him there was Elgno Hen.

XLIII. Upon the resolution there came a failing
From the dread of a furious horseman:
Will there be another compared with Urien?

XLIV. Decapitated is my lord, his opponents are powerful:
Warriors will not love his enemies:
Many sovereigns has he consumed.

XLV. The ardent disposition of Urien! it is sadness to me:
There is commotion in every region.
In pursuit of Llovan Llawdivro.

XLVI. Gentle gate! thou art heard afar;
There is scarcely another deserving praise,
Since Urien is no more.

XLVII. Many a hunting-dog and fine grown hawk
Have been trained on its flow,
Before Erlleon became desolate.

XLVIII. This hearth, deserted by the shout of war,
More congenial on its floor would have been
The mead, and loquacious drinkers.

XLIX. This hearth, will not nettles cover it?
While its defender lived,
More congenial to it were those who made requests.

L. This hearth, will it not be covered by the greensward?
In the lifetime of Owain and Elphin,
Its cauldron boiled the prey.

LI. This hearth, will it not be covered with musty fingers?
More congenial around its viand would have been
The gashing sword of the dauntless.

LII. This hearth, will not the slender brambles cover it?
Burning wood used to be on it,
Which Reged was accustomed to give.
LIII. This hearth, will not thorns cover it?
More congenial on it would have been the mixed group
Of Owain's social retinue.
LIV. This hearth, will it not be covered over by the ants?
More accustomed it was to bright torches,
And harmless festivities.
LV. This hearth, will it not be covered with dock-leaves?
More congenial on its floor would have been
The mead, and loquacious drinkers.
LVI. This hearth, will it not be turned up by the swine?
More congenial to it would have been
The joy of men, and the circling horns of banquet.
LVII. This hearth, will it not be scratched up by the fowl?
Want would not approach it
In the lifetime of Owain and Urien.
LVIII. This buttress, and that one there,
More congenial around them would have been
The joy of a host, and the tread of a minstrel.

J. Poems Relating to Urien and His Son Owen

XLVI. BOOK OF TALIESSIN XVIII.

A rumour has come to met from Calchvynyd,
A disgrace in the south country, a praiseworthy pillage.
And he will give to a lion the fierceness of his baptism.
Full is his strath of joyful produce.
The people are satiated with warfare, the strangers are satiated,
A battle of encroachment, during the excessive heat of the country,
A wonder of Cymry that relate it.
Let the cattle of the son of Idno come to Dyved.
And let no one dare not to come.
10 To pay a hundred cows I will give one calf.
The slaughter of thy foes about thy country,
Like fire it heats a vapour where it happens to be.
When we made an expedition to the land of Gwydno,
There was a corpse delicately fair between the gravel and the pebbles on the bank.
When he returned in the autumn from the country of Clydesmen,
The cow did not low to her calf.
Will greet Mabon from another country,
A battle, when Owain defends the cattle of his country.
A battle in the ford of Alclud, a battle in the Gwen,
20 A battle, in conjunction of tumult to them.

A battle against Rodawys of snowy-white aspect,
Brandishing of spears and black, and bright sheets,
A battle on this side of the gleaming guiding heart of oak.
A shield in hand, the camp trembling,
Saw Mabon on the fair portion of Reidol.
Against the kine of Reged they engaged,
If they had wings they would have flown.
Against Mabon without corpses they would not go.
Meeting, they descend and commence the battle.
30 The country of Mabon is pierced with destructive slaughter.
When Owain descends for the kine of his father,
There broke out lime, and wax, and hawthorn.
Is it not fair prey for any one to take a bald cow?
Support each other against men with ruddy spears.
Against the four-way-spreading conflagration,
Against the mighty rising.
Against gore on flesh,
Against a dismal straining.
A rumour came to me,
40 From the bright lands of the South.
Splendid and liberal chiefs declare
That thou shalt not be addressed by vulgar ones.
About the ford of the boundary, about the alders his battle-places.
When was caused the battle of the king, sovereign, prince,
Very wild will the kine be before Mabon.
From the meeting of Gwrgun.
The resting-place of the corpses of some was in Run.
There was joy, there will be for ravens.
Loud the talk of men after
50 Battle. Escaped not the shield of Owain.
With notched shield an opposing in battle tumult,
Cattle would not run about without crimson faces.
Crimson were the kine of Bender, and great his grace,
Gore surrounding the top of his head.
And a white face conspicuous the gasping.
The golden saddle (was) drenched in gore, as to its appearance.
The Gwentians praise the booty, the booty was extended,
The booty in front of the eager battle of the eager strangers.
A booty of heads with forked branches. On the shields
60 Awfully the blades are falling about the head.
A battle in front of Owain, great, great his rage.
A fine day, they fell, men, defending (their) country.
There rested the extreme-impelling advantage of their father.

XLVII. THE AFFAIR OF ARGOED LLWYFAIN. - BOOK OF TALIESSIN XXXV.

IN the morning of Saturday there was a great battle,
From when the sun rose until it gained its height.
Flamdwyn hastened in four hosts
Godeu and Reged to overwhelm.
They extended from Argoed to Arvynyd.
They retained not life during one day.
Flamdwyn called out again, of great impetuosity,
Will they give hostages? are they ready?
Owen answered, Let the gashing appear,
10 They will not give, they are not, they are not ready.
And Ceneu, son of Coel, would be an irritated lion
Before he would give a hostage to any one.
Urien called out again, the lord of the cultivated region,
If there be a meeting for kindred,
Let us raise a banner above the mountain,
And advance our persons over the border.
And let us raise our spears over the heads of men,
And rush upon Flamdwyn in his army,
And slaughter with him and his followers.
20 And because of the affair of Argoed Llwyfain,
There was many a corpse.
The ravens were red from the warring of men.
And the common people hurried with the tidings.
And I will divine the year that I am not increasing.
And until I fail in old age,
In the sore necessity of death,
May I not be smiling,
If I praise not Urien.

XLVIII. THE DEATH-SONG OF OWAIN. - BOOK OF TALIESSIN XLIV.

Text, vol. ii. p. 199. Notes, vol. ii. p. 417.
THE soul of Owain son of Urien. May its Lord consider its need.
The chief of Reged, the heavy sward conceals him. His knowledge was not shallow.
A low cell (contains) the renowned protector of bards, the wings of dawn were the flowing of his lances.
For there will not be found a match for the chief of the glittering west.
The reaper of the tenacious foes. The offspring of his father and grandfather.
When Flamdwyn killed Owain, there was not one greater than he sleeping.
A wide number of Lloegyr went to sleep with light in their eyes.
And those that fled not instantly were beyond necessity.
Owain valiantly chastised them, like a pack (of wolves) pursuing sheep.

10 A worthy man, upon his many-coloured trappings, he would give horses to those that asked.
While he hoarded hard money, it was not shared for his soul.
The soul of Owain, son of Urien.

K. Poems Relating to the Battle of Ardderyd

XLIX. BLACK BOOK OF CAERMARTHEN I.

I. How sad with me, how sad!
Have Cedwyv and Cadvan perished?
Glaring and tumultuous was the slaughter;
Perforated was the shield from Try-wruyd.
TALIESSIN.
II. It was Maelgwn that I saw combat-ing,
His household before the tumult of the host is not silent.
MYRDIN.
III. Before two men in Nevtur will they land,
Before Errith and Gurrith on a pale white horse.
The slender bay they will undoubted-ly bear away.
Soon will his retinue be seen with Elgan.
Alas for his death! a great journey they came.
TALIESSIN.
IV. Rys, the one-toothed, a span was his shield;
Even to thee has complete prosperity come.
Cyndur has been slain; beyond meas-ure they deplore;
Men that were generous while they lived have been slain;
Three men of note, whose. esteem was great with Elgan.
MYRDIN.
V. Through and through, in excess and excess they came,

From yonder and yonder there came to me Bran and Melgan;
Slay, in their last conflict, Diwel
The son of Erbin, and his men, they did.
TALIESSIN.
VI. The host of Maelgwn, it was fortu-nate that they came--
Slaughtering men of battle, penetrat-ing the gory plain,
Even the action of Ardderyd, when there will be a crisis,
Continually for the hero they will prepare.
MYRDIN.
VII. A host of flying darts, reeking will be the gory plain;
A host of. warriors, vigorous and ac-tive will they be;
A host, when wounds will be given, a host, when flight will take place,
A host, when they will return to the combat.
TALIESSIN.
VIII. The seven sons of Eliffer, seven heroes when put to proof,
They will not avoid seven spears in their seven divisions.
MYRDIN.
IX. Seven blazing fires, seven oppos-ing armies,
The seventh Cynvelyn in every fore-most place.
TALIESSIN.

188

X. Seven thrusting spears, seven rivers-ful
Of the blood of chieftains will they fill.
MYRDIN.
XI. Seven score generous ones have gone to the shades;
In the wood of Celyddon they came to their end.
Since I, Myrdin, am next after Taliessin,
Let my prediction become common.

L. BLACK BOOK OF CAERMARTHEN XVII.

I. SWEET appletree of delightful branches,
Budding luxuriantly, and shooting forth renowned scions,
I will predict before the owner of Machreu,
That in the valley of Machawy on Wednesday there will be blood,--
Joy to Lloegyr of the blood-red blades.
Rear, O little pig! there will come on Thursday
Joy to the Cymry of mighty battles,
In their defence of Cymminawd, with their incessant sword-thrusts.
On the Saxons there will be a slaughter with ashen spears,
And their heads will be used as balls to play with.
I prophesy truth without disguise,--
The elevation of a child in a secluded part of the South.
II. Sweet appletree, a green tree of luxurious growth,
How large are its branches, and beautiful its form!
And I will predict a battle that will make me shriek
At Pengwern, in the sovereign feast, mead is appropriate. [1]
III. Sweet appletree, and a yellow tree;
Grow at Tal Ardd, without a garden surrounding it;
And I will predict a battle in Prydyn,
In defence of their frontier against the men of Dublin;
Seven ships will come over the wide lake,
And seven hundred over the sea to conquer.
Of those that come, none will go to Cennyn,
Except seven half-empty ones, according to the prediction.
IV. Sweet appletree that luxuriantly grows!
Food I used to take at it base to please a fair maid,
When, with my shield on my shoulder, and my sword on my thigh,
I slept all alone in the woods of Celyddon.
Hear, O little pig! now apply thyself to reason,
And listen to birds whose notes. are pleasant,
Sovereigns across the sea will come on Monday;
Blessed will the Cymry be, from that design.
V. Sweet appletree that grows in the glade!
Their vehemence will conceal it from the lords of Rydderch,
Trodden it is around its base, and men are about it.
Terrible to them were heroic forms.

Gwendydd loves me not, greets me not;
I am hated by the firmest minister of Rydderch;
I have ruined his son and his daughter.
Death takes all away, why does he not visit me?
For after Gwenddoleu no princes honour me;
I am not soothed with diversion, I am not visited by the fair;
Yet in the battle of Ardderyd golden was my torques,
Though I am now despised by her who is of the colour of swans.
VI. Sweet appletree of delicate bloom,
That grows in concealment in the woods!
At break of day the tale was told me,
That the firmest minister is offended at my creed,
Twice, thrice, four times, in one day.
O Jesus! would that my end had come
Before the death of the son of Gwendydd happen on my hand!
VII. Sweet appletree, which grows by the river-side!
With respect to it, the keeper will not thrive on its splendid fruit.
While my reason was not aberrant, I used to be around its stem
With a fair sportive maid, a paragon of slender form.
Ten years and forty, as the toy of lawless ones,
Have I been wandering in gloom and among sprites.
After wealth in abundance and entertaining minstrels,
I have been (here so long that) it is useless for gloom and sprites to lead me astray.
I will not sleep, but tremble on account of my leader,
My lord Gwenddoleu, and those who are natives of my country.
After suffering disease and longing grief about the words of Celyddon,
May I become a blessed servant of the Sovereign of splendid retinues!
VIII. Sweet appletree of delicate blossoms,
Which grows in the soil amid the trees!
The Sibyl foretells a tale that will come to pass--
A golden rod of great value, will, for bravery,
Be given to glorious chiefs before the dragons;
The diffuser of grace will vanquish the profane man.
Before the child, bold as the sun in his courses,
Saxons shall be eradicated, and bards shall flourish.
IX. Sweet appletree, and a tree of crimson hue,
Which grow in concealment in the wood of Celyddon;
Though sought for their fruit, it will be in vain,
Until Cadwaladyr comes from the conference of Cadvaon,
To the Eagle of Tywi and Teiwi rivers;
And until fierce anguish comes from Aranwynion,
And the wild and long-haired ones are made tame:
X. Sweet appletree, and a tree of crimson hue,
Which grow in concealment in the wood of Celyddon;

Though sought for their fruit, it will be in vain,
Until Cadwaladyr comes from the conference of Rhyd Rheon,
And Cynan to meet him advances upon the Saxons;
The Cymry will be victorious, glorious will be their leader.
All shall have their rights, and the Brython will rejoice,
Sounding the horns of gladness, and chanting the song of peace and happiness!

[1] The following lines are added at the bottom of the page:--
And around Cymminawd, a deadly hewing down
By a chief of Eryri--hatred will remain.

L. The Gododin Poems

LI. BOOK OF ANEURIN I.

THIS THE GODODIN.   ANEURIN COMPOSED IT.
I. OF manly disposition was the youth,
Valour had he in the tumult;
Fleet thick-maned chargers
Were under the thigh of the illustrious youth;
A shield, light and broad,
Was on the slender swift flank,
A sword, blue and bright,
Golden spurs, and ermine.
It is not by me
That hatred shall be shown to thee;
I will do better towards thee,
To celebrate thee in poetic eulogy.
Sooner hadst thou gone to the bloody bier
Than to the nuptial feast;
Sooner hadst thou gone to be food for ravens
Than to the conflict of spears;
Thou beloved friend of Owain!
Wrong it is that he should be under ravens.
It is evident in what region
The only son of Marro was killed.
II. Caeawg, the leader, wherever he came,
Breathless in the presence of a maid would he distribute the mead;
The front of his shield was pierced, when he heard
The shout of battle, he would give no quarter wherever he pursued;
He would not retreat from the combat, until he caused
Blood to stream; like rushes would he hew down the men who would not yield.

The Gododin does not relate, in the land of Mordai,
Before the tents of Madawg, when he returned,
Of but one man in a hundred that came back.
III. Caeawg, the combatant, the stay of his country,
Whose attack is like the rush of the eagle into the sea, when allured by his prey;
He formed a compact, his signal was observed;
Better was his resolution performed: he retreated not
Before the host of Gododin, at the close of day.
With confidence he pressed upon the conflict of Manawyd;
And regarded neither spear nor shield.
There is not to be found a habitation that abounded in dainties,
That has been kept from. the attack of the warriors.
IV. Caeawg, the leader, the wolf of the strand,
Amber wreaths encircled his brow;
Precious was the amber, worth wine from the horn.
He repelled the violence of ignoble men, and blood trickled down;
For Gwynedd and the North would have come to his share,
By the advice of the son of Ysgyrran,
Who wore the broken shield.
V. Caeawg, the leader, armed was he in the noisy conflict;
His was the foremost part of the advanced division, in front of the hosts.
Before his blades fell five battalions.
Of the men of Deivyr and Brenneich, uttering groans:
Twenty hundred perished in one hour.
Sooner did his flesh go to the wolf, than he to the nuptial feast;
He sooner became food for the raven, than approached the altar;
Before he entered the conflict of spears, his blood streamed to the ground.
It was the price of mead in the hall, amidst the throng.
Hyveidd Hir shall be celebrated as long as there will be a minstrel.
VI. The men went to Gododin with laughter and sprightliness,
Bitter were they in the battle, displaying their blades
A short year they remained in peace.
The son of Bodgad, by the energy of his hand, caused a throbbing.
Though they went to churches to do penance,
The old, and the young, and the bold-handed,
The inevitable strife of death was to pierce them.
VII. The men went to Gododin, laughing as they moved:
A gloomy disaster befell their army;
Thou slayest them with blades, without much noise:
Thou, powerful pillar of living right, causest stillness.
VIII. The men went to Catraeth, loquacious was their host;
Fresh mead was their feast, and also their poison.
Three hundred were contending with weapons;
And after sportive mirth, stillness ensued!

Though they went to churches to do penance,
The inevitable strife of death was to pierce them.
IX. The men went to Catraeth, fed with mead, and drunk.
Firm and vigorous; it were wrong if I neglected to praise them.
Around the red, mighty, and murky blades
Obstinately and fiercely fought the dogs of war.
If I had judged you to be on the side of the tribe of Brenneich,
Not the phantom of a man would I have left alive.
A friend I have lost, myself being unhurt;
He openly opposed the terrible chief--
The magnanimous hero did not seek the dowry of his father-in-law;
The son of Cian of Maen Gwyngwn.
X. The men went to Catraeth with. the dawn;
They dealt peaceably with those who feared them.
A hundred thousand and three hundred engaged in mutual overthrow.
Drenched in gore they served as butts for lances;
Their post they most manfully defended
Before the retinue of Mynyddawg Mwynvawr.
XI. The men went to Catraeth with the dawn;
Regretted are their absence and their disposition;
Mead they drank, yellow, sweet, ensnaring.
In that year many a minstrel fell.
Redder were their swords than their plumes.
Their blades were white as lime, their helmets split into four parts,
Before the retinue of Mynyddawg Mwynvawr.
XII. The men went to Catraeth with the day:
Have not the best of battles their disgrace?
They made biers a matter of necessity.
With blades full of vigour in defence of Baptism.
This is best before the alliance of kindred.
Exceedingly great was the bloodshed and death, of which they were the cause,
Before the army of Gododin, when the day occurred.
Is not a double quantity of discretion the best strengthener of a hero?
XIII. The man went to Catraeth with the day:
Truly he quaffed the foaming mead on serene nights;
He was unlucky, though proverbially fortunate:
His mission, through ambition, was that of a destroyer.
There hastened not to Catraeth
A chief so magnificent
As to his design on the standard.
Never was there such a host
From the fort of Eiddyn,
That would scatter abroad the mounted ravagers.
Tudvwlch Hir, near his land and towns,

Slaughtered the Saxons for seven days.
His valour remained until he was overpowered;
And his memory will remain among his fair associates.
When Tudvwlch, the supporter of the land, arrived,
The station of the son of Cilydd became a plain of blood.
XIV. The man went to Catraeth with the dawn;
To them were their shields a protection.
Blood they sought, the gleamers assembled:
Simultaneously, like thunder, arose the din of shields.
The man of envy, the deserter, and the base,
He would tear and pierce with pikes.
From an elevated position, he slew, with a blade,
In iron affliction, a steel-clad commander;
He subdued in Mordai those that owed him homage;
Before Erthgi armies groaned.
XV. Of the battle of Catraeth, when it shall be related,
The people will utter sighs; long has been their sorrow.
There will be a dominion without a sovereign, and a murky land.
The sons of Godebawg, an upright clan,
Bore, streaming, long biers.
Sad was the fate, just the necessity,
Decreed to Tudvwlch and Cyvwlch Hir.
Together they drank the clear mead
By the light of the rushes,
Though pleasant to the taste, its banefulness lasted long.
XVI. Before Echeching, the splendid Caer, he shouted:
Young and forward men followed him;
Before, on the Bludwe the horn was poured out
In the joyful Mordai;
Before, his drink would be bragget;
Before, gold and rich purple he would display;
Before, high-fed horses would bear him safe away;
Gwrthlev and he, when he poured out the liquor,
Before, he would raise the shout, and there would be a profitable diminution;
He was a bear in his march, always unwilling to skulk.
XVII. And now the early leader,
The sun is ascending,
The sovereign from which emanates universal light.
In the heaven of the Isle of Prydain.
Direful was the flight before the shaking
Of the shield in the direction of the victor;
Bright was the horn
In the hall of Eiddyn;
With pomp was he invited
To the feast of the intoxicating mead;

He drank the beverage of wine
At the meeting of the reapers;
He drank transparent wine,
With a daring purpose.
The reapers sing of war,
War with the shining wing;
The minstrels sang of war,
Of harnessed war,
Of winged war.
No shield was unexpanded
In the conflict of spears;
Of equal eye they fell
In the struggle of battle.
Unshaken in the tumult,
Without dishonour did he retaliate;
His will had to be conciliated
Ere became a green sward
The grave of Gwrvelling the great.
XVIII. Qualities they will honour.
Three forward (chiefs or bands) of Novant,
A battalion of five hundred;
Three chiefs and three hundred;
There are three Knights of battle.
From Eiddyn, arrayed in golden armour,
Three loricated hosts.
Three Kings wearing the golden torques;
Three bold Knights.
Three equal battles;
Three of the same order, mutually jealous.
Bitterly would they chase the foe;
Three dreadful in the conflict;
Lions, that would kill dead as lead.
There was in the war a collection of gold;
Three sovereigns of the people.
Came from the Brython,
Cynri and Cenon
And Cynrain from Aeron,
To greet with ashen lances.
The Deivyr distillers.
Came there from the Brython,
A better man than Cynon,
A serpent to his sullen foe?
XIX. I drank mead and wine in Mordai,
Great was the quantity of spears
In the assembly of the warriors.

He prepared food for the eagle.
When Cydywal sallied forth, he raised
The shout with the green dawn, and dealt out tribulation;
Splintered shields about the ground he left,
With darts of awful tearing did he hew down;
In the battle, the foremost in the van
The son of Syvno wounded; the astronomer knew it.
He who sold his life,
In the face of warning,
With sharpened blades committed slaughter;
But he himself was slain by crosses and spears.
According to the compact, he meditated an attack,
And admired a pile of carcases
Of gallant men of toil,
Whom in the upper part of Gwynedd he pierced.
XX. I drank wine and mead in Mordai,
And because I drank, I fell by the side of the rampart; the fate of allurement.
Colwedd the brave was not without ambition.
When all fell, thou didst also fall.
Thus, when the issue comes, it were well if thou hadst not sinned.
Present, it was related, was a person of a daring arm.
XXI. The men went to Catraeth; they were renowned;
Wine and mead from golden cups was their beverage,
That year was to them of exalted solemnity;
Three warriors and three score and three hundred, wearing the golden tor-
ques.
Of those who hurried forth after the excess of revelling,
But three escaped by the prowess of the gashing sword,
The two war-dogs of Aeron, and Cenon the dauntless,
And myself from the spilling of my blood, the reward of my sacred song.
XXII. My friend in real distress, we should have been by none disturbed,
Had not the white Commander led forth (his army):
We should not have been separated in the hall from the banquet of mead,
Had he not laid waste our convenient position.
He who is base in the field, is base on the hearth.
Truly the Gododin relates that after the gashing assault,
There was none more ardent than Llivieu.
XXIII. Scattered, broken, of motionless form, is the weapon,
To which it was highly congenial to prostrate the horde of the Lloegrians.
Shields were strewn in the entrance, shields in the battle of lances;
He reduced men to ashes,
And made women widows,
Before his death.
Graid, the son of Hoewgi,

With spears,
He caused the effusion of blood.
XXIV. Adan was the hero of the two shields
Whose front was variegated, and motion like that of a war-steed.
There was tumult in the mount of slaughter, there was fire,
Impetuous were the lances, there was sunshine,
There was food for ravens, for the raven there was profit.
And before he would let them go free,
With the morning dew, like the eagle in his pleasant course,
He scattered them on either side as they advanced forward.
The Bards of the world will pronounce an opinion on men of valour.
No ransom would avail those whom his standard pursued.
The spears in the hands of the warriors were causing devastation.
And ere was interred under his horses,
One who had been energetic in his commands,
His blood had thoroughly washed his armour:
Buddvan, the son of Bleiddvan the Bold.
XXV. It were wrong to leave him without a memorial, a great wrong.
He would not leave an open gap through cowardice;
The benefit of the minstrels of Prydain never quitted his court.
On the calends of January, according to his design.
His land was not ploughed, since it lay waste.
He was a mighty dragon of indignant disposition,
A commander in the bloody field after the banquet or wine;--
Gwenabwy, the son of Gwen, of the strife of Catraeth.
XXVI. True it was, as songs relate,
No one's steed overtook Marchleu.
The lances of the commander
From his prancing horse, strewed a thick path.
As he was reared to bring slaughter and support.
Furious was the stroke of his protecting sword;
Ashen shafts were scattered from the grasp of his hand.
From the stony pile;
He delighted to spread destruction.
He would slaughter with a variegated sword from a furze-bush;
As when a company of reapers comes in the interval or fine weather,
Would Marchleu cause the blood to flow.
XXVII. Issac was sent from the southern region;
His conduct resembled the flowing sea;
He was full of modesty and gentleness,
When be delightfully drank the mead.
But along the rampart of Offer to the point of Madden,
He was not fierce without heroism, nor did he attempt scattering without
effecting it,

His sword resounded in the mouths of mothers;
He was an ardent spirit, praise be to him, the son of Gwyddneu.
XXVIII. Ceredig, lovely is his fame;
He would gain distinction, and preserve it;
Gentle, lowly, calm, before the day arrived
In which he learned the achievements of the brave:
May it be the lot of the friend of songs to arrive
In the country of heaven, and recognise his home!
XXIX. Ceredig, amiable leader,
A wrestler in the impetuous fight;
His gold-bespangled shield was conspicuous on the battle-field,
His lances were broken, and shattered into splinters,
The stroke of his sword was fierce and penetrating;
Like a man would he maintain his post.
Before he received the affliction of earth, before the fatal blow.
He had fulfilled his in guarding his station.
May he find a complete reception
With the Trinity in perfect unity.
XXXI When Caradawg rushed to battle,
Like the woodland boar was the gash of the hewer;
He was the bull of battle in the conflicting fight;
He allured wild dogs with his hand.
My witnesses are Owain the son of Eulad,
And Gwryen, and Gwyn, and Gwryad.
From Catraeth, from the conflict,
From Bryn Hydwn, before it was taken,
After having clear mead in his hand,
Gwrien did not see his father.
XXXI. The men marched with speed, together they bounded onward;
Short-lived were they--having become drunk over the clarified mead.
The retinue of Mynyddawg, renowned in a trial,
Their life was the price of their banquet of mead;--
Caradawg and Madawg, Pyll and Ieuan,
Gwgawn and Gwiawn, Gwyn and Cynvan,
Peredur with steel arms, Gwawrddur and Aeddan.
A defence were they in the tumult, though with shattered shields,
When they were slain, they also slaughtered;
Not one to his native home returned.
XXXII. The men marched with speed, together were they regaled
That year over mead; great was their design:
How sad to mention them! how grievous the longing for them!
Their retreat was poison; no mother's son nurses them.
How long the vexation and how long the regret for them--
For the brave men of the wine-fed region!
Gwlyged of Gododin, having partaken of the inciting

Banquet of Mynyddawg, performed illustrious deeds,
And dear was the price he gave for the purchase of the conflict of Catraeth.
XXXIII. The men went to Catraeth in battle-array and with shout of war,
With the strength of steeds, and with dark-brown harness, and with shields,
With uplifted javelins, and sharp lances,
With glittering mail, and with swords.
He excelled, he penetrated through the host,
Five battalions fell before his blade;
Ruvawn Hir,--he gave gold to the altar,
And gifts and precious stones to the minstrel.
XXXIV. No hall was ever made so loquacious,--
So great, so magnificent for the slaughter.
Morien procured and spread the fire,
He would not say that Cenon would not make a corpse
Of one harnessed, armed with a pike, and of wide-spread fame.
His sword resounded on the top of the rampart.
No more than a huge stone can be removed from its fixed place
Will Gwid, the son of Peithan, be moved.
XXXV. No hall was ever so full of delegates:
Had not Moryen been like Caradawg,
With difficulty could he have escaped towards Mynawg.
Fierce, he was fiercer than the son of Fferawg;
Stout was his hand, he set flames to the retreating horsemen.
Terrible in the city was the cry of the multitude;
The van of the army of Gododin was scattered;
In the day of wrath he was nimble--and was he not destructive in retaliating?
The dependants of Mynyddawg deserved their horns of mead.
XXXVI. No hall was ever made so immovable
As that of Cynon of the gentle breast, sovereign of valuable treasures.
He sat no longer at the upper end of the high seat.
Those whom he pierced were not pierced again;
Sharp was the point of his lance;
With his enamelled armour he penetrated through the troops;
Swift in the van were the horses, in the van they tore along.
In the day of wrath, destruction attended his blade,
When Cynon rushed forward with the green dawn.
XXXVII. A grievous descent was made on his native place;
He repelled aggression, he fixed a boundary;
His spear forcibly pushed the laughing chiefs of war:
Even as far as Effyd reached his valour, which was like that of Elphin;
Eithinyn the renowned, an ardent spirit, the bull of conflict.
XXXVIII. A grievous descent was made on his native place,
The price of mead in the hall, and the feast of wine;
His blades were scattered about between two armies,

Illustrious was the knight in front of Gododin.
Eithinyn the renowned, an ardent spirit, the bull of conflict.
XXXIX A grievous descent was made in front of the extended riches;
The army dispersed with trailing shields.--
A shivered shield before the herd of the roaring Beli.
A dwarf from the bloody field hastened to the fence;
On our part there came a hoary-headed man to take counsel.
On a prancing steed, bearing a message from the golden-torqued leader.
Twrch proposed a compact in front of the destructive course:
Worthy was the shout of refusal;
We cried, "Let heaven be our protection;
Let his compact be that he should be prostrated by the spear in battle."
The warriors of the far-famed Aclud
Would not contend without prostrating his host to the ground.
XL. For the piercing of the skilful and most learned man,
For the fair corpse which fell prostrate on the ground,
For the falling of the hair from off his head,
From the grandson of the eagle of Gwydien,
Did not Gwyddivg defend with his spear,
Resembling and honouring his master?
Morieu of the sacred song defended
The wall, and deposed the head
Of the chief in the ground, both our support and our sovereign
Equal to three men, to please the maid, was Bradwen,
Equal to twelve was Gwenabwy the son of Gwen.
XLI. For the piercing of the skilful and most learned man,
He bore a shield in the action;
With energy did the stroke of his sword fall on the head.
In Lloegyr he caused gashings before three hundred chieftains.
He who takes hold of a wolf's mane without a club
In his hand, must naturally have a brave disposition under his cloak.
In the engagement of wrath and carnage
Bradwen perished--he did not escape.
XLII. A man moved rapidly on the wall of the Caer,
He was of a warlike disposition; neither a house nor a city was actively en-
gaged in battle.
One weak man, with his shouts,
Endeavoured to keep off the birds of battle.
Surely Syll of Mirein relates that there were more
That had chanced to come from Llwy,
From around the inlet of the flood;
Surely he relates that there were more
At an early hour,
Equal to Cynhaval in merit.

XLIII. When thou, famous conqueror!
Wast protecting the ear of corn in the uplands
Deservedly were we said to run like men of mark.
The entrance to Din Drei was not guarded.
Such as was fond of treasure took it;
There was a city for the army that should venture to enter.
Gwynwyd was not called, where he was not.
XLIV. Since there are a hundred men in one house,
I know the cares of distress.
The chief of the men must pay the contribution.
XLV. I am not headstrong and petulant.
I will not avenge myself on him who drives me.
I will not laugh in derision.
Under foot for a while,
My knee is stretched,
My hands are bound,
In the earthen house,
With an iron chain
Around my two knees.
Yet of the mead from the horn,
And of the men of Catraeth,
I, Aneurin, will compose,
As Taliesin knows,
An elaborate song,
Or a strain to Gododin,
Before the dawn of the brightest day.
XLVI. The chief exploit of the North did the hero accomplish;
Of a generous breast was he, liberal is his progeny;
There does not walk upon the earth, mother has not borne
Such an. illustrious, powerful, iron-clad warrior.
By the force of the gleaming sword he protected me,
From the dismal earthen prison he brought me out,
From the place of death, from a hostile region:--
Ceneu, the son of Llywarch, energetic, bold.
XLVII. He would not bear the reproach of a congress,
Senyllt, with his vessels full of mead;
He enriched his sword with deeds of violence;
He enriched those who rushed to war;
And with his arm made pools (of blood).
In front of the armies of Gododin and Brennych.
Fleet horses were customary in his hall.
There was streaming gore, and dark-brown harness.
A long stream of light there was from his hand.
And like a hunter shooting with the bow
Was Gwen; and the attacking parties mutually repulsed each other,

Friend and foe by turns;
The men did not cut their way to flee,
But they were the general defenders of every region.
XLVIII. Llech Lleutu and Tud Lleudvre
The course of Gododin,
The course of Ragno, close at hand,
The hand that was director of the splendour of battle,
With the branch of Caerwys.
Before it was shattered
By the season of the storm, by the storm of the season,
To form a rank in front of myriads of men,
Coming from Dindywydd,
Excited with rage,
Deeply did they design,
Sharply did they pierce,
Wholly did the host chant,
Battered was their shield;
Before the bull of conflict
Their van was broken.
XLIX. His languid foes trembled greatly,
Since the battle of most active tumult,
At the border of Banceirw,
Around the border of Bancarw;
The fingers of Brych will break the bar,
For Pwyll, for Disteir, for Distar,
For Pwyll, for Roddig, for Rychwardd,
A strong bow was spent by Rys in Riwdrech.
They that were not bold did not attain their purpose
None escaped that was once overtaken and pierced.
L. It was no good deed that his shield should be pierced.
On the side of his horse;
Not meetly did he place his thigh
On the long-legged, slender, gray charger.
Dark was his shaft, dark,
Darker was his saddle.
Thy man is in his cell,
Gnawing the shoulder of a buck;
May he have the benefit of his hand!
Far be he!
LI. It was well that Adonwy came to Gwen;
Gwen was left without Bradwen.
Thou didst fight, kill, and burn,
Thou didst not do worse than Moryen;
Thou didst. not regard the rear or the van.
Of the towering figure without a helmet.

Thou didst not observe the great swelling sea of knights.
That would hew down, and grant no quarter to the Saxons.
LII. Gododin, in respect of thee will I demand
The dales beyond the ridges of Drum Essyd.
The slave to the love of money is without self-control.
By the counsel of thy son let thy valour shine forth.
It was not a degrading advice.
In front of Tan Veithin,
From twilight to twilight, the edge gleamed.
Glittering exterior had the purple of the pilgrim.
Gwaws, the defenceless, the delight of the bulwark of battle, was slain.
His scream was inseparable from Aneurin.
LIII. Together arise the associated warriors,
To Catraeth the loquacious multitude eagerly march;
The effect of mead in the hall, and the beverage of wine.
Blades were scattered between the two armies.
Illustrious was the knight in front of Gododin:--
Eithinyn the renowned, an ardent spirit, the bull of conflict.
LIV. Together arise the associated warriors,
Strangers to the country, their deeds shall be heard of.
The bright wave murmured along on its pilgrimage,
While the young deer were in full melody.
Among the spears of Brych thou couldst see no rods.
Merit does not accord with the rear.
Moryal in pursuit will not countenance evil deeds,
With his steel blade ready for the effusion of blood.
LV. Together arise the associated warriors.
Strangers to the country, their deeds shall be heard of.
There was slaughtering with axes and blades,
And there was raising large cairns over the men of toil.
LVI. Together arise the warriors, together met,
And all with one accord sallied forth;
Short were their lives, long is the grief of those who loved them.
Seven times their number of Lloegrians they had slain;
After the conflict women raised a lamentation;
Many a mother has the tear on her eyelash.
LVII. No hall was ever made so faultless
Nor a hero so generous, with the aspect of a lion of the greatest course,
As Cynon of the gentle breast, the most comely lord.
The city, its fame extends to the remotest parts;
It was the staying shelter of the army, the benefit of flowing melody.
In the world, engaged in arms, the battle-cry,
And war, the most heroic was he;
He slew the mounted ravagers with the sharpest blade;
Like rushes did they fall before his hand.

Son of Clydno, of lasting fame! I will sing
To thee a song of praise without limit, without end.
LVIII. From the banquet of wine and mead
They deplored the death
Of the mother of Hwrreith.
The energetic Eidiol.
Honoured her in front of the hill,
And before Buddugre,
The hovering ravens
Ascend in the sky.
The foremost spearmen fall
Like a virgin-swarm around him
Without the semblance of a retreat
Warriors in wonder shook their javelins,
With pallid lips,
Caused by the keenness of the destructive sword.
Wakeful was the carousal at the beginning of the banquet;
To-day sleepless is
The mother of Reiddun, the leader of the tumult.
LIX. From the banquet of wine and mead
They went to the strife
Of mail-clad warriors: I know no tale of slaughter which accords
So complete a destruction as has happened.
Before Catraeth, loquacious was the host.
Of the retinue of Mynyddawg, the unfortunate hero,
Out of three hundred but one man returned.
LX. From the banquet of wine and mead they hastened,
Men renowned in difficulty, careless of their lives;
In bright array around the viands they feasted together;
Wine and mead and meal they enjoyed.
From the retinue of Mynyddawg I am being ruined;
And I have lost a leader from among my trite friends.
Of the body of three hundred men that hastened to
Catraeth, alas! none have returned but one alone.
LXI. Pressent, in the combat of spears, was impetuous as a ball,
And on his horse would he be, when not at home;
Yet illusive was his aid against Gododin.
Of wine and mead he was lavish;
He perished on the course;
And under red-stained warriors
Are the steeds of the knight, who in the morning had been bold.
LXII. Angor, thou who scatterest the brave,
Like a serpent thou piercest the sullen ones,
Thou tramplest upon those that are clad in strong mail
In front of the army:

Like an enraged bear, guarding and assaulting,
Thou tramplest upon spears.
In the day of conflicts
In the swampy entrenchment:
Like Neddig Nar,
Who in his fury prepared
A feast for the birds,
In the tumultuous fight.
Upright thou art called from thy righteous deed,
Before the director and bulwark of the course of war,
Merin, and Madyen, it is fortunate that thou wert born.
LXIII. It is incumbent to sing of the complete acquisition
Of the warriors, who around Catraeth made a tumultuous rout.
With confusion and blood, treading and trampling.
The strength of the drinking horn was trodden down, because it had held mead;
And as to the carnage of the interposers
Cibno does not relate, after the commencement of the action.
Since thou hast received the communion thou shalt be interred.
LXIV. It is incumbent to sing of so much renown,
The loud noise of fire, and of thunder, and of tempest,
The noble manliness of the knight of conflict.
The ruddy reapers of war are thy desire,
Thou man of might! but the worthless wilt thou behead,
In battle the extent of the land shall hear of thee.
With thy shield upon thy shoulder thou dost incessantly cleave
With thy blade (until blood flows) like refined wine from glass vessels.
As money for drink, thou art entitled to gold.
Wine-nourished was Gwaednerth, the son of Llywri.
LXV. It is incumbent to sing of the illustrious retinue,
That, after the fatal impulse, filled Aeron.
Their hands satisfied the mouths of the brown eagles,
And prepared food for the beasts of prey.
Of those who went to Catraeth, wearing the golden torques,
Upon the message of Mynyddawg, sovereign of the people,
There came not without reproach on behalf of the Brython,
To Gododin, a man from afar better than Cynon.
LXVI. It is incumbent to sing of so skilful a man;
Joyous was he in the hall; his life was not without ambition;
Bold, all around the world would Eidol seek for melody;
For gold, and fine horses, and intoxicating mead.
Only one man of those who loved the world returned,--
Cynddilig of Aeron, the grandson of Enovant.
LXVII. It is incumbent to sing of the illustrious retinue
That went on the message of Mynyddawg, sovereign of the people,

And the daughter of Eudav Hir, the scourge of Gwananhon,
Who was appareled in purple robes, certain to cause manglings.
LXVIII. The warriors celebrated the praise of Nyved,
When in their presence fire was lighted.
On Tuesday, they put on their dark-brown garments;
On Wednesday, they polished their enamelled armour;
On Thursday, their destruction was certain;
On Friday, was brought carnage all around:
On Saturday, their joint labour did no execution;
On Sunday, their blades assumed a ruddy line;
On Monday, was-seen a pool knee-deep of blood.
Truly, the Gododin relates that, after the toil,
Before the tents of Madawg, when he returned,
Only one man in a hundred came back,
LXIX. Early rising in the morn
There was a conflict at the Aber in front of the course,
The pass and the knoll were in conflagration.
Like a boar didst thou lead to the mount,
There was treasure for him that was fowl of it; there was room;
And there was the blood of dark-brown hawks.
LXX. Early rising in an instant of time,
After kindling a fire at the Aber in front of the fence,
After leading his men in close array,
In front of a hundred he pierced the foremost.
It was sad that you should have caused a gushing of blood,
Like the drinking of mead in the midst of laughter.
It was brave of you to stay the little man
With the fierce and impetuous stroke of the sword.
How irresistible was he when he would kill
The foe! would that his equal could be found!
LXXI. He fell headlong down the precipice;
Song did not support his noble head:
It was a violation of privilege to kill him when bearing the branch,
It was the usage that Owain should ascend upon the course,
And extend, before the onset, the best branch,
And that he should pursue the study of meet and learned strains.
An excellent man was he, the assuager of tumult and battle,
His grasp dreaded a sword;
In his hand he bore an empty corselet.
O sovereign, dispense rewards
Out of his precious shrine.
Eidol, with frigid blood and pallid countenance,
Spreading carnage, his judgment was just and supreme,
Owner of horses
And strong trappings,

And ice-like shields;
Instantaneously he makes an onset, ascending and descending.
LXXII. The leader of war with eagerness conducts the battle,
A mighty country loves mighty reapers.
Blood is a heavy return for new mead.
His cheeks are covered with armour all around,
There is a trampling of accoutrements--accoutrements are trampled.
He calls for death and brings desolation.
In the first onset his lances penetrate the targets,
And for light on the course, shrubs blaze on the spears.
LXXIII. A conflict on all sides destroyed thy cell;
And a hall there was to thee, where used to be poured out
Mead, sweet and ensnaring.
Gwrys make the battle clash with the dawn;
The fair gift of the tribes of the Lloegrians;
Punishment he inflicted until a reverse came.
May the dependants of Gwynedd hear of his renown.
Gwananhon will be his grave.
The lance of the conflict of Gwynedd,
The bull of the host, the oppressor of sovereigns,
Before earth pressed upon him, before he lay down;
Be the extreme boundary of Gododin his grave!
LXXIV. An army is accustomed to be in hardships.
Mynawg, the bitter-handed leader of the forces,
He was wise, ardent, and stately:
At the social banquet he was not at all harsh.
They removed the valuable treasures that were in his possession:
And not the image of anything for the benefit of the region was left,
We are called! Like the sea is the tumult in the conflict;
Spears are mutually darting--spears all equally destructive;
Impelled are sharp weapons of iron, gashing even the ground,
And with a clang the sock falls on the pate.
A successful warrior was Fflamddur against the enemy.
LXXV. He supported war-horses and war-harness.
Drenched with gore on red-stained Catraeth
Is the shaft of the army of Dinus,
The angry dog of war upon the towering hill.
We are called to the honourable post of assault;
Most conspicuous is the iron-clad Heiddyn.
LXXVI. Mynawg of the impregnable strand of Gododin,
Mynawg, for him our cheeks are sad:
Before the raging flame of Eiddyn he turned not aside.
He stationed men of firmness at the entrance,
He placed a thick covering in the van,
Vigorously he descended upon the furious foe;

He caused devastation and sustained great weight.
Of the retinue of Mynyddawg there escaped none
Except one frail weapon, tottering every way.
LXXVII. Since the loss of Moryed there was no shield-bearer,
To support the strand, or to set the ground on fire;
Firmly did he grasp in his hand a blue blade,
A shaft ponderous as a chief priest's crozier;
He rode a gray stately-headed. courser,
And behind his blade there was a dreadful fall of slaughter;
When overpowered, he did not run away from the battle.
He poured out to us sparkling mead, sweet and ensnaring.
LXXVIII. I beheld the array from the high land of Adoyn;
They descended with the sacrifice for the conflagration;
I saw what was usual, a continual running to the town,
And the men of Nwythyon entirely lost;
I saw men in complete order approaching with a shout;
And the heads of Dyvynwal and Breych, ravens devoured them.
LXXIX. Blessed conqueror, of temper mild, the bone of the people,
With his blue streamer displayed, while the foes range the sea.
Brave is he on the waters, most numerous his host;
With a bold breast and loud shout they pierced him.
It was his custom to make a descent before nine armaments,
In the face of blood, of the country, and of the tribes.
I love the victor's throne which was for harmonious strains,
Cynddilig of Aeron, the lion's whelp!
LXXX. I could wish to have been the first to fall in Catraeth,
As the price of mead in the hall, and the beverage of wine;
I could wish to have been pierced by the blade,
Ere he was slain on the green plain of Uffin,
I loved the son of renown, who caused blood to flow,
And made his sword descend upon the violent.
Can a tale of valour before Gododin be related,
In which the son of Ceidiaw has not his fame as a man of war?
LXXXI. It is sad for me, after our toil,
To suffer the pang of death through indiscretion;
And doubly grievous and sad for me to see
Our men falling from head to foot,
With a long sigh and with reproaches.
After the strenuous warriors of our native land and country,
Ruvawn and Gwgawn, Gwiawn and Gwlyged,
Men most gallant at their posts, valiant in difficulties,
May their souls, now after the conflict,
Be received into the country of heaven, the abode of tranquillity.
LXXXII. He repelled the chain through a pool of blood,
He slaughtered like a hero such as asked no quarter.

With a sling and a spear; he flung off his glass goblet
Of mead; in the presence of sovereigns he overthrew an army.
His counsel prevailed wherever he spoke.
A multitude that had no pity would not be allowed
Before the onset of his battle-axes and sword;
Sharpened they were; and his sounding blade was carefully watched.
LXXXIII. A supply of an army,
A supply of lances,
And a host in the vanguard,
With a menacing front:
In the day of strenuous exertion,
In the eager conflict,
They displayed their valour.
After intoxication,
And the drinking of mead,
There was no deliverance.
They watched us
For a while;
When it shall be related how the attack
Of horses and men was repelled, it will be pronounced the decree of fate.
LXXXIV. Why should so much anxiety come to me?
I am anxious about the maid--
The maid that is in Arddeg.
There is a precipitate running,
And lamentation along the course.
Affectionately have I deplored,
Deeply have I loved,
The illustrious dweller of the wood!
And the men of Argoed.
Woe to those who are accustomed
To be marshalled for battle!
He pressed hard upon the hostile force, for the benefit of chieftains,
Through. rough woods,
And dammed-up waters,
To the festivities,
At which they caroused together: he conducted its to a bright fire,
And to a white and fresh hide.
Gereint front the south raised a shout;
A brilliant gleam reflected on the pierced shield.
Of the lord of the spear, a gentle lord
Attached to the glory of the sea.
Posterity will accomplish
What Gereint would have done.
Generous and resolute wert thou!

LXXXV. Instantaneously his fame is wafted on high,
Irresistible was Angor in the conflict,
Unflinching eagle of the forward heroes;
He bore the toil, brilliant was his zeal;
He outstripped fleetest horses in war;
But he was mild when the wine from the goblet flowed.
Before the new mead, and his cheek became pale,
He was a man of the banquet over delicious mead from the bowl.
LXXXVI. With slaughter was every region filled;
His courage was like a fetter:
The front of his shield was pierced.
Disagreeable is the delay of the wrathful
To defend Rywoniawg.
The second time they raised the shout, and were crushed
By the war-horses with gory trappings.
An immovable army will his warlike nobles form,
And the field was reddened when he was greatly enraged.
Severe in the conflict, with a blade he slaughtered
Sad news from the battle be brought
And a New-year's song he composed.
Adan, the son of Ervai, there was pierced,
Adan! the haughty boar, was pierced,
One damsel, a maid, and a hero.
And when he was only a youth he had the rights of a king.
Being lord of Gwyndyd, of the blood of Glyd Gwaredawg.
Ere the turf was laid on the gentle face
Of the generous dead, now undisturbed,
He was celebrated for fame and generosity.
This is the grave of Garthwys Hir from the land of Rywoniawg.
LXXXVII. The coat of Dinogad was of various colours,
And made of the speckled skins of young wolves.
"Whistle! whistle!" the juggling sound!
I fain would dispraise it; it is dispraised by eight slaves.
When thy father went out to hunt,
With his pole on his shoulder, and his provisions in his hand,
He would call to his dogs of equal size,--
"Catch it! catch it! seize it! seize it!"
He would kill a fish in his coracle,
As a noble lion kills (his prey).
When thy father went up to the mountain
He would bring back the head of a roebuck, the head of a wild boar, the head
of a stag,
The head of a spotted moor-hen from the mountain,
The head of a fish from the falls of Derwennyd.
As many as thy father could reach with his flesh-hook,

Of wild boars, lions, and foxes.
None would escape except those that were too nimble.
LXXXVIII. If distress were to happen to me through extortion,
There would not come, there would not be to me anything more calamitous.
No man has been nursed in a hall who could be braver
Than he, or steadier in battle.
And on the ford of Penclwyd his horses were the best;
Far-spread was his fame, compact his armour;
And before the long grass covered him beneath the sod,
He, the only son of Ffervarch, poured out the horns of mead.
LXXXIX. I saw the array from the headland of Adoyn,
Carrying the sacrifice to the conflagration;
I saw the two who from their station quickly fell
By the commands of Nwython greatly were they afflicted.
I saw the men, who made a great breach, with the dawn at Adoyn;
And the head of Dyvynwal Vrych, ravens devoured it.
XC. Gododin, in respect of thee will I demand
In the presence of a hundred that are named with deeds of valour.
And of Gwarchan, the soil of Dwywei of gallant bravery,
Let it be forcibly seized in one region.
Since the stabbing of the delight of the bulwark of battle,
Since earth has gone upon Aneurin,
My cry has not been separated from Gododin.
XCI. Echo speaks of the formidable and dragon-like weapons,
And of the fair game which was played in front of the unclaimed course of
Gododin.
He brought a supply of wine into the tents of the natives,
In the season of the storm, when there were vessels on the sea,
When there was a host on the sea, a well-nourished host.
A splendid troop of warriors, successful against a myriad of men,
Is coming from Dindywydd in Dyvnwydd.
Before Doleu in battle, worn out were their shields, and battered their hel-
mets.
XCII. With slaughter was every region filled.
His courage was like a fetter;
The front of his shield was pierced.
Disagreeable is the delay of the brave
To defend Rywyniawg.
The second time they reposed, and were crushed
By the war-horses with gory trappings.
An immovable army will his warlike and brave nobles form,
When they are greatly affronted.
Severe in the conflict with blades he slaughtered;
Sad news from the battle he brought;
And all hundred New-years' songs he composed.

Adan, the son of Urvai, was pierced;
Adan, the haughty boar, was pierced;
One damsel, a maid, and a hero.
And when he was only a youth he had the rights of a king,
Lord of Gwyndyd, of the blood of Cilydd Gwaredawg
Eve the turf was laid on the face of the generous dead,
Wisely collected were his treasure, praise, and high-sounding fame.
The grave of Glorthyn Hir from the highlands of Rywynawg.
XCIII. For the piercing of the skilful and most learned man,
For the fair corpse which fell prostrate on the ground,
Thrice six persons judged the atrocious deed early in the morning;
And Morien lifted up his ancient lance,
And, shouting, unbent his tight-drawn bow
Towards the Gwyr, and the Gwyddyl, and Prydein.
Towards the lovely, slender, bloodstained body
The sigh of Gwenabwy, the soil of Gwen.
XCIV. For the afflicting of the skilful and most learned man,
There was grief and sorrow, when he fell prostrate on the ground;
His banner showed his-rank, and was borne by a man at his side.
A tumultuous scene was beheld in Eiddyn, and on the battle-field.
The grasp of his hand prevailed
Over the Gynt, and the Gwyddyl, and Pryden,
He who meddles with the mane of a wolf without a club in his hand,
He must naturally have a brave disposition under his cloak.
The sigh of Gwenabwy, the son of Gwen.

LII. BOOK OF ANEURIN II.

HERE BEGINNETH THE GORCHAN OF TUDVWLCH.
THEY assemble in arms, the ranks are formed, tumult approaches;
In front are the warlike, in front the noble, in front the good;
While the trenches are full of motion, around are heard the curved horns,
and are seen the curved falchions;
To the praise of the king with the host whose presence is devastation.
I saw dark gore arising on the stalks of plants, on the clasp of the fetter,
On the bunches, on the sovereign, on the bush, and the spear:
And ruddy was the sea-beach; and on the sea-beach, and in Ewionydd
And Gwynheidyd splendid excess prevailed.
The crowd made a firm stay before the ceremony, like the checking of excess.
10 Uplifted were the shields around the front of the aged when the excess
prevailed.
A wolf in his lifetime was Bleiddiad, unrestrained in his bravery.
Active were the glittering shafts with the aspect of a serpent, from the radi-
ance of serpents.
Wounded thou art, commander of rulers, and delight of females.

Thou lovedst partly to live: I wish thou livedst, O thou of victorious energy!
Unjustly oppressed bull (of conflict), I deplore thy death, thou who wert fond of the tumult!
In the face of the sea, in the front rank of men, around the pit of battle
Bran combats in Cynwyd.
A wave burst forth which afflicted the world.
He refused to the tribes of the country, and for the benefit of the infantry,
20 Four multitudes, four military troops of the world.
The shields were in splinters, and the blade in the hair of one from the square,
The man who poured the expressed mead out of the blue horns,
A man of quality, surrounded with purple, the stay or armies.
It was the performance of Tudvwlch of severe aspect, whose standard was of the colour of the blood of grapes.
By reason of mead free drunk, a multitude went over the boundary.
In the action at the goal, for the preservation of law.
Cynan, the energetic chief from Mona, acted justly as regards the higher orders.
Tudvwlch and Cyvwlch made breaches in the heights of Caers;
With Mynyddawg disastrous did their wassails prove.
30 A year of longing for the men of Catraeth is cherished by me;--
Their steel blades, their mead, their vehemence, and their fetters.
They assemble in arms, the ranks are formed; do I not hear the tumult?
AND SO IT ENDETH.

LIII. BOOK OF ANEURIN IV.
HERE NOW BEGINNETH THE GORCHAN OF CYNVELYN.

WERE I to praise,
Were I to sing,
The Gwarchan would cause high shoots to spring,
Stalks like the collar of Trych Trwyth,
Monstrously savage, bursting and thrusting through,
When he was attacked in the river
Before his precious things.
Carn Gaffon burst through,
Before the cairns of Riwrhon,
10 Those that delighted in war,
Whose bones were short, their horsemen shorter.
Gylvach burst through
The assaults of heroism.
Fury against the Angles is just;

It is right to kill; it is right to crush those who are crushing.
Before the congenial splendour
There will be light for furthering the project,
And ability to descend
To every daring enterprise,
20 Through nail, through snare,
Through trapdoor, and fetters,
And gold spread abroad;
And deep sorrow will happen
To Gwynassedd the yellow.
His blood will be around him
Concealed will be the froth
Of the splendid yellow mead;
Again there will be blood around him
Before the battles of Cynvelyn,--

30 From the indignation of Cynvelyn,
The uplifted pillar of wrath,
Food-provider for the birds.
With pendent stirrups
Will the graceful ones return,
Under the thigh of the heroes,
As swift as sprites move
On a pleasant lawn.
Sovereign of the land of song!
It is mine to lament him,
40 Until I come to the silent day!
The foe asked for
A long-handled weapon!
More powerful than the highly-
honoured lays
Is the Gwarchan of Cynvelyn.
The Gorchan of Cynvelyn, to make
the region weep.
A man of fortitude from Gwynedd has
departed his country!
The brave are lamented;
Let the Caer of Eiddin deplore
The dread and illustrious men
clothed in splendid blue.
50 Brilliant is thy ruddy gem--is it not
precious?
Flowing panegyric is due to the hors-
es
Of Eithinyn--are they not splendid?
The Gwarchan of Cynvelyn on Go-
dodin!

Has he not, for a man, performed a
reasonable part?
His heavy spear, adorned with gold,
he bestowed on me;
Be it for the benefit of his soul!
His son Tegvan shall be honoured
In numbering and in partitioning, the
grandson of Cadvan,
The pillar of ardency.
60 When weapons were hurled
Over the heads of battle-wolves,
Soon would he come in the day of
distress.
Three men and three score and three
hundred
To the conflict of Catraeth went forth;
Of those who hastened
From the mead of the cup-bearers,
three only returned,--
Cynon, and Cadreith, and Cadlew of
Cadnant;
And me, on account of my blood they
deplored,
Son of the omen pile, my ransom they
contributed,
70 Of pure gold, and steel, and silver.
For their heroism they received no
protection.
The Gwarchan of Cynvelyn will cele-
brate their contribution.

HERE ENDETH THE GWARCHAN OF CYNVELYN.

LIV. BOOK OF ANEURIN V.

Every ode of the Gododin is equivalent to a single song, according to the priv-
ilege of poetical composition. Each of the Gwarchans is equal to three hun-
dred and sixty-three songs, because the number of the men who went to Ca-
traeth is commemorated in the Gorchans; and as no man should go to battle
without arms, so no bard ought to contend without that poem.
Here now begins the Gwarchan of Maelderw. Taliessin sung it, and it is a
privileged ode. His three Gwarchans are equal in poetical competition to all
the odes in the Gododin.

214

The noise of two Abers around the Caer!
Arouse thyself to arms and splendour!
Cold is the passing and repassing of the breach of battle.
Lover of fame, seekest thou to sleep?
The variegated texture, the covering of heroism,
For the shelterless assault shall be woven.
The breach that has been attempted will not be effected.
Bear the patient exertion of heroism.
Sharply in arms he used to frown,
10 But mildly allured he the intellectual world.
A man that will run when thou pursuest,
Will have the rounded house of the sepulchre for his bed.
Call together, but do not reproach the over-anxious;
And meddle not with the fierce and violent.
Let him who has a just claim break the boundary.
He does not calculate upon praise
Who defends his shelter.
Praise is the meed of those who have made impressions.
The victor gazed towards the fair one.
20 Of bright and prominent uplifted front,
On the ruddy dragon, the palladium of Pharaon,
Which will in the air accompany the people.
Dead is every one that fell on his mouth
In the repulsion of the march of Teth and Teddyd.
Courteous was the great retinue of the wall, of ashen spears.
To the sea thou mayst not come;
But neither thy retreat nor thy counsel will fail,
Thou magnanimous soul in the defence of his boundaries.
No more can they extricate themselves,
30 Extricate themselves before the barrier of Eiddyn.
Cenan, the fair wall of excellence,
Placed a sword on the entrenchment of warriors.
Victorious was the chief
In dispossessing the sovereign,
The inconstant
Gray-headed chief of ministers,
Whose counsels were deep.
The mutually sweet will not produce the mutually bitter.
I have mutually wished,
40 I do mutually wish for the repose of Eulli
The fair aspect of which is filled with deep interest,
On the course on a serene morning.
It allures me, it plays upon my strong desire.
I will ask the men for a dwelling,
In order to lessen the loss.

Happiness was lost and recovered.
The Northern Run, chieftain, thou hast caused to withdraw
The fat one in returning thou wilt cause to return to me.
They call more for large trees than for honeysuckles.
        (*Three lines untranslated*).
Let the sovereign stand firm between the looks of Dremrudd,
The ruddy glancer, whose purpose cannot be viewed for a sufficient time,
Whose purpose cannot be viewed for a sufficient time,
By those who with impunity plough the noisy sea.
First to be satisfied is the pale one,
The eccentric, whose throne is of complete form.
Before he was covered, Gownddelw
60 Was a tall man of great worth like Maelderw.
I will extol him who wields the spear,
Whose course is like that of the ruler of the mount,
The pervader of the land, by whose influence I am moved.
With active tumult did he descend to the ravine between the hills,
Nor was his presence a running shadow.
Whatever may befall the high land,
Disgrace shall never happen to the assembled train.
I. It is well that Adonwy came, Adonwy to those that were left.
What Bradwen did, thou hast done; thou didst kill and burn,
Thou didst not keep the rear or the van.
I know the aspect of thy helmet. I have not seen from sea
To sea a worse knight than Odgur.
II. Three hundred golden-torqued ones hastened along
To engage in the conflict; a sally ensued;
And though they were killed, they also killed;
And unto the end of the world honoured they shall be;
And of those who went in mutual amity,
Alas! except one man none escaped.
III. Three hundred wearing the golden torques,
Fond of valorous toil, and headlong in the course;
Three hundred haughty ones,
Unanimous, and equally armed.
Three hundred prancing horses
Did with them hasten.
Three chiefs and three hundred,
Alas! none returned.
IV. Furious in the battle, unreceding in distress;
In the conflict there was no peace if he acted vigorously;
In the day of wrath, shunning was no part of his work;
The aspect of a boar had Bleiddig son of Eli;
Wine was quaffed in brimful vessels of glass;
And the day of battle, exploits did he achieve

On Arvwl Cann, before he died.
Ruddy-tinted carnage used to attract him:
V. Vigorously in the front of battles would he cause the crimson fluid to flow,
Powerful as an instrument in battle,
And splendidly covered with mail.
Report informs me
That the dexterous blade
Will not be manifested
To the diffident.
VI. He would reduce men to ashes,
And make wives widows,
Before his death,--
Breint, son of Bleiddgi;
With spears would he
Cause blood to flow.
VII. Great is the design of him who conceals his vigorous attack;
His weapon he will conceal
Like a hidden treasure.
When all ascended, thou descendest.
Ceneu Gwyn, the blood of the dead how didst thou shed!
Three years and four,
Thou, guardian, didst put on magnificent raiment.
And to protect thee,
Though a youth, it was not right for me, for thou didst not retreat.
Pressent narrates that he was carried away with the arms.
VIII. When he repaired to his native country, his fame was spread abroad;
He poured out the wine, the golden-torqued man!
He would give a gorgeously fine suit to a brave person,
And check a hundred men, courteous hero!
And send away the progeny of a foreign knight;--
The only son of Cian from beyond Bannawg.
Never did in Gododin tread on the surface of the fosse,
While he was, any one more ardent than Lliv.
IX. Anger, the scatterer of the brave, serpent with the piercing pike,
An immovable stone in front of the army;
Accustomed to the preparation of attacks,
And greatly to reward the assaulting lance.
Perfect art thou called from thy just deed,
Leader, director, and bulwark of all that are of the same language:
Tudvwlch, the subduer in battle, the destroyer of Caers.
X. Anger, the scatterer of the brave, serpent with the piercing pike in the front of the army;
Perfect art thou called from thy just deed.
Faithful art thou called from thy faithful deed.

Leader, director, and the bulwark of every tribe,
Meryn, son of Madyeith, it is well that thou art born!
XI. Gwolowy secured a gray wolf, whose roaring was as that of water.
Angor, the scatterer of the brave, an immovable stone in the front of the army.
Ruddy radiance, and horses, and men were in front of Gododin,
Whence so rapidly ascends the address
Of the Bard of the Cymry, Tottarth, in front of Garth Merin.
XII. His shield, with endurance, he would not lower
Before the face of any one; wrong he would not encourage.
Urgent were the requests for horses in the entrance.
The gold of the heroes, the crowd of holly lances covered it with gore,
While his comrade was pierced, he pierced others;
Disgrace to thee he would not bring:
Active in martial valour, he made a noble display,
When he carried away the famous Cyhuran of Mordei.
XIII. Falsely it was said by Tudleo,
That no one's steeds were overtaken by Marchlew,
As he was reared to bring support to all around:
Powerful was the stroke of his sword on the adversary;
Eagerly ascended the ashen spear from the grasp
Of his hand, from the narrow summit of the awful pile.
XIV. Direct us to heaven, the wished-for home of order!
Woe to us on account of constant lamentation and grief!
When the strangers came from Dineiddyn,
Every wise man was banished the country.
In the contention with Lloegyr of various conflicts,
Nine score for every one were made prostrate.
An array of horses, harness, and silken robes,
Gwaednerth arranged conspicuously from the battle.
XV. From the retinue of Mynyddawg that hastened
In splendid order around the store of beverage regaled they themselves,
From the banquet of Mynyddawg, my mind has become sad,
Because of those of my true kinsmen I have completely lost.
Of three hundred golden-wreathed heroes, who marched to Catraeth,
Alas! except one man none escaped.
XVI. The retinue of Gododin rode on
Swan-coloured horses with quivering manes and drooping harness,
And in front of the host, the throng descended,
In defence. of his generalship, and the mead of Eiddyn,
By the advice of Mynyddawg.
The shields were moved about,
The lances fell
Upon fair brows,

While the men were languidly dropping like fruit from the tree.
They bore no reproach, men that did not skulk.
XVII. Have I not drunk mead on the march,
A banquet of wine before Catraeth as a preservative?
When he made slaughter with his unyielding lance
In the conflict, it was no inglorious sight to see where thou wert.
A monster wag no frightful object to thee while effecting deliverance,
Terrible and shielded Madawg Elved.
XVIII. When they fairly met, there was no escaping for life.
Dialgur of Arvon fetched bright gold at the request
Of the Brython. High-mettled were the horses of Cynon.
XIX. Llech Lleudu, and Tud Lleuvre,
The course, the course of Gododin.
A hand! a hand! a counsel! a counsel!
A tempest over the sea! a vessel from beyond sea!
The host of Heidiliawn, the host of Meidlyawn, a degenerate host,
Moving from Dindywydd.
Battered was the shield before the bull of conflict, the van was broken.
XX. Golden-mailed warriors were there on the walls of the Caer;
Slow was the excess, but the tumult of battle was not dilatory.
One feeble man with his shouts kept away
The birds of the region, like Pelloid Mirain.
No one living will relate what happened
At Lliw, about the banks of Llwch Llivanad;
No one living will relate of any one to whom in the day of conflict
Cynaval was not equal in merit.
XXI. No achievement to-day around Neimyn!
The same covering envelopes men of the noblest descent.
A numerous host engaged in battle which is worth relating,
The son of Nwython killed of the golden-torqued ones
A hundred chieftains, as far as it is related, the vehemence
Was greater than when a hundred men went to Catraeth.
He was like a mead-fed hero with a large heart.
He was a man of hosts; energetic was he in his coat of mail,
He was a man of conflict, fierce was he on the ridge of Cavall.
No man among a thousand brave warriors
Handled a spear, or a shield, or a sword, or a dagger,
Who was a braver man than Neim the son of Nwython.
XXII. While there was a drop, they were like three lions in purpose;
In the battle three brave, prompt, active lions.
Bribon who wielded the thick lance,
XXIII. Accustomed was he to defend Gododin against a hero,
In the van of battle, against vehement ones,
Accustomed was he, in the manner of Alan, to be swift;
Accustomed was he before a horde of depredators to make a descent;

Accustomed was the son of Golystan, though he was
A sovereign, to listen to what his father said;
Accustomed was he, in the interest of Mynyddawg, to have a perforated shield,
And a ruddy lance, before the vigorous chief of Eiddyn.
XXIV. The rulers did not celebrate the praise of the holy one.
Before the attack of the numerous host, the battle was broken through.
Like a raging fire through combustibles.
On Tuesday, they put on their splendid robes;
On Wednesday, bitter was their assembly;
On Thursday, messengers formed contracts;
On Friday, there were carnage and contusion;
On Saturday, they dealt mutual blows;
On Sunday, they were pierced by ruddy weapons;
On Monday, a pool of blood, knee-deep, was seen.
The Gododin, after tedious toil, cannot relate it.
Before the tents of Madawg after the return.
XXV. A grievous descent was made in front of the hoarded riches;
The first to chase them was a person renowned for activity;--
Gwannannon, honoured in the mead banquet, whose prowess I will extol;
And next to him the brave-minded and heroic
Eithinyn the renowned, the son of Bodw.
XXVI. Men of excess went with them,
Who had been revelling in wine and mead,
In the banquet of Mynyddawg.
We are greatly grieved at the loss
Of a man of such terrible energy;
Like thunder from heaven was the clashing of his shield,
From the agitation caused by Eithinyn;
XXVII. Swift and heroic he was when at early dawn
He would arise to lead his band;
But whether leading or following
Before a hundred he stood prominent.
He was so disposed to (assault) them,
As to drink mead or wine;
He was so unsparing,
When he transfixed the foes,
And forward was his course towards them.
XXVIII. Rapidly and heroically with the dawn they marched
To the conflict, with the commander in front of the course;
Gwair was greeted by the fluid gore
In the van of the battle;
He was a beloved friend
In the day of distress.

The defence of the mountain, the place,
And the forward beam of war, wore a murky hue.
XXIX. His lances were seen among the hosts
Vigorously employed for mutual defence against the foe;
Before the din of his shields they concealed themselves,
They lay hid before Eiddyn, the lofty hill;
And of as many as he found none returned;
Of him the truth is related and sung:
Obstinately would he pierce armour, when he caused a trembling;
And he whom he pierced, would not be pierced again.
Repeated are the lamentations that his presents are gone;
His friends were as numerous as bees;
And before he was covered under the sward of the earth,
He caused the mead to flow.
XXX.   (*Five lines untranslated.*)
The Gododin will not relate at the early dawn
Of any to whom Cynaval was not equal.
XXXI. Blade weapons, broad and ruddy, were abundant before he was covered,
The hero who filled the plain with slaughtered men.
He was a joyous chief, an unflinching wolf-like hero, a firm wolf
In the camp, with a submissive retinue blessing him;
Before he was arrested, he was not feeble.
Perfect art thou called from thy righteous deed;
Leader, director, and bulwark of all that are of the same language,
Tudvwlch, the subduer in battle, the destroyer of Caers.
XXXII. The slayer of hosts is gone to the black glebe:
A piece of earth has made
Sweet bitter to the people.
Withered leaves are driven too and fro on his patrimony;
It was not for the advantage of the country that the sod (should cover him);
The bull of conflict never retreated the width of an acre.
Sad is the fate that it should thus be!
XXXIII. He pierced upwards of three hundred of the foe,
He slaughtered the centre and the extreme;
He was worthy to be at the head of an army, most gentle;
He fed his horses upon barley in winter,
Black ravens croaked on the wall
Of the beautiful Caer. He was an Arthur
In the midst of the exhausting conflict,
In the assault in the pass, like Gwernor the hero.
XXXIV. I ought to sing to Cynon with the flesh-spears:
In action, and before the desolating spears of Aeron,
His hand was reckoned at the head of hoary heroes.
To me was distributed the best fare among the daring ones,

To the advantage of Mynyddawg, knight of the people,
He appointed me to harass the enemy
On Catraeth, where the golden-torqued heroes were loquacious.
They pierced and slaughtered those who stood before them;
Whelps committed ravages about their territories.
There was scarcely in the lists, on the part of the Brython,
At Gododin, from a distance a man better than Cenon.
XXXV. It is incumbent on me to celebrate the complete acquisition
Of our warriors, who around Catraeth made a tumultuous rout,
With confusion, and blood, and treading, and trampling,
Where valour was trampled, and vengeance taken because of the contribu-
tion of mead.
As to the carnage of the combatants,
Cibno does not relate after the excitement of battle.
Since he has received the communion he shall be interred.
XXXVI. Birds were allured (*untranslated*).
> (*One line untranslated.*)
He put on gold before the battle-shout, in the front rank of the accomplished
heroes.
> (*Three lines untranslated.*)
Cibno the son of Gwengad had a long and splendid retinue.
XXXVII. I owe a complete song to the dog of Gwerunyd.
Let joy be in the chamber.   *   *   *

LV. SONG TO ALE - BOOK OF TALIESSIN XX.

I.

THE qualities shall be extolled
Of the man that. chained the. wind.
When his powers come,
Extremely noisy the elements;
For ever will thy impulse be,
Thou dost pervade
The tide of darkness and day.
The day, there will be a shelter to me,
The night, it will be rested.
10 Softness is praised.
From a great Guledig.
The great God caused
The sun of summer, and its excessive
heat;
And he caused
The abundance of the wood and field.
He is the powerful cause of the
stream,
Flowing abundantly.
He is the powerful cause of every
kindness;
God redeemed me
20 And before they come,
The people of the world to the one
hill,
They will not be able to do the least,
Without the power of the King.
He shall steep it in the Llyn,
Until it shall sprout.
He shall steep it another time
Until it is sodden.
Not for a long time will be finished
30 What the elements produce.
Let his vessels be washed,
Let his wort be clear.
And when there shall be an exciter of

song,
Let it be brought from the cell,
Let it be brought before kings.
In splendid festivals.
Will not oppose every two
The honey that made it.
God's departure in me,
40 As long as the world is in being,
The mildest is the Trinity.
The provocative of the drunkard is
drunkenness.
The fishes might show
The capacity of the lodgments
Of the gravel of the salt sea,
Before it overwhelms the strand.
The gravel of the salt sea
Below the sand
Will conceal me from the privileged
one.
Myself he will deliver.
50 No one will be satisfied,
Without the power of the Trinity.

II.

Qualities they will honour
In the boundary of Garant.
The mighty ones, without desire,
from the reeking
Marsh will remove,
When the string of harmony re-
sounds,
Or the shades of night approach,
The hidden retreat from day.
Do the skilful in song know
Where the powerful artist is con-
cealed?
10 That will give me a robe
From the gate when he ascends.
When the chief leads, in winter,
What melody is commenced together.
In choosing loud fame,
With haste the fortunate will run,
He will awake the sleeper.
He will merit Carawg

Of the many-citied Cymry,
The father of Caradawg;
20 The sound of the Meneivians,
The sound of Mynawg of Mona.
The great terrible perjured
Gwentians, long-haired.
On account of Caer Wyrangon.
Who will pay the precious reward?
Is it Maelgwn from Mona?
Or shall it come from Aeron?
Or Coel or Canawon?
Or Gwrweddw or his sons?
30 His enemies shall not exult
From the hostages of Ynyr.
To him will resort the minstrels
The star of magnificent stars,
Have I not disarmed the mystery?
In Mordei Uffin,
In the seas of Gododin,
He is a sharer of varied words,
The raven of the morning divining.
I am an aged exile,
40 I am of joyful talents,
And the stroke of malice.
Mine, the praising of Urien,
Of splendid purity of life.
Very keen his conduct of hosts,
The ruddy-reaping of the steep.
Ruddyn formed them,
At the battle in Harddnenwys,
It was Ynyr that broke them to piec-
es.
A hundred festivals holding
50 A hundred friends be defended.
I saw mighty men,
Who hastened to the shout of war;
I saw blood on the ground
From the assault of swords.
They tinged with blue the wings of
the dawn;
They threw off the spears.
Three hundred festivals complete of
the renowned
Ynyr, on the earth indeed there will
be redness.

M. Poems Relating to Cadwallawn

LVI. BOOK OF TALIESSIN XLIX.

A BRIGHT festivity
About the two lakes,
The lake on my side.
The side about the Caer,
The Caer in urgency
Has been described.
A comely flight from it;
And the legion of the band
Augmented stones.
10 The dragon will flow around,
Above the places,
Vessels of liquor,
Liquor in golden horns,
Golden horns in hand,
Hand on the knife,
The knife on the rallying point.
Truly I implore thee,
Victorious Beli,
Son of Manogan, the king,
20 That will preserve the qualities
Of the honey isle of Beli,

He had a right to it.
Five chiefs there will be,
Of the Gwyddyl Ffichti,
Of a sinner's disposition,
Of the race of the knife.
Five others there will be,
Of the Norddmyn's place,
The sixth a wonderful king,
30 From sowing to reaping.
The seventh proceeded
To land over the flood.
The eighth of the line of Dyvi.
Shall not be separated from prosperi-
ty,
Before the shout of Venni.
The calls of Eryri.
With difficulty thou wilt come.
Let us implore Eloi,
When we may be with Celi,
40 A dwelling of heaven will be to
me.

LVII. BOOK OF TALIESSIN L.

MAY God exalt over the community of Brython
The sign of gladness of a host from Mona,
There is a contention among the active patriots of Gwynedd.
Of bright radiancy, from every battle to have pledges,.
Powys will become grave in embraces.
Men, great-craving, will act on their laws.
Two hosts will go, they will be consonant.
Of one disposition, of one word, harmonious, compact.
They will divide justly the people of Ceredigiawn.
10 When thou seest men few about Llyn Aeron.
When will be heavy Tywi and Teivi rivers,
They will make battle in haste about Llys Llonion.
What he saw he left over-laden.
He protected not cities from indignations.

A man warm, a man that guards, a man of impulse.
He was not an utterly clownish man, Rieddon.
When Cadwallawn came
Over the ocean of Iwerdon,
He regulated heaven as high creator.
20 Songsters, soon may I hear their cares,
An army of horsemen so harassing about Caer Llion,
And the revenge of Idwal on Aranwynyon,
And playing at ball with heads of Saxons.
There will be troubled the Cat Vreith and its strange language,
From the ford at Taradyr, as far as Porth Wygyr in Mona.
A youth brought them to Dinas Maon.
From the time when is defended the honey and clover
They leave their noise and contention,
30 Not unpledged to raise anger against enemies.
May God exalt over the community of Brython.

LVIII. RED BOOK OF HERGEST XV.

I. CADWALLAWN, before he came,
Fought, to our ample satisfaction,
Fourteen great battles,
For fairest Prydein,
And sixty skirmishes.

II. Cadwallawn encamped on Ceint;
Birds presaged the troubles of Lloegyr;
I His hand was open, and honour flowed.

III. Cadwallawn encamped on Yddon,
The fierce affliction of his foes,
A lion prosperous over the Saxons.

IV. Cadwallawn the illustrious
Encamped on Digoll Mount,
For seven months and seven battles daily.

V. Cadwallawn encamped on the Havren,
And on the further side of Dygen,
And the devourers were burning Meigen.

VI. Cadwallawn encamped on the Wy,
The multitude, after passing the water,
Followed to the battle of shield.

VII. Cadwallawn encamped by the well
Of Bedwyr; before soldiers he cherished virtue;
There Cynon showed how to assert the right.

VIII. Cadwallawn encamped on the Tav;
Very numerous I see
The sharers in the fame of the powerful chief.

IX. Cadwallawn encamped on the Tawy;
He had the hand of slaughter in the breach;
Illustrious was he, eager he sought the conflict.

X. Cadwallawn encamped beyond the Caer
Of Caew, with an army urgent in tumult
A hundred battles, and the breaking of a hundred Caers.

XI. Cadwallawn encamped on the Cowyn;
The hand was weary of the rein;

The men of Lloegyr, numerous their complaints.

XII. Cadwallawn encamped this night In the extremity of the region of Penvro,
For refuge to retreat where the difficulty was great.

XIII. Cadwallawn encamped on the Teivi;
The blood mixed with the brine;
The fury of Gwynedd violently raged.

XIV. Cadwallawn encamped on the river Duffyrdd,
He made the eagles full:
After the battle gifts were conferred.

XV. Cadwallawn encamped, my brother,
In the upper part of the country of Dunawd;

His wrath was violent in the gushing fight.

XVI. Cadwallawn encamped on Menin,
The lion with a numerous host,
Great the tumult, extremely harassing to the rear.

XVII. From the plotting of strangers and iniquitous
Monks, as the water flows from the fountain,
Sad and heavy will be the day for Cadwallawn.

XVIII. The trees have put on the gay robes
Of summer; let wrath be hastened by fate;
Let us meet around Elved.

N. Predictive Poems Relating to Cadwaladyr

LIX. THE OMEN OF PRYDEIN THE GREAT - BOOK OF TALIESSIN VI.

I.

THE Awen foretells the hastening of
The multitude, possessed of wealth and peace;
And a bountiful sovereign, and eloquent princes.
And after tranquillity, commotion in every place,
Heroic men raising a tumult of fierce contention.
Swift the remorse of defending too long.
The contention of men even to Caer Weir, the dispersion of the Allmyn.
They made great rejoicing after exhaustion,
And the reconciling of the Cymry and the men of Dublin,
10 The Gwyddyl of Iwerdon, Mona, and Prydyn,
Cornwall and Clydemen their compact with them.
The Brython will be outcasts, when they shall have done,
Far will be foretold the time they shall be.
Kings and nobles will subdue them.
The men of the North at the entry surrounding them,
In the midst of their front they will descend.

II.

Myrdin foretells these will meet,
In Aber Peryddon, the stewards of the kings
And though there be no right of slaughter they complain.
20 Of one will of the mind they will refuse.
Stewards their taxes would collect;
In the treasures of Cymry, there was not that they would pay.
One that is a proprietor says this.
There will not come one that will pay in slavery.
The great Son of Mary declareth, when if did not break out
Against the chief of the Saxons and their fondness,
Far be the Cychmyn to Gwrtheyrn of Gwynedd.
He drove the Allmyn to banishment.
No one will attain to anything, but what earth will deprive.
30 They know not what may be passing in every outlet.
When they bought Thanet, through lack of discretion,
With Hors and Heng who were in their career,
Their prosperity has been derived from us without honour.
After a secret, the captive was worked upon at the Ynver.
Drunkenness will be pleased with much liquor of mead,
Poverty will bear with the death of many.
Terrors will bear with the tears of women;
An enervated chief will excite a wailing.
The sorrow of the world will bear with much irritation.
40 When the Cechmyu of Thanet are our kings,
May the Trinity ward off the blow that is intended.
To agitate the land of the Brython, and the Saxons at variance.
Sooner may their kings be in banishment,
Than the Cymry should go into exile.

III.

The great Son of Mary declareth, when will not break out
The Cymry against the surmise of a baron, and princes;
Foremost ones in asking, examples, one law they complain,
One meeting, one council, of one voice they are.
There were none, however great, who did not speak.
50 Except to dispense with surmises they would not agree.
To God and David they recommended themselves.
Let him pay, let him refrain from a refusal to Allmyn.
Let them make ill reports of the wants of the townsman.
The Cymry will meet the Saxons.
For various mutual consumption and resistance.
Of the excessively great army, when they have experience,
And on the hill, at the blades and shout, they will tremble,

And on the Gwy severe rencounters will follow them.
And a banner will come, rough it will descend.
60 And like the budded blossoms the Saxons will fall.
The Cymry gathering strength with union of actions.
First and last the Granwynyon were in a strait,
The stewards to the value of their deceit prostrating them.
Their army in the running of blood surrounding them.
Others on their feet through woods will retreat.
Through the ramparts of the city they will flee.
A war without returning to the land of Prydyn.
The council will be broken by hand, like the sea they will glide away.
The stewards of Caer Ceri dishonoured complain.
70 Some the valley and hill do not decline,
To Aber Peryddon they came not well.
Tremendous taxes they collect.
Nine score hundred men they descend.
Great mockery, except four, they did not return.
Tranquillity to their wives they say,
Their shirts full of gore they wash.
The Cymry, foremost in asking, profuse of soul,
The men of the South will defend their taxes,
With sharp-ground blades utterly they will kill.
80 There will be no advantage to the physician from what they do.
The armies of Cadwaladyr, mighty they come,
The Cymry were exalted, a battle they made.
A slaughter without measure they assailed.
In the end of their taxes, death they know.
Others, large branches they planted.
For age of ages their taxes they will not leave off.
In wood, in plain, on hill,
A candle in the dark will go with them.
Cynan opening a forward way in every descent.
90 Saxons against the Brython, woe they will sing.
Cadwaladyr a pillar with his princes.
Though prudence utterly attending to them.
When they drop their covering over their support.
In affliction, and the crimson gore on the cheeks of the Allmyn.
At the end of every expedition spoil they lead.
The Saxon on journey as far as Caer Wynt formerly who sooner skulked?
Happy they, the Cymry, when they say,
The Trinity delivered us from the former trouble.
Let not Dyved or Glywyssyg tremble.
100 The praise of stewards will not affect kings,
Nor shall the councils of the Saxons obtain what they say.
Meads shall not cause drunkenness with us,

Without the payment by fate of what we have.
From orphaned sons and others a few
Through the intercession of David and the saints of Prydeyn,
As far as the stream of Arlego they will flee out.

IV.

The Awen foretells, the day will come,
When he will come to summon to one council,
One company, one council, and Lloegyr being burnt,
110 In the hope of detracting our most comely army.
And the song of another country will flee always.
He knows not a hiding-place for my goods, and where will be a shelter?
They raise a barking, like a bear from the mountain.
To pay flattery their country will bleed.
Again shall come the toil of spears, fierce and sharp:
The friend shall not spare the body of his companion.
Again shall come the head of a salmon without brains;
Again shall come widowed women and spare horses.
Again shall come a terrible shout from the assault of the warriors,
120 And many hands unequal before scattering armies.
The messengers of death met together,
When stood carcases according to their origin,
The tax will be avenged and the value daily,
And the many messages on the false army.

V.

The Cymry have prevailed through the rencounter,
Completely unanimous: of one voice, of one faith.
The Cymry have prevailed to cause battle.
And the tribes of many a country they will collect,
And the holy banner of David they will raise,
130 To lead the Gwyddyl through the dark blue sea.
And the faction of Dublin with us stood,
When they come to the battle, they will not deny themselves;
They will ask the Saxons what they seek:
How much of debt from the country they hold?
Whence is their route when they settled?
Whence their generation? from what land did they come?
Since the time of Gwrtheyrn they trample upon us.
Truth will not be obtained in the land of discord.
Did they not trample entirely on the privilege of our saints?
140 Did they not entirely break through the miracles of David?
The Cymry will keep themselves, when they visit.
The Allmyn will not go from the places they stand on,

Until they shall have paid seven times the value of what they did.
And death shall scatter to the value of their wrong.
The kin of Garmawn will pay of honour,
In four years and four hundred.
Valiant men long-haired, the Lord will incite:
And a driving of the Saxons from Iwerdon there will be.
Thence will come from Lengo, a wanton fleet,
150 The battle was ruined, the armies were torn.
There will come from Alclud, men, bold, faithful,
To drive from Prydein bright armies.
There will come from Llydaw, a seasonable ally,
Warriors from their war-horses will not regard their origin.
Saxons on all sides into disgrace will come;
Their age has passed away; there is not a country.
Death has been accomplished to the black auxiliary.
Disease and duty will deliver us,
After gold and silver and what is congenial.
160 Let a bush be their shelter in reward of their bad faith.
Let the sea be, let an anchor be, their counsellors.
let gore be, let death be, their auxiliary.
Cynan and Cadwaladyr, mighty in armies;
They will, be honoured until judgment: prosperity will attend them.
Two tenacious chiefs; profound their counsel.
Two that will overcome the Saxons, with the aid of the Lord.
Two generous ones, two treasurers of a merchant's country.
Two fearless ones, ready, of one fortune, of one faith.
Two exalters of Prydein of bright armies.
170 Two bears do not know shame barking daily.
Druids foretell what great things will happen.
From Mynaw to Llydaw in their hands will be.
From Dyved to Thanet they will possess.
From the light to the ground along their Abers.
Their chief partly paid for the land.
A nakedness on Cynon, Saxons will not be.
The Gwyddyl will return to their native country,
The Cymry will raise up a mighty auxiliary.
Armies about ale from the tumult of soldiers.
180 And the kings of God that have kept their faith
Will summon to every fleet: trouble will end;
And Cynan will reconcile them with each other.
Cynon will not call in as combatants,
Save the Cechmyn of Cadwaladyr, and his merchants.
Like a Cymro, joyful of speech he will be,
About the afflicted isle swarms will cease;
When the carcases stand according to their race,

Even to Aber Santwic it will be noised,
That the Allmyn are about to emigrate abroad,
190 One after another, breaking afresh upon their race.
The Saxons at anchor on the sea always,
The Cymry venerable until doomsday shall be supreme
They will not seek books nor be covetous of poets.
The presage of this isle will be no other than this.
We will praise the King that created heaven and earth.
May David be a leader to the combatants.
Ynyr in Gelli Caer for God be is;
He will not die, he will not run away, he will not exhaust;
He will not fade, he will not fail, he will not bend, he will not tremble.

LX. BOOK OF TALIESSIN XLVII.

THE Awen foretells the hastening of
The multitude, possessed of wealth and peace,
And a bountiful sovereign, and eloquent princes,
And after tranquillity, commotion in every place.
The seven sons of Beli arose.
Caswallawn, and Lludd, and Cestuddyn,
Diwed, Plo, Coll, Iago from the land of Prydyn.
A country boiling will be made as far as Balaon.
Tired out their nails, ready for journeying their reins.
10 Borderers of a ravaging country.
The Cymry lost all their bounty.
In the alliance of the sovereign's servants,
Llyminawg will appear
Who will be an ambitious man,
To subdue Mona,
And to ruin Gwynedd,
From its extremity to its centre.
From its beginning, from its end,
And to take its pledges.
20 Persevering his face,
He will submit to none,
Whether Cymry or Saxons.
A person will come from concealment,,
That will make an universal stain of red,
And a battle of strifes.
Another will come,
Far-extending his armies,
A triumph to the Brython.

231

I. TRULY there will be to me a Roman friend.
Possibly from the son of another man he will cause
Before him that he heard the expanding tumult.
And an army and flow of blood on his enemy.
And let horses sound, and the multitude (be) merciful.
They would cut, they would greatly assemble in the sword of conflict.
Ravens and eagles adore blood.
The ruddy path of the violent bear is fearless.
Let Cadwaladyr rise ardent and gleaming
On the face of the embattled hosts of vigorous countries.
II. Truly there will be to me a day-share of frailties,
A vow of prophecy in the first beginning.
Years victorious, an excess of extensive rights.
When winter overspreads, sharp the steering of ships.
Confined the flow of harmony, courteous, respiring.
Glorious the appearance of the torrent on the top of the waves.
The swans resort round the morsel on the face of the surges.
Bear and lion empty the bright pools.
The boundary depends upon crimson spears.
Too much is sought chastisement, a caution to the fronts.
Before his ranks and great possessions,
Creeds fall, collars are broken by the crowds in front.
To the combat of Cadwaladyr, of splendidly-read fame,
There arose a dragon from the south,
By a free youth he was slain on a Thursday.
III. Truly there will be to me bounteous heroism,
A royal eulogy of fame of great abundance.
A path thick, abundant, broad its form.
Until there be seven languages to the king of Gwynedd,
Until exhausting tumult passes away,
A king fond of a sleepless covering,
Violence on Angles, and a journey to banishment,
Through a sea will glide their offspring.
IV. Truly there will be to me one having a right to Mona.
Glorious the protection of the dragon to the people of the Brython.
Chief of armies, a respecter of breastplated men.
Deep, the prophecy divine of the Druids.
They would pitch their tents on Tren and Taranhon.
They would lie in ambush, to take Mona.
Far to go away be it a length from Iwerdon.
Fair the honour to liberate the Cæsarians.
V. Predict a scene of unlovely discord.
I know when a battle was caused over wine and mead

A bear from Deheubarth barking at Gwynedd.
Defending too long wonderful superfluity.
Its fortified uplands were prepared,
On the calends of winter placing lands.
The mutual reflection on shields in the shout of the sword,
To the combat of Cadwaladyr on the lord of Gwynedd.
VI. Truly it will come, this will come to pass.
All Lloegyr will lose their possessions by us.
Seeing the aspects of the speckled white men,
Between the shafts of arrows and white iron,
A shouting on the sea, a lance-darting trembling of slaughter--
They will languish in the ocean, beyond the broad lake,
Sea and isles will be their gain.
VII. Truly there will come to me from beyond Hafren
Repelled of Prydein, a king of destiny.
A mild ruler of armies, numerous his progeny.
A kingdom suitable, hateful from ice.
The common people of the world truly will be joyful.
They possess energies, a tribe of rich men.
The flash flamed over the region of Hafren.
Let the Cymry be collected splendidly
To the combat of Cadwaladyr; be joyful
The chief minstrels with the glory of the battle.
VIII. Truly he will come
With his host and ships,
And searing shields,
And changing lances,
And after a valiant shout,
His will will be done.
May the circle of Prydein
Be enflamed there.
The dragon will not hide himself,
However many may come.
Not light the praise
Of conquering Dyved.
He will bear likewise
Over the effusions of Reged.
The creator, possessor of treasure,
Generous, daring his flow,
Immense his battle.
By airing the skin
Of Cadwaladyr, an active work.

O. Poems Connected with Powys

LXII. SATIRE OF CYNAN GARWYN SON OF BROCHWAEL.

BOOK OF TALIESSIN XXIII.

CYNAN, the exciter of battle,
Bestowed on me treasure,
For not false the glory
Of the stout hunting dogs of the do-
main.
A hundred steeds of equal pace,
Silver their covering.
A hundred legions in green
Of one front running together.
A hundred urchins in my bosom.
10 And a battalion of cats.
A sword with sheath of stone.
A fist-cell better than any.
A hundred Cynan had,
Hateful not to see,
From the vales of Cadell.
In battle they were not shaken.
To the battle on Wy there resorted
Spears innumerable.
The Gwentians were slain,
20 With the gore-drenched blade.
A battle in Mona, great, fair,
Hovering over, and praised
Over the Menei, there went
Horses and confident ones.
A battle on the hill of Dyved.

Slaughter stings in motion.
Nor were seen
The kine before the countenance of
any one.
Let the son of Brochuael boast,
30 He will declare his wish.
Let Cornwall greet,
The younger will not praise fate.
The incomprehensible will depress
In the day that is praised by me,
My patron of Cynan.
Battles arose.
A woeful spreading flame,
There raises up a great fire.
A battle in the country of Brachan,
40 A warring scene of tumult,
Miserable princes.
Were made to tremble before Cynan.
The breastplate being transfixed,
Like a ruler, they cried out,
Cyngen of perfect song
Thou wilt help with thy wide country.
A saying was heard.
Every one in his red place,
Be the circle red, they say ironically,
50 They, will enslave thy Cynan.

LXIII. RED BOOK OF HERGEST XVI.

I. STAND forth, maidens, and survey
the land
Of Cyndylan; Llys Pengwern, is it not
in flames?
Woe to the youth that longs for good
fellowship.
II. One tree with the tendril on it
Is escaping it may be,
But what God shall have willed, let it
come!

III. Cyndylan, with heart like the ice
of winter,
With thrust of wild boar through his
head,
Thou hast dispensed the ale of Tren!
IV. Cyndylan, with heart like the fire
of spring,
By the common oath, in the midst of
the common speech,
Defending Tren, that wasted town!

V. Cyndylan, bright pillar of his country,
Chain-bearer, obstinate in fight,
Protected Tren, the town of his father!
VI. Cyndylan, bright intelligence departed,
Chain-bearer, obstinate in the host,
Protected Tren as long as be was living.
VII. Cyndylan, with heart of greyhound,
When he descended to the turmoil of battle,
A carnage he carved out.
VIII. Cyndylan, with heart of hawk,
Was the true enraged
Cub of Cyndrwyn, the stubborn one.
IX. Cyndylan, with heart of wild boar,
When he descended to the onset of battle,
There was carnage in two heaps.
X. Cyndylan, hungry boar, ravager,
Lion, wolf fast holding of descent,
The wild boar will not give back the town of his father.
XI. Cyndylan! while towards thee fled
His heart, it was a great festival
With him, like the press of the battle!
XII. Cyndylan of Powys purple gallant is he!
The strangers' refuge, their life's anchor,
Cub of Cyndrwyn, much to be lamented!
XIII. Cyndylan, fair son of Cyndrwyn,
No fitting garb is the beard about the nose,
Will a man be no better than a maid?
XIV. Cyndylan! a cause of grief thou art
Set forward will not be the array,
Around the pressure of the covert of thy shield!

XV. Cyndylan, keep thou the slope
Till the Lloegrians come to-day,
Anxiety on account of one is not fitting.
XVI. Cyndylan, keep thou the top
Till the Lloegrians come through Tren,
'Tis not called a wood for one tree!
XVII. My heart has great misery
In joining together the black boards,
Fair is the flesh of Cyndylan, the common grief of a hundred hosts!
XVIII. The Hall of Cyndylan is dark
To-night, without fire, without bed!
I'll weep a while, afterwards I shall be silent.
XIX. The Hall of Cyndylan is dark
To-night, without fire, without candle!
Except God, who will give me patience?
XX. The Hall of Cyndylan is dark
To-night, without fire, without light,
Let there come spreading silence around thee!
XXI. The Hall of Cyndylan! dark
Its roof, after the fair assemblage!
Alas, it makes not well its end!
XXII. The Hall of Cyndylan! art thou not
Without seemliness? in the grave is thy shield!
As long as he was living there was no break in the shingle.
XXII. The Hall of Cyndylan is forlorn
To-night, since there has been no one owning it,
Ah! death will not leave me long!
XXIV. The Hall of Cyndylan is not pleasant
To-night, on the top of Carrec Hytwyth,
Without lord, without company, without feast!

XXV. The Hall of Cyndylan is gloomy
To-night, without fire, without songs--
Tears are the trouble of my cheeks!
xxvi. The Hall of Cyndylan is gloomy
To-night, without family,
   *   *   *   *   *
XXVII. The Hall of Cyndylan pierces
me
To see it, without roof, without fire.
Dead is my chief, myself alive!
XXVIII. The Hall of Cyndylan lies
waste
To-night, after warriors contended,
Elvan, Cyndylan Caeawc!
XXIX. The Hall of Cyndylan is piercing
cold
To-night, after the honour that befel
me.
Without the men, without the women
it sheltered.
XXX. The Hall of Cyndylan is still
To-night, after losing its elder.
The great merciful God! what shall I
do?
XXXI. The Hall of Cyndylan! dark is its
roof
Since the destruction by the Loegri-
ans
Cyndylan and Elvan of Powys.
XXXII. The Hall of Cyndylan is dark
To-night, of the children of
Cyndrwyn,
Cynon and Gwiawn and Gwyn.
XXXIII. The Hall of Cyndylan pierces
me
Every hour, after the great gathering
din at the fire
Which I saw at thy fire-hearth!
XXXIV. The eagle of Eli, loud his cry:
He has swallowed fresh drink,
Heart-blood of Cyndylan fair!
XXXV. The eagle of Eli screams aloud
To-night, in the blood of fair men he
wallows!

He is in the wood, a heavy grief to
me!
XXXVI. The eagle of Eli I bear
To-night, bloody is he, I defy not,
He is in the wood, a heavy grief to
me!
XXXVII. The eagle of Eli, let him afflict
To-night the vale of illustrious
Meissir,
Brochwael's land, long let him affront
it!
XXXVIII. The eagle of Eli keeps the
seas;
He will not course the fish in the
Aber.
Let him call, let him look out for the
blood of men!
XXXIX. The eagle of Eli traverses
The wood at dawn to feast,
His greed, may his boldness prosper
it!
XL The eagle of Pengwern with the
gray horn-beak,
Very loud his echoing voice,
Eager for the flesh.
XLI. The eagle of Pengwern with the
gray horn-beak,
Very loud his call of defiance,
Eager for the flesh of Cyndylan!
XLII. The eagle of Pengwern with the
gray born-beak,
Very loud his clamour,
Eager for the. flesh of him I love!
XLIII. The eagle of Pengwern! from
afar is his call
To-night, for the men of blood is his
look-out,
Truly will Tren be called the ruined
town!
XLIV. The eagle of Pengwern! from
afar let him call
To-night, for the blood of men let him
look out,
Truly will Tren be called the town of
flame!

XLV. The churches of Bassa! there rests
To-night, there ends, there shrinks within himself,
The shelter in battle, heart of the men of Argoed!

XLVI. The churches of Bassa are en-riched
To-night, my tongue hath done it!
Ruddy are they, overflowing my grief!

XLVII. The churches of Bassa are close neighbouring
To-night to the heir of Cyndrwyn,
Graveyard of Cyndylan fair!

XLVIII. The churches of Bassa are lovely
To-night, their clover hath made them so,
Ruddy are they, overflowing my heart!

XLIX. The churches of Bassa have lost their privilege
Since the destruction by the Lloegri-ans
Of Cyndylan and Elvan of Powys.

L. The churches of Bassa are to make an end
To-night; the warriors are not to con-tinue.
He knows who knoweth all things, and I here know.

LI. The churches of Bassa are still
To-night, and I am to cry!
Ruddy are they, overflowing is my lament.

LII. The White Town in the bosom of the wood!
There has ever been of its lustyhood,
On the surface of the grass, the blood!

LIII. The White Town in the country side!
Its lustyhood, its gray thoughtfulness,
The blood under the feet of its warri-ors!

LIV. The White Town in the valley!
Joyful its troop with the common spoil
Of battle, its people, are they not gone?

LV. The White Town between Tren and Trodwyd!
More common was the broken shield
Coming from battle than the evening ox.

LVI. The White Town between Tren and Traval.
More common was the blood
On the surface of the grass than the ploughed fallow.

LVII. Alas, Ffreuer! how sad is it
To-night, after the loss of kindred.
By the mishap of my tongue were they slain.

LVIII. Alas, Ffreuer! how languid she is
To-night, after the death of Elvan,
And the eagle of Cyndrwyn, Cyndylan.

LIX. It is not the death of Ffreuer that separates me
To-night from the enjoyment of the social circle.
I will keep awake, I will early weep.

LX. It is not the death of Ffreuer that pierces me with pain.
From the beginning of night till mid-night
I will keep awake, I will weep with the dawn.

LXI. It is not the death of Ffreuer that stares me
To-night, and causes my checks to be yellow,
And the red tears to flow over the bedside.

LXII. It is not the death of Ffreuer that I am tormented with
To-night, but myself, being feebly

sick,
My brothers and my country I mourn.
LXIII. Fair Ffreuer! there are brothers who cherish thee,
And who have not sprung from the ungenerous;
They are men who cherish no timidity.
LXIV. Fair Ffreuer! to thee have been brothers;
When they heard the meeting of armies
Their confidence would not fail them.
LXV. I and Ffreuer and Medlan,
While there may be battle in every place,
Are not concerned if our side be not slain.
LXVI. The mountain, were it still higher
I will not covet, there to lead my life.
Light of valuable things is my clothing.
LXVII. Parallel with the Avaerwy,
The Tren enters the Trydonwy,
And the Twrch falls into the Marchnwy.
LXVIII. Parallel with the Elwydden,
The Trydonwy flows into the Tren,
And the Geirw flows into the Alwen.
LXIX. Before my covering was made of the hide
Of the hardy goat, intent I was on carnage;
I was made drunk with the mead of Bryum.
LXX. Before my covering was made of the hide
Of the hardy goat, the young goat to the holly,
I was made drunk with the mead of Tren.
LXXI. After my brethren from the region of the Hafren,
And about the two banks of the Dwyryw,
Woe is me, God, that I am alive!
LXXII. After well-trained horses and garments of ruddy hue,
And the waving yellow plumes,
Slender is my leg, a covering is not left me.
LXXIII. The cattle of Edeyrniawn went not astray,
And with none did they go away,
In the lifetime of Gorwynion, a man of Uchnant.
LXXIV. The cattle of Edeyrniawn went not astray,
And with none did they wander,
In the lifetime of Gowrynion, a man . . .
Reproach is known to the herdsman.
The price is shame and refusal.
On such as come to disgrace it will befall.
I know what is good,
The blood of one hero for another.
LXXV. Were it the wife of Gyrthmwl, she would be languid
This day; loud would be her scream;
She would deplore the loss of her heroes.
LXXVI. The soil of Ercal is on courageous men,
On the progeny of Moryal,
And after Rys great lamentation.
LXXVII. The hawk of Heledd calls unto me
"O God! why is it that to thee have been given
The horses of my country and their land?
LXXVIII. The hawk of Heledd will greet me
"O God I why is it that to thee are given the dark coloured harness
Of Cyndylan and his forty horses?"
LXXIX. Have I not gazed with my eyes on pleasant land

From the conspicuous seat of Gor-
wynion?

Long the course of the run, longer my
recollection.

LXXX Have I not gazed from Dinlle
Wrecon on the patrimony of Ffreuer,
With grief for its social enjoyment?

LXXXI. A horseman from a Caer be-
low,
He was slow in his complaints.
A man of Sannair--

LXXXII. Slain were my brothers all at
once--
Cynan, Cyndylan, Cynwraith--
In defending Tren, a town laid waste.

LXXXIII. A tribe would not tread on
the nest
Of Cynddylan; he would never flinch
a foot;
His mother nursed no weakling son.

LXXXIV. Brethren I have had who
never were dejected,
Who grew up like hazel saplings;
One by one, they are all gone.

LXXXV. Brethren I have had whom
God has taken
From me; my misfortune caused it.
They would not purchase glory by
false means.

LXXXVI. Thin the gale, thick the ru-
mour,.
Sweet the furrows; thou that made
them remain not;
Those who have been are no more.

LXXXVII. What is heard by God and
man,
What is heard by young and old,
Disgrace of beards, let the flier loose.

LXXXVIII. While it lives the flier will
fly
With garments waiting for the battle-
field,
And with blue blades the chief was
enlivened.

LXXXIX. I wonder the bright fort is no
more
After its defenders notoriously skilful
In the lair of the boar there is break-
ing of pignuts.

XC. They are neither mist nor smoke,
Nor warriors in mutual defence.
In a meadow slaughter is bad.

XCI. I listened in the meadow to the
clatter of shields.
A fortress is no restraint to the
mighty,
The best of men, Caranmael.

XCII. Caranmael, pressure there is on
thee;
I know thy retreat from battle.
A mark is wont on the brow of a
combatant.

XCIII. Accustomed to exert a liberal
hand,
The son of Cyndylan, retainer of
praise,
The last man of Cyndrwyn, Caran-
mael.

XCIV. Devoid of zeal was he,
And his patrimony was sequestrated,
Who sought Caranmael for a judge.

XCV. Caranmael, intimate with exer-
tion,
Son of Cyndylan of ready fame,
Was not a judge, though he would
wist to be.

XCVI. Where Caranmael put on the
corselet of Cyndylan,
And pushed forward his ashen spear,
A Frank should not deprive him of his
head.

XCVII. The time when I fared on rich
viands
I would not lift my thigh
For a man that complained of a sore
disease.

XCVIII. Brothers I also have had
That would not complain of pestilen-

tial diseases:
One was Elvan, Cyndylan another.
XCIX. Hair is not gracefully worn, is it not becoming
A man in the heat of conflict?
My brethren were not clamorous.
C. But for death and its fearful afflictions,
And the pang of the blue blades,
I will not be clamorous either.
CI. The plain of Maodyn, is it not covered with frost?
Since the destruction of him who was of benevolent purpose
On the grave of Eirinwed thick the snow.
CII. The mound of Elwyddan, is it not drenched with rain,
And the plain of Maodyn below it?
Cynon ought to deplore him.
CIII. Four equal brothers to me have been,

And each was the head of a family.
Tren knows to itself no owner.
CIV. Four equal brothers to me have been,
And to each chief there was vigour.
Tren knows no congenial owner.
CV. Four equal courageous and comely
Brothers to me have been from Cyndrwyn.
There is not to Tren the possession of enjoyment.
CVI. Fly thee hence, and array thyself
Thou art not wont to rise with the dawn.
Am I not wounded by a spike from the comer of thy bag?
CVII. Fly thee hence and hide thyself
Thou art not of sinless conversation..
Prostration is useless, thy creeping will cause a noise.

P. Poems Which Mention Henry, or the Son of Henry

LXIV. A DIALOGUE BETWEEN MYRDIN AND HIS SISTER GWENDYDD. - RED BOOK OF HERGEST I.

I. I have come to thee to tell
Of the jurisdiction I have in the North;
The beauty of every region has been described to me.
II. Since the action of Ardderyd and Erydon,
Gwendydd, and all that will happen to me,
Dull of understanding, to what place of festivity shall I go?
III. I will address my twin-brother Myrdin, a wise man and a diviner,
Since he is accustomed to make disclosures
When a maid goes to him.

IV. I shall become the simpleton's song:
It is the ominous belief of the Cymry.
The gale intimates
That the standard of Rydderch Hael is unobstructed.
V. Though Rydderch has the pre-eminence,
And all the Cymry under him,
Yet, after him, who will come?
VI. Rydderch Hael, the feller of the foe,
Dealt his stabs among them,
In the day of bliss at the ford of Tawy.
VII. Rydderch Hael, while he is the enemy

Of the city of the bards in the region of the Clyd;

Where will he go to the ford?

VIII. I will tell it to Gwendydd.

Since she has addressed me skilfully,

The day after to-morrow Rydderch Hael will not be.

IX. I will ask my far-famed twin-brother,

The intrepid in battle,

After Rydderch who will be?

X. As Gwenddoleu was slain in the blood-spilling of Ardderyd,

And I have come from among the furze,

Morgant Mawr, the son of Sadyrnin.

XI. I will ask my far-famed brother,

The fosterer of song among the streams,

Who will rule after Morgant?

XII. As Gwenddoleu was slain in the bloodshed of Ardderyd,

And I wonder why I should be perceived,

The cry of the country to Urien.

XIII, Thy head is of the colour of winter boar;

God has relieved thy necessities

Who will rule after Urien?

XIV. Heaven has brought a heavy affliction

On me, and I am ill at last,

Maelgwn Hir over the land of Gwynedd.

XV. From parting with my brother pines away

My heart, poor is my aspect along my furrowed cheek;

Now, after Maelgwn, who will rule?

XVI. Run is his name impetuous in the gushing conflict;

And fighting in the van of the army,

The woe of Prydein of the day!

XVII. Since thou art a companion and canon

Of Cunllaith, which with great expense we support,

To whom will Gwynedd go after Run?

XVIII. Run his name, renowned in war;

What I predict will surely come to pass,

Gwendydd, the country will be in the hand of Beli.

XIX. I will ask my far-famed twin-brother,

Intrepid in difficulties,

Who will rule after Beli?

XX. Since my reason is gone with ghosts of the mountain,

And I myself am pensive,

After Beli, his son Iago.

XXI. Since thy reason is gone with ghosts of the mountain,

And thou thyself art pensive,

Who will rule after Iago?

XXII. He that comes before me with a lofty mien,

Moving to the social banquet;

After Iago, his son Cadvan?

XXIII. The songs have fully predicted

That one of universal fame will come;

Who will rule after Cadvan?

XXIV. The country of the brave Cadwallawn,

The four quarters of the world shall hear of it;

The heads of the Angles will fall to the ground,

And there will be a world to admire it.

XXV. Though I see thy cheek so direful,

It comes impulsively to my mind,

Who will rule after Cadwallawn?

XXVI. A tall man holding a conference,

And Prydein under one sceptre,

The best son of Cymro, Cadwaladyr.

XXVII. He that comes before me mildly,

His abilities, are they not worthless?
After Cadwaladyr, Idwal.
XXVIII. I will ask thee mildly,
Far-famed, and best of men on earth,
Who will rule after Idwal?
XXIX. There will rule after Idwal,
In consequence of a dauntless one
being called forth,
White-shielded Howel, the son of
Cadwal.
XXX. I will ask my far-famed twin-
brother,
The intrepid in war,
Who will rule after Howel?
XXXI. I will tell his illustrious fame,
Gwendydd, before I part from thee;
After Howel, Rodri.
XXXII. Cynan in Mona will be,
He will not preserve his rights;
And before the son of Rodri may be
called,
The son of Cealedigan will be.
XXXIII. I will ask on account of the
world,
And answer thou me gently;
Who will rule after Cynan?
XXXIV. Since Gwenddoleu was slain
in the bloodshed of
Ardderyd, thou art filled with dismay;
Mervyn Vrych from the region of
Manaw.
XXXV. I will ask my brother re-
nowned in fame,
Lucid his song, and he the best of
men,
Who will rule after Mervyn?
XXXVI. I will declare, from no malevo-
lence,
The oppression of. Prydein, but from
concern;
After Mervyn, Rodri Mawr.
XXXVII. I will ask my far-famed twin-
brother,
Intrepid in the day of the war-shout;

Who will rule after the son of Rodri
Mawr?
XXXVIII. On the banks of the Conwy
in the conflict of Wednesday,
Admired will be the eloquence
Of the hoary sovereign Anarawd.
XXXIX. I will address my far-famed
twin-brother,
Intrepid in the day of mockery,
Who will rule after Anarawd?
XL. The next is nearer to the time
Of unseen messengers;
The sovereignty in the band of How-
el.
XLI. The Borderers have not been,
And will not be nearer to Paradise.
An order from a kiln is no worse than
from a church.
XLII. I will ask my beloved brother,
Whom I have seen celebrated in
fame,
Who will rule after the Borderers?
XLIII. A year and a half to loquacious
Barons, whose lives shall be short-
ened;
Every careless one will be dispar-
aged.
XLIV. Since thou art a companion and
canon of Cunllaith,
The mercy of God to thy soul!
Who will rule after the Barons?
XLV. A single person will arise from
obscurity,
Who will not preserve his counte-
nance;
Cynan of the dogs will possess Cym-
ry.
XLVI. I will ask thee on account of the
world,
Answer thou me gently,
Who will rule after Cynan?
XLVII. A man from a distant foreign
country;
They will batter impregnable Caers
They say a king from a baron.

XLVIII. I will ask on account of the world,
Since thou knowest the meaning;
Who will rule after the Baron?
XLIX. I will foretell of Serven Wyn,
A constant white-shielded messenger,
Brave, and strong like a white encircled prison;
He will traverse the Countries of treacherous sovereigns;
And they will tremble before him as far as Prydein.
L. I will ask my blessed brother,
For it is I that is inquiring it,
Who will rule after Serven Wyn?
LI. Two white-shielded Belis
Will then come and cause tumult;
Golden peace will not be.
LII. I will ask my far-famed twin-brother,
Intrepid among the Cymry,
Who will rule after the two white-shielded Belis?
LIII. A. single passionate one with a beneficent mien,
Counselling a battle of defence;
Who will rule before the extermination?
LIV. I will ask my far-famed twin-brother,
Intrepid in the battle,
Who is the single passionate one
That thou predictest then?
What his name? what is he? when will he come?
LV. Gruffyd his name, vehement and handsome:
It is natural that he should throw lustre on his kindred;
He will rule over the land of Prydein.
LVI. I will ask my far-famed twin-brother,
Intrepid in battles,
Who shall possess it after Gruffyd?

LVII. I will declare from no malevolence,
The oppression of Prydein, but from concern;
After Gruffyd, Gwyn Gwarther.
LVIII. I will ask my far-famed twin-brother,
The intrepid in war,
Who will rule after Gwyn Gwarther?
LIX. Alas! fair Gwendydd, great is the prognostication of the oracle,
And the tales of the Sybil;
Of an odious stock will be the two Idases;
For land they will be admired; from their jurisdiction, long animosity.
LX. I will ask my far-famed twin-brother,
Intrepid in the battles,
Who will rule after them?
LXI. I will predict that no youth will venture;
A king, a lion with unflinching hand,
Gylvin Gevel with a wolf's grasp.
LXII. I will ask my profound brother,
Whom I have seen tenderly nourished,
After that who will be sovereign?
LXIII. To the multiplicity of the number of the stars
Will his retinue be compared;
He is Mackwy Dau Hanner.
LXIV. I will ask my unprotected brother,
The key of difficulty, the benefit of a lord--
Who will rule after Dan Hanner?
LXV. There will be a mixture of the Gwyddelian tongue in the battle,
With the Cymro, and a fierce conflict;
He is the lord of eight chief Caers.
LXVI. I will ask my pensive brother,
Who has read the book of Cado,
Who will rule after him?

LXVII. I say that he is from Reged,
Since I am solemnly addressed;
The whelp of the illustrious Henri,
Never in his age will there be deliverance.

LXVIII. I will ask my brother renowned in fame,
Undaunted among the Cymry,
Who will rule after the son of Henri?

LXIX. When there will be a bridge on the Tav, and another on the Tywi,
Confusion will come upon Lloegyr,
And I will predict after the son of Henri,
Such and such a king and troublous times will be.

LXX. I will ask my blessed brother,
For it is I that is inquiring,
Who will rule after such and such a king?

LXXI. A silly king will come,
And the men of Lloegyr will deceive him;
There will be no prosperity of country under him.

LXXII. Myrdin fair, of fame-conferring song,
Wrathful in the world,
What will be in the age of the foolish one?

LXXIII. When Lloegyr will be groaning,
And Cymir full of malignity,
An army will be moving to and fro.

LXXIV. Myrdin fair, gifted in speech,
Tell me no falsehood;
What will be after the army?

LXXV. There will arise one out of the six
That have long been in concealment;
Over Lloegyr he will have the mastery.

LXXVI. Myrdin fair, of fame-conferring stock,

Let the wind turn inside the house,
Who will rule after that?

LXXVII. It is established that Owein should come,
And conquer as far as London,
To give the Cymry glad tidings.

LXXVIII. Myrdin fair, most gifted and most famed,
For thy word I will believe,
Owein, how long will he continue?

LXXIX. Gwendydd, listen to a rumour,
Let the wind turn in the valley,
Five years and two, as in time of yore.

LXXX. I will ask my profound brother,
Whom I have seen tenderly nourished,
Who will thence be sovereign?

LXXXI. When Owein will be in Manaw,
And a battle in Prydyn close by,
There will be a man with men under him.

LXXXII. I will ask my profound brother,
Whom I have seen tenderly nourished,
After that who will be sovereign?

LXXXIII. A ruler of good breeding and good will he be,
Will conquer the land,
And the country will be happy with joy.

LXXXIV. I will ask my profound brother,
Whom I have seen tenderly nourished,
After that who will be sovereign?

LXXXV. Let there be a cry in the valley
Beli Hir and his men like the whirlwind;
Blessed be the Cymry, woe to the Gynt.

LXXXVI. I will ask my far-famed twin-brother,

Intrepid in battles,
After Beli who will be the possessor?
LXXXVII. Let there be a cry in the Aber,
Beli Hir and his numerous troops;
Blessed be the Cymry, woe to the Gwyddyl.
LXXXVIII. I will address my farfamed twin-brother
Intrepid in war;
Why woe to the Gwyddyl?
LXXXIX. I will predict that one prince will be
Of Gwynedd, after your affliction;
You will have a victory over every nation.
XC. The canon of Morvryn, how united to us
Was Myrdin Vrych with the powerful host,
What will happen until the wish be accomplished?
XCI. When Cadwaladyr will descend,
Having a large united host with him,
On Wednesday to defend the men of Gwynedd,
Then will come the men of Caer Garawedd.
XCII. Do not separate abruptly from me,
From a dislike to the conference;
In what part will Cadwaladyr descend?
XCIII. When Cadwaladyr descends
Into the valley of the Tywi,
Hard pressed will be the Abers
And the Brython will disperse the Brithwyr.
XCIV. I will ask my profound brother,
Whom I have seen tenderly nourished;
Who will rule from thenceforth?
XCV. When a boor will know three languages
In Mona, and his son be of honoura-
ble descent,
Gwynedd will be heard to be abounding in riches.
XCVI. Who will drive Lloegyr from the borders
Of the sea, who will move upon Dyved?
And as to the Cymry, who will succour them?
XCVII. The far-extended rout and tumult of Rydderch,
And the armies of Cadwaladyr,
Above the river Tardennin,
Broke the key of men.
XCVIII. Do not separate abruptly from me,
From dislike to the conference,
What death will carry off Cadwaladyr?
XCIX. He will be pierced by a spear from the strong timber
Of a ship, and a hand before the evening;
The day will be a disgrace to the Cymry.
C. Do not separate abruptly from me
From dislike to the conference,
How long will Cadwaladyr reign?
CI. Three months and three long years,
And full three hundred years
With occasional battles, he will rule.
CII. Do not separate abruptly from me
From dislike to the conference,
Who will rule after Cadwaladyr?
CIII. To Gwendydd I will declare;
Age after age I will predict;
After Cadwaladyr, Cynda.
CIV. A hand upon the sword, another upon the cross,
Let every one take care of his life;
With Cyndav there is no reconciliation.

CV. I will foretell that there will be one prince
Of Gwynedd, after your affliction,
You will overcome every nation.
CVI. And as to the tribe of the children of Adam,
Who have proceeded from his flesh,
Will their freedom extend to the judgment?
CVII. From the time the Cymry shall be without the aid
Of battle, and altogether without keeping their mien,
It will be impossible to say who will be ruler.
CVIII. Gwendydd, the delicately fair,
The first will be the most puissant in Prydein;
Lament, ye wretched Cymry!
CIX. When extermination becomes the highest duty,
From the sea to the shoreless land,
Say, lady, that the world is at an end.
CX. And after extermination becomes the highest duty,
Who will there be to keep order?
Will there be a church, and a portion for a priest?
CXI. There will be no portion for priest nor minstrel,
Nor repairing to the altar,
Until the heaven falls to the earth.
CXII. My twin-brother, since thou hast answered me,
Myrdin, son of Morvryn the skilful,
Sad is the tale thou hast uttered.
CXIII. I will declare to Gwendydd,
For seriously hast thou inquired of me,
Extermination, lady, will be the end.
CXIV. What I have hitherto predicted
To Gwendydd, the idol of princes.
It will come to pass to the smallest tittle.

CXV. Twin-brother, since these things will happen to me,
Even for the souls of thy brethren,
What sovereign after him will be?
CXVI. Gwendydd fair, the chief of courtesy,
I will seriously declare,
That never shall be a sovereign afterwards.
CXVII. Alas I thou dearest, for the cold separation,
After the coming of tumult,
That by a sovereign brave and fearless
Thou shouldst be placed under earth.
CXVIII. The air of heaven will scatter
Rash resolution, which deceives, if believed:
Prosperity until the judgment is certain.
CXIX. By thy dissolution, thou tenderly nourished,
Am I not left cheerless?
A delay will be good destiny when will be given
Praise to him who tells the truth.
CXX. From thy retreat arise, and unfold
The books of Awen without fear;
And the discourse of a maid, and the repose of a dream.
CXXI. Dead is Morgeneu, dead Cyvrennin
Moryal. Dead is Moryen, the bulwark of battle;
The heaviest grief is, Myrdin, for thy destiny.
CXXII. The Creator has caused me heavy affliction;
Dead is Morgeneu, dead is Mordav,
Dead is Moryen, I wish to die.
CXXIII. My only brother, chide me not;
Since the battle of Ardderyd I am ill;

It is instruction that I seek;
To God I commend thee.
CXXIV. I, also, commend thee,
To the, Chief of all creatures
Gwendydd fair, the refuge of songs.
CXXV. The songs too long have tarried
Concerning universal fame to come;
Would to God they had come to pass!
CXXVI. Gwendydd, be not dissatisfied;
Has not the burden been consigned
to the earth?
Every one must give up what he
loves.
CXXVII. While I live, I will not forsake
thee,
And until the judgment will bear thee
in mind;
Thy entrenchment is the heaviest
calamity.

CXXVIII. Swift is the steed, and free
the wind;
I will commend my blameless brother
To God, the supreme Ruler;
Partake of the communion before thy
death.
CXXIX. I will not receive the communion
From excommunicated monks,
With their cloaks on their hips;
May God himself give me communion!
CXXX. I will commend my blameless
Brother in the supreme Caer;
May God take care of Myrdin!
CXXXI. I, too, will commend my
blameless
Sister in the supreme Caer;--
May God take care of Gwendydd.
Amen!

LXV. A FUGITIVE POEM OF MYRDIN IN HIS GRAVE - RED BOOK OF HERGEST II.

THE man that speaks from the grave
Has been instructed that before seven years,
The horse of Eurdein of the North will die.
II. I have quaffed wine from a bright glass
With the lords of fierce war;
My name is Myrdin, son of Morvryn.
III. I have quaffed wine from a goblet
With the lords of devouring war;
Myrdin is my deserving name.
IV. When opposition will come upon a black wheel,
To destroy Lloegyr of exhausted course,
Bitter will be their enmity in defending
The White Mount; at the White Mount distress there will be,
And long regret to the nation of the Cymry.
V. There will be no protection in the recesses of Ardudwy,
In the maritime region of the Cymry,
From the renowned Boar of the intrepid host.
VI. When the red one of Normandy will come
To charge the Lloegrians with enormous expense,

There will be a tax upon every prediction,
And a castle at Aber Hodni.
VII. When the strong-freckled one will come
As far as Ryd Bengarn,
Men will be disgraced, hilts worn out:
The chief noble of Prydein will be their chief in judgment.
VIII. When Henri will come to claim
Mur Castell on the border of Eryri,
Disturbance beyond sea will call him.
IX. When the pale weak one will come to claim London,
Upon unhandsome horses,
He will call forth the lordship of Caergein.
X. Scarce the acorns, thick the corn,
When there will suddenly appear
A king, a youth, woo to such as tremble!
XI. There will be a youth of great renown,
Who will conquer a thousand cities;
Like the life of tender shoots will be that of the king I from a youth.
XII. Strong towards the weak will he be,
Weak towards the strong of the uplands;--
A ruler from whose coming worse it will fare.
XIII. There will be a state when they will delight in wantonness,
When women will be a soft herd,
And a host of young children at confession.
XIV. There will be a state when they will delight in order;
Even the churl will do a good turn;
The maid will be handsome, and the youth resolute.
XV. There will be a state towards the end of the age,
When from adversity the young will fail,
And in May cuckoos die of cold.
XVI. There will be a state when they will delight in hunting-dogs,
And build in intricate places
And a shirt without great cost cannot be obtained.
XVII. There will be a state when they will delight in oaths;
Vice will be active, and churches neglected;
Words as well as relies will be broken,
Truth will disappear, and falsehood spread
Faith will be weak, and disputings on alternate days.
XVIII. There will be a state when they will delight in clothes;
The counsellor of a lord will be a vagrant of a bailiff;
Empty-handed the bard, gay the priest;
Men will be despised, refusals frequent.
XIX. There will be a state without wind, without rain,
Without too much ploughing, without too much consuming,
Land enough will one acre be for nine.

XX. When the men will come without manliness,
And corn grow in the place of trees,
In peace everywhere feasts will be prevalent.
XXI. When the cubit shall be held in esteem, trees in spring
There will be after the chief of mischief:
Let the cowhouse post be worse than a coulter.
XXII. Wednesday, a day of enmity,
Blades will be completely worn out;
They will conceal two in the blood of Cynghen.
XXIII. In Aber Sor there will be a council,
On men after the devastation of battle,
A happy ruler is a leader in the camp.
XXIV. In Aber Avon will be the host of Mona,
And Angles after that will be at Hinwedon;
His valour will Moryon long preserve.
XXV. In Aber Dwvyr the leader will not hold out,
When that which will be performed by Gwidig will take place,
And after the battle of Cyvarllug.
XXVI. A battle will be on the river Byrri,
And the Brython will be victorious;
The men of Gwhyr will perform acts of heroism.
XXVII. In Aber Don a battle will ensue,
And the shafts will be unequal,
And crimson blood on the brow of Saxons.
Servile is thy cry, thou Gwendydd!
Have told it me the ghosts
Of the mountain, in Aber Carav.

LXVI. BLACK BOOK OF CAERMARTHEN XVI.

I. BLESSED is the birch in the valley of the Gwy,
Whose branches will fall off one by one, two by two,
It will remain when there will be a battle in Ardudwy,
And the lowing together of cattle about the ford of Mochnwy,
And spears and shouting at Dyganwy,
And Edwin bearing sway in Mona,
And youths pale and light
In ruddy clothes commanding them.
II. Blessed is the birch in Pumlumon,
Which will see when the front of the stag shall be exalted,
And which will see the Franks clad in mail,
And about the hearth food for whelps,
And monks frequently riding on steeds.
III. Blessed is the birch in the heights of Dinwythwy,
Which will know when there shall be a battle in Ardudwy,

And spears uplifted around Edrywy,
And a bridge on the Taw, and another on the Tawy,
And another, on account of a misfortune, on the two banks of the Gwy,
And the artificer that will make it, let his name be Garwy;
And may the principal of Mona have dominion over it.
Women will be under the Gynt, and men in affliction.
Happier than I is he who will welcome
The time of Cadwaladyr: a song he may sing!

LXVII. BLACK BOOK OF CAERMARTHEN XVIII.

O little pig! thou happy little pig!
Bury not thy snout on the top of the mountain;
Burrow in a secluded place in the woods,
For fear of the hunting dogs of Rydderch, the champion of the faith.
And I will prognosticate, and it will be true,
As far as Aber Taradyr, before the usurpers of Prydein,
All the Cymry will be under the same warlike leader;
His name is Llywelyn, of the line
Of Gwynedd, one who will overcome.
II. Listen, O little pig! it is necessary to go,
For fear of the hunters of Mordei, if one dared,
Lest we be pursued and discovered;
And should we escape, I shall not complain of fatigue,
And. I will predict, in respect of the ninth wave,
And in respect of the single white-bearded person, who exhausted Dyved,
Who erected a chancel in the land for those of partial belief,
In the upland region, and among wild beasts.
Until Cynan comes to it, to see its distress,
Her habitations will never be restored.
III. Listen, O little pig! I cannot easily sleep,
On account of the tumult of grief which is upon me;
Ten years and forty have I endured pain;
Evil is the joy which I now have.
May life be given me by Jesus, the most trustworthy
Of the kings of heaven, of highest lineage!
It will not be well with the female descendants of Adam,
If they believe not in God, in the latter day.
I have seen Gwenddoleu, with the precious gifts of princes,
Gathering prey from every extremity of the land;
Beneath my green sod is he not still!
The chief of sovereigns of the North, of mildest disposition.
IV. Listen, O little pig! it was necessary to pray,
For fear of the five sovereigns from Normandi;
And the fifth going over the salt sea,

To conquer Iwerdon with its pleasant towns;
He will cause war and confusion,
And ruddy arms and groanings in it.
And they, certainly, will come from it,
And do honour on the grave of Dewi.
And I will predict that there will be confusion
From the fighting of son and father, the country shall know it;
And that there will be to the Lloegrians the falling of cities,
And that deliverance will never be to Normandi.
V. Listen, O little pig! be not drowsy;
There comes to us a sad report
Of petty chieftains full of perjury
And husbandmen. that are close-fisted of the penny.
When there shall come over the sea men completely covered with armour,
With war-horses under them, having two faces,
And two points on their terribly destructive spears;
There will be ploughing without reaping in the world of war;
The grave will be better than life to all the wretched;
Horns will be on the women of the four quarters;
When the vigorous young men shall become corpses,
There will be a severe morning in Caer Sallawg.
VI. Listen, O little pig! thou pig of peace!
A Sibyl has told me a wonderful tale;
And I will predict a summer full of fury,
Between brothers, treachery from Gwynedd.
When a pledge of peace shall long be required from the land of Gwynedd,
There shall come seven hundred ships of the Gynt with the north wind;
And in Aber Dau their conference will be.
VII. Listen, O little pig! thou blessed little pig!
A Sibyl has told me it tale which frightens me;
When Lloegyr shall encamp in the land of Ethlin,
And make Dyganwy a strong fort,
By the . . . of Lloegyr and Llywelyn,
There will be it child on the shoulders . . . baggage.
When Deinoel, the son of Dunawd Deinwyn, becomes enraged,
The Frank shall flee the way he does not seek;
In Aber Dulas their support will be exhausted,
Of a ruddy hue will be their garments around them.
VIII. Listen, O little pig! listen to the calls for attention!
For the crime of the necessitous God will make remissions.
. . . what is becoming, be it mine,
And what is . . . let him seek.
IX. Listen, O little pig! it is broad daylight,
Hark thou to the song of water-birds whose notes are loud!
To us there will be years and long days,

And iniquitous rulers, and the blasting of fruit,
And bishops sheltering thieves, churches desecrated,
And monks who will compensate for loads of sins.
X. Listen, O little pig! penetrate into Gwynedd;
Have a partner when thou goest to rest.
Little does Rydderch Hael know to-night at his feast
What sleeplessness last night I bore.
The snow was up to my knee, owing to the wariness of the chief,
Icicles hung to my hair; sad is my fate!
Tuesday will come, the day of fierce anger,
Between the ruler of Powys, and the region of Gwynedd.
When the beam of light will arise from its long repose,
And defend from its enemy the frontiers of Gwynedd.
Unless my Maker will grant me a share of his mercy,
Woe to me that I have existed, miserable will be my end!
XI. Listen, O little pig! utter not a whisper,
When the host of war marches from Caermarthen,
To support, in the common cause, two whelps
Of the line of Rys, the stay of battle, the warlike commander of armies,
When the Saxon shall be slain in the conflict of Cymmerau,
Blessed will be the lot of Cymry, the people of Cymrwy.
XII. Listen, O little pig! blessed little pig of the country!
Do not sleep in the morning, burrow not in the fertile region,
Lest Rydderch Hael and his cunning dogs should come,
And before thou couldst reach the wood, thy perspiration trickled down.
XIII. Listen, O little pig! thou blessed pig!
Hadst thou seen as much severe oppression as I have,
Thou wouldst not sleep in the morning, nor burrow on the hill.
When the Saxons repose from their serpent cunning,
And the castle of Collwyn is resorted to from afar,
Clothes will be smart, and the black pool clear.
XIV. Listen, O little pig! hear thou now;
When the men of Gwynedd lay down their great work,
Blades will be in hands, horns will be sounded,
Armour will be broken before sharp lances.
And I will predict that two rightful princes
Will produce peace from heaven to earth--
Cynan, Cadwaladyr, thorough Cymry.
May their councils be admired.
The laws of the country, and the exclusion of troubles,
And the abolition of armies and theft;
And to us then there shall be a relief after our ills,
And from generosity none will be excluded.
XV. Listen, Q little pig! is not the mountain green?
My cloak is thin for me there is no repose;

Pale is my visage, Gwendydd does not come to me.
When the men of Bryneich will bring their army to the shore,
Cymry will conquer, glorious will be their day.
XVI. Listen, O little pig! thou brawny pig!
Bury not thy snout, consume not Mynwy;
Love no pledge, love no play.
And an advice I will give to Gwenabwy,
"Be not an amorous youth given to wanton play."
And I will predict the battle of Machawy,
When there will be ruddy spears. in the Riw Dydmwy,
From the contention of chieftains; breast will heave on the saddles;
There will be a morning of woe, and a woeful visitation;
A bear from Deheubarth will arise,
His men will spread over the land of Mynwy.
Blessed is the lot that awaits Gwendydd,
When the Prince of Dyved comes to rule,
XVII. Listen, O little pig! are not the buds of thorns
Very green, the mountain beautiful, and beautiful the earth?
And I will predict the battle of Coed Llwyvein,
And ruddy biers from the attack of Owein,
When stewards shall make short disputes,
When there will be perjury and treachery amongst the children of the land;
And When Cadwaladyr comes to conquer
Mona, the Saxons shall be extirpated from lovely Prydein.
XVIII. Listen, O little pig! great wonders
Will be in Prydein, and I shall not be concerned;
When come the inhabitants of the regions about
Mona to question the Brython, there will be troublesome times;
A successful leader will uplift radiant spears,
Stout Cynan, appearing from the banks of the Teiwi,
Will cause confusion in Dyved;
May there be to him for riches melody in it!
XIX. Listen, O little pig! how wonderful it is
That the world is never long in the same condition!
How far the Saxons proclaim the cause of strife
With the generous Brython, the sons of trouble!
And I will predict before the end
The Brython uppermost of the Saxons; the Picts say it;
And then will come upon its the spirit of joyfulness,
After having long been of a tardy disposition.
XX. Listen, O little pig! hear thou the melody
And chirping of birds by Caer Reon.
One I have that I would place on Mynydd Maon,
To view the comely forms of the lovely ones.
And I will predict a battle on the wave,

And the battle of Machawy, and a battle on a river,
Ant] the battle of Cors Vochno, and the battle of Minron,
And the battle of Cymminawd, and the battle of Caerlleon,
And the battle of Abergwaith, and the battle of Ieithion;
And when there shall be an end of music at the land's end;
A child will arise, and good there will be to the Brython.
XXI. Listen, O little pig! a period will come,
How miserable that it should come, but come it will!
Maids will be bold, and wives wanton;
They will love, but will not revere their kindred;
Liberal will not the prosperous be towards one another.
Bishops will be of a different language, worthless, and faithless.
XXII. Listen, O little pig! thou little speckled one!
List to the voice of sea-birds, great is their energy!
Minstrels will be out, without their appropriate portion;
Though they stand at the door, a reward will not come,
I was told by a sea-gull that had come from afar,
That strange sovereigns will make their appearance;
Gwyddyl, and Brython, and Romani
Will create discord and confusion,
And in the name of gods will come into it,
And vigorously fight on both banks of the Tywi.
XXIII. Listen, O little pig! thou stout-armed little one!
Hark to the voice of sea-birds, whose clamour is great.
Minstrels will be out, without an honourable portion,
There will be repugnance to hospitality; a youth will have his own opinion,
Without protection of countenance, without an honourable portion.
When two brothers will be two Idases for land,
From their claim will be cherished a lasting feud.
XXIV. Listen, O little pig! to me it is of no purpose
To hear the voice of water-birds, whose scream is tumultuous,
Thin is the hair of my head, my covering is not warm;
The dales are my barn, my corn is not plenteous;
My summer collection affords me no relief,
Before parting from God, incessant was my passion.
And I will predict, before the end of the world,
Women without shame, and men without manliness.
XXV. Listen, O little pig! a trembling pig!
Thin is my covering, for me there is no repose,
Since the battle of Ardeleryd it will not concern me,
Though the sky were to fall, and sea to overflow.
And I will predict that after Henri
Such and such a king in troublesome times.
When there shall be a bridge on the Taw, and another on the Tywi,
There will be an end of war in it.

LXVIII. RED BOOK OF HERGEST XX.

THE fleet of Mona, the seat of misfortune,
Prevents bloodshed, with the noise of oars around her.
A greater influx will be into the Conwy on account of distress,
The men of the eagle of Eryri having fallen.
Without ardour they were in the time of heat before becoming silent,
Cymry without energy against injustice.
The dragon of prediction is the son of Henri;
For a year was be desired before the assembling of hosts,
Wolf of the mighty, mighty his retainers:
10 The retinue of the world will for a time be a sign from the Invisible.
The country will be constant to the ruler of Normandi,
The bane of Prydein, there will be anxious concern because of his birth,
With a constancy like the revolving of a wheel.
Chief of bards of every region, as to thy ancient claims
I will address thee by signs.
How often dost thou communicate with the youthful hero,
The heroic youth, amiable in society?
Supremely high will be the voice of fame on the blue sea,
When the youths of Brythyon come to their privilege;
20 And Owein will be the ruler of the kingdom,
A ruddy man in the ruddy scene, the joy of Gwynedd,
Of brave ancestors, the progeny of Mervyn, the bulwark of sovereignty.
A crowned young hero, on the point of effecting deliverance.
Known to God is my wish.
That the Allmyn should commence their flight with a bloody fate,
And with destruction so precipitate, so violent, so terrible!
Extremely offensive is every naked truth, be it certain
That distracted men have come contending about towns.
A heap of ruddy carcases by the peaceless blade has been deserved; and cer-
tainly such is the case.
30 Every record, every juncture, every man, and every triumph,
Christ has conferred upon me the advantage of knowing.
The Lloegrians are unfit in the conflict of blades,
An enervated rabble to contend in battle.

LXIX. RED BOOK OF HERGEST XIX.

Soon it will happen that kindred by nature will be in the shout of war,
Soon will happen many a cut from the tournament;
Soon will come between Saxons a recoil
From mutual wounding, irreverent burying and ministering;
Soon will the men of Manaw come to obtain praise,
And the North they will certainly make without peace.

Soon will be in Prydein anxiety and want,
And around Lloegyr they will loudly complain;
For the falling of the son of Henri they will be amazed;
10 So great in the dispersion will be the trepidation!
Scattered over seas, a number of legions they will chase away.
Tumult will be on the borders, arrogance they will not respect.
And I will predict that they will energetically shout;
The innocent like the guilty, they will hew down.
With great ambition the navy of Lloegyr they will attack;
Barbarous hosts, plunder they will seek;
With open violence they will reduce towers,
And strongholds they will make weak.
In front of the host of the tournament,
20 For the contention of one day a myriad will fall;
On the seas they will openly cause destruction.
As for me, I will predict that children will not multiply,
And it is not I that conceal that they will not be dispersed.
An age of repose the Creator will cause to be, and their extinction;
The Brythyon will scatter them, chief they will be.
Tribulation will ensue from the anger of relatives,
And the Saxons will be joyful when they see it.
The omen promises to shorten it while they will be.

LXX. RED BOOK OF HERGEST XXI.

I.

CHRIST JESUS! who art in complete possession of light,
The strength of the feeble Christian in the gloom;
Christ, the mysterious One! in order to produce seriousness
May utterance be given to my bardic lays;
May my bards, when they chant, be attended to;
May my bardic word from the golden chair be kept;
May my poem above books be read.
As a canon by him who chants the Paternoster.
Believe in God, and God will not reject thee;
10 Believe! from his court no vanity will affect thee;
Believe that He suffered on a Friday,
And that He arose to overcome a host.
From the mutual sullenness of royal chiefs a tumult shall be heard;
By virtue of unity, the compact of Rosser,
May the Saxons hasten away before distress!
On the borders a standing army will be complained of.
Unprofitable Maelenydd will be molested,
Lawless, with rights, without a Caer.

20 Around the land of Mael a long battle will be heard;
Around the banks of Gwyran there will be a gory scene;
Around Buallt eager will be the tumult at the close of day,
Beards in flight from mortal cowardice.
Around Aber Cammarch may be greeted
The chief, the joy of his retinue.
Then will the poet be free from anxiety,
From celebrating the completion of splendid actions,
From the primitive language, penance, and paternosters,
From the value of respect when thou art addressed.
30 Ask of the Supreme Being, from the depth of adoration,
Of adoration, success from above the light,
To the steel against Lloegyr which corrupts the paternoster,
To his friends, his flag, and his standard.
A man from concealment, prompt, brave, and wrathful,
Will appear, to command a multitude;
He will cause terror at the commencement,
And easily break the boundary on a Friday,
Friday: believe it is no falshood.
The Saxons will retreat from his oppression over the country.
40 About Aber Cammarch there will be ignominy,
Excessive tumult, shouting, blades, and men in battle-array.
And a splendid banner, it is no error,
And a dragon causing the death of a leader:
Lloegrians will be uttering doleful lamentations,
And men in the dire shout bewailing their brains.
A man over Lloegyr which corrupts religion,
Will come to command his army;
He will cause a happy beginning.
For a long time, as regards the land, he will disappear,
50 The hero of a disturbed country.
There will be a mutual sharpening of blades, a mutual havoc concerning baptism.
It will be time like doomsday; and gifts will be given to the poet,
The action will be heard all over the land.
His driving and impelling forces will have no end.
His gifts, according to established rights, he will pour forth.
Let us deserve and love Caer Leriydd,
Because of the voice of Cod whose favour is unfeigned.
Until we shall have been long through.
60 Purity is a state of freedom from frailty.
Precious will be the gifts of baptism from my Lord,
Seek mercy, for fear of the element of discord.

II.

Around Buallt the troops of the public host
Cause a tumult: there is complaint for each destruction.
When disbanded let the hordes of Henri fly.
Obscure is the top of the Caer where ruins meet.
Alun, the foremost in beauty, is all commotion,
Dispersion, ruin, and disgrace are all over it:
70 The slaughter shocks one when thou relatest it;
To relate its severe loss thou canst not,
From the contention of a baron of short co-operation,
There will be a white corpse, without head, without beauty,
There will be spare horses, worthless to be destroyed.
And men with unfriendly looks about Ceri,
And loud uproar, and thrusting, and shouting,
And groaning in every . . .
Actively will the sons of Cymry call upon Dewi
Who loveth peace and mercy . . .

III.

80 Fellow-ranger of the green woods!
Painful, piercing grief affects me.
Conflicts are pangs of anguish to the upright.
The life of a man is pursued like that of a wretch,
By the strong ones of Lloegyr who corrupt equity.
Let us meet them and see their death!
The union of Saxons is but for a night;
Of ignoble descent they are in the banquet of mead;
They make compacts without mutual entertainment and sociality;
And break them with a violent rupture:
90 Barons whose co-operation is of short duration.
And the ruler of what land in Gwyned, inferior in speech,
Can relate the fatigue and trouble of pursuing them?
Look if you can see any paltry spoil.
The tumult of slaughter is heard again.
Let reparation be made if there is military law.
It is peaceless treachery if a man is to be denied the hope
Of being brought to God at once.
Hosts get rich on full march.
A plaintiff is strong while investigating his claim.
100 A man was killed by an unlucky obstruction.
True, it is incumbent on the innocent to die,
But it is a disgrace before God to cause his death.
There is a deliverer ten times to the brave.
God will be pleased when every language shall have ceased.

Health by means of penance is a painful restriction.
May he give us through hope,
In the end, mercy through a just compact! Amen.

III. Miscellaneous Poems from The Black Book of Caermarthen

Q. Poems Attributed to Other Early Bards

LXXI. MEIGANT - BLACK BOOK OF CAERMARTHEN II.

A DREAM I happen to see last night; clever is he that can interpret it.
It shall not be related to the wanton; he that will not conceal it shall know it not.
It is an act of the gentle to govern the multitude. Pleasure is not the wealth of a country.
Have I not been under the same covering with a fair maid of the hue of the billow of the strand?
Labour bestowed on anything good is no pain, and the remembrance of it will last.
Worse is my trouble to answer him who is not acquainted with it.
It is no reparation for an evil deed, a desistence after it is done.
One's benefit does not appear when it is asked for in a round about way: thou hadst better keep to what there is.
And associate with the virtuous, and be resolute as to what may happen.
10 He that frequently commits crime will at last be caught.
He that will not relate a thing fully, will not find himself contradicted.
Riches will not flourish with the wicked. Mass will not be sung on a retreat.
A sigh is no protection against the vile. He that is not liberal does not deserve the name.
. . . .

LXXII. CUHELYN - BLACK BOOK OF CAERMARTHEN III.

GOD supreme, be mine the Awen! Amen; fiat!
A successful song of fruitful praise, relating to the bustling course of the host,
According to the sacred ode of Cyridwen, the goddess of various seeds,
The various seeds of poetic harmony, the exalted speech of the graduated minstrel,
Cuhelyn the bard of elegant Cymraec utterly rejects.
A poem for a favour, the gift of friendship, will not be maintained. .
But a composition of thorough praise is being brought to thee,
Splendid singer in a choir, and of a song equal in length and motion.

Appropriate and full were the tuneful horns, gloriously ascended the conflagration

10 Of the nation of the border, whose troops were of the same pace and simultaneous movement.

Praise the here, whose gift is large, the benefit of humble suitors,

Light is the rebuke of the rallying-point of relatives, the winner of praise,

A skilful fastener, for a hundred calends, the accumulator of heat;

A fierce frowning wolf, whose inflexible disposition is law, accustomed to jurisdiction.

Eidoel was a man extremely brave, very choice and full of wisdom;

A leader as regards the Brython, full of knowledge and prudence, fiery in his wrath;

Accustomed to hatred, accustomed to harmony, and to the high seat in the banquet of mead;

Partaker of the intoxicating wine, a knight of the list, a place of limitation;

A lord who is the measurer of the wall, the delight of the four quarters, the great centre power;

20 A knight of stout conduct, a knight of virtuous conduct, with warriors full of rage;

A guardian celebrated in song, a fine panegyric, the blandishment of language.

Odious was his death by Nognaw. Am I not agitated? The active and eloquent one will I praise;

A contented ruler, a restless guardian, energetic and wise.

A company of active reapers, melodious poetry, and the assuaging of wrath

A talented hero, like a furious wave over the strand,

The marrow of fine songs, a contemplative mind, a sacred mystery;

A servitor with knowledge, the possession of mead, in agreeable eulogy;

Music which has melody like that of a golden organ, a place of retirement;

The action of law against violence, the admirable vigour of the brave, the energy of the Supreme Being.

30 A blessing I will venture to ask, a blessing I will pray for, I will bind myself thereby;

The wonderful rush of the gale, the pervasion of fire, the war of youth;

One deserving of ruddy gold, one liberal of praise furrowed (with age), a free wing;

Ready affluence, a rill in a pleasant shelter, a reward for a panegyric.

The most deserving will yield, he will keep his refuge from the insult of the enemy:

He has completely kept the law, completely shown his disposition before the placid Ogyrven.

For a good turn from me, may the gift of Cuhelyn give satisfaction of mind.

XXIII. BLACK BOOK OF CAERMARTHEN IV.

ACCORDING to the sacred ode of Cyridwen, the Ogyrven of various seeds,--
The various seeds of poetic harmony, the exalted speech of the graduated minstrel,
Cuhelyn the wise, of elegant Cymraec, an exalted possession,
Will skilfully sing; the right of Aedan, the lion, shall be heard.
A song of fulness, worthy of a chair, a powerful composition it is.
From suitors may he receive eulogy, and they presents from him;
The bond of sovereigns, the subject of contests in harmonious song.
Splendid are his horses, hundreds respect him, the skilful seek the chieftain,
The circle of deliverance, the nation's refuge and a treasure of mutual reproach.
10 To banter with him, who is of a venerable form, I would devoutly desire;
A broad defence, like a ship to the suppliant, and a port to the minstrel,
Quick as lightning, a powerful native, a chief whose might is sharp;
A luminary of sense, much he knows, completely he accomplishes.
May the hero of the banquet, through peace, enforce tranquillity from this day.

LXXIV. THE CYNGHOGION OF ELAETH - BLACK BOOK OF CAERMARTHEN XX.

I. NOW gone are my ardour and liveliness;
If I have erred, I truly acknowledge it;
May the Lord not inflict upon me severe pain!
II. May not the Lord inflict severe pain
On man for his anger and passion.
A reprobate of Heaven is reprobate of earth.
III. Let sinful mortal believe in God,
And wake at midnight;
Let him who offends Christ sleep not.
IV. Let not a son of man sleep for the sake of the passion
Of the Son of God, but wake up at the early dawn;
And he will obtain heaven and forgiveness.
V. Pardon will he obtain, who will call upon
God, and despise Him not,
And heaven the night he dies.
VI. If a son of man dies without being reconciled
To God ' for the sins which he has committed,
It is not well that a soul entered his flesh.
VII. It is not common for the mischievous to employ himself in converse
With God, against the day of affliction,
The bold thinks that he shall not die.
　　　Now gone--

I. NOT to call upon God, whose favour defends
Both the innocent and the angels,
Is too much of false pride;
Woe to him that does it openly in the world.
II. I love not treasure with traces of dwellings no longer existing;
Everything in the present state is like a summer habitation.
I am a man to Him whose praise is above all things,
To the most high God who made me.
III. I love to praise Peter, who can bestow true peace,
And with him his far-extending virtues;
In every language he is, with hope, acknowledged
As the gentle, high-famed, generous porter of heaven.
IV. God I will implore to grant a request,
Lord, be Eloi my Protector!
That to my soul, for fear of torments,
Be the whole protection of all the martyrs.
V. Of God I will ask another request,
That my soul, to be safe from the torments of enemies,
And held in remembrance, may have
The protection of the Virgin Mary and the holy maidens.
VI. Of God I will ask a request also,
Just is be, and able to defend me,
That to my soul, for fear of terrible torments,
Be the protection of the Christians of the world.
VII. Of God I will ask a considerate request,
That, being ready and diligent at all matins,
To my soul, for fear of punishment,
May be the protection of God and all the saints.
     Not to call upon God--

R. Anonymous Poems on Religious Subjects

LXXVI. BLACK BOOK OF CAERMARTHEN V.

A SKILFUL composition, the pattern being from God,
A composition, the language, beautiful and pleasant, from Christ.
And should there be a language all complete around the sun,
On as many pivots as there are under the sea,
On as many winged ones as the Almighty made,
And should every one have thrice three hundred tongues,
They could not relate the power of the Trinity.
A diligent man in prosperity will receive no punishment.

Let communion be ready against the Trinity.
10 Let him be ill and ailing when his flesh becomes weak,
That he may puff his disguise.
Woe to thee, man of passion; if the world were given me,
Unless thou wert to deliver thyself, thou wouldst be satiated of the evil.
Art thou not at liberty as regards what thy mind loves?
Furious thy violent death, thy being borne on the wattled frame;
More wretched thy end, thy interment in the grave,
And being trodden by feet in the midst of soil and sod.
Unequalled thy journey, thy separation from thy companions.
Faithless and useless body, think of thy soul!
20 Body, thou wouldst not hear when others spoke.
What gavest thou of thy wealth before private confession?
What gavest thou of thy riches before the close and silent pit?
And what thou hadst intended, thou hast left undone
And thou sawest not how many thou shouldst have loved.
And a benefit it would have been as regards the passions of the people.
And the good would have come to so much prosperity.
When thou of thy freedom purchasest a hundred things, they are uncertain,
And vanish as suddenly as the motion of eyelid.
Hast thou noticed that they love sinisterly while seeking violence?
30 Thou respectedst not Friday, of thy great humility
Thou chantedst not a paternoster at matins or vespers,
A paternoster, the chief thing to be repeated: meditate on nothing
Except the Trinity.
Thou shouldst pay what is equal to three seven paternosters daily.
What has been and is not, and their life has not passed away.
Thou art more accustomed to the roaring of the sea than to the preaching of
the evangel.
Must thou not go to the pile, because thou hast not been humble?
Thou respectedst neither relics, nor altars, nor churches.
Thou didst not attend to the strains of bards of harmonious utterance.
40 Thou didst not respect the law of the Creator of heaven before death.
A strange mixture didst thou employ in thy speech.
Woe is me that I went with thee to our joint work!
Woe is me when I am about to praise thee!
When I came to thee, small was my evil,
But it came to me from thy grovelling co-operation.
As for them, none will believe us respecting thy appearance of enjoyment.

LXXVII. BLACK BOOK OF CAERMARTHEN VI.

SOUL, since I was made in necessity blameless
True it is, woe is me that thou shouldst have come to my design,
Neither for my own sake, nor for death, nor for end, nor for beginning.

It was with seven faculties that I was thus blessed,
With seven created beings I was placed for purification;
I was gleaming fire when I was caused to exist;
I was dust of the earth, and grief could not reach me;
I was a high wind, being less evil than good;
I was a mist on a mountain seeking supplies of stags;
10 I was blossoms of trees on the face of the earth.
If the Lord had blessed me, He would have placed me on matter.
 Soul, since I was made--

LXXVIII. BLACK BOOK OF CAERMARTHEN VII.

LET us not reproach one another, but rather mutually save ourselves.
Certain is a meeting after separation,
The appointment of a senate, and a certain conference,
And the rising from the grave after a long repose.
The mighty God will keep in his power the man of correct life,
And will let fire upon the unholy people,
And lightning and thunder and wide-spread death.
Neither a solitary nor a sluggard shall pass to a place of safety.
And after peace there shall be the usages of a kingdom;
10 The three hosts shall be brought to the overpowering presence of Jesus:
A pure and blessed host like the angels;
Another host, mixed, like the people of a country;
The third host, unbaptized, a multitude that directly after death
Will proceed in a thick crowd to the side of devils,
Not one of them shall go, owing to their hideous forms,
To the place where there are flowers and dew on the pleasant land,
Where there are singers tuning their harmonious lays,
Happy will be their cogitations with the ruler of the glorious retinue;
Where the Apostles are in the kingdom of the humble,
20 Where the bounteous Creator is on his glorious throne.
May a disposition for the grave be given us; exalted is a relationship to Him;
And. before we are gathered together to mount Olivet,
May those who have fallen be victorious over death;
And work like theirs may we also do; for at the judgment day
The wonders, greatness, and puissance of the Creator none can relate.

LXXIX. BLACK BOOK OF CAERMARTHEN IX.

Text, vol. ii. p. 10. Notes, vol. ii. p. 330.
LET God be praised in the beginning and the end.
Who supplicates Him, He will neither despise nor refuse.
The only son of Mary, the great exemplar of kings,
Mary, the mother of Christ, the praise of women.

The sun will come from the East to the North.
Intercede, for thy great mercy's sake,
With thy Son, the glorious object of our love,
God above us, God before us, God possessing (all things).
May the Father of Heaven grant us a portion of mercy;
10 Puissant Sovereign, may there be peace between us without refusal;
May we reform and make satisfaction for our transgressions,
Before I go to the earth to my fresh grave,
In the dark without a candle to my tribunal,
To my narrow abode, to the limits assigned to me, to my repose;
After my horse, and indulgence in fresh mead,
And social feasting, and gallantry with women.
I will not sleep; I will meditate on my end.
We are in a state the wantonness of which is sad;
Like leaves from the top of trees it will vanish away.
20 Woe to the niggard that hoards up precious things;
And unless the Supreme Father will support him,
Though he is allowed to have his course in the present world, his end will be dangerous.
He knows not what it is to be brave, yet will he not tremble in his present state;
He will not rise up in the morning, will utter no greeting, nor will he sit;
He will not sing joyfully nor ask for mercy.
Bitter will, in the end, be the retribution
Of haughtiness, arrogance, and restlessness.
He pampers his body for toads and snakes
And lions, and conceives iniquity.
30 And death will come upon hoary age;
He is insatiable in the assembly and in the banquet.
Old age will draw nigh, and spreads itself over thee.
Thy ear, thy sight, thy teeth, they will not return;
The skin of thy fingers will wrinkle,
And age and hoariness will affect thee.
May Michael make intercession for us, that the Father of heaven may dispense us His mercy!
The beginning of summer is a most pleasant season, tuneful the birds, green the stalks of plants,
Ploughs are in the furrow, oxen in the yoke,
Green is the sea, variegated the land.
40 When cuckoos sing on the branches of pleasant trees,
May my joyfulness become greater.
Smoke is painful, sleeplessness is manifest.
Since my friends are returned to their former state
In the hill, in the dale, in the islands of the sea,
In every direction that one goes, in the presence of the blessed Christ there is

no terror.

It was our desire, our friend, our trespass

To penetrate into the land of thy banishment.

Seven saints and seven score and seven hundred did he pierce in one convention.

With Christ the blessed they sustain. no apprehension of evil.

50 A gift I will ask, may it not be refused me by the God of peace.

Since there is a way to the gate of the Supreme Father,

Christ, may I not be sad before thy throne!

LXXX. BLACK BOOK OF CAERMARTHEN X.

HAIL, glorious Lord!

May church and chancel bless Thee!'

And chancel and church!

And plain and precipice!

And the three fountains there are,

Two above wind, and one above the earth,

May darkness and light bless Thee!

And fine silk and sweet trees!

Abraham the chief of faith did bless Thee.

10 And life eternal.

And birds find bees.

And old and young.

Aaron and Moses did bless Thee.

And male and female.

And the seven days and the stars.

And the air and the ether.

And books and letters.

And fish in the flowing water.

And song and deed.

20 And sand and sward.

And such as were satisfied with good.

I will bless Thee, glorious Lord!

Hail, glorious Lord!

LXXXI. BLACK BOOK OF CAERMARTHEN XI.

I. I WILL extol Thee, the Trinity in the mysterious One,

Who is One and Three, a Unity of one energy,

Of the same essence and attributes, one God to be praised.

I will praise Thee, great Father, whose mighty works are great;

To praise Thee is just; to praise Thee is incumbent on me,

The produce of poetry is the right of Eloi.

Hail, glorious Christ!

Father, and Son, and Spirit! Lord,

God, Adonai!

II. I will extol God, who is both One and Two,

Who is Three without any error, without its being easily doubted;

Who made fruit, and rill, and every gushing stream;

God is his name, being two Divine Ones to be comprehended;

God is his name, being three Divine Ones in his energy;

God is his name, being One; the God of Paul and Anhun.

III. I will extol One, who is both Two and One.

Who is, besides, Three, who is God Himself,

Who made Mars and Luna, and male and female,
And ordained that the shallow and the abyss should not be of equal depth;
Who made heat and cold, and sun and moon,
And letters in the wax, and flame in the candle,
And affection to be one of the senses, and lovely woman late,
And caused the burning of five Caers, and an erring consort.

LXXXII. BLACK BOOK OF CAERMARTHEN XII.

IN the name of the Lord, mine to adore, whose praise is great.
I will praise the great Ruler, whose blessing is great on an alms-deed;
The God that defends us, the God that made us, the God that will deliver us,
The God of our hope, blessed, perfect, and pure is his true happiness.
God owns us; God is above, the Triune King,
God has been felt a support to us in affliction;
God has been, by being imprisoned, in humility.
May the blessed Ruler make us free against the day of doom,
And bring us to the feast, for the sake of his meekness and lowliness,
10 And happily receive us into Paradise from the burden of sin,
And give us salvation, for the sake of his agony and five wounds,
Terrible anguish! God delivered us when he assumed flesh.
Man would have been lost, had He not ransomed him, according to his glorious ordinance.
From the bloody Cross came redemption to the whole world.
Christ the mighty Shepherd, his merits will never fail.

LXXXIII. BLACK BOOK OF CAERMARTHEN XIII.

HERE is a graciously disposed King, who is wonderful in the highest degree,
Who is chief above the children of Adam,
Who is a happy and most mighty defence,
Who is generous, glorious, and most pure,
Whose claim is most strong and binding.
What is heard of him, and what is true, that will I celebrate.
To the great God, to the condescending and most compassionate God,
To the blessed God a sacred song I will sing.
Until I become a blameless man to God, I will consider the substance,
10 About the sin which Adam. shined.
About sin before the judgment I am very anxious,
Against the day of appointment, when all men shall come
From their graves in their strength and greatest vigour,
As they were when they were in their very prime,
In one host to the one place most pleasant,
Even to the top of one hill, in order to be judged.
Among this multitude may I attain the merit

Of being protected by a retinue of the nine orders of Heaven.
My God! what a gathering!
20 My Lord God! may my bardic lore
Affect the bonds of the universe!
My great Superior! my Owner!
The object of my reverence! before going to the sod, before going to the gravel,
Permit thou me to indite a composition
To thy praise, before my tongue becomes mute,
And my memory like Job, who spoke
Unto his wife concerning her dragonic obedience.
When the servant of God on a certain day came
To him to the contest with his wife,
30 Before the blow he gave a handful
Of what had peeled from the surface of his flesh.
And since the presents which any one gave were now acceptable,
The merciful God made a gift of charity
In pure gold, the treasure of the Trinity.
In a fainting state he sits, and there praises God.
Blessed was he to be plagued! Now said Sin,
"Thou knowest how to conceal the perfidy of the mysterious Being."
The love-diffusing Lord of heaven, the Creator, take thou to praise Him,
That thou mayest reach the fair and happy region,
40 Happy, pleasant, free, and greatly deserving praise.
Loving wine, love thou the gentle, preserve the truth.
Eva did not preserve the sweet apple-tree which God commanded her,
For her transgression He was not reconciled to her,
But manifest pain he inflicted upon her.
Some wonderful covering of a flinty dress she put on herself;
The Maker of heaven caused her, in the midst of her riches, to make herself bare.
And a second miracle did the bountiful Lord, who hears being praised.
When she wished to avoid being caught,
The way in which she fled was where
50 There was a ploughman ploughing the ground,
With men in attendance. The mysterious Trinity has spoken it.
Then went the faultless mother of splendid gifts
With her happy husband. A crowd of men
Afterwards came to ask.
In an entertainment,
"Hast thou seen a woman and a son with her?"
And say thou, for the record's truth,
And he will not refuse our request,
That thou didst see us going without her
60 To a certain spot, and the blessing of God be on it!

Upon that came a destitute rabble, a race of the disposition of Cain,
A fierce and iniquitous multitude are they;
A tower was sought, in order to seek the mysterious Being,
Then said one who was deformed and unwitty, to the man whom thou seest,-
"Hast thou seen the men of the city of giants
Going by thee without turning?"
I did see them when I harrowed the fair land,
Where you see the reaping.
What the children of Cain now did, was
70 To turn away from the reapers.
Through the intercession of Mary Maria,
And her knowledge communicated to her by God,
There were defending them, besides herself,
The Holy Spirit and her sanctity.

LXXXIV. BLACK BOOK OF CAERMARTHEN XXV.

AS long as we sojourn among excess and pride,
Let our work be perfect;
Let us seek deliverance through faith,
And religion and belief, as long as there is a belief in
God through obtaining faith,
And by doing great penance daily,
Soul, why askest thou me
What my end, and will the grave be my portion?

LXXXV. BLACK BOOK OF CAERMARTHEN XXIX.

I. A BLESSING to the happy youth and to the fair kingdom!
Large is the wave, capacious the breast.
God is his name in the depth of every language.
Thou with energy didst overshadow the pure Mary;
Well hast Thou come in human form.
Behold here the Son of glorious hope,
Whose death proceeded from Idas.
He was, by his treachery and disgraceful conduct,
A deluder in the gentle service of his Lord;
Cunning was he, but he was not wise;
And until the judgment I know not his destination.
If a bard were every poet that is
On earth, on the brine and on the cultivated plain,
On the sand and on the seas, and in the stars of astronomy,
The giver with the gentle and ready hand being judge,
More than they could I should wish, and also do,
To relate the power and bounty of the Creator.
Great God! to-day is thy majesty extolled.
II. The blessing of the nine hosts of heaven on the mysterious
Creator, the mighty God and dominator,

Who has created the light of gladness,
And generous brightness of the sun in the day,
Like the Christian's lamp, it shines above the deep,
A thousand times greater than the moon.
And a third wonder is, the agitation of the sea;
How it ebbs, how it swells,
How it goes, how it comes, how it rolls, how it settles;
How long will it go, or how will it be?
At the end of seven years,
The Creator will check its course,
Until it comes to its former state.
We will worship him who causes it, the mighty
God, the Son of Mary, who created heaven and earth.
When thou camest on Easter eve
From Uffern, what was thy portion became liberated;
Creator of heaven! may we purchase thy loving-kindness!

S. Poems Relating to Yscolan

LXXXVI. BLACK BOOK OF CAERMARTHEN XXVI.

I. BLACK thy horse, black thy cope,
Black thy head, black thyself,
Yes, black I art thou Yscolan?
II. I am Yscolan the scholar,
Slight is my clouded reason,
There is no drowning the woe of him who offends a sovereign.
III. For having burnt a church, and destroyed the cattle of a school,
And caused a book to be submerged,
My penance is a heavy affliction.
IV. Creator of the creatures, of supports
The greatest, pardon me my iniquity!
He who betrayed Thee, deceived me.
V. A full year was given me
At Bangor on the pole of a weir;
Consider thou my suffering from sea-worms.
VI. If I knew what I now know
As plain as the wind in the top branches of waving trees,
What I did I should never have done.

LXXXVII. BLACK BOOK OF CAERMARTHEN XXVII.

I.

I. THE first word that I will utter
In the morning when I get up,
"May the Cross of Christ be as a vesture around me."

II. What belongs to my Creator I will put on
To-day, in one house will I attend.
He is not a God in whom I will not believe.
III. I will dress myself handsomely,
And believe in no omen which is not certain;
He that created me will strengthen me.
IV. I have a mind to see sights,
Intending to go to sea;
May a useful purpose become a treasure!
V. I have a mind for all advice,
Intending to go to sea;
May the purpose be useful, Lord!
VI. Let the raven uplift its wing,
With the intention of going far away;
May a useful purpose become better!
VII. Let the raven uplift its wing,
With. the intention of going to Rome;
May a useful purpose become glorious!
VIII. Saddle thou the bayard with the white bridle,
To course Hiraethawg with its quaking grass:
Creator of Heaven! God must be with us!
IX. Saddle thou the bayard with the short hair,
Free in the conflict, quick in his pace;
Where the nose is, there will be snorting.
X. Saddle thou the bayard with the long bound,
Free in the conflict, pleasing in his pace;
The sneering of the vicious will not check the brave.
XI. Heavy the consistence of the earth, thick leaves its cover;
Bitter the drinking-horn of sweet mead;
Creator of Heaven! prosper my business!
XII. From the progeny of the sovereign and victor,
Gwosprid, and Peter chief of every language,
Saint Ffraid, bless us on our journey!
XIII. Thou, Sun, to him intercession and vows are made,
Lord, Christ the Mysterious, the pillar of beneficence!
May I make satisfaction for my sin and actions.

II.

I asked to secular priests,
To their bishops and their judges,
"What is the best thing for the soul?"
The Paternoster, and consecrated wafers, and a holy
Creed, he who sings them for his soul,
Until the judgment will be accustomed to the best thing.
Smooth the way as thou goest, and cultivate peace,

And to thee there will be no end of mercy.
Give food to the hungry and clothes to the naked,
10 And say thy devotions:
From the presence of devils thou hast escaped.
The proud and the idle have pain in their flesh,
The reward of going to excess:
Beware of sifting what is not pure.
Excess of sleep, and excess of drunkenness, and too much beverage
Of mead, and too much submission to the flesh,
These are six bitter things against the judgment.
For perjury in respect of land, and the betrayment of a lord,
And the scandalising of the bounteous,
20 At the day of judgment let there be repentance.
By rising to matins and nocturns,
Awaking, and interceding with the saints,
Shall every Christian obtain forgiveness.

IV. Miscellaneous Poems from the Book of Aneurin

T. Poem Containing Ancient Proverbs

LXXXVIII. BOOK OF ANEURIN III.

HERE BEGINNETH THE GWARCHAN OF ADEBON.
THE apple will not fall far from the apple-tree.
The diligent cannot prosper with the prodigal.
The naked will not be bold among thistles.
All, when made to swear overmuch, will fail.
Would I love him who would love the rapacious?
Death will not occur twice.
His speech is of no use to the dumb.
Thou wilt not delight to put one of the same language in fear.
The horses of an effeminate person are his dainties.
10   .   .   .   .
At home peace has been lost.
Be thy mansion large, thou wert a hero in the day of conflict.
As long as there will be things to seek for thee there will be seekers.
High stones, a reaping to the foe.
The conclusion of the Gwarchan of Adebon.
AND SO ENDETH THE GWARCHAN OF ADEBON.

V. Miscellaneous Poems from the Book of Taliessin

U. Poems Relating to The Life & Opinions of Taliessin

LXXXIX. THE FOLD OF THE BARDS - BOOK OF TALIESSIN III.

MEDITATING were my thoughts
On the vain poetry of the bards of
Brython.
Making the best of themselves in the
chief convention.
Enough, the care of the smith's
sledge-hammer.
I am in want of a stick, straitened in
song,
The fold of the bards, who knows it
not?
Fifteen thousand over it
Adjusting it.
I am a harmonious one; I am a clear
singer.
10 I am steel; I am a druid.
I am an artificer; I am a scientific one.
I am a serpent; I am love; I will in-
dulge in feasting
I am not a confused bard drivelling,
When songsters sing a song by
memory,
They will not make wonderful cries;
May I be receiving them.
Like receiving clothes without a
hand,
Like sinking in a lake without swim-
ming,
The stream boldly rises tumultuously
in degree.
20 High in the blood of sea-board
towns.
The rock wave-surrounded, by great
arrangement,
Will convey for us a defence, a pro-
tection from the enemy.
The rock of the chief proprietor, the
head of tranquillity.
The intoxication of meads will cause
us to speak.
I am a cell, I am a cleft, I am a restora-
tion,
I am the depository of song; I am a
literary man;
I love the high trees, that afford a
protection above,
And a bard that composes, without
earning anger;
I love not him that causes contention
30 He that speaks ill of the skilful
shall not possess mead.
It is a fit time to go to the drinking,
With the skilful men, about art,
And a hundred knots, the custom of
the country,
The shepherd of the districts, support
of gates,
Like going without a foot to battle.
He would not journey without a foot.
He would not breed nuts without
trees,
Like seeking for ants in the heath.
Like an instrument of foolish spoil,
40 Like the retinue of an army with-
out a head,
Like feeding the unsheltered on li-
chen.
Like ridging furrows from the coun-
try
Like reaching the sky with a hook,
Like deprecating with the blood of
thistles,
Like making light for the blind,
Like sharing clothes to the naked,

Like spreading buttermilk on the
sands,
Like feeding fish upon milk,
Like roofing a hall with leaves,
50 Like killing a tortoise with rods.
Like dissolving riches before a word.
I am a bard of the hall, I am a chick of

the chair.
I will cause to loquacious bards a
hindrance.
Before I am dragged to my harsh re-
ward,
May we buy thee, that wilt protect us,
thou son of Mary.

XC. HOSTILE CONFEDERACY - BOOK OF TALIESSIN VII.

A BARD there is here, who has not
sung, what he shall have to sing;
Lot him sing; when he shall have fin-
ished,
An astrologer then he may be.
The generous ones refuse me.
There will not be one that will give.
Through the language of Taliessin,
It was a bright day
When Kian did
Praise the multitude.
10 There will be a slaughter, let there
be the speech of Avagddu.
But if he ingeniously brings
The requisites forward,
Gwiawn will declare,
O the deep that will come
He would make the dead alive,
And destitute of wealth he is.
They will not make their cauldrons,
That will boil without fire.
They will make their metals
20 In age of ages.
Thy pace that bears thee
From the deep of panegyric,
Is it not the hostile confederacy?
What its custom?
So much of national song
Your tongue has given.
Why will ye not recite an oration
Of blessing over the liquor of bright-
ness?
The theme of every one's rhapsody.
30 I shall be there according to cus-
tom,

He was a profound judge.
He came after his periodical custom,
The third of the equal judges.
Three score years
I have supported an earthly scene,
In the water of law and the multitude.
In the element of lands.
A hundred servants surrounded,
A hundred kings made vows.
40 A hundred they are that went,
A hundred they are that came.
A hundred minstrels sang,
And he foretold of them.
Lladdon, the daughter of the stream,
Little was her desire
For gold and silver,
Who is the living one that left her?
Blood on the breast;
He will probably be spoken of,
50 He will be greatly praised.
I am Taliessin,
I will delineate the true lineage
Continuing until the end,
In the pattern of Elphin,
Is not the tribute
Of counted gold a debt?
When is hated and not loved,
Perjury and treason,
I desire not advantage,
60 Through the fluctuation of our
song.
The brother that freely greets,
From me no one shall know.
The wise man of the primary science,
The astrologer reasoned,

About wrath, about the resolvent,
About the man describing windings.
About men well versed in praise.
Let us proceed, God it is,
Through the language of Talhaearn,
70 Baptism was the day of judgment,
That judged the characteristics
Of the force of poetry.
He and his virtue gave
Inspiration without mediocrity,
Seven score Ogyrven
Are in the Awen.
Eight score, of every score it will be one.
In the deep it will cease from ire;
In the deep it will be excessively angry;
80 In the deep, below the earth;
In the sky, above the earth.
There is one that knows
What sadness is,
Better than joy.
I know the law of the graces of
The Awen, when it flows,
Concerning skilful payments,
Concerning happy days,
Concerning a tranquil life,
90 Concerning the protection of ages.
Concerning what beseems kings; how long their consolation.
Concerning similar things, that are on the face of the earth.
Magnificent astronomy, when communicated,
Sees all that is high.
When the mind is active,
When the sea is pleasant,
When the race is valiant,
When the high one is supplicated,
Or the sun when it is given,
100 When it covers the land.
Covering land of what extent?
When was drawn the bird of wrath,
The bird of wrath when it was drawn.
When the earth is green.

Who chaunted songs?
Songs who chaunted?
If true, who has considered them?
It has been considered in books,
110 How many winds, how many streams,
How many streams, how many winds.
How many rivers in their courses,
How many rivers there are.
The earth, what its breadth;
Or what its thickness.
I know the noise of the blades,
Crimson on all sides, about the floor.
I know the regulator,
Between heaven and earth;
120 When an opposite hill is echoing,
When devastation urges onward,
When the silvery (vault) is shining,
When the dell shall be gloomy.
The breath when it is black,
When is best that has been.
A cow, when it is horned,
A wife, when she is lovely,
Milk, when it is white,
When the holly is green,
130 When is bearded the kid
In the multitude of fields,
When it is bearded,
When the cow-parsnip is created,
When is revolving the wheel,
When the mallet is flat,
When is spotted the little roebuck,
When the salt is brine,
Ale, when it is of an active quality.
When is of purplish hue the alder.
140 When is green the linnet,
When are red the hips,
Or a woman when restless,
When the night comes on.
What reserve there is in the hour of flowing,
No one knows whence the bosom of the sun is made ruddy.
A stain on a new garment,

It is difficult to remove it.
The string of a harp, why it com-
plains,
The cuckoo, why it complains, why it
sings.
150 Why keepeth the agreeable,
Why have led the camp
Gereint and Arman.
What brings out the sparkle
From bard working of the stones.
When is sweet-smelling the goat's-
beard plant;
When the crows are of a waxen line.
Talhayarn is
The greatest astronomer.
What is the imagination of trees.
160 From the muse the agreement of
a day.
I know good and evil.
. . . .
. . . .
The bowl of whom has flowed,
What dawn has finished,
Who preached,
Eli and Eneas:
I know the cuckoos of summer,
(Where) they will be in the winter.
170 The Awen I sing,
From the deep I bring it,
A river while it flows,
I know its extent;
I know when it disappears;
I know when it fills;
I know when it overflows;
I know when it shrinks;
I know what base
There is beneath the sea.
180 I know their equivalent,
Every one in its retinue;
How many were heard in a day,
How many days in a year.
How many shafts in a battle,
How many drops in a shower.
Mildly he divided them.
A greater mockery, the partial stir-
ring up of disgrace,
The vicious muse of Gwydyon.
I know the one,
190 That filled the river,
On the people of Pharaoh.
Who brought the windings
Of present reasons.
What was the active patience,
When heaven was upreared.
What was a sail-staff
From earth to sky.
How many fingers about the caul-
dron,
About one, about the hand,
200 What name the two words
Will not deliver in one cauldron.
When the sea is turning round,
When black are the fish.
Marine food shall be their flesh,
Until it is transformed,
When fish shall contain it.
When the foot of the white swan is
black,
Four-sided the sharp spear.
The tribe of heaven will not put
down.
210 Which are the four elements.
Their end is not known.
What pigs, or what wandering of
stags.
I salute thee, Bard of the border.
May he increase thee, (whose) bones
(are of) mist
(Where) two cataracts of wind fall.
My mind has been expressed
In Hebrew, in Hebraic.
In Hebraic, in Hebrew,
Laudatu Laudate Jesu.
220 A second time was I formed.
I have been a blue salmon.
I have been a dog; I have been a stag;
I have been a roebuck on the moun-
tain.
I have been a stock, I have been a
spade;

I have been an axe in the hand;
I have been a pin in a forceps,
A year and a half;
I have been a speckled white cock
Upon hens in Eiddyn.
230 I have been a stallion over a stud.
I have been a violent bull,
I have been a buck of yellow hue,
As it is feeding.
I have been a grain discovered,
Which grew on a hill.
He that reaped me placed me,
Into a smoke-hole driving me.
Exerting of the hand,
In afflicting me,
240 A hen received me,
With ruddy claws, (and) parting comb.

I rested nine nights.
In her womb a child,
I have been matured,
I have been an offering before the Guledig,
I have been dead, I have been alive.
A branch there was to me of ivy,
I have been a convoy,
Before God I have been poor.
250 Again advised me the cherisher
With ruddy claws; of what she gave me
Scarcely can be recounted;
Greatly will it be praised.
I am Taliessin,
I will delineate the true lineage,
That will continue to the end,
In the pattern of Elphin.

XCI. THE CHAIR OF TALIESSIN - BOOK OF TALIESSIN XIII.

Text, vol. ii. p. 151. Notes, vol. ii. p. 403.

I AM the agitator
Of the praise of God the Ruler.
With respect to the concerns of song,
The requisites of a profound speaker,
A bard, with the breast of an astrologer.
When he recites
The Awen at the setting in of the evening.
On the fine night of a fine day.
Bards loquacious the light will separate.
10 Their praise will not bring me to associate,
In the strath, on the course
With aspect of great cunning.
I am not a mute artist,
Conspicuous among the bards of the people.
I animate the bold,
I influence the heedless
I wake up the looker on,

The enlightener of bold kings.
I am not a shallow artist,
20 Conspicuous among kindred bards,
The likeness of a subtle portion,
The deep ocean (is) suitable.
Who has filled me with hatred?
A prize in every unveiling,
When the dew is undisturbed,
And the wheat is reaped,
And the bees are gentle,
And myrrh and frankincense,
And transmarine aloes.
30 And the golden pipes of Lleu,
And a curtain of excellent silver,
And a ruddy gem, and berries.
And the foam of the sea.
Why will the fountain hasten
Water-cresses of purifying juicy quality?
What will join together the common people?

Wort, the nobility of liquor.
And a load that the moon separates
The placid gentleness of Merlyn.
40 And philosophers of intelligence
Will study about the moon.
And the influence of an order of men,
Exposed to the breeze of the sky.
And a soddening and effusion,
And a portion after effusion,
And the coracle of glass
In the hand of the pilgrim,
And the valiant one and pitch,
And the honoured Segyrffyg,
50 And medical plants.
A place of complete benefit,
And bards and blossoms.
And gloomy bushes,
And primroses and small herbs,

And the points of the tree-shrubs.
And deficiency and possession,
And frequent pledging.
And wine overflowing the brim,
From Rome to Rossed.
60 And deep still water,
Its stream the gift of God.
Or if it will be wood the purifier,
Fruitful its increase.
Let the brewer give a heat,
Over a cauldron of-five trees,
And the river of Gwiawn,
And the influence of fine weather,
And honey and trefoil,
And mead-horns intoxicating
70 Pleasing to a sovereign,
The gift of the Druids.

XCII. SONG TO THE WIND - BOOK OF TALIESSIN XVII.

GUESS who it is.
Created before the deluge.
A creature strong,
Without flesh, without bone,
Without veins, without blood,
Without head, and without feet.
It will not be older, it will not be
younger,
Than it was in the beginning.
There will not come from his design
10 Fear or death.
He has no wants
From creatures.
Great God! the sea whitens
When it comes from the beginning.
Great his beauties,
The one that made him.
He, in the field, he, in the wood,
Without hand and without foot.
Without old age, without age.
20 Without the most jealous destiny
And he (is) coeval
With the five periods of the five ages.
And also is older,

Though there be five hundred thou-
sand years.
And he is as wide
As the face of the earth,
And he was not born,
And he has not been seen.
He, on sea, he, on land,
30 He sees not, he is not seen.
He is not sincere,
He will not come when it is wished.
He, on land, he, on sea,
He is indispensable,
He is unconfined,
He is unequalled.
He from four regions,
He will not be according to counsel.
He commences his journey
40 From above the stone of marble.
He is loud-voiced, he is mute.
He is uncourteous.
He is vehement, he is bold,
When he glances over the land.
He is mute, he is loud-voiced.
He is blustering.

Greatest, his banner
On the face of the earth.
He is good, he is bad,
50 He is not bright,
He is not manifest,
For the sight does not see (him).
He is bad, he is good.
He is yonder, he is here,
He will disorder.
He will not repair what he does
And he sinless,
He is wet, he is dry,
He comes frequently
60 From the heat of the sun, and the
coldness of the moon.
The moon is without benefit,
Because less, her heat.
One Person has made it,
All the creatures.
He owns the beginning
And the end without falsehood.
Not skilful, the minstrel
That praises not the Lord.
Not true, the songster
70 That praises not the Father.
Not usual will a plough be
Without iron, without seed.
There was not a light
Before the creation of heaven;

There will not be a priest,
That will not bless the wafer;
The perverse will not know
The seven faculties.
Ten countries were provided,
80 In the angelic country.
The tenth were discarded,
They loved not their Father.
A loveless shower
In utter ruin.
Llucufer the corrupter,
Like his destitute country
Seven stars there are,
Of the seven gifts of the Lord.
The student of the stars
90 Knows their substance.
Marca mercedus
Ola olimus
Luna lafurus
Jubiter venerus
From the sun freely flowing
The moon fetches light.
Remembrance is not in vain,
No cross if not believed.
Our Father! Our Father!
100 Our relative and companion.
Our Sovereign, we shall not be sepa-
rated.
By the host of Llucufer.

XCIII. SONG TO MEAD. - BOOK OF TALIESSIN XIX.

I WILL adore the Ruler, chief of every place,
Him, that supports the heaven: Lord of everything.
Him, that made the water for every one good,
Him, that made every gift, and prospers it.
May Maelgwn of Mona be affected with mead, and affect us,
From the foaming mead-horns, with the choicest pure liquor,
Which the bees collect, and do not enjoy.
Mead distilled sparkling, its praise is everywhere.
The multitude of creatures which the earth nourishes,
10 God made for man to enrich him.
Some fierce, some mute, he enjoys them.
Some wild, some tame, the Lord makes them.
Their coverings become clothing.

For food, for drink, till doom they will continue.
I will implore the Ruler, sovereign of the country of peace,
To liberate Elphiñ from banishment.
The man who gave me wine and ale and mead.
And the great princely steeds, beautiful their appearance,
May he yet give me bounty to the end.
20 By the will of God, he will give in honour,
Five five-hundred festivals in the way of peace.
Elphinian knight of mead, late be thy time of rest.

XCIV. SONG TO THE GREAT WORLD. - BOOK OF TALIESSIN LV.

I WILL adore my Father,
My God, my strengthener,
Who infused through my head
A soul to direct me.
Who has made for me in perception,
My seven faculties.
Of fire and earth,
And water and air,
And mist and flowers,
10 And southerly wind.
Other senses of perception
Thy father formed for me.
One is to have instinct
With the second I touch,
With the third I call,
With the fourth I taste,
With the fifth I see,
With the sixth I hear.
With the seventh I smell.
20 And I foresay,
Seven airs there are,
Above the astronomer,
And three parts the seas.
How they strike on all sides.
How great and wonderful,
The world, not of one form,
Did God make above,
On the planets.
He made Sola,
30 He made Luna,
He made Marca
And Marcarucia,
He made Venus,
He made Venerus,
He made Severus,
And the seventh Saturnus,
The good God made
Five zones of the earth,
For as long as it will last.
40 One is cold,
And the second is cold,
And the third is heat,
Disagreeable, unprofitable.
The fourth, paradise,
The people will contain.
The fifth is the temperate,
And the gates of the universe.
Into three it is divided,
In the minstrelsy of perception.
50 One is Asia,
The second is Africa,
The third is Europa,
The baptism of consolation,
Until doomsday it will continue,
When everything will be judged.
My Awen has caused me
To praise my king.
I am Taliessin,
With a speed flowing as a diviner.
60 Continuing to the end
In the pattern of Elphin.

XCV. SONG TO THE LITTLE WORLD. - BOOK OF TALIESSIN LVI.

THE beautiful I sang of, I will sing.
The world one day more.
Much I reason,
And I meditate.
I will address the bards of the world,
Since it is not told me
What supports the world,
That it falls not into vacancy.
Or if the world should fall,
10 On what would it fall?
Who would uphold it?

The world, how it comes again,
When it falls in decay,
Again in the enclosing circle.
The world, how wonderful it is,
That it falls not at once.
The world, how peculiar it is,
So great was it trampled on.
Johannes, Mattheus,
20 Lucas, and Marcus,
They sustain the word
Through the grace of the Spirit.

XCVI. JUVENILE ORNAMENTS OF TALIESSIN. - BOOK OF TALIESSIN IX.

I WILL address my Lord,
To consider the Awen.
What brought necessity
Before the time of Ceridwen.
Primarily through my life
Poverty has been.
The wealthy monks
Why will they not speak to me?
Why will they not cause me to tremble?
10 One hour that I was not followed,
What disappearance of smoke?
Why sang he evil?
What fountain breaks out
Above the covert of darkness?
When the reed is white,
When it is a moonlight night.
Another was not sung,
It was shaken out,
When is apt to be forward
20 The noise of waves on the shore.
In the vengeance of the ocean,
A day will reach to them.
When a stone is so heavy,
When a thorn is so sharp.
Knowest thou which is best?
Its base or its point,
Who caused a partition
Between man and frigidity?

Whose is the wholesomest sore?
30 The young or the old?
Knowest thou what thou art
When thou art sleeping?
Whether a body or a soul,
Or a secresy of perception?
The ingenious minstrel,
Why does he not inform me?
Knowest thou where should be
The night waiting the passing of the day?
Knowest thou a sign,
40 How many leaves there are?
Who uplifted the mountain,
Before the elements fell?
Who supports the structure
Of the earth for a habitation?
The soul of whom is complained of?
Who has seen it, who knows?
I wonder in books
That they know not truly
The soul, what is its seat.
50 What form its limbs,
Through what part it pours out.
What air it respires?
A war petulant,
A sinner endangered.
A wonder in mockery,
What were its dregs.

Which is the best intoxication,
Of mead or of bragget?
When their happiness
60 Was protected by the God of Trinity
Why should I utter a treatise,
Except of thee?
Who caused coin
Of current silver?
When is so current
A ear so prickly;
Death having a foundation,
In every country is shared.
Death above our head,
70 Wide is its covering,

High above the canopy of heaven.
Man is oldest when he is born.
And is younger (and) younger continually,
What is there to be anxious about,
Of the present attainment?
After a want of property,
Does it not make to us a shortness of life?
Enough of sadness,
The visitation of the grave.
80 And the One that made us,
From the supreme country,
Be he our God, and bring us
To him at the end!

XCVII. THE ELEGY OF THE THOUSAND SONS. - BOOK OF TALIESSIN II.

I. I WILL offer a prayer to the Trinity,
May the Eternal grant me to praise thee!
In the present course, dangerous
Our work; destruction is a slight impulse of wrath.
They reckon of the saints a tribe,
King of heaven, may I be eloquent about thee!
Before the separation of my soul from my flesh.
Thou particularly knowest in what is my sin.
II. Thy entreaty before the paternal governance
May there be to me from the Trinity mercy!
I adore, I earnestly long for the elements of blood,
Nine degrees of the mystic troops of heaven,
And the tenth, saints a preparation of sevens.
Heroic numberer of languages,
A conspicuous sea-shoal of goodly increase.
A number that God will watch with

extreme love.
In heaven, in earth, at the end,
In straits, in expanse, in form,
In body, in soul, in habit,
Prudence (is) far from the presence of kings.
j adore thee, Ruler of the land of peace.
Let my soul be in a condition of life;
For ever in (his) court;
A servant of heaven (to be), he will not refuse me.
III. Apostles and martyrs,
Youths, supplicants of glory,
And Solomon (that) served God:
Of pure speech, of pure walk, thy quality
And a verdant gift will come to me.
As long as I keep my faculties.
Numbers there were clean and holy,
Steps, golden columns of the church.
And many writers have declared,
Skilled in the fully-holy books,
For the multitude discarded anxiety.
May my soul be defended from it!
IV. A number there were in the inconcurrence

Of Uffern, a cold refuge;
During the five ages of the world,
Until when Christ loosened the bond-
age.
From the deep shore of the abyss of
evil
Many God brought through protec-
tion,
Two thousand sons of the children of
Ilia.
A bimatu et infra
Slew the amistra.
Edris ertri kila
The tears of Rachel, it was seen that a
plague
Had come to Jerusalem.
V. The number of the saints of Amori-
ca,
And a number in the form of Toronia,
That had broken the advanced Caer of
Roma.
And Poli and Alexandria
And Garanwys and Indra
Tres partes divicia
Asicia, Affrica, Europa.
VI. The number of the saints in Ca-
pharnaum, Marituen, and Naim,
And Zabulon and Cisuen and Ninifen
and Neptalim
In Dubriactus and Zorim
In it prophesied Christ, the son of
Mary, daughter of Joachim;
From the chief temple of the chief in-
fidel nation.
VII. The number of the saints of
Erechalde,
The fame far of the castle of Maria.
That broke not again Syloe
Ecclesie retunde
Phalatie cesarie
Amanion amabute,
And the valleys of Bersabe.
And before the Christian religion the
men of Cartasine,
And the severely just ones of Retunde,

The languages, Greek and Hebrew,
And Latin, men of gleaming pervasion.
VIII. The number of saints in scores,
Valiant men, golden their party.
Before kings a career of praise,
Warriors, no one was before them in
demanding.
In straits, in expanse, in every need,
May they be a city to our body and
our soul!
IX. The number of the saints of
Sicomorialis,
And isle of Deffrobani.
And the holy multitude that blessed
Water, wine, hostile men destroyed.
And entreating his exalted weight,
Under the stars, saints he planted.
X. The number of the saints that the
upper region holds,
Effectus re inferior
A superare superior
And armonim and thyfor
And the valley of Enor and Seger,
And Carthage the greater and the less,
And the green isle, the boundary of
the sea.
XI. The number of the saints of the
Isle of Prydein,
And Iwerdon, a gentle portion.
Multitudes, of beautiful works,
Believed, served with us.
XII. The number of saints, a synod
without desire,
From God the divine prophesy.
In every tongue they compose,
About the earth they were,
And so many wisely prophesied
Christ, and before he was, they were.
XIII. The number of the saints of the
East,
And the concord of the nation of Ju-
dah.
Languages of Greek and Hebrew,
And Latin, men of gleaming pervasion.

XIV. Seven scores, seven scores, seven hundreds of saints,
And seven thousands and seven ten scores,
November a number implored,
Through martyrs good they came.
Fifteen scores of saints there were
And three thousand children of Morialis.
In these Decembers above relatives
Over the head of Jesus utter sighs.
XV. Twelve thousand in the convention
Believed through the voice of John.
They worship, they deserve a portion,
In heaven they will not be angry.
XVI. Nine thousand saints received
Baptism, and religion, and confession.
Notwithstanding death the punishment of people (is) heat,
Uffern, cold its refuge.
If the Lord hath satisfied us,
Through the head of Peter was made the destitute.
XVII. Qui venerunt angli
In natale Domini
Media nocte in laudem
Cum pastoribus in Bethleem.
Nivem angli de celo
Cum Michaele archanglo
Qui precedunt precelio
Erga animas in mundo
Am nivem nivem angeli.
Precedunt confirmati
Vnistrati baptizati
Usque in them judicii.
Quando fuit Christus crucifixus ut sibi
Ipsi placuisset venissent ibi in auxilium
Plusquam duodecim legiones angelorum.
Toto orbe terrarum.
Jesus Christus videntem in agonia in mundo.
Ut sint nostri auxilium
Duodecim milia miliantem
Ante tribunal stantem.
Qui laudantie laudantium
Tues mores rex regum.
XVIII. The number that have been, and will be,
Above heaven, below heaven, how many there are.
And as many as have believed in revelation,
Believed through the will of the Lord.
As many as are on wrath through the circles,
Have mercy, God, on thy kindred.
May I be meek, the turbulent ruler,
May I not endure, before I am without motion.
Grievously complaineth every lost one,
Hastily, claimeth every needy one.
An exceedingly displeased mind will not run
From (its) present course, when I am angry.
I will declare when I am in the gravel,
From the maintenance of gifts,
From being numbered, from going to be a martyr
In the reckoning of Saint Segerno.
From a word when sin may be to me,
Let there be no sigh from those that hear me.

XCVIII. THE PLEASANT THINGS OF TALIESSIN. - BOOK OF TALIESSIN IV.

A PLEASANT virtue, extreme, penance to an extreme course;
Also pleasant, when God is delivering me.
Pleasant, the carousal that hinders not mental exertion;

Also pleasant, to drink together about horns.
Pleasant is Nud, the superior wolf-lord;
Also pleasant, a generous one at Candlemas tide.
Pleasant, berries in the time of harvest;
Also pleasant, wheat upon the stalk.
Pleasant, the sun moving in the firmament;
10 Also pleasant, the retaliators of outcries.
Pleasant,, a steed with a thick mane in a tangle;
Also pleasant, crackling fuel.
Pleasant, desire, and silver fringes;
Also pleasant, the conjugal ring.
Pleasant, the eagle on the shore of the sea when it flows;
Also pleasant, sea-gulls playing.
Pleasant, a horse with gold-enamelled trappings;
Also pleasant to be holiest in a breach.
Pleasant, liquors of the mead-brewer to the multitude;
20 Also pleasant, a songster generous, amiable.
Pleasant, the open field to cuckoos and the nightingale;
Also pleasant when the weather is serene.
Pleasant, right, and a perfect wedding;
Also pleasant, a present that is loved.
Pleasant, a meal from the penance of a priest;
Also pleasant to bring to the altar.
Pleasant, mead in a court to a minstrel,
Also pleasant, the limiting a great crowd.
Pleasant, the catholic clergy in the church,
30 Also pleasant, a minstrel in the hall.
Pleasant to bring back the divisions of a parish;
Also pleasant to us the time of paradise.
Pleasant, the moon, a luminary in the heavens;
Also pleasant where there is a good rememberer.
Pleasant, summer, and slow long day;
Also pleasant to pass out of chastisement.
Pleasant, the blossoms on the tops of the pear-trees;
Also pleasant, friendship with the Creator.
Pleasant, the solitary doe and the fawn;
40 Also pleasant, the foamy horseblock.
Pleas-ant, the camp when the leek flourishes;
Also pleasant, the charlock in the springing corn.
Pleasant, a steed in a leather halter;
Also pleasant, alliance with a king.
Pleasant, the hero that destroys not the yielding;
Also pleasant, the splendid Cymraec language.
Pleasant, the heath when it is green;
Also pleasant, the salt marsh for cattle.

Pleasant, the time when calves draw milk;
50 Also pleasant, foamy horsemanship.
And what is pleasant to me is no worse.
And. the paternal horn by mead-nourished payment.
Pleasant, the directing of fish in the pond;
Also pleasant, calling about to play.
Pleasant, the word that utters the Trinity;
Also pleasant, extreme penance for sin.
Pleasant, the summer of pleasantness;
Communion with the Lord, in the day of judgment.

XCIX. BOOK OF TALIESSIN V.

O GOD, the God of formation,
Ruler, strengthener of blood.
Christ Jesus, that guards,
Princes loud-proclaiming go their
course.
For a decaying acquisition.
It will not make me without shares,
The praising thy mercy.
There hath not been here;
O supreme Ruler;
10 There hath not been; there will
not be,
One so good as the Lord.
There hath not been born in the day
of the people
Any one equal to God.
And no one will acknowledge
Any one equal to him.
Above heaven, below heaven,
There is no Ruler but he.
Above sea, below sea,
He created us.
20 When God comes
A great noise will pierce us,
The day of judgment terribly.
Messengers from the door,
Wind, and sea, and fire.
Lightning and thunder.
A number without flattery.
The people of the world groaning
Will be concealed. A reaching arm
will be brought.

Will be concealed the sea and stars,
30 When the Father descends,
To take vengeance with his hosts
With trumpets penetrating into the
four regions.
And to set the sea on fire.
The nations of the world will be
burnt,
Until they are reduced to ashes.
Was burnt the desert portion
Before his great presence.
He will draw a stream
Before his front rank.
O Kings will shudder (that) day,
Woe awaits them!
When the recompenser shall appear,
Let the heaven appear below.
A ruddy wind will be brought
Out to the cinder,
Until the world is as desolate
As when created.
Saint Peter says it,
The day of the earth;
50 There will come a Saturday,
The earth in one furnace.
Saturday, a clear morning
The love-diffusing (Lord) will sepa-
rate us.
The land of worldly weather,
A wind will melt the trees:
There will pass away every tranquil-
lity

When the mountains are burnt.
There will be again inhabitants
With horns before kings;
60 The mighty One will send them,
Sea, and land, and lake.
There will be again a trembling ter-
ror,
And a moving of the earth,
And above every field,
And ashes the rocks will be;
With violent exertion, concealment,
And burning of lake.
A wave do ye displace,
A shield do ye extend
70 To the travelling woe,
And violent exertion through grief.
And inflaming through fury
Between heaven and earth.
When the Trinity shall come
To the field of its majesty,
The host of heaven about it,
An extensive tribe near it,
Songs and minstrels.
And the hymns of angels,
80 Will raise from the graves,
They will entreat from the beginning
They will entreat together publicly,
On so great a destiny.
Those whom the sea has destroyed
Will make a great shout,
At the time when cometh
He, that will separate them.
As many as are mine,
Let them go to the right.
90 Those that have done evil,
Lot them go to the left side.
Do not thy passions counteract
What thy lips utter?
Thy going in thy course into valleys,
Dark. without lights.
And mine were his words.
And mine were his languages.
And mine was his bright country,
And their hundred fulnesses.
100 The hundredth country present.

I have not been without battle.
Bitter affliction was frequent
Between me and my cousins.
Frequent trials fell
between me and my fellow-
countrymen.
There was frequent contention
Between me and the wretched.
This ever overcame me,
Man would never do it.
110 (Those) that placed me on the
cross
I knew when young.
That drove me on the tree,
My head hung down.
Stretched were my two feet,
So sad their destiny.
Stretched with extreme pain
The bones of my feet.
Stretched were my two arms,
Their burden will not be.
120 Stretched were my two shoul-
ders,
So diligently it was done.
Stretched were the nails,
Within my heart.
Stretched was the spiking,
Between my two eyes.
Thick are the holes
Of the crown of thorns in my head.
The lance was struck
And my side was pierced.
130 It will be struck to you also,
As your right hand (struck me).
To you there will be no forgiveness,
For piercing me with spears.
And the Ruler we knew not
When thou wert hung.
Ruler of heaven, Ruler of every peo-
ple!
We knew not, O Christ! that it was
thou.
If we had known thee,
Christ, we should have refrained
from thee.

140 A denial will not be received
From the race of the lower country.
Ye have committed wickedness
Against the Creator.
A hundred thousand angels
Are to me witnesses,
Who came to conduct me
After my hanging,
When hanging cruelly,
Myself to deliver me
150 In heaven there was trembling
When I had been hung.
When I cried out Eli!
God love-prospering above heaven.
And sing ye, the two Johns,
Before me the two primary parts.
With two books in your hands,
Reading them.
There would not come a great diffi-
culty

. . . .
160 And yours will be flattery,
The value of your foolish speech.
Dissolution will close.
Upon you to moist Uffern.
Christ Jesus high hath founded three
hundred thousand years,
Since he is in life,
And a second thousand before the
cross
Shone Enoch.
Do not the brave know
The greatness of their progeny?
170 A country present will meet thee,
And while it may possibly be yours,
Three hundred thousand years save
one,
A short hour of the day of everlasting
life.

C. BOOK OF TALIESSIN XXVII.

ON the face of the earth his equal was not born,
Three persons of God, one Son gentle, strong Trinity.
Son of the Godhead, Son of the Manhood, one son wonderful.
Son of God, a fortress, Son of the blessed Mary, a good son to see.
Great his destiny, great God supreme, a glorious portion.
Of the race of Adam, and Abraham he was born.
Of the race of the Lord, a portion of the eloquent host, was he born.
He brought by a word the blind and deaf from every ailment.
A people gluttonous, vain, iniquitous, vile, perverse,
10 We have risen against the Trinity, after redemption,
The Cross of Christ clearly, a breastplate gleaming against every ailment.
Against every hardship may it be certainly a city of protection.

V. Poems Relating to Jewish History.

CI. THE PLAGUES OF EGYPT - BOOK OF TALIESSIN XXII.

THE Hebrews took upon the sons of
Israel,
High in mind,
A joint number in succession.
They approached.

God kept vengeance
On the people of Pharaonus.
Ten plagues paining
Before their being drowned
In the bottomless sea.

10 The first plague, fish destroying
With unusual cold.
The second plague, frogs abundant,
They filled the rivers,
The houses and furniture,
And couches,
And closets of meat.
The third, gnats,
Bold and sharp, were arranged.
The fourth, a: sharp watery humour
90 Strikes in the manner of winged insects.
Next were devoured
The fruits of the trees and the field
By a crop of flies.
The fifth, murrain.
On all the children
Of the Egyptians,
Animals were destroyed.
With a heavy disease
They were all smitten.
30 The sixth, without deceit,

Sweating imposthumes,
The scars of ants.
The seventh, thunder,
Hail and fire,
And rain destructive.
Wind blasting the tops,
On leaves and shrubs.
The eighth, locusts,
Broad their ears,
40 Devouring flowers.
The ninth, prodigious
To be spoken of, terrible,
Like waves floating
Black darkness.
With a countenance gloomy.
Tenth, in the night
The greatest affliction
On the People of the tribes,
Christ Jesus, Christians, are prostrate
50 Until they are in shelter.
The six hundred warriors
Of the Hebrew soldiers.

CII. THE ROD OF MOSES - BOOK OF TALIESSIN XXIV.

FROM every return his host of brothers he rencountered,
Advantage acknowledged to Christ the Ruler, portion of praise.
The glorious God sits on the lap of Mary his counterpart.
The course of truth, perfect nobility, a pattern of thee.
Rods of Jesse, thy people Judah rencountered,

. . . .

Dexterous Lord, courteous, faultless, of gentle concord.
In respect of the earth, in the temple of Solomon, foundation of impulse,
10 The door of Paradise; shepherd of God; profoundly he reigned.
Was it not heard from learned prophets
That the birth of Jesus had taken place; during his life,
That there would be life to all kings, a life prepared or ready.
Before thou wouldst have caused, if I had not recorded the danger.
He brought what was bright; he did not cease from the earth.
On the sea deep, when descended thy emotion.
A country native, brought not the greatly-kind; be to me from thee
The greatness of thy tribulation be to me thy grace, rods of Jesse,
And the grace of Jesus, glittering its flowers.
20 Great miracle in his mind from the gifts of God,
He was a judge; a judge he was; a dexterous divine.

A man of counsel to every obedient one against falsehood.
He is a bright tenure of a number of generations.
. . . .
Bold will be the opposition to the only Son of Mary, to worship the Lord.
The youth ready to assist, from God he sprang, whether he be knowing,
whether he be simple.
Thy foreholding, coeval with perfect trees,
Had been expanded beautifully from the lap of Jesus.
30 . . . .
And to give grace, the king of sons,
A new melody men will not greatly listen to.
True his grace, a youth of support, without a lord.
The evolver of every elevation before Druids.
Nudris they knew not, a gentle sight to see Mabon.
They brought frankincense and hard gold from Ethiopia.
O fate-impelling God, O God the ruler, king of the states of progression!
The cruel Herod was not oppressive in the shroud of death.
Thy pained failure, a country owning sons,
40 When the Lord went away, when overwhelmed
Nilus, and a wintry blast brought Herod to the grave.
Perfect nobleness in the city of Nazareth,
He went not to a country possessing melody.
There will be a resuscitation; may I be bold in thy grace, in the country of the
exalted company.
The birth of the Lord was brought by the possessor of a legion of angels.

CIII. BOOK OF TALIESSIN XXIX.

AND God the possessor, God the regulator, merciful diviner,
Great., wonderful, when thou protectedst me through the wave.
The hosts of Moses, sovereign Lord, woe their dispersion!
Pharaoh and his host perceived them, cursing the cause,
And to sea thou madest new the cause.
Did he not allure them through an inundation that drowns birds?
From where the sun rises to the west there was land.
Thou wouldst protect those that thou lovest from every prison
Except hosts, vehement their shout, heavy their din.
10 And protect us also from the miseries of Uffern fierce.
And God the possessor, God the regulator, merciful diviner,
Thine is the country of heaven, it is in peace that thou lovest.
There is not weariness, nor want in thy country, Lord.
No one will be ordered; no one will be an enemy to another.
I would have known, if I had understood, for shame,
That thou lovest, the Holy Trinity, any one that is skilful.
Bards disparage you; they love much for ever.

That was not vile, the Israel which thou placedst in the hand of David.
Alexander had a large number of men.
20 He would not have been strong, had he not thy friendship,
With his armies and great battles and his tortuous hosts.
When they came to the land they were sad in their death.
Solomon the judge contained the land, he was better than they.
Son of kings. He was accustomed to riches for his auxiliary.
The sons of Jacob were rich on their land;
What they liked, they shared according to the word of the Lord.
Abel, innocent, was prosperous, and took the faith,
His brother Cain was headstrong, evil his counsel.
Aser and Soyw in the clear air, their co-operators.
30 A star-angel conducteth a number before their warriors,
With the wand of Moses, him and his hosts on their land.

. . . .

The talkative and dumb and wise and bold were redressed,
Ruler protect, one protection to those that deserve death.
I also will praise the abode of hosts, the dwelling of blessedness,
I also will praise the best repository that overflows the world.
The chief kingdom that Jonah brought from the centre of junction,
The nation of Nineveh, he was a man that joyfully preached.
Queens over sea had the shadow of the Lord, that protected them,
40 And Maria Mary, daughter of Anna, great her penitence.
Through thy generosity and mercy, King of the world!
May there be to us, in the cities of heaven, admission to thee.

CIV. BOOK OF TALIESSIN LI.

THE eternal Trinity
Made the element,
And after the element,
Adam wonderfully.
And after Adam,
Well he made Eva.
The blessed Israel
The mighty Spirit made.
Ardent the suggestion,
10 Clear the reasoning.
Twelve towns of Israel, rising equally high,
Twelve sons of Israel, the generous God made.
Twelve sons of Israel were nursed together.
Twelve good, blameless, three moth-ers nursed them.
One person created them, the Creator made them.
As he will do as he pleases, who is supreme.
Twelve sons of Israel made the love diffuser.
As he will do as he pleases, who is Lord.
Twelve sons of Israel made the Lord.
20 As he will do as he pleases, who is skilful.
Twelve-sons of Israel bore reward
Of the mission of Jesus.
And one father there was to them.
And three mothers to them.
From them came grace

And good offspring.
And Mary, good, created,
And Christ, my strengthener,
Lord of every fair country,

30 And I will call on and sing to thee
every day;
For has been my desire
Friendship with thee.

W. Poems Relating to Legends of Alexander the Great

CV. THE CONTRIVED WORLD - BOOK OF TALIESSIN XXVI.

HE was dexterous that fairly ruled over a country,
He was most generous, with most beautiful queens,
He was a violent poison of woe to his fellow-countrymen.
He broke upon Darius three times in battle.
And he will not be a dwarf shrub in the country of the plumed Darius.
Strenuous, far he conquered, the wood-pushing overtook
Alexander; in the golden fetters of woe he is imprisoned.
He was not long imprisoned; death came.
And where he had moving of armies,
10 No one before him was exalted,
To go to the grave, rich and prosperous, from the pleasure,
The generous Alexander took him there.
The land of Syr and Siryol, and the land of Syria,
And the land of Dinifdra, and land of Dinitra;
The land of Persia and Mersia, and the land of Canna;
And the isles of Pleth and Pletheppa;
And the state of Babilon and Agascia
Great, and the land of Galldarus, little its good.
Until the earth produced, sod was there.
20 And they do their wills by hunting them.
They render hostages to Europa.
And plunder the countries of the peoples of the earth.
Furiously they pierce women, they impel here,
Before the burned ones there was a devastation of modesty,
Of battles when the sorrow was mentioned.
They satisfy the ravens, they make a head of confused running,
The soldiers of the possessor of multitudes, when they are mentioned.
Nor a country to thy young men, when it is destroyed,
There will not be for thy riddance, a riddance of burthen.
30 From the care of the fetter and its hardship.
A hundred thousand of the army died from thirst:
False their plans with their thousands.
Was poisoned his youth before he came home.
Before this, it would have been better to have been satisfied.
To my lord land-prospering, a country glorious,
One country may the Lord, the best region connect.

May I reform, may I be satisfied. Be with thee the fulness,
And as many as hear me, be mine their unity.
May they satisfy the will of God before the clothing of the sod.

CVI. BOOK OF TALIESSIN XXVIII.

I WONDER that there is not pro-
claimed
An acknowledgment of heaven to the
earth.
Of the coming of a giant Ruler,
Alexander the Great.
Alexander, possessor of multitudes.
Passionate, iron-gifted,
Eminent for sword-strokes.
He went under the sea,
Under the sea he went,
10 To seek for science.
Whoever seeks science,

Let him be clamorous in mind.
He went above the wind,
Between two griffins on a journey,
To see a sight.
A sight he saw,
The present was not sufficient.
He saw a wonder.
A superiority of lineage with fishes.
20 What he desired in his mind,
He had from the world.
And also at his end
With God, mercy.

VI. Miscellaneous Poems from The Red Book of Hergest

X. Poems Attributed to Llywarch Hen

CVII. RED BOOK OF HERGEST V.

I. LET the cock's comb be red; naturally loud
Be his voice, from his triumphant bed:
Man's rejoicing, God will recommend.
II. Let the swineherds be merry at the sighing
Of the wind; let the silent be graceful;
Let the vicious be accustomed to misfortune.
III. Let the bailiff impeach; let evil be a tormentor;
Let clothes be fitting;
He that loves a bard, let him be a handsome giver.
IV. Let a monarch be vehement, and let him be brave;
And let there be a hurdle on the gap;
He will not show his face that will not give.
V. Fleet let the racers be on the side
Of the mountain; let care be in the bosom;
Unfaithful let the inconstant be.
VI. Let the knight be conspicuous; let the thief be wary;
The rich woman may be deceived;
The friend of the wolf is the lazy shepherd.

VII. Let the knight be conspicuous: fleet be the horse;
Let the scholar be ambitious;
Let the prevaricating one be unfaithful.
VIII. Let cows be round-backed; let the wolf be gray;
Let the horse over barley be swift;
Like gossamer will he press the grain at the roots.
IX. Let the deaf be bent; let the captive be heavy
Nimble the horse in battles;
Like gossamer will he press the grain the ground.
X. Let the deaf be dubious; let the rash be inconstant;
Let the mischievous wrangle;
The prudent need but be seen to be loved.
XI. Let the lake be deep; let the spears be sharp;
Let the brow of the sick be bold at the shout of war;
Let the wise be happy--God commends him.
XII. Let the exile wander; let the brave be impulsive;
Let the fool be fond of laughter.
XIII. Let the furrows be wet; let bail be frequent;
Let the sick be complaining, and the one in health merry;
Let the lapdog snarl; let the hag be peevish.
XIV. Let him that is in pain cry out; let an army be moving;
Let the well-fed be wanton;
Let the strong be bold; let the hill be icy.
XV. Let the gull be white; let the wave be loud;
Let the gore be apt to clot on the ashen spear.
Let the ice be gray; let the heart be bold.
XVI. Let the camp be green; let the suitor be reproachless;
Let there be pushing of spears in the defile;
Let the bad woman be with frequent reproaches.
XVII. Let the hen be clawed; let the lion roar;
Let the foolish be pugnacious;
Let the heart be broken with grief.
XVIII. Let the tower be white; let the harness glitter;
Let there be beauty--many will desire it;
Let the glutton hanker; let the old man mediate.

CVIII. RED BOOK OF HERGEST VI.

I. USUAL is wind from the south; usual is noise;
In the village usual for the weakling to be slender;
Usual for a man to inquire after news.
Usual for a foster-child to have dainties.
II. Usual is wind from the east; usual for a man with swelling breast to be
Proud; usual for the thrush to be among thorns;

Usual against oppression is an outcry;
Usual for crows to find flesh in a nook.
III. Usual is wind from the north; usual for maids to be
Lovely; usual, a handsome main in Gwynedd;
Usual for a prince to provide a feast;
Usual after drinking is derangement of the senses.
IV. Usual is wind from the sea; usual for the high tide to
Overflow; usual for a sow to breed vermin;
Usual for swine to turn up the ground for earth-nuts.
V. Usual is wind from the mountain; usual a plash
In the plain; usual to find thatch in the meadows
. . . .
Usual are leaves, tender shoots, and trees.
VI. Usual an eagle's nest in the top of the oak,
And in the congress-house, men of renown;
The eye of the fond one is on whom he loves.
VII. Usual is the day with a. blazing fire in the hurried season
Of winter, with the eloquent men of spears;
Usual for the hearth of the faithless to be a desert.
VIII. Dried is the reed; there is flood in the brook;
The commerce of the Saxon is with money;
Unhappy is the soul of the mother of unfaithful children.
IX. The leaf is driven by the wind;
Woe to it as to its fate;
It is old--this year it was born.
X. Though it may be small, yet ingeniously
Do the birds build in the summit of trees
Of equal age will be the good and the happy.
XI. Cold and wet is the mountain; cold and gray the ice;
Trust in God--he will not deceive thee;
Persevering patience will not leave thee long afflicted.

CIX. RED BOOK OF HERGEST VII.

I. THE Calends of winter, hard is the grain;
The leaves are on the move, the plash is full;
In the morning before he sets off,
Woe to him that trusts to a stranger.
II. The Calends of winter, the time of pleasant gossiping,
The gale and the storm keep equal pace;
It is the work of the wise to keep a secret.
III. The Calends of winter, the stags are lean,
Yellow, the tops of birch, deserted the summer dwelling;
Woo to him who for a trifle deserves disgrace.

IV. The Calends of winter, the tops of the branches are bent;
Uproar from the mouth of the vicious is common;
Where there is no natural gift there will be no learning.
V. The Calends of winter, blustering is the weather,
Unlike the beginning of summer;
Except God, there is none that divines.
VI. The Calends of Winter, gay the plumage of birds;
Short the day; loud the cuckoos;
Mercifully has the most beneficent God made them.
VII, The Calends of winter, it is hard and dry;
Very black is the raven, quick the arrow from the bow;
At the stumbling of the old, the smile of the youth is apt to break out.
VIII. The Calends of winter, lean is the stag:
Woe to the weak! if he chafes, it will be but for a short while;
Truly better is amiability than beauty.
IX. The Calends of winter, bare is where the heath is burnt,
The plough is in the furrow; the ox at work;
Amongst a hundred there is hardly a friend.

CX. RED BOOK OF HERGEST VIII.

1. ENTANGLING is the snare, clustered is the ash;
The ducks are in the pond; white breaks the wave;
More powerful than a hundred is the counsel of the heart.
II. Long the night, boisterous is the sea-shore;
Usual a tumult in a congregation;
The vicious will not agree with the good.
III. Long the night, boisterous is the mountain,
The wind whistles over the tops of trees;
Ill-nature will not deceive the discreet.
IV. The saplings of the green-topped birch
Will extricate my foot from the shackle;
Disclose not thy secret to a youth.

V. The saplings of oaks in the grove
Will extricate my foot from the chain;
Disclose no secret to a maid.
VI. The saplings of the leafy oaks
Will extricate my foot from the prison;
Divulge no secret to a babbler.
VII. The saplings of bramble have berries on them;
The thrush is on her nest;
And the liar will never be silent.
VIII. Rain without, the fern is drenched;
White the gravel of the sea; there is spray on the margin;
Reason is the fairest lamp for man.
IX. Rain without, near is the shelter,
The furze yellow; the cow-parsnip withered and dry;
God the Creator! why hast thou made a coward?
X. Rain without, my hair is drenched;
Full of complaint is the feeble; steep

the cliff;
Pale white is the sea; salt is the brine.
XI. Rain without, the ocean is
drenched;

The wind whistles over the tops of
the reeds;
After every feat, still without the ge-
nius.

CXI. RED BOOK OF HERGEST IX.

I. BRIGHT are the ash-tops; tall and white will they be
When they grow in the upper part of the dingle;
The languid heart, longing is her complaint.
II. Bright is the top of the cliff at the long midnight hour;
Every ingenious person will be honoured.
It is the duty of the fair one to afford sleep to him in pain.
III. Bright are the willow-tops; playful the fish
In the lake; the wind whistles over the tops of the branches;
Nature is superior to learning.
IV. Bright the tops of the furze; have confidence
In the wise; and to the unwise be repulsive;
Except God, there is none that divines.
V. Bright the tops of the clover; the timid has no heart;
Jealous ones weary themselves out;
Usual is care upon the weak.
VI. Bright the tops of reed-grass; furious is the jealous,
And he can hardly be satisfied;
It is the act of the wise to love with sincerity.
VII. Bright the mountain-tops; from the bluster of winter,
Withered and drooping is the tall grass;
Against famine there is no bashfulness.
VIII. Bright the mountain-tops; intruding is the cold of
Winter; brittle are the reeds; rime is over the grave;
Imprudence committed violence in banishment.
IX. Bright the tops of the oak; bitter the ash-branches;
Sweet the cow-parsnip, the wave keeps laughing;
The cheek will not conceal the anguish of the heart.
X. Bright the tops of the dogrose; hardship has no formality;
Let every one preserve his purity of life.
The greatest blemish is ill-manners.
XI. Bright the tops of the broom; let the lover make assignations;
Very yellow are the clustered branches;
Shallow ford; the contented is apt to enjoy sleep.
XII. Bright the tops of the apple-tree; circumspect is
Every prudent one, a chider of another;
And after loving, indiscretion leaving it.

XIII. Bright the tops of the apple-tree; circumspect is
Every prudent one; in the long day a stagnant pool is malarious;
Thick is the veil on the light of the blind prisoner.
XIV. Bright the hazel-tops by the hill of Digoll;
Unafflicted will be every squabby one;
It is an act of the mighty to keep a treaty.
XV. Bright the tops of reeds; it is usual for the sluggish
To be heavy, and the young to be a learner;
None but the foolish will break the faith.
XVI. Bright the tops of the lily; let every bold one be a servitor;
The word of a family will prevail;
Usual with the faithless, a broken word.
XVII. Bright the tops of the heath; usual is miscarriage
To the timid; water will be intrusive in front of the shore;
Usual with the faithful, an unbroken word.
XVIII. Bright the tops of rushes; cows are profitable,
Running are my tears this day;
Comfort for the miserable there is not.
XIX. Bright the tops of fern, yellow
The charlock; how reproachless are the blind;
How apt to run about are youngsters!
XX. Bright the tops of the service-tree; accustomed to care,
Is the aged one, and bees to the wilds
Except God, there is no avenger.
XXI. Bright the tops of the oak; incessant is the tempest;
The bees are high; brittle the dry brushwood;
Usual for the wanton to laugh excessively.
XXII. Bright the tops of the grove; constantly the trees
And the oak-leaves are falling;
Happy is he who sees the one he loves.
XXIII. Bright the tops of the oaks; coldly purls the stream;
Let the cattle be fetched to the birch-enclosed area;
Abruptly goes the arrow of the haughty to give pain.
XXIV. Bright the tops of the hard holly, and others; let gold be distributed;
When all fall asleep on the rampart,
God will not sleep when He gives deliverance.
XXV. Bright the tops of the willows; inherently bold
Will the war-horse be in the long day, when leaves are abounding;
Those that have mutual friendship will not despise one another.
XXVI. Bright the tops of rushes; prickly will they be
When spread under the pillow;
The wanton mind will be haughty.
XXVII. Bright the tops of the hawthorn; confident is the sight of the steed;
It is usual for a lover to be a pursuer;
May the diligent messenger do good.

XXVIII. Bright the tops of cresses; warlike is the steed;
Trees are fair ornaments for the ground;
Joyful the soul with what it loves.
XXIX. Bright is the top of the bush; valuable the steed;
It is good to have discretion with strength;
Let the unskilful be made powerless.
XXX. Bright are the tops of the brakes; gay the plumage
Of birds; the long day is the gift of the light;
Mercifully has the most beneficent God made them.
XXXI. Bright the tops of the meadow sweet; and music
In the grove; bold the wind, the trees shake;
Interceding with the obdurate will not avail.
XXXII. Bright the tops of the elder-trees; bold is the solitary songster;
Accustomed is the violent to oppress;
Woe to him who takes a reward from the hand.

CXII. RED BOOK OF HERGEST X.

I. SITTING high upon a hill, battle-inclined is
My mind, and it does not impel me onward:
Short is my journey, my tenement is laid waste.
II. Sharp is the gale, it is bare punishment to live;
When the trees array themselves in gay colours
Of summer; violently ill I am this day.
III. I am no hunter, I keep no animal of the chase;
I cannot move about:
As long as it pleases the cuckoo, let her sing!
IV. The loud-voiced cuckoo sings with the dawn,
Her melodious notes in the dales of Cuawg:
Better is the lavisher than the miser.
V. At Aber Cuawg the cuckoos sing,
On the blossom-covered branches:
The loud-voiced cuckoo, let her sing a while!
VI. At Aber Cuawg the cuckoos sing,
On the blossom-covered branches:
Woe to the sick that hears their contented notes.
VII. At Aber Cuawg the cuckoos sing:
The recollection is in my mind!
There are that hear them that will not bear them again!
VIII. Have I not listened to the cuckoo on the ivied tree?
Did not my shield hang down?
What I loved is but vexation; what I loved is no more.
IX. High above the merry oak,
I have listened to the song of birds.
The loud cuckoo--every one remembers what he loves.
X. Songstress with the solacing song! her voice is grief exciting:
Subject to wander, with the flight of the hawk,
The loquacious cuckoo at Aber Cuawg.
XI. The birds are clamorous; humid are the glens:
Let the moon shine; cold the midnight hour:
Distracted is my mind from the torment of disorder.

XII. White-topped is the cliff; long the midnight hour:
Every ingenious one-will be honoured:
I owe the indulgence of sleep to old age.
XIII. The birds are clamorous; the beach is wet:
Let the leaves fall; the exile is unconcerned:
I will not conceal it, I am ill this night.
XIV. The birds are clamorous; the strand is wet:
Clear is the sky; large the wave:
The heart is palsied with longing.
XV. The birds are clamorous; the strand is wet:
Conspicuous is the wave with its ample range:
What was formed in my youth,
I could love, if I could have it again.
XVI. Clamorous are the birds on the scent;
Loud the cry of dogs in a desert;
Again clamorous are the birds.
XVII. In the beginning of summer, gay are all varied seeds!
When the warriors hasten to the conflict,
I do not go, infirmity will not leave me.
XVIII. In the beginning of summer, it is glorious on the course,
When the warriors hasten to the field of battle;
I shall not go, infirmity separates me.
XIX. Hoary is the mountain summit; the tops of the ash are brittle:
From the Abers the fair wave is impelled:
Laughter is far from my heart.
XX. What is it to me this day at the end of the month?
In the social banquet I have left it:

Distracted is my mind; a fever has made choice of me.
XXI. Quick is the sight of the sentinel;
Let the idle use courtesy:
Distracted is my mind; disease preys upon me.
XXII. Riches like a bowl encircling mead,
The happy man will not wish for:
It is a precious thing to know patience.
XXIII. Riches like a bowl round the cheering beverage,
The gliding stream, the refreshing shower,
And the deep ford: the mind is stirred to treachery.
XXIV. To foment treachery is an iniquitous deed;
There will be pain where there will be purifying;
It is to sell a little for much.
XXV. Let the wicked be fomenting treachery;
When God will judge, at the long day,
Dark will be falsehood, truth clear.
XXVI. There is danger in repelling the graduated visitor;
Men are joyous over the beverage:
Frail is the reed, of riches an emblem.
XXVII. Hear the wave of sullen din, and loud,
Amidst the pebbles and gravel:
Distracted is my mind from delirium this night.
XXVIII. Branching is the top of the oak; bitter the taste of the ash:
Sweet the cow-parsnip; the wave is laughing:
The cheek will not conceal the affliction of the heart.
XXIX. The heaving sigh tells upon me,
After my experience . . . . .
God will not bestow on the wicked what is good.

XXX. To the wicked what is good will not be given;
But sorrow and anxiety:
God will not undo what he is doing,
XXXI. The son of sickness has been a brisk youth, he had
An active share in the court of the king;
May God be propitious to the diviner!
XXXII. As to what is being done, it will come to pass,
Let him that reads it consider:
What is detested by man here, is detested by God above.

CXIII. RED BOOK OF HERGEST XIII.

I. MAENWYN, when I was of thy age,
My garment should not be trodden under foot,
My land should not be ploughed without blood.
II. Maenwyn, when I was opposed to thee,
With youth attendant on me,
The foe would not break my boundary.
III. Maenwyn, while I was in pursuit of thee,
Following my youth,
The foe loved not the fury of my resentment.
IV. Maenwyn, while I was young and plump,
Addicted to fierce slaughter,
I would perform the acts of a man, though I was but a youth.

V. Maenwyn, take thy aim discreetly;
There is need of advice on him who is in error:
Let Maelgwn provide another mayor.
VI. My choice is a portion, with its sheath on it,
And sharp-pointed as a thorn;
It is not labour lost for me to whet a stone.
VII. A present was bestowed on me from the vale
Of Mewyrniawn, concealed in a bucket,
A sharp iron projecting from the hand.
VIII. Blessed be the solitary hag,
That said from the door of her cell,
"Maenwyn, do not deliver up thy knife."

Y. Poems Beginning "Eiry Mynyd."

CXIV. RED BOOK OF HERGEST IV.

I. MOUNTAIN snow--every region is white;
The raven is accustomed to sing.
No good will come from long sleeping.
II. Mountain snow--white the ravine;
From the assault of the wind trees will bend.
Many a two may mutually love,
But never come together.

III. Mountain snow--the wind scatters it;
Broad the moon's orb, green the dock-leaves.
The mischievous man is seldom without claim.
IV. Mountain snow--fleet the hart;
Common in Prydein is a daring race.
Understanding is necessary for the alien.

301

V. Mountain snow--the hart in the warmth;
Ducks in the pond, white the foam.
Slow is the aged, and easily overtaken.
VI. Mountain snow--the hart is roaming;
The countenance smiles on whom one loves.
As long as a tale is told me,
I know where there is disgrace.
VII. Mountain snow--the strand is white and pebbly;
The fishes in the ford may go to the cavern.
Odious is he that imposes burdens.
VIII. Mountain snow--the hart in the retreat;
It is usual for a chieftain to have splendid arms,
. . . .
And for misfortune to fall on the beard.
IX. Mountain snow--the hart is plump and round;
I have said a great deal; if I am not mistaken,
This is unlike a summer day.
X. Mountain snow--the hart is hunted;
The wind whistles over the eaves.
Sin is a very great heap.
XI. Mountain snow--the hart is leaping;
The wind whistles over the high white wall.
It is natural the calm should be graceful.
XII. Mountain snow--the hart in the vale;
The wind whistles above the housetop.
Evil will not conceal itself where it is.
XIII. Mountain snow--the hart on the strand;

The aged has lost his juvenility.
. . . makes a man captive.
XIV. Mountain snow--the hart in the bush;
Thoroughly black the raven; swift the young roebuck.
If one is free and healthy, it is strange there should be complaining.
XV. Mountain snow--the hart in the rushes;
Cold the quagmire; the mead is in the brewing-tub.
The injured is accustomed to complain.
XVI. Mountain snow--variegated the front of the tower;
Let the cattle seek shelter.
Woe to the wife that should get a bad husband.
XVII. Mountain snow--variegated the side of the cliff;
Dried the stalk; the water-lily droops.
Woe to the man that should have a bad wife.
XVIII. Mountain snow--the hart in the ditch;
Congenial to the thief is long night.
Let the bees sleep in the shelter.
XIX. Mountain snow--slow is
The growth of the liverwort.
The sluggard will not soon avenge an injury.
XX. Mountain snow--the fish in the lake;
Proud the hawk; people cluster around monarchs.
Every one cannot get what he wishes.
XXI. Mountain snow--red the top of the fir;
Wrathful the push of many spears.
Alas, for longing, my brethren
XXII. Mountain snow--swift the wolf;
The side of the desert he will penetrate.

Every blemish is common on the destitute of zeal.

XXIII. Mountain snow--not slow the hart;
Rain falls from the sky.
Sorrow produces complete depression of spirits.

XXIV. Mountain snow--noisy the roebuck;
The waves wash the margin of the strand;
Let the skilful conceal his design.

XXV. Mountain snow--the hart in the glen;
Summer will be placid; calm the lake.
The gray-bearded in frost has a strong support,

XXVI. Mountain snow--variegated the breast of the goose;
Strong my arm and shoulder.
I pray that I may not be a hundred years old.

XXVII. Mountain snow--bare the stalk-tops;
Bent the branches of trees; the fish are in the deep.
Where there is no learning there will be no natural gift.

XXVIII. Mountain snow--the fish in the ford;
Let the lean and stooping stag seek the sheltered vale.
Longing for the dead will not avail.

XXIX Mountain snow--the hart in the wood;

The discreet will not walk on foot.
The timid causes many a delay.

XXX. Mountain snow--the hart on the slope;
The wind whistles over the ash-tops.
A third foot for the aged is his stick.

XXXI. Mountain snow--the hart is upon it;
The ducks are in the lake; white the water-lily.
The vicious is not disposed to listen.

XXXII. Mountain snow--ruddy the feet of hens;
Shallow the water; it makes much noise.
The disgrace that is boasted of is augmented.

XXXIII. Mountain snow--nimble the hart;
Hardly anything in the world interests me.
Admonition to the depraved will not avail.

XXXIV. Mountain snow--white its fleece;
. . . .

XXXV. Mountain snow--white the roofs of houses;
If the tongue were to relate what the bosom knows,
None would be neighbours.

XXXVI. Mountain snow--let the wise move about in the day;
Let every pensive one be ill, every bush bare.
It is usual that the unwise should have all faults.

CXV. RED BOOK OF HERGEST III.

Llewelyn and Gwrnerth were two penitent saints at Trallwng in Powys; and it was their custom to meet together during the last three hours of the night and the first three hours of the day to say their matins, and the hours of the day besides. And once upon a time Llewelyn, seeing the cell of Gwrnerth shut, and not knowing why it was so, composed an Englyn.

I. MOUNTAIN snow--wind about the bush;
It is the Creator of heaven that strengthens me.
Is it asleep that Gwrnerth is?
II. Mountain snow--God above all things;
It is to Him I will pray.
No; I cannot sleep.
III. Mountain snow--wind about the house;
It is so thou speakest.
What, Gwrnerth, causes that?
IV. Mountain snow--wind from the south;
I will utter prime words.
Most probably it is death.
V. Mountain snow--white-topped the vale;
Every one is mild to him by whom he is cherished.
May the Creator of heaven deliver thee!
VI. Mountain snow--white-topped the tree;
I will speak differently.
There is no refuge against the decree of Heaven.
VII. Mountain snow--every rite should be observed
For fear of distressing anxiety in the day of doom.
Shall I have the communion as a favour?
VIII. Mountain snow--wind about the house;
It is so thou speakest.
Alas I my brother, must that be?
IX. Thou highly-gifted! thee I love;
It is to God I will pray.
Llewelyn, it is high time I should receive it.
X. Mountain snow-wind about the hill;

The Creator of heaven will have me.
Is it asleep Llewelyn is?
XI. Mountain snow--wind from the south;
I will utter prime words.
No; I am chanting my hours.
XII. Mountain snow--it is easily known
When the wind turns round a wall.
Knowest thou who says it?
XIII. Mountain snow--thou bold of speech,
It is so thou speakest.
I know not, unless thou wilt say.
XIV. Mountain snow--every assistance
Will receive becoming praise;
Thy brother Gwrnerth is here.
XV. Foremost in the tumult and in energetic action
Is every brave one, being impelled by his Awen;
What, Gwrnerth, is best for thee?
XVI. The first thing to be aimed at in every usage and action congenial to the brave,
Is a pure life unto the day of judgment;
The best that I have found is almsgiving.
XVII. Thou highly gifted with good qualities,
The canon is on thy lips;
Tell we what alms the best.
XVIII. Bold the Awen; there is wind over the lake
When the wave beats around the eminence;
The best is meat for hunger.
XIX. If meat I cannot obtain,
And with my hands cannot get in,
Say what shall I then do?
XX. Foremost in the tumult and in energetic action
Is every brave one, impelled by his

Awen;
Give clothing to keep from nakedness.
XXI. My clothes I will give,
And myself commend to God;
What recompense shall I then receive?
XXII. What good things thou givest on every opportunity
Bold in thy privilege keep thy countenance;
And thou shalt have heaven a hundredfold.
XXIII. Since with the early dawn I love thee,
It is in the form of verse I am asking,
With God what one thing is most odious?
XXIV. Advantage, and Awen, and equality
When water will run tip the ascent;
The worst of deceit where there is confidence.
XXV. If I practise deceit through confidence

And to God Supreme confess,
What punishment will befall me?
XXVI. Shouldst thou practise deceit through confidence,
Without faith, without religion, without belief,
Thou shalt have sevenfold penance.
XXVII. I will with the dawn believe thee,
And for God's sake will ask,
How shall I obtain heaven?
XXVIII. Good and evil are not alike,
As wind and smoke when contending;
Do good for the sake of God, who is not wrathful.
XXIX. Bold is the Awen of every one that is patronised;
Horses are apt to run much about in hot weather.
The end of all things is confession.
XXX. What thou doest from all excess,
From deception, and oppression, and arrogance,
For God's sake make a full confession.

Tyssilio, the son of Brochwael Ysgythrog, composed these verses concerning Gwrnerth's coming to perform his devotions with Llewelyn the saint, his companion; and they are called the Colloquy of Llewelyn and Gwrnerth.

Z. Poems on Various Subjects

CXVI. RED BOOK OF HERGEST XVIII.

LIKE a wheel revolving immense courses,
A weakening affliction is the severe compulsion of taxes,
The unjust imposition of the ardent dragon of the mountains.
Terrible is the conflict about the ports and ferries,
And the hostilities of chieftains to chieftains.
It is natural that Franks should be highly elated: they will come on a Thursday;
And for a lady's complaint there will be wars;
And the country will be wasted, and without land;
And the key of Rome will be in the hands of commanders;

10 And the Allmyn will be unable to make assaults;
And there will be happiness to the Venedotians, who will resort to the South;
And weakness to the Saxon from his treaties,
And long depravity from want of laws;
And Lloegyr will be enfeebled by the treachery of its chiefs,
And the thrusting of Franks, and tumult in ships,
And the battle of Dovyr hastening death,
A wonder for a long life to such as will hear it.
There will be a wounding through the community owing
to the disappearance of the partisans
Of the guileless dragon, dark and light.
20 Powerful chiefs of noble descent.
And may He give us of his bounty a pledge
Of a portion of his feast for ever without privation!
Amen.

CXVII. THE VIATICUM OF LLEVOED WYNEBGLAWR - RED BOOK OF HERGEST XXIV.

I. THE wealth of the world, let it go, it will come,
As long as it is esteemed.
Necessity equalises affliction,
There will be fair weather after rain.
It is often the case that persons fostered by the same are unlike.
The brave will play though blood way be shed.
Every coward will be trampled upon;
Every strong one will be allowed to pass.
The happy is pleased with harmonious sounds,
Which God will freely pour upon him.
II. The wealth of the world, let it go, it will come;
May God provide what suffices!
Loud is the noise of the wave against the land;
When called, it recedeth from it.
Listless is the man that sees not,
That is not concerned, that cares not what may be.
Where justice is not practised, it is not entertained in the country.

Mass will not be sting on a flight.
Let him be a wolf that dareth deceive.
Desirous will the scholar be that Llawddino should prosper.
III. The wealth of the world, let it go, it will come.
Desire calls for the return of liberty.
The height of the young will increase.
Lying praise will not be borrowed.
The slave and the free are not of the same design.
Empty the country, where there is no religion.
There will be a return which will not be repeated.
Cold does not agree with the hoary.
The unbeliever does not think of God.
No one that does not improve is called skilful.
Let us observe and acquire religion,
Until we have relationship with Christ.
IV. The unsociable man is uncomely in the place of gathering.
Trouble in the upland, enmity in the vale.

A refusal is better than a false promise.

In one's actions servility is supererogatory.

The sweet is seldom unpleasant.

The evil done by a fellow will survive after he has passed away.

An excuse is not usually regarded.

Good cannot be had without deserts.

The four quarters open deeply in four different ways.

It is a saying that death is better than trouble.

Bad is sin from its being far pursued.

It is good in distress to support a monastery.

God of Heaven! woe to the daring one that does not believe thee!

Son of Mary! endowed with undefiled genius,

It is a good work to hope in thee;

Before the world thou art mentioned.

V. The wave hastens forward; let it beat the shore.

The fuel of wrath is impulsive.

Watch-stones form the best history.

The wisdom of a host, and deception through laughter.

Let fundamental knowledge be accurate.

Let the weakling be slow, let the niggard die.

The evil alliance of Gall Cynnin.

With a wanton a secret will not long remain.

Blood will cause blood to flow,

The froward will meet with contention.

Let the weak be set at large.

The iniquitous will lose his clan.

Except God, there is no one that knows the future.

Its lord is the chief cause of prosperity to a country.

VI. The wave hastens forward; the beach repels.

Light pain will soon be relieved;

The multitude will bustle about the mead-liquor.

Let him who ejects every one from his frontier cease to exist.

Let the obstinate be cut off.

Whoso purchases heaven will not be confounded.

How curious thou art that any should mention it.

The trees have put on a beauteous robe.

A mirror is not visible in the dark.

A candle will not preserve from cold.

He is not happy who is not discreet.

The favour of the Supreme Being will not deceive.

VII. He who cultivates not wisdom as the chief foundation,

What will put a bird to flight he will not do.

Cold is the sway of winter; bare the sea-shore.

Better is what is easy than the encountering of difficulties.

Reproach will not mend what is evil.

Many a boastful word will cause embarrassment.

To the bosom, while it goes about;

From haste it cannot be known where it will go.

The Trinity will retaliate arrogance.

Great God! how good a Being thou art!

VIII. Fleet is the steed; clear is every strand;

The desire of the high-minded one is chivalry.

No one reaps from his contrivance.

Every one is not born wise.

The mind is not bold in a ship on the strand.

There will be no peace between dry

sticks and the flame.
Let a man live without evil conduct,
Courteous to song, I confer benefits
on those in a state of excommunica-
tion.
No naked one will be very energetic.
There is no law unless there be su-
premacy.
A king will challenge spoil.
The furious, his death is certain.
Is it not customary that cowardice
should harbour from death.
Let the brave escape from his conflict.
Intoxicated the dumb; every barbari-
an is a bravado.
A city will extinguish a wilderness.
The talkative loves easy work.
Every one is praised according to his
work.
God loves not the hopeless.
Fortune is the best assistance.
IX. In spring the land is partly bare,
If people are turbulent, their shout is
deceitful.
In calm reflection riches are despised.
What is not often seen is neglected.
He that is faithless, his presumption
will be contemned.
It is a complete share that is longed
for.
Let the woman that is never asked
appear demure.
Disgrace is apt to follow long celiba-
cy.
He that will not completely conceal
himself, will be completely taken
away.
From a long restraint comes com-
plaint.
What seemeth good to God is certain.
He that is brave, his praise will be
heard abroad.
From a little comes enrichment.
Blessed is he to whom are given
The favour of God and long life.

www.ingramcontent.com/pod-product-compliance
Lightning Source LLC
Chambersburg PA
CBHW030912090426
42737CB00007B/171